INTERVENTIONS: NEW STUDIES
IN MEDIEVAL CULTURE

Ethan Knapp, Series Editor

INVENTION AND AUTHORSHIP IN MEDIEVAL ENGLAND

∽

ROBERT R. EDWARDS

THE OHIO STATE UNIVERSITY PRESS
COLUMBUS

Copyright © 2017 by The Ohio State University.
All rights reserved.

Library of Congress Cataloging-in-Publication Data
Names: Edwards, Robert, 1947– author.
Title: Invention and authorship in medieval England / Robert R. Edwards.
Other titles: Interventions: new studies in medieval culture.
Description: Columbus : The Ohio State University Press, [2017] | Series: Interventions: new studies in medieval culture | Includes bibliographical references and index.
Identifiers: LCCN 2017005170 | ISBN 9780814213407 (cloth ; alk. paper) | ISBN 0814213405 (cloth ; alk. paper)
Subjects: LCSH: Authorship—History—To 1500. | Authors, Medieval. | Invention (Rhetoric)—History—To 1500. | Literature, Medieval—History and criticism. | English literature—Middle English, 1100–1500—History and criticism.
Classification: LCC PN144 .E35 2017 | DDC 809/.89420902—dc23
LC record available at https://lccn.loc.gov/2017005170

Cover design by Janna Thompson-Chordas
Text design by Juliet Williams
Type set in Adobe Minion Pro

Cover image: Auteur de "Tristan" et copiste, Bibliothèque nationale de France (BnF), Français 97, fol. 215v, late fifteenth century.

∞ The paper used in this publication meets the minimum requirements of the American National Standard for Information Sciences—Permanence of Paper for Printed Library Materials. ANSI Z39.48-1992.

9 8 7 6 5 4 3 2 1

For Patrick,
who asked the first question

CONTENTS

Acknowledgments		ix
Introduction		xi

PART 1: INVENTIONS

Prelude	Bede and the Denial of Authorship	3
Chapter 1	Walter Map: Authorship and Counter-Authorship	9
Chapter 2	Marie de France: Signature and Invention	33

PART 2: AUTHORSHIP DIRECT AND OBLIQUE

Chapter 3	John Gower: Scriptor, Compositor, Auctor	63
Chapter 4	Geoffrey Chaucer: Imitation and Refusal	105

PART 3: CONSTRUCTING A CANON

Chapter 5	Simulating Authorship: Thomas Hoccleve and John Lydgate	149
Chapter 6	Thomas Hoccleve: "Sum of the doctrine"	163
Chapter 7	John Lydgate and the "Stile Counterfet"	176
Afterword	The Afterlife of Medieval Authorship	197

Bibliography	205
Index	225

ACKNOWLEDGMENTS

THIS BOOK had its beginnings in conversations and teaching. I am grateful to Patrick Cheney for giving me the occasion to think about authorship and for sustaining a long-running discussion of the critical issues it entails. As the book took shape, I was fortunate to have other generous colleagues to ask for advice and guidance. I thank Emily Grosholz, James Simpson, Ralph Hanna III, Norris Lacy, R. F. Yeager, James L. W. West III, Caroline D. Eckhardt, Scott Smith, and Wolfram Keller. Two readers for The Ohio State University Press have made valuable suggestions to strengthen the book. I hope I have used all the counsel available to me wisely; any errors that remain are mine. My debts to other scholars, those who have defined the field and those who have moved inquiry forward, will be evident in the text and the notes. I have also had the welcome opportunity to teach the materials of authorship and medieval literary culture in graduate seminars and undergraduate courses. In their writing and comments, my students have been fair arbiters of what helps and what makes sense in criticism and interpretation, and I hope their own intellectual work has benefited from the exchanges.

My research has had generous support from my home institution in the forms of a sabbatical leave and research funding. I thank Susan Welch, Dean of the College of the Liberal Arts at The Pennsylvania State University, and my department heads in English and Comparative Literature, Mark Morrisson and Caroline D. Eckhardt, respectively. Chad Schrock, Sarah Breckenridge Wright, Gabriel Ford, Danielle Netzer, Emily Fogel, Samuel McMillan, and Theodore Chelis have done splendid work in contributing to research for the book and reading chapters multiple times. I wish to offer my thanks to my editor at The Ohio State University Press, Eugene O'Connor, and to Ethan Knapp for including the book in his series, Interventions: New Studies in Medieval Culture. My enduring debt is to my wife, Emily, and our children: Benjamin, Robert, William, and Mary-Frances. Their support, belief, and good will have made all the difference in a long project that had to find its own direction.

A portion of chapter 1 originally appeared in my article "Walter Map: Authorship and the Space of Writing," *New Literary History* 38 (2007): 273–92; an early version of chapter 2 appeared as "Marie de France's *Lais* and *Le livre Ovide*," *Mediaevalia* 26 (2005): 57–82; parts of chapter 4 are reworkings of my essay "Authorship, Imitation, and Refusal in Late-Medieval England," which originally appeared in *Medieval and Early Modern Authorship*, edited by Guillemette Bolens and Lukas Erne (Tübingen: Narr, 2011), 51–73. I am grateful to the editors and publishers for permission to include these materials.

INTRODUCTION

IN THIS BOOK, I examine forms of literary authorship in medieval England. I seek, on the one hand, to extend the findings of a body of scholarship that has traced a key feature of literary culture in the medieval and Early Modern periods—the emergence of the author as a visible figure within literary practice and in its many contexts. I attempt, on the other, to interpret authorship as both an external condition of writing and an internal element of textual meaning. Authorship connects the social, political, and cultural significance of works with the craft of figuration and aesthetic representation. For modern interpreters, it is a middle term between historical context and the works of imagination and thus a tool for criticism. The central argument I want to advance is that literary authorship develops in medieval England from discrete acts of invention—that is, from the discovery of expressive possibilities within and against established conventions of reading and writing. As this description implies, authorship is at once rhetorical and literary, historical and poetic.

It will be immediately clear that my inquiry involves, in every instance, essentially contested terms—authorship as a concept and practice, the literary as a discursive mode, and medieval England as a place, nation, and period. To speak of authorship is, in one sense, merely a stylistic convenience, an economical phrasing or shorthand to designate what is in fact a multiform practice. I approach it in this book as a discursive field rather than a concept with a single definition and subsequent applications. Authorship is an idea continually in play in medieval culture and modern accounts of its historical formulations. The sources for medieval authorship lie predominantly in commentary on the Latin Bible and on the classical writers whose works formed the basis of the educational curriculum in Late Antiquity and the Middle Ages.[1] Exegesis and pedagogy offer frames that analyze and generate writing in classical languages and European vernaculars situated variously at the center and on the margins of diverse official cultures. Yet the historical development of authorship, as scholarship has shown, begins in tensions within the logic of the institutional frames of commentary and pedagogy. From the High Middle Ages onward, these developments accelerate in European vernaculars, including those of England.

The literary, as John Burrow has remarked, is a problematic quality to distinguish with precision or consistency in the medieval period.[2] The formal features of the literary appear not just in belletristic or imaginative writing but in historical, religious, and didactic compositions. A figure like Geoffrey of Monmouth troubles the boundaries of history and fiction for his contemporaries no less than for later readers. William Langland writes poetry founded on figurative language and aesthetic strategies of representation with social and religious meanings that are finally inseparable from each other and from his mode of expression. Richard Rolle is recognized as an author in both Latin and English of spiritual works that circulated under his name and served as a source for excerpts, citations, and allusions.[3] One practical difference marking the literary in the works I examine is a primary rather than instrumental commitment to imagination, expression, and the allusive resources of language, even if the conventional aims of pleasure and profit provide an expected rationale. The literary aligns with the fictive as a mode of composition, and it presents fictional creations—imaginative worlds, often secular but not necessarily

---

1. The *auctores* of the curriculum described by the twelfth-century Benedictine master Conrad of Hirsau include Christian writers (Avianus, Prosper, Prudentius, Sedulius, and Theodolus), Aesop, Boethius, and Donatus in addition to the canonical prose writers and poets of antiquity; see Quain, "Mediaeval *Accessus ad auctores*," 216.

2. Burrow, *Medieval Writers*, 12. Burrow finds a counterpart to modern discussions of poetic and literary language in medieval uses of eloquence regardless of the truth claims of any particular discursive mode. The modern discussion proceeds from the formalist principles and efforts to define literariness early in the twentieth century. Wogan-Browne et al., *Idea of the Vernacular*, xv, in their illustrations of literary theory in Middle English, choose to blur distinctions between literary texts and other texts.

3. Watson, *Richard Rolle*, 257–70. Renevey, *Language, Self and Love*, 66–67, delineates Rolle's career under the terms *interpres*, *auctor*, and "messager." Hanna, "Rolle and Related Works," 19–31, remarks that Rolle is "the first real 'author' in Middle English" (19).

so—as meaningful sites of knowledge and reflection.⁴ In this respect, literary authorship is a special case—on balance, a minority case—within a wider practice of authorship in medieval writing.⁵ Put in a slightly different way, it is a potential arising from dominant modes of textual authority. In the prelude of part 1 of this book, I show that Bede's description of his own writing is an exquisitely balanced account of precisely that potential—one that signals the recognized features of authorship yet refuses to take the step of claiming authorship directly.⁶ The writers who concern me elsewhere in this book similarly locate their authorship in relation to larger established institutional practices and modes of discourse. Literary authorship operates in their works as a repeatedly negotiated, functional difference rather a stably defined mode of writing.⁷

Authorship "in medieval England"—the third contested term of my inquiry—develops across the boundaries of jurisdictions and time. English writers adapt conventions of authorship from the exegetical and pedagogical sources of pan-European Latin clerical culture. They draw, too, on forms of authorship elaborated in medieval European vernaculars.⁸ In a narrow sense, my topic is medieval literary authorship as theorized in Western Europe and practiced in England across three languages of record—Latin, French, and English. It thus excludes Gaelic, Welsh, Norse, and Scots writers and their associated traditions.⁹ The two writers discussed in part 1—Walter Map and Marie de France—put immediate pressure on what authorship in medieval England might mean. Map is a Welsh marcher from a family with a long history of royal service; Marie asserts, "Si sui de France." Both dwell in a court

---

4. Ashe, *Early Fiction in England*, xv–xix, rightly observes that fiction is contractual, predicated on an agreement shared by writers and readers with the stipulations about truth claims of fiction fully known to each party.

5. Cannon, *Grounds of English Literature*, 46, makes the strongest recent objection against taking one class of literary objects to represent all literary objects. His specific concern is with post-Conquest writing in English, but the principle applies broadly in literary history.

6. Bede's influence in England after the Scandinavian invasions of the ninth century reflects, in this context, his earlier reception as an author on the Continent from the Carolingian age onward.

7. Conrad, adapting Bernard of Utrecht's *Commentum in Theodolum*, holds that authors, poets, historians, commentators, prophets (*vates*), expositors, and homilists share the common activity of composing texts. The differences he enumerates, however, are functional rather than systematic. Thus an author's augmentation ("auctor ab augendo") of historical records, the words of earlier writers, and established doctrine through the act of writing ("stilo suo") is not strictly comparable to a poet's speaking ("dicat") false things for true or occasionally mixing ("commisceat") the true and the false; see *Accessus ad auctores*, ed. Huygens, 59, 75–76.

8. The exemplary case is Dante; see Ascoli, *Dante and the Making of a Modern Author*.

9. See Lees, *Cambridge History of Early Medieval English Literature* for reconsiderations of links with Anglo-Scandinavian, Gaelic, and Welsh traditions.

that governed a cross-channel empire whose ideology held that Angevin dominion was continuous with earlier English dynasties and that identity was formed by history rather than ethnicity.[10] Historians continue to debate the point at which a sense of English national identity appears.[11] What Map and Marie demonstrate for the literary sphere is that English writing is formulated by authors within institutions and jurisdictions who negotiate the margins rather than the center of official culture.

The practice of medieval English authorship takes a distinctive form in its revisionary performance and repertoire of accompanying gestures. The writers who best represent authorship in post-Conquest and late medieval England approach it obliquely as revisionary, belated, and often fraught. There is no writer who claims authorship in a way comparable to Jean de Meun's continuation of Guillaume de Lorris in the second half of the *Roman de la Rose*, where the event of Jean's succession is marked as both present and already prophesied. What we find in medieval England is a self-reflexive, performative negotiation of authorship that links external reception and literary standing to internal, textual meaning. That such a negotiation is staged repeatedly across time and historical periods reflects, I believe, the structural conditions of invention rather than a unified medieval English tradition as such, carried forward from Angevin to Ricardian and Lancastrian and even Tudor writers. Yet the model of authorial negotiation is diachronic as well as synchronic and structural. We can use it to gauge literary works over time in order to see, for example, how Angevin writers answer the problem of establishing literary authorship that subsequently challenged Ricardian and Lancastrian writers. This model allows us as well to weigh later poetic confrontations with an English national tradition, configured specifically by authorship, as it engaged writers like Stephen Hawes and John Skelton in the shift from late medieval to Tudor literary culture.

One feature that emerges prominently in the invention of literary authorship in medieval England is the complex agency exercised by writers. The description of authorship that I have sketched involves, if nothing else, a strong sense of agency. Composition itself implies agency; the Latin terms *fictor* and *formator* and the vernacular *maker* designate agents who effect a primary transformation of language and ideas into a work transmitted as a

---

10. Ashe, *Fiction and History*, 24, argues for the generative influence of insular court writing on continental French literature.

11. Gillingham, *English in the Twelfth Century*, 123–44, proposes that by 1140 a perception of an integrated nation had begun to appear. Turville-Petre, *England the Nation*, 7, contends, "In thirteenth-century England it took considerable efforts of distortion to shape both the land and the people into a vision of a single community."

text. The fourfold etymology devised for *auctor* by medieval commentators describes forms of textual agency. Scholarship has long observed (and occasionally disputed) Leo Spitzer's influential distinction between a biographical and "empirical" first-person "I" within medieval texts in order to locate one conventional form of agency: on this view, the biographical is unknown, irretrievable, or irrelevant, while the empirical is "impersonal," thereby serving as "a representative of mankind."[12] Spitzer uses poet and author as interchangeable terms, and his distinction between the biographical and empirical "I" has deep investments in modernist aesthetics as well as medieval poetics. In Spitzer's formulation, individual literary creation and tradition recede in favor of the message that a writer conveys through his transparent, instrumental agency on behalf of mankind rather than himself or herself. By contrast, the agency I find working in medieval English texts consciously foregrounds the decision to write within traditions and conventions that are neither strictly biographical nor impersonally representative.[13] Nor is such agency merely self-reflexive and inward. It connects aesthetic representation, however allusive and self-conscious the text may be on close reading, to ethics, social belief, politics, and conditions of production; it is always situated.

In these terms, authorship marks a self-projection through writing—a signature transmitted by a work—that carries into multiple dimensions of cultural prestige and power. As a corollary, authorship is performative in a strong sense, for it claims a place in relation to earlier writers and works, even if (as often) it rhetorically disavows responsibility for making the claim. And from this it follows that a writer's agency has as much to do with reception as self-representation and assertion. Authorship is a demand for standing and intelligibility: to be an author is to be recognized and regarded as such.[14] It is construed, as Jocelyn Wogan-Browne and her collaborators write, as "participation in an intellectually and morally authoritative tradition."[15] The inventional techniques for devising literary authorship depend on a careful reading of prior texts and models of discourse and on imagining how such sources might be reshaped in new conceptual and expressive forms.[16] Within

---

12. Spitzer, "Note on the Poetic and the Empirical 'I,'" 416.

13. Lerer, *Traditions*, proposes that tradition is an activity, operating in a conflated temporality of past and present, "passing on but also giving up" (2) power and control; it is insistently partial—a selection from a broad array of models made to establish a working canon, a "complex of fits and starts, of things begun and rediscovered" (46–47).

14. Van Dyke, *Chaucer's Agents*, 31, notes the tendency to emphasize the separate functions exercised by authors within the unstable theoretical distinctions of medieval authorship.

15. Wogan-Brown et al., *Idea of the Vernacular*, 4.

16. Nowlin, *Chaucer, Gower, and the Affect of Invention*, 1–35, emphasizes the alignment of invention with affect in a common structure of movement, emergence, and becoming: the

this dual framework—hermeneutic and mimetic—medieval academic literary commentary, which seemingly presents an established structure of definitions and stable distinctions, comprises a discursive field, a mixed array of commonplaces about authorship, used by turns literally and metaphorically. Writers become authors not just by creating works but by consciously placing themselves through their works within the interpretive structure of a literary system; they operate between and among its heuristic categories. Moreover, the alignment of invention and imitation with the external apparatus of commentary makes authorship an internal feature of medieval literary works, a source and not just a condition of meaning.

Before the mid-fourteenth century, authorship in medieval England has a discontinuous record; throughout, however, it is structured and made intelligible by specific moments that occur within literary works and cultural systems. My discussion focuses accordingly on writers who place themselves and their works in literary and poetic contexts linked to secular institutional structures, notably courts, patrons, and elite reading communities, including religious communities. In mapping the field of authorship from the twelfth to the late fifteenth century and slightly beyond, I begin from five working assumptions. First, authorship is multiple rather than unitary—no single model defines the field. Second, the lexicon and concepts of authorship that writers invoke are themselves heterogeneous and frequently inconsistent; they grow by accretion rather than successive and systematic reformulations of literary doctrine. Third, writers appropriate the discourses of authorship selectively and even opportunistically, sometimes in a calculated troping or abuse of terms and ideas. In other words, authorship is as much practice as program. Fourth, authorship is conditioned, though not determined, by contexts (patrons who warrant composition, reading communities, contemporary writers, and literary forebears). Fifth, authorship is an orchestration of belatedness, and it operates through a poetics of revision and imitation. I shall return to these points in the chapters that follow: my aim is not to devise a single theory of medieval English literary authorship but to interpret a multiform practice that indirectly constitutes a national tradition and continues over the period divisions between the Middle Ages and the Renaissance.

RECOVERING MEDIEVAL AUTHORSHIP

The study of medieval authorship has an immediate background in the critique of representation mounted by Roland Barthes and Michel Foucault in

---

discovery of material parallels the recognition of feeling.

the late 1960s. This background is important not because it bears directly on medieval authorship but because it affects what we have come to regard as an adequate account of medieval authorship—namely, a set of literary precepts open to critical analysis but contained within a strong sense of periodization. Barthes regards the author as an invention of European modernity ("un personnage moderne"), who has since been displaced by language and writing as the generative sources of expression. Viewed analytically, Barthes contends, the author is the past of his own book, whose meaning is to be found in the present understanding of the reader.[17] Foucault, recognizing that writing itself might paradoxically serve as a surrogate for the author, argues that authorship has a classificatory aim and stabilizes the relations of works and texts.[18] The author function that he elaborates holds that discourses, authorship prominent among them, are objects of appropriation; authorship operates in multiple rather than universal and constant ways, it is constructed and differentiated by fields, and it applies not to individuals but culturally constructed subjects occupying positions within dynamic systems of symbolic production.

For scholars seeking to recover or reconstruct medieval authorship based on periodization, Barthes and Foucault offer a provocation over history, and they force a turn toward the theoretical groundings of authorship. Barthes contentiously defines the author as a post-medieval figure who is aligned with the sovereign individual of modern science, religious reform, and emerging capitalism. Spitzer's distinction between the biographical and empirical "I" and his ready substitution of the terms poet and author provide a line of demarcation that reinforces Barthes's conventional period division between the Middle Ages and the Renaissance. For his part, Foucault explicitly declines the opportunity to write a sociohistorical analysis of authorship. He turns, however, to the late classical precedent of Saint Jerome for the procedures used to establish a canon of writings based on the value, conceptual coherence, stylistic unity, and historical dating furnished by an author.[19] He also mentions but does not develop the crucial link between authorship and authority to explain how a work acquires prestige and explanatory power. While framing the terms of debate on modern authorship, Barthes and Foucault give a direction to later accounts of medieval authorship by focusing on the importance of literary and cultural systems. Unlike theories of the poet, in which the powers of imagination and creation may transcend contexts, theories of authorship are essentially situated in historical frameworks and discursive structures. Authorship functions, then, as a relation to tradition and literary antecedents. It is by nature revisionary. The text it produces is, in Barthes's phrase, "un tissu de

---

17. Barthes, "La mort de l'auteur," 61.
18. Foucault, "Qu'est-ce qu'un auteur?" 73–104; rpt. in *Dits et écrits: 1954–1988*, 1:789–821.
19. See Vessey, "From *Cursus* to *Ductus*," 59, for a critique of Foucault's handling of Jerome.

citations, issues des mille foyers de la culture" (65). Authorship represents, in Foucault's formulation, not an origin or source of meaning but a structural constraint, a stabilizing point of reference, regulating the circulation and transformations of fiction. The "ideological function" of the author turns dialectically on the simultaneous proliferation and control of meaning.[20]

Efforts to produce a historical rather than a theoretical account of medieval authorship have a practical starting point in M.-D. Chenu's brief mapping of the derivation and semantic interplay of the terms *auctor, actor,* and *autor*.[21] Later scholarship on European vernaculars—notably, Douglas Kelly's study of medieval French literature and Sebastian Coxon's work on medieval German writers—has traced the influence of the literary systems behind Chenu's definitions on representations of authorship.[22] For Middle English writers, Burrow examines the backgrounds of literary culture in ways that bear directly on authorship. The writer Laȝamon (fl. 1200), he notes, constructs a scene of authorship as he describes himself compiling his book from a Latin copy of Bede's *Historia Ecclesiastica,* the Old English translation of Bede, and Wace's *Roman de Brut.* Burrow observes, "All the evidence suggests that Middle English literature is largely the work of men writing on parchment, wax tablets, or paper, and often like Laȝamon, consulting the writings of others in the process."[23] In Laȝamon's scene, as in other accounts, authorship is material as well as conceptual.[24]

Current understandings of authorship are grounded in the medieval practices of exegesis and pedagogy and in the relation of these practices to vernacular writing. They respond to the demands for historical and theoretical definition by demonstrating that historical models of authorship are already significantly theoretical. Two foundational texts have shaped discussion in recent decades: Alastair Minnis's *Medieval Theory of Authorship* (1984) and Rita Copeland's *Rhetoric, Hermeneutics, and Translation in the Middle Ages* (1991). It is crucial to grasp not just the historical procedures these studies describe but the analytical framework that they establish for subsequent historical and critical approaches to medieval English authorship. Both studies move away, initially at least, from the prescriptive *artes* of medieval rhetoric

---

20. Foucault elaborates the ideological function in a variant ending of the essay (*Dits et écrits,* 1.811).
21. Chenu, "Auctor, Actor, Autor," 81–86; cf. Müller, "Auctor—Actor—Author," 17–31; and Maranini, "'Proprie quidem compilare,'" 675–89.
22. Kelly, *Medieval* Opus; idem, *Conspiracy of Allusion*; Coxon, *Presentation of Authorship.*
23. Burrow, *Medieval Writers,* 28.
24. Already in Nennius's Prologue to *Historia Brittonum* (ninth century), traditional accounts are supplemented by the compilation of other textual records, including those of the Romans, Church Fathers, Scots, and Saxons.

and poetics to the broad framework for interpreting the works that inform medieval culture—the Bible in the first instance and then the pagan *auctores*, who provide the basic materials of educational curricula and thereby shape the conditions of literacy. Literacy in this instance does not refer to an abstract skill utilized indifferently across a range of texts. It is a practice in which reference, allusion, citation, and resonance are already in place to support the transmission and uncoding of textual meaning. Medieval literacy functions through and against the paradigms of literary intertexts.

Minnis argues for the central importance of medieval commentaries, prologues, and introductions to a historical understanding of literary composition in the medieval period. These sources do not prescribe a content or substance so much as furnish an idiom and conceptual scheme that writers "regarded as being sophisticated enough (and of course distinguished enough) to provide a basis for the description and justification of their own writings," even if the uses made of them move in directions not envisioned in their original purposes.[25] In Minnis's analysis of the commentary tradition, the key development is the emergence of high status and respect for the didactic and literary strategies of the human author within the interpretive framework applied to Scipture: "*auctoritas* moved from the divine realm to the human" (vii). *Auctor* and *auctoritas*, Minnis insists, are intrinsically linked. An author's work must be respected and believed; it has to answer the requirements of intrinsic worth (predominantly doctrinal orthodoxy) and authenticity (a connection to a named writer).

Minnis's account of the etymologies and functions applied to a medieval *auctor* makes it clear that they represent a spectrum of literary production rather than a single, determinate role. Grammarians and encyclopedists variously derive *auctor* from Latin *augere* ("to increase"), *agere* ("to do or perform"), *auieo* ("to tie or bind"), and Greek *autentim* ("authority"). As Jan Ziolkowski notes, a juridical sense of an *auctor* is written into the earliest extant formulations of Roman law, where an *auctor* is the guarantor of a truth or of a right capable of being held or transferred.[26] In these ways, writers expand their sources for composition, transform the materials through creation, bind poetic lines together in feet and verses, and provide a juridical point of origin and responsibility to which works and other forms of discourse can be traced. The widely cited distinctions made by Bonaventure in his commentary on Peter Lombard's *Sentences* identify a series of positions in the making of a book. The *scriptor* writes another's words without adding his own,

---

25. Minnis, *Medieval Theory of Authorship*, xi.
26. Ziolkowski, "Cultures of Authority," 425.

a *compilator* assembles passages from other works without adding his own words, a *commentator* adds his own words in a subordinate position in order to clarify the words of another, and an *auctor* writes his own words, which hold a prime place, while adding those of others for confirmation. Burrow points out that *translator* would be a logical addition to Bonaventure's listing.[27] Except for the *scriptor* who, in theory, merely reproduces the words of a given text, each of these functions requires invention, hence the critical understanding of an antecedent text and a formal idea of what a fully realized work might be. Yet even the *scriptor* can exercise an authorial role, sometimes in the metaphor of writing dictation from a greater source, as in Dante's turning to divine *materia* for which he is a scribe (*Paradiso* 10.27), and other times in providing institutional legitimacy by writing down and regulating "visionary authors"—notably women writers—outside a dominant tradition.[28] All these positions involve complex forms of agency in the execution of a work, an operation of judgment and will within textual conventions.

Minnis traces an important historical shift that occurs in the emphases of the commentary tradition as new forms of academic prologues appear in the twelfth and thirteenth centuries; the forms derive from classical and late classical models and appear prominently in the High Middle Ages.[29] The Type C prologue to commentaries, for instance, identifies the part of philosophy to which a work is assigned, usually ethics, which addresses human will, choice, and action.[30] The Aristotelian prologue of the thirteenth century adapts the schema of material, efficient, formal, and final causes to literary analysis. Minnis rightly stresses the far-reaching implications of this development: the human *auctor* becomes a secondary efficient cause in the writing of scripture, a mortal counterpart, parallel but subordinate to the divine author. In this *duplex causa efficiens*, the human author undertakes activity that is both literary and moral. He serves instrumentally in the composition of works, while his actions are viewed in an exemplary mode, as in the case of the psalms and David. He is the juridical source for *originalia*, the body of work confidently

---

27. Burrow, *Medieval Writers*, 30.

28. Summit, "Women and Authorship," 97, observes that the male scribes who record the works of medieval women visionaries not only produce a text but also serve as mediators of institutional authority and guarantors that the works can be absorbed within the official discourse that they seemingly wish to disavow. The transcribers of Margery Kempe's book are a case in point. For discussion of how scribal copying and other forms of transmission constitute an "authorship of readers," see Cornish, *Vernacular Translation*, 44–69.

29. Classifications established in Hunt, "Introduction to the 'Artes,'" 85–112; and Quain, "Mediaeval *Accessus ad auctores*," 228–42.

30. Minnis extends his study of the complications of an ethical poetics in "Trouble with Theology," 20–37.

ascribed to him and thereby available for gauging arguments in the context of doctrine and known authority.

The new prominence of the human author coincides, in Minnis's account, with a shift in interest from the allegorical to the literal level. The literal level includes rhetorical figures such as metaphor, simile, and parable—language used properly and figuratively to denote and signify. It is the human author who constructs the literal sense. His efforts are divided between devising a *forma tractandi* or *modus agendi* (a way of proceeding that correlates with style and appropriate modes of discourse) and a *forma tractatus* (the literary structure and *ordinatio* of a work that arranges material to achieve an end or objective). According to Minnis, commentators recognized that the *modus agendi* differed among books of the Bible; accordingly, multiple forms of literary analysis, including rhetorical analysis, were required.[31] What occurs decisively in the development of exegesis is the recognition that sacred and profane poetry share a common ground that becomes visible by the early fourteenth century in the analysis of style and discursive modes.[32] It is not the case that the sacred page and profane writing have somehow become equivalent or indistinguishable. Rather, the major finding that Minnis presents is that the idioms and interpretive schemes of commentary in the late Middle Ages migrate from the Bible to pagan authors and on to vernacular writers because of their focus on the human *auctor* as an agent—a maker of texts and a figure within textual culture.

Copeland, like Minnis, traces and weighs the effects of changes in the literary systems that support authorship. Her focus is on translation, the mode of authorial production that Burrow adds to supplement the functions that Bonaventure distinguishes in making a book.[33] Translation includes paraphrase, imitation, and other textual reworkings in the pedagogical tradition as well as rendering from one language to another within a program of cultural transference. Copeland situates these activities on the shifting disciplinary borders of grammar and rhetoric. The conventional aims of grammatical teaching in antiquity and the Middle Ages—proper usage and commentary on the elements of poetic texts—extend into the substantive analysis of subject matter (particularly history), which rhetoric claimed as its domain. Similarly, rhetorical invention, the initiating and foundational step in generating discourse, appropriates the grammatical techniques of commentary on the

---

31. Minnis, *Medieval Theory of Authorship*, observes, "The *modus sacrae Scripturae* is essentially a rhetorical mode" (126).

32. Ibid., 141.

33. Ellis, "Translation," 443–58, extends the point by replacing Bonaventure's hypothetical maker of a book with a translator.

poets (*enarratio poetarum*). Commentary and imitation intersect, Copeland observes, in translation, which both produces texts from earlier authoritative models and marks differences from those models. Within these terms, authorship is revisionary and rivalrous; it absorbs and contests its ostensible sources as models and signs of cultural prestige.

The relations that Copeland traces historically involve a structural dynamic that carries forward to authorship as a whole. Translation, hermeneutics, and invention necessarily reconfigure the sources they are designed to serve. The ostensible aim of their service is preservation and continuity, but the effect of their procedures is to highlight what can be changed and made new to a greater and lesser degree. Copeland identifies translation as primary when it emphasizes exegesis and seeks to refine the stylistic possibilities of the vernacular, and she labels it as secondary when it stresses the inventional process of the translation in the vernacular. These distinctions chart a synchronic and theoretical movement from detailed textual commentary on a source text to the creation of a counterpart to the source. In the process, translation comes to stand as a placeholder for a broad class of works created out of difference.[34] The grammarian's exegesis supports this development—a conceptual slippage as much as a disciplinary encroachment—by the rhetorical process of rewriting the text according to an interpretation of its meaning.[35] Copeland points out that the location of meaning outside the text is a governing principle of Christian commentary on the Bible, and she tracks the ways that textual commentary employs the rhetorical canons of invention and disposition to generate difference and the possibility of rewriting. Rhetoric retains the strong sense in Copeland's account of a practice that seeks to produce a synthetic and substantive understanding of texts, yet rhetoric also becomes performative and self-reflexive, enacting and foregrounding the interpretive procedures of textual commentary. In these shifts, then, Copeland identifies a place of authorial agency in addition to the literary roles of the *compilator* and *auctor* that scholars have long identified in medieval writers. Commentator and translator alike hold a position of authorial agency in making works.

The literary systems that shape medieval theories of authorship find their strongest historical purchase in the shift from Latin to vernacular writing. The historical dimension does not arise simply from the supposed stability of Latin and the mutability of European vernaculars. (Latin tradition has its own variations, and vernaculars prove themselves, as often as not, conservative and internally regulated.) Rather, the vernacular makes its special claim to the his-

---

34. Copeland, *Rhetoric, Hermeneutics, and Translation*, 93.
35. Ibid., 76.

torical because of its belatedness—specifically, because its belatedness signals a relation to cultural authority. Dante is a paradigmatic figure for his appropriation of literary systems to the vernacular lyric (in the *Vita nuova, De vulgari eloquentia,* and *Convivio*) and to his *Commedia* (in the *accessus* provided by the "Epistle to Can Grande"). Minnis and Copeland point to Gower and Chaucer as important examples in medieval England. Minnis notes Gower's adaptation of the prophetic voice as a *forma tractandi* in the *Vox clamantis* and his use of the academic prologue in both the *Vox* and the *Confessio Amantis*. He identifies the *Prologus* of the *Confessio* as an extrinsic prologue concerned with wisdom and the beginning of Book 1 (lines 1–92) as an intrinsic prologue focused on the human *auctor*. The *Confessio,* as Minnis shows, not only employs but also exploits the paratexts of academic commentary to examine the ethical components of love (its principle *materia*) and relate those moral lessons to the political challenges of governance. Copeland dramatically reverses direction by taking Book 7—Gower's schematization of learning and a mirror for princes—as the key to the *Confessio*. She finds in the analytical divisions of Gower's exegetical structure a pattern of meaning that serves directly as the *materia* that Gower invents as an author. From this she traces both the logic of grouping narratives within the penitential framework of the Seven Deadly Sins and the differences from sources and intertexts (Ovid most prominent among them) that reveal Gower's narratives as works of translation already shaped by interpretation.

Chaucer presents Minnis and Copeland with a more difficult case of vernacular appropriation. Minnis notes Chaucer's use of the critical vocabulary associated with literary exegesis and his adoption of compilation as a literary form and authorial activity. The compiler, he says, is a figure responsible not for the stories he gathers but for the arrangement he gives them. At stake here is Chaucer's frequent disavowal of what he reports, of which the salient example is perhaps the pilgrim-narrator's claim in the *Canterbury Tales* to "telle a tale after a man" (I.731)—that is, to repeat the stories of his fictional characters in their own words and thus make them the authorities he collects, cites, and disavows as needed. The effect, Minnis observes, is that "the 'lewd compilator' has become the compiler of the 'lewd.'"[36] Copeland focuses on a different *compilatio*—the *Legend of Good Women*—as her major illustration of Chaucer's redirection of authorial conventions. Like Minnis, she notes Chaucer's adaptation of vocabulary and apparatus from exegesis, but she directs her interests to the two differing Prologues to the poem, which represent "Chaucer's most

---

36. Minnis, *Medieval Theory of Authorship,* 203.

sustained examination of vernacular authorship."³⁷ The F and G Prologues, she says, serve as *accessus* in much the same way as do scholastic introductions to Ovid's *Heroides*, but they work prospectively and make interpretation of the stories itself the material invented by the poet-narrator. This shift in the object of invention grounds a collection centered on classical heroines understood and represented through vernacular authorship, not Latin authority. It displaces the canonical sources of narrative for the inventional power of the translator, producing stories distinguished precisely by their difference from their sources.

Subsequent accounts of medieval English authorship build on the work of Minnis and Copeland. In an overview of approaches, Stephen Partridge notes that the focal points for inquiry have been paratexts, self-reflexive devices, intertextuality, the material text, and reception.³⁸ Wogan-Browne and her collaborators, focusing on the adaptations and reception of theoretical schemes, note that the "theoretical components are self-evidently included for local and strategic purposes" and "heavily situated."³⁹ Most studies concentrate on the rhetorical postures in these materials that were open to writers in the fourteenth and fifteenth centuries. Graham Caie notes the rise of named vernacular authors in the period and suggests that a change occurs in the effects produced by modesty topoi, the claims to be a compiler or maker, and the literary tactics of disavowal: "Many [declarations of modesty] are deliberately drawing attention to the process of composition and by playing with these modesty topoi they are *confirming* not *denying* their originality and power of creativity."⁴⁰ The evidence of this change, for Caie, lies in the presentation and *ordinatio* of manuscripts where a hierarchy of scripts prevails and where glosses and commentaries (as in the Ellesmere Chaucer) are the marks of privileged, authoritative, or canonical texts.

Vincent Gillespie examines a group of authorial poses, including the fiction of authorial intent, which he describes, drawing on Copeland and Stephen Melville, as a "holding category" for the interpretation that is supplied by the magisterial reader in the commentary tradition.⁴¹ For Gillespie, the figure of the classical orator lends the probity required for claims to authorship and implicitly complements the moral authority of biblical authors identified by Minnis. Accordingly, Dante presents the poet, if not precisely the author, as a

---

37. Copeland, *Rhetoric, Hermeneutics, and Translation*, 186.
38. Partridge and Kwakkel, *Author, Reader, Book*, 4.
39. Evans et al., "Notion of Vernacular Theory," in Wogan-Browne et al., *Idea of the Vernacular*, 316.
40. Caie, "'I do not wish to be called auctour,'" 13–14.
41. Gillespie, "Authorship," 138.

theologian and, in conjunction with Petrarch, as an advocate for a protohumanist poetics, while Machaut and fourteenth-century French writers offer a position for representing authorial subjectivity within courtly culture. Gillespie sees both a promotion and critique of laureate status in late medieval English writers, who enact an "abnegation of authorial responsibility" (152) that ends, as in Chaucer's *House of Fame,* with stories telling themselves.

Anthony Bale, like Caie, finds an important development in the naming of authors in the late Middle Ages. Naming identifies a work worth reading and distinguishes it from other discursive forms (what he calls "subliterary forms" such as ballads, lyrics, and the contents of commonplace books).[42] Authors, even those fictitious and invented, can serve as a shadow presence in high literary culture, as in the case of Chaucer's Lollius or Mandeville. In religious and mystical writing, however, the stakes are considerably higher, for authorship as a practice carried out by figures like Margery Kempe, who makes her book by dictating to male scribes, reveals a deep ambivalence between the written word and divine mystery. Bale also remarks the commodification of authors that appears in late medieval England as a corollary of naming. Particularly in the laureate tradition promoted by John Lydgate for Chaucer and for himself, authors are conferred "a kind of celebrity" in their rhetorical positions, which secures their "brand value."[43] For the literary tradition, the English national author advanced in Early Modern print culture is already substantially present in fifteenth-century poetic and manuscript culture.

One valuable finding in the continuing research is that highly nuanced distinctions operate within authorship, beyond such contrasts as Latin and vernacular, imaginative and practical, popular and elite, or written and oral. Stephanie Trigg distinguishes the poet as a social performer in oral culture from the writer who shapes and constructs texts within literary tradition and the author who defines his reception.[44] Kellie Robertson proposes that a writer's literary production occupies a third space between labor and leisure, as located by the colophons to the first and third recensions of Gower's *Confessio Amantis* and to the *Vox Clamantis* ("inter labores et ocia") or by the ambivalent reflection on language as work added to the C-text of *Piers Plowman* (Passus 6).[45] Copeland argues, in a subsequent study of rhetoric and authorship, that the figure of *insinuatio,* by which an orator distances himself from the objectionable materials he must argue, supports the claims of a writer's fiction to offer meaning in its own right. *Insinuatio,* in this sense, complements

---

42. Bale, "From Translator to Laureate," 923.
43. Ibid., 927, 930; citing Meyer-Lee, *Poets and Power,* 52.
44. Trigg, *Congenial Souls,* 44–55.
45. Robertson, "Authorial Work," 447.

and complicates the juridical sense of authorship; it strategically displaces the locus of responsibility for discourse beyond the author to his sources in a chain of substitution and authority.[46]

Several important studies look at the afterlife of medieval authorship as a way of defining its features. A. C. Spearing revises the itinerary from medieval to Renaissance.[47] Chaucer's English disciples, he argues, construct a form of authorship in their treatment of Chaucer that redirects his poetry from its connections with Italian protohumanism and produces a "father Chaucer" who subsequently dominates the field of elite literary production. This figure serves the ambitions of Hoccleve, Lydgate, and others by enabling their succession in a literary genealogy that parallels Lancastrian political succession; it serves the aims of Tudor writers by offering in Chaucer an obsolete poet to be honored and replaced by modernity. Seth Lerer traces Chaucer's fifteenth-century reception through reading, imitation, and material production.[48] Chaucer's authority, he contends, shapes and overmatches his readers at the same time that it generates a laureate poetics, which finds its most powerful means of expression in print culture and its full social and political expression in Early Modern writers. Robert Meyer-Lee foregrounds the relationship of authors to political authority and finds two distinctive modes operating in late medieval England— a posture of abjection and begging in Hoccleve and a laureate status inhabited, though not overtly claimed, by Lydgate.[49] On this reading, Lydgate's example, in counterpoint with Hoccleve's subordination, drives authorial self-presentation, patronage, and cultural prestige far into the Early Modern period. The rethinking of the medieval-Early Modern divide in recent decades, notably in formulations like James Simpson's revolutionary and reformist models of historical transition, inevitably puts pressure on these accounts of medieval authorship.[50] The crucial shift for my inquiry is from the development of medieval into Early Modern forms to the uses of medieval authorship by Early Modern writers.

AUTHORSHIP AND LITERARY HISTORY

I stated earlier that literary authorship in medieval England emerged within a discontinuous literary history. Authorship does not have a founding moment followed by successive phases of elaboration. It operates, rather, in complex

---

46. Copeland, "Insinuating Authors."
47. Spearing, *Medieval to Renaissance*, 1–14.
48. Lerer, *Chaucer and His Readers*, 3–21.
49. Meyer-Lee, *Poets and Power*, 1–11.
50. Simpson, *Reform and Cultural Revolution*, 35–36; cf. Cummings and Simpson, *Cultural Reformations*, 1–9.

temporalities, sometimes disarticulated and other times overlapping (both conditions hold for insular Latin, French, and English literary traditions). Old English literature had a robust vernacular tradition but no focus on authorship as such. Anglo-Latin writing of the Old English period produces one exception—important because it is finally a refusal of authorship—in Bede's biographical notice, which functions as a summative *rectractatio* setting out his corpus of works. In a sense, then, authorship is a delayed effect, one of many, from the disruption of Latin and vernacular insular traditions and from the reshaping of the institutional structures that supported those traditions. The Norman Conquest of 1066, unlike the Danish monarchy in place from 1016 to 1042, displaced literary culture and began a process that would channel Anglo-Saxon writing and its achievements as a cosmopolitan vernacular with few counterparts toward an antiquarian project during its afterlife in the eleventh and twelfth centuries.[51] Christopher Cannon describes the period 1066–1300 as a time of formal invention and experiment in the English vernacular because writers were unaware of each other and isolated from vernacular models and examples.[52] Literary historians debate the precise effects of the Conquest on literary culture as well as national identity.[53] What seems beyond dispute, however, is that the Conquest brought a new administrative order, one both political and ecclesiastical, and that this change directly affected the institutional arrangements supporting literary production, recording, transmission, and reception.[54]

Consequently, the literary history that might otherwise frame the emergence of medieval English authorship is a record of survivals and discontinuities until the mid-fourteenth century and arguably well into the fifteenth century. Provincial as well as metropolitan centers support writing that ranges from secular and religious compositions to didactic and historical works; the boundaries marking off these modes are at once visible and permeable. Latin, French, and English serve as the principal languages of official record and imaginative expression, though they are not the only languages of poetry.[55] They have shared and separate histories that shift dynamically in relation to each other across the medieval period. The influence is not unidirectional, for

---

51. For an overview and critical discussion, see Lerer, "Old English," 7–34; and Treharne, "Categorization, Periodization," 247–73 on the "adaptive" character of writing in English. Swan, "Old English Textual Activity," 151, says that Old English writing in the twelfth century "could be seen as a kind of subculture."

52. Cannon, *Grounds of English Literature*, 7.

53. For an overview of the positions, see Ashe, *Fiction and History*, 1–15.

54. Clanchy, *From Memory to Written Record*.

55. The twelfth-century Anglo-French prose description of Britain, *De Bretaine*, enumerates five historical languages (British, English, Scottish, Pictish, and Latin) and adds Norman and French as a sixth; quoted from Wogan-Browne et al., *Vernacular Literary Theory*, 15–18.

patronage and reading communities often determine the choice of linguistic medium for a writer, notably along the lines of gender. In the interplay of languages, the locus of authority shifts, too, so that, at certain points, Latin and French effectively serve as classical languages—that is, languages conveying the materials of classical antiquity. And insular writing in French clearly serves as a source not only for Middle English translations and adaptations but also for canonical forms and subject matter that become dominant in continental French literature.[56] Against this background, it is impossible to write a unitary history of authorship in medieval England, to impose a coherence in which, as Cannon suggests, history as an explanatory narrative substitutes itself for the past.[57] We must look instead to moments when writers claim authorship and locate themselves in relation to literary culture, more often than not in a subtle and ambivalent relation. These moments are not simply exemplary but constitutive; they are the primary record of writers acting within historical contexts to inaugurate themselves as authors. Even if we possessed a continuous literary history from the Old English period to the Tudor period, the study of authorship would necessarily return to such moments as the concrete particulars of historical agency.[58]

My examination of medieval English literary authorship begins in part 1 with two writers associated with the court of Henry II. Chapter 1 focuses on the courtier, secular clerk, and satirist Walter Map. Map understands authorship as a claim made simultaneously against and within the structure of high literary culture. Henry's court privileged history and didactic writing, and Map devises his authorship as an alternative to these dominant forms, producing what I describe as a counter-authorship. He consciously positions himself as a writer on the margins rather than at the center of literary discourse (the court as center is displaced and unrecognizable for Map). His subject matter is the "friuola narracio" dismissed or ignored in established genres and canons. The texts he produces in his *De nugis curialium* (*Courtiers' Trifles*)—a compilation of satire, anecdote, legend, romance, and exhortation—find their meaning in readers with the hermeneutic skills and agility to match his inventions. A "modern" gleefully mistaken for an "ancient" in his most successful piece of literary imitation, the "Dissuasio Valerii," Map writes the ambivalence

---

56. See Ashe, *Fiction and History*, 23, for a summary.
57. Cannon, *Grounds of English Literature*, 25.
58. Lerer, "Epilogue," 231–34, makes a similar point about the mechanisms by which literary history becomes intelligible. Extending John Guillory's claim (*Cultural Capital*) that canons exercise authority by a principle of selection that sets works in relation to each other, Lerer sees systems of retrieval (the organization of library holdings and personal collections) and anthologies (particularly important for medieval works) as concrete embodiments of explanation by particulars.

of authorship into his own narratives and metafiction. He does not establish a tradition as such. Rather, he invents a model of authorship ostensibly decentered from authority and working the margins of literary culture. It is a model that later medieval English writers will repeatedly discover on their own terms and in their own contexts of writing and reception.

Chapter 2 examines the authorship that Marie de France invents for herself by inscribing her presence in her works and by imagining a new formulation of Ovidian elegy. Marie is the starting point for English Ovidianism. Across her corpus, with striking consistency, the prologues and epilogues of Marie's works situate her writing within the conventions of authorship. She is a compiler and translator between traditions as well as texts. The *Fables* arrive for her through a (fictonal) chain of transmission from Greek to Latin to English, and their mobility as a work symbolizes authorial translation itself. Similarly, her poems on Saint Patrick and Saint Audrey (if the latter is rightly attributed to her) are relocated from Latin sources to vernacular texts and from monastic to lay contexts of reception. In all these works, Marie explicitly intends to be seen and remembered as the author. The full effects of her claim to authorship become visible in the revisionary practices of the *Lais*, which reinvent Ovid's erotic teachings within a different social structure and set of relations. In the *Ars amatoria* and *Remedia amoris*, Ovid imagines a four-stage program devised to find a lover, capture her, extend the period of pleasure in a love affair, and terminate it when a lover grows tiresome. In its insistence on craft and technique (*ars*), the Ovidian program is an exercise in self-mastery and poetic authorship as well as erotic conquest. The *magister amoris* is a practitioner and victim of his craft and thus becomes a subject as well as the author of his story. Marie revises the Ovidian program and dismisses its illusion that control emanates from a systematic intention and fully realized design—in short, from a narrative imagined and then executed. In an iconic burning of *Le livre Ovide*, usually taken to represent the *Remedia amoris*, Marie commits herself to the *materia* of Ovid's third phase, the extended interim of erotic pleasure. As she compiles her stories from Celtic sources and transfers them from oral form to writing, she foregrounds at the same time the thematic and rhetorical resources of elaboration, adornment, and delay to rewrite Ovid within the contexts of twelfth-century baronial culture.

In the late fourteenth century, Middle English writing consolidates its place as a literary medium and a vibrant national and at times cosmopolitan tradition. Part 2 concentrates on the two poets who connect the literary achievements of their works to the role of the author. Chapter 3 examines the works of John Gower, the poet who most overtly seeks to become an author in trilingual medieval England. Throughout his career, Gower employs the textual apparatus of biblical and classical commentary to frame his poems. He sees his major works—the *Mirour de l'Omme, Vox Clamantis,* and *Confessio Amantis*—as comprising a literary canon, and he generates paratexts to sustain the structure of his canon, even as the works themselves undergo development, revision, and recontextualization.[59] Authorship figures internally in the *Mirour* and *Vox* through the voice of an exemplary self, preacher, and prophet. It is marked externally in Gower's glosses in the *Confessio* and his creation of the persona of a lover whose final dismissal from erotic service coincides with Gower's return to his earlier body of didactic writing. Gower is also the custodian of his reputation as an author. Here he has precedents in Map obliquely and Marie explicitly, while his contemporaries embed their authorship within their fictions. Moreover, after completing the *Confessio*, Gower creates a secondary and parallel canon of shorter poems, again in three languages, that stands as a commentary and extension of his major poems.

Chapter 4 analyzes the ambivalent and unreproducable authorship devised by Geoffrey Chaucer. Chaucer was recognized as an author by his contemporaries, who respond as much to his early poetry as to *Troilus and Criseyde* and his translation of Boethius. Their recognition of him is matched by Chaucer's own composition of embedded poetic catalogues that list and classify his works. Chaucer's inscription of himself as an author proceeds, however, by imitation and refusal. Imitation sets him visibly in relation to literary traditions, canons, and forebears. Refusal is a mechanism of agency that does not cancel imitation but allows instead a revisionary poetics. Chaucer directs this twin process to both vernacular and classical writing. The vernacular is a medium and alternative for classical sources, but it is also an established tradition with named authors, canonical forms, and cultural prestige. The arc of his career runs from revisionary poetics to self-sustaining fiction. Chaucer initially claims authorship in a courtly sphere by redacting the vernacular into the works for which his contemporaries recognize him. At mid-career, he imitates classical sources by rewriting antiquity as an imaginative sphere parallel to courtly culture. The discursive forms that he redirects in this project are epic and elegy; he appropriates the fictions of authorship devised for each. In the *Canterbury Tales*, he conceives a radically different form of authorship. As a compiler and translator, he speaks "proprely" and tells a tale "after a man" (and woman) who is not an external authority but a character in his own fiction. The extrinsic and internal dimensions of authorship from the commentary tradition and vernacular practitioners reach a vanishing point in Chaucer's erasure of himself as the agent responsible for his texts.

---

59. Wogan-Browne et al. find a parallel to Gower in Reginald Pecock's concern to present a unified canon of his works (*Idea of the Vernacular*, 15).

The poetic achievements of Gower, Chaucer, and Langland leave no immediate models of authorship available to succeeding writers. In part 3, my interest lies, accordingly, in the efforts in the early fifteenth century to fabricate alternate links with Gower and Chaucer as literary authors (the Langland tradition, broadly speaking, comprises poems of controversy and dissent rather than literary authorship). In chapter 5, I consider the means that Thomas Hoccleve and John Lydgate use to connect themselves to their vernacular masters. Our current understanding rightly emphasizes that discipleship and literary genealogy position Hoccleve and Lydgate as poetic heirs, particularly as heirs to Chaucer. Their mechanism of succession is what I will call a simulation of authorship. Hoccleve and Lydgate, I argue, see their literary forebears as an occasion, a rhetorical topic for invention; they recontextualize them selectively and partially, and present these counterfeit versions as the authorial models that are reproduced deferentially and belatedly in their own works. This process occurs, moreover, in parallel with fictions of patronage that similarly appropriate and reproduce occasions for writing—some commissioned, others imagined, but all structured by a revisionary poetics. It runs in tandem, moreover, with the politics of succession driving Lancastrian anxieties over descent and royal legitimation.

Chapter 6 looks closely at Hoccleve's overdetermined roles as scribe, commentator, compiler, translator, and first-person author. In all these, Hoccleve visibly exploits the commonplaces of authorship. The works he produces, however, are notably partial and defective. The effect is not simply to evoke his authorial models as warrants for writing but to display his products as reproductions and substitutes for the originals. Lydgate, as I show in chapter 7, follows a similar strategy. The courtly poems in his minor canon, traditionally (if wrongly) separated from his religious and instructional writing, are a performance of authorship within recognized genres and forms, troping Chaucer's dream poems in particular. The "epic project" of writing the narratives of Thebes (*The Siege of Thebes*), Troy (*Troy Book*), and Rome (*The Serpent of Division*)—a metanarrative of aristocratic selfhood, chivalric institutions, and statecraft promoted by Lancastrian sponsorship—stands as a counterpart to Chaucer's classicizing poems, which Lydgate repeatedly invokes. In *Fall of Princes*, his last major work, Lydgate undertakes his most intricate negotiation of authorship. He translates, in an active sense, the exemplary narratives of *de casibus* tragedy from Laurent de Premierfait's aristocratic French audience, from Boccaccio's original Latin work and its French redactions, and from Duke Humphrey's ambitions as patron to the larger political aims of a civic humanism founded on the arts of language. For both Hoccleve and Lydgate, the outcome of their authorial inventions is a literary history whose origins lie in the agency of belatedness and whose effect is to produce a tradition that serves sixteenth-century English writers as a past to be evoked and, inevitably, superseded.

In the afterword, I discuss briefly the uses made of medieval English literary authorship on the moving borders of the Early Modern period. Tudor and early Elizabethan writers saw in medieval works a national literary tradition based on a multiform practice of authorship; there were immediate connections for them in fifteenth-century writers and a more distant founding triumvirate in Gower, Chaucer, and Lydgate. What kinds of ambition and agency could a national tradition serve construed in this way? In Stephen Hawes's *Pastime of Pleasure,* infused as it is with Lydgate, we see an effort to sustain forms of medieval authorship within early humanist courtly culture, a culture that Lydgate partially (but only partially) anticipates. In John Skelton's *Garlande or Chapelet of Laurell,* the medieval English authors are placeholders for the fame and laureate status that Skelton bestows on himself in direct self-inauguration. Hawes and Skelton give us two moments in a literary history that becomes fully legible with the authorship of Edmund Spenser. But these moments are not the only ones that limn the afterlife of medieval English authorship. Legislation in 1543 effectively defines a medieval English canon for the nation by limiting the printing of medieval authors to Chaucer and Gower and condemning others as "papist, retrograde, unworthy of dissemination," while the revival of medieval forms in the 1550s under Queen Mary supports a Catholic religious tradition.[60] As the reception history suggests in bold strokes and fine detail, medieval practices of authorship simultaneously constitute Renaissance authorial programs and remain unresolved within them.

My focus in this book is on the reciprocal and defining pressures that shape literary authorship in key instances from the visible reestablishment of English literary culture in the later twelfth century to the engagement with medieval forms within sixteenth-century humanism. This is a process that occurs within a discontinuous literary history and across three languages of record. I do not offer a survey or catalogue of authorship for this period. My interest lies, rather, in writers who claim authorship within and against dominant practices. Authorship is for them a position of belatedness, an inventive dialectic of agency and appropriation from below and from outside. It functions in relation to literary tradition and forms of cultural authority while, at the same time, resituating and recontextualizing both of them. In this respect, authorial invention significantly overlaps imitation in the shifting measures of rivalry and deference that generate a counterpart to a canonical source, inter-

---

60. Lerer, "Literary Histories," 81.

text, or genre. In the great interlocked scenes of authorial self-inauguration—Statius's sending the *Thebaid* to track the footsteps of the *Aeneid*, Dante's inclusion of himself in the *bella scuola* of the ancient poets, Chaucer's adaptation of the scene from Dante in the bidding prayer of *Troilus and Criseyde*—the objective and the energies are insistently revisionary. To be an author is to occupy and transform an already inhabited imaginative space within a literary system that structures orders of knowledge, belief, and desire.

PART 1

Inventions

PRELUDE

Bede and the Denial of Authorship

IN THE final chapter of his *Ecclesiastical History of the English People*, the Venerable Bede inserts a biographical notice of his life and works (5.24). The notice is the most extensive and nuanced account of authorship by an English writer before the Norman Conquest. The life Bede describes, structured by study and monastic observance, is exclusively institutional. He is born within the holdings of Monkwearmouth, enters the monastery as an oblate at age seven, and devotes himself throughout to reflection on scripture: "omnem meditandis scripturis operam dedi."[1] The pleasures he records, between the duties of monastic discipline and liturgy, are learning, teaching, and writing: "semper aut discere, aut docere, aut scribere dulce habui." Though earlier Latin and vernacular writers have a sense of working within their traditions of composition, Bede's account is arguably the earliest formal representation of authorship in English literary history. Its importance lies, however, not as a determining origin for later medieval conceptions of authorship but as a point of orientation that reveals the stakes of authorship and its multiple formulations.

Bede's account is particularly notable for its nuanced lexicon of authorship, which distinguishes various modes of textual production within a comprehensive project of writing. As Emily V. Thornbury points out, in Old

---

1. Bede, *Bede's Ecclesiastical History of the English People*, 566.

English and Anglo-Latin usage, the terms applied to poets and writers align composition with larger functions, chiefly social and political.[2] Bede arranges the *History* as a compilation ("Haec de historia ecclesiastica ... digessi") gathered from the writings of the ancients, the traditions of his predecessors, and his own direct knowledge. Weaving together sources is a literary practice continuous with monastic discipline. Thus, for his own needs and those of his brethren, he compiles brief annotations on scripture from the Church Fathers ("breuiter anotare") or adds his own comments ("superadicere curaui") to the meaning and interpretation they offer.[3] His list of works includes commentary on the prophets excerpted from Jerome ("distinctiones capitulorum ex tractu beati Hieronomi excerptas") and whatever he found in Augustine's works on Paul, transcribed in order ("cuncta per ordinem transscribere curaui"). He translates Paulinus's metrical work on St. Felix into prose ("in prosam transtuli") and corrects the sense, as far as he is able, of the life and passion of St. Anastasius ("prout potui, ad sensum correxi"), which had already been badly translated and incompetently emended. He composes both poetic and prose lives of St. Cuthbert ("prius heroico metro et postmodum plano sermone, descripsi"), an *opus geminatum* with substantial revision from the hexametrical to the prose version.[4] In addition, he undertakes a careful annotation of the established Hieronymian martyrology ("diligenter adnotare studui") and supplements his treatise on metrics with a study of the rhetorical figures used in scripture.

For the other works listed in the passage by title or topic (the majority of Bede's forty-four entries), the understood verb in Bede's account is "I composed" or simply "I wrote." The Old English translation of the *History* made in the late ninth or early tenth century supplies these verbs as required for the commentary on Genesis ("ic sette") and the history of the abbots ("ic awrat"). The translation is also a significant document for Bede's reception and recontextualization, for it condenses Bede's broad authorial lexicon in order to make him a source of composition, hence an author in his own right. His arrangement of the *History* (Latin "digessi") is expressed as his making the work (Old English "ic gedyde").[5] His brief annotations of the Fathers are

---

2. Thornbury, *Becoming a Poet in Anglo-Saxon England*, 11–36. Thornbury points out that Aldhelm is the only Anglo-Saxon writer to be called a *scop*, in a single instance that also describes him as "bonus auctor" (24).

3. Westgard, "Bede and the Continent in the Carolingian Age and Beyond," 201–15, observes that the autobiographical sketch envisions a wide audience, including clerical and political elites.

4. Bede refers to the double work earlier in the *History* 4.28.

5. Bede, *Old English Version of Bede's Ecclesiastical History of The English People*, 480.

rendered by the doublets *writan* and *settan*: "I wrote and composed" ("ic ... wrat 7 sette"). The excerpts from Jerome on the prophets are not mentioned, while the transcription of Augustine's remarks on Paul combines copying and compilation in a single term: "ic awrat." Similarly, the lives of Cuthbert, rendered from verse to prose (Latin "descripsi"), are written ("ic awrat"), and the *History* itself is explicitly composed by its author ("ic on fif bec gesette").[6] Bede's annotation of the martyrology, which gave it a historical or narrative form, is made emphatically the product of his writing: "ic geornlice awrat."[7]

Bede's listing of his works follows the model of Gregory of Tours (*Libri historiarum* 10.31.18) as well as the more distant influences of Augustine's *Retractationes* and the career summaries of classical writers, of which Vergil's is the most notable.[8] His literary career intriguingly parallels the one that he sketches for Caedmon in his *History* (4.22), which tallies Caedmon's works sequentially from creation through apocalypse and emphasizes those that turn mankind from love of the world to the love and exercise of good works.[9] Caedmon, as Bede makes clear, is a figure of grace ("Uisumque est omnibus caelestem ei a Domino concessam esse gratiam"). Bede, by contrast, describes himself as a figure who performs all the functions associated with medieval textual production—transcription, commentary, compilation, translation, redaction, composition.[10] Despite the parallels, then, Caedmon as a poet is distinguished from Bede as an author. The different functions that Bede enumerates for himself match and even extend beyond the activities of authorship defined in the High Middle Ages through the roles of the scribe, compiler, commentator, and author.[11] Bede's account also reflects the fourfold sense of author derived etymologically by medieval grammarians: someone who creates (*agere*), aug-

---

6. Miller, *Collation*, 595, records the variant of *awrat* for *gesette* in the entry for Bede's *History*.

7. Lapidge, "Saintly Life in Anglo-Saxon England," 250–51, on Bede's martyrologium. The variant reads, "ic gesette martyloigium [*sic*]" and later for the book of Bede's epigrams, "Ic wrat bóc epigrāmatum" (Miller, *Collation*, 595).

8. Wallace-Hadrill, *Bede's* Ecclesiastical History of the English People, 203. Bede uses Augustine's *Retractationes* as a guide for his *Retractatio in Actus Apostolorum*, which alters and corrects parts of his *Expositio in Actus Apostolorum*.

9. Vessey, "From *Cursus* to *Ductus*," 93–94.

10. The brief listing of Aldhelm's writings (5.18), including his *opus geminatum*, suggests an earlier Latin model to match the vernacular model of Caedmon. Bede also gives an account of Gregory the Great's writings (2.1). He describes Adamnan's book on the holy places (5.15–16), substituting portions of his own redaction of the work for the original (*Ecclesiastical History*, 508n2).

11. Bonaventure, quaestio 4, proem to commentary on Peter Lombard's *Sentences*; quoted in Burrow, *Medieval Writers*, 29–31.

ments (*augere*), binds together (*auieo*), and bears responsibility for a piece of discourse (*autentim*).[12]

In its immediate historical context, Bede's practice reflects a significant reformulation of classical authorship. In Roman tradition, writers are in the earliest cases subordinate artisans or outside professionals and only later aristocrats named as authors; their literary works circulate in a network of patronage and have public life, chiefly political and military honors, as their objective.[13] The most prominent successors to this tradition are late classical Christian writers like Augustine, Ambrose, Jerome, and Cassiodorus, who led secular and public lives at some point. Shaped entirely by monastic discipline, Bede appropriates the transformation of classical authorship by redirecting literary composition from an instrument of pagan worldly ambition and elite Christian pastoral teaching to a means for sustaining a different social reality, the *alter orbis* of spiritual and intellectual withdrawal that divides him from both the world and ascetic monasticism.[14] He thereby embeds authorship within specific collective experience and social performance, from the transcription and compilation of sources through to the reception of works. Bede's final scene of authorship, conveyed by his pupil Cuthbert's letter on his death, portrays Bede teaching, dictating, and translating John's gospel into English.[15] Moreover, Bede textualizes authorship—that is, he directs the various functions associated with composition toward the objective of creating a written text. The prefatory letter to bishop Acca of Hexham in Bede's commentary on Luke concentrates composition and textual production in the figure of a writer who is also an amanuensis and copyist ("ipse mihi dictator simul notarius et librarius").[16] In this respect, the Old English translation of the *History*, in its lexical focus on writing and composition, does not betray an impoverished or reductive understanding of the range of authorship that Bede maps for himself in the Latin text. In fact, it accurately describes demanding intellectual tasks—for example, Bede's effort to express the literal and allegorical senses of the Fathers and to correct the garbled text of Anastasius's life and passion. Rather, the concentrated lexicon of the translation advances, in its own terms, the objective of portraying Bede as an author.

---

12. Minnis, *Medieval Theory of Authorship*, 10–12. In the prefatory letter to King Ceolwulf that accompanies the *History*, this last sense is the one that Bede attaches to *auctores*, by which he means the sources from which he has written ("in his quae scripsi").

13. Farrell, "Greeks Lives and Roman Careers in the Classical *Vita* Tradition," 34–35.

14. Frantzen, "Englishness of Bede, from Then to Now," 229–30. Kendall, "Bede and Education," 110–12, stresses a break from the ascetic tradition in favor of scholarship and learning.

15. Cuthbert, "Epistola de obitu Bedae," in Bede, *Ecclesiastical History*, 583.

16. Bede, *In Lucae Evangelium Expositio*, 7.

Bede's powerful integration of writing is only one of many forms and modes of authorship. In one sense, the master narrative of medieval English authorship is the unraveling of Bede's extraordinary synthesis of the functions and institutional site of writing. I begin with his account because it furnishes terms and fundamental concepts for an historical and critical understanding. Chief among these are the power of tradition as a source for writing and interpretation, the active reworking of texts through techniques of invention and imitation, the shifting relation of Latin and vernacular languages as forms of cultural authority, particularly through translation, and the contextual grounding supplied by audience and reception. In addition, Bede names himself as an author and is recognized as such in England and on the Continent.[17] Bede's terms and concepts do not, of course, come down in an unbroken historical succession. The Scandinavian incursions of the ninth century and the Norman Conquest of the twelfth century profoundly disrupt historical continuity and reconfigure the lines of influence. The incursions divide Old English literature in Latin and the vernacular into at least two periods.[18] Bede's work substantially returns to England from its continental circulation after the destruction of the institutional structures that originally made it possible. The Conquest effects a dislocation rather than a break in English literary culture, for earlier Latin and vernacular traditions persist in complex ways, just as indigenous social structures remain in place while the upper echelons of political and ecclesiastical administration are replaced.[19] Bede is a figure who must be assimilated into Anglo-Norman historiography, while the Old English literary tradition proves resilient, if not wholly vital, until the thirteenth century.

The narrative of Bede's authorship is silent, however, in one key respect. In the exemplary story of Caedmon, Bede describes a process of composition working through grace that reproduces essential aspects of medieval grammatical education. Caedmon learns from scripture through translators ("per interpretes") and transposes the content into English poems of technical accomplishment and aesthetic effect. Translation was a pedagogical feature of late classical and medieval curricula, and so was the exercise of reworking the same materials in verse and prose, as Bede and Aldhelm demonstrate.[20] The striking feature of Bede's account is the cancellation of fiction. Caedmon receives the art of poetry ("canendi artem") through divine grace and consequently is unable to compose on other topics: "Vnde nil umquam friuoli et superuacui poematis facere potuit, sed ea tantummodo, quae ad religionem

---

17. Cooper, "Choosing Poetic Fathers," 30–33.
18. Wormald, "Anglo-Saxon Society and Its Literature," 1.
19. Lerer, "Old English," 7–34; Cannon, *Grounds of English Literature*, 17–49.
20. Hanna et al., "Latin Commentary," 363–421.

pertinent, religiosam eius linguam decebant" [Hence he could never compose any foolish or trivial poems but only those which were concerned with devotion and so were fitting for his devout tongue to utter].[21] Caedmon's secular life, Bede goes on to observe, taught him no secular songs at all ("nil carminum aliquando didicerat"). *Friuolus* and *superuacuus* conventionally designate the literary and even comprise an aesthetic, a counter-classical sensibility with roots in Ovid and a robust medieval heritage.[22] The Old English equivalents to these terms make clear the nature of the literary for Bede's near contemporaries and readers: "leasunge, ne idles leoþes" [lies and superfluous poems].

The problem that Bede suppresses here is the place of literary fiction within the mechanisms of authorship and the institutional structures of scribal culture. In his account, the problem is situated in the vernacular. Caedmon stands outside the practice of secular composition; the story of his divine inspiration suggests that the secular topics he cannot improvise probably refer to folk tradition and popular poetry, symbolized in Bede's story by the harp circulating at the feast that Caedmon abandons. At the same time, Bede himself is shaped by a deep classicism—the informing presence of classical writers, particularly Vergil, within grammatical training and in the writings of the Church Fathers who are his *auctores*. Though educational reforms in the early Middle Ages propose Christian writers as counterparts or replacements for classical Latin writers, the conditions of literacy that Bede develops in his authorship depend on a curriculum based substantially on poetic fiction. Bede represents himself, however, as committed only to the project of scriptural study and commentary. Fiction thus provides the test case for medieval authorship, already present and acknowledged yet unassimilated and inadmissible. The closest Bede comes to it are stories of wonder and marvel from the hagiographical tradition. Though scribal culture preserves vernacular heroic narratives, only the fragmentary prose translation of *Apollonius of Tyre* seems to reflect an awareness of imaginative literary discourse in Old English; the last act mentioned is Apollonius's composing and depositing two books about his journey. It is in post-Conquest England that literary fiction emerges definitively as a crafted imaginative work created by an author, stabilized by genre, presented as a text, and directed to specific, often exclusive audiences.[23]

---

21. Bede, *Bede's Ecclesiastical History of the English People*, 414–15.
22. Johnson, "Problem of the Counter-Classical Sensibility," 123–51.
23. Nykrog, "Rise of Literary Fiction," 593–614. For the place of fiction within post-Conquest historiography, see Otter, *Inventiones: Fiction and Referentiality in Twelfth-Century English Historical Writing*; and Rollo, *Glamorous Sorcery: Magic and Literacy in the High Middle Ages*.

CHAPTER 1

Walter Map

Authorship and Counter-Authorship

THE WRITINGS of Walter Map, collected in his *De Nugis Curialium* (*Courtiers' Trifles*), represent one of the earliest efforts to devise literary authorship in medieval England. Map's book is firmly, if ambivalently, rooted in the court of Henry II. Map opens with a partial comparison of the Angevin court with hell and repeatedly asserts his alienation, even as the court remains the source for public life and the defining context for writing. Map says that he writes at the insistence of an otherwise unidentified addressee, Geoffrey, who may be a contemporary or merely a convenient fiction.[1] His book evidently had no history of circulation as a complete work. Parts of it circulated independently, however. The "Dissuasio Valerii ad Ruffinum," one of the books of "wikked wyves" read to Chaucer's Wife of Bath (*Canterbury Tales* III.685), was a staple of medieval antifeminist literature. It is the topic of multiple commentaries in the fourteenth century, including those of the Franciscan John Ridewall and the Dominican Nicholas Trevet.[2] Map's monastic satires and perhaps all of Distinctio 3, a thematically integrated unit of stories, may have circulated, too.[3] The unique textual witness is a fourteenth-century manuscript whose arrange-

---

1. Türk, *Nugae curialium*, 177, identifies Geoffrey as the secular clerk Geoffrey Ridel, royal administrator, chief justice, controversialist, and later bishop of Ely.
2. Ridewall, *Un commentaire de la "Dissuasio Valerii" de Gautier Map*.
3. Hinton, "Walter Map's *De Nugis Curialium*," 125n8.

ment of materials is arguably not authorial.[4] Nonetheless, Map inscribes a variety of audiences as potential and imagined readers—palace bureaucrats in need of recreation, a recalcitrant friend, an unsympathetic public from which he hides his identity as a modern rather than ancient author.

Map writes at a historical moment and in a cultural milieu where satire enjoyed a particularly rich expression.[5] Henrician satire operated across a number of forms—epistolary, instructional, and imaginative. Peter of Blois wrote, withdrew, and revised a monitory letter to Henry's courtiers asserting his own recognition that "courtly life is the death of the soul."[6] John of Salisbury and Gerald of Wales wove criticism of the court into treatises designed to educate monarchs in principles of statecraft. Nigel of Canterbury wrote a tract against courtiers and court clerics as well as the *Speculum Stultorum*, his satiric beast epic of the ass Brunellus. Unlike his contemporaries, though, Map places authorship and writing rather than moral correction at the center of his work.[7] Peter's invective, as he admits in his later retraction, equates the court with the world in general and draws on a broad tradition of contempt for the world. Writers of princely instruction base their precepts and political theory on moral philosophy, especially the cultivation of moderation and other virtues that separate a king from a tyrant. If Map shares with these writers a recourse to exemplarity, his interest lies more in the textuality of narratives than in their application.

Map had a contemporary reputation as a wit and storyteller. Sebastian Coxon proposes that Map's wit both claimed a license for provocative materials and advanced his authorship in elite circles.[8] But Map's interests ranged well beyond satirical topics. The *De nugis* emerges as a compilation of discursive modes, academic *modi tractandi* as well as popular forms—secular and

---

4. Map, *De nugis curialium*, ed. and trans. James, rev. Brooke and Mynors, xxiv–xxxii, makes the case based on internal references that Distinctiones 4 and 5 originally began the book and that Distinctiones 1, 2, and 3 followed. Henceforth I cite the introduction to James's edition as Brooke. In his review of the edition, Christopher M. McDonough generally accepts Brooke's view but notes the anomaly of leaving the epilogue of Distinctio 4 in place if it was intended to end the book (295). In his review, A. G. Rigg argues that Map's final plan for the book is essentially reflected in the unique manuscript (Oxford, Bodley MS 851): Distinctiones 1–3 were nearly finished, Distinctio 4 was still being used as it is preserved, and most of Distinctio 5 (up to the duplicate opening in 5.7) was "probably nearly complete" (182).

5. Jaeger, *Origins of Courtliness*, 55, identifies Henry II's court as the most prolific center of the curial satire that emerged in the mid-twelfth century.

6. Peter of Blois, Letter 14, *Patrologia Latina* 207:43. Peter moderates his views of the court and the roles of clerics in Letter 150 (*Patrologia Latina* 207:439–42). For discussion of Letter 14, see Cotts, *Clerical Dilemma*, 269–88.

7. Dronke, *Medieval Poet*, 308, sees Peter of Blois as more seriously engaged in satire than Map or John of Salisbury.

8. Coxon, "Wit, Laughter, and Authority," 41–43.

ecclesiastical anecdote, legend, history, folklore, ghost story, gossip, polemic, informal ethnography, romance, novella, moralization, and exhortation.[9] The mixture of genres and discursive modes within a project of writing looks forward to the inclusion of multiple sources and forms within a narrative frame by later medieval writers like John Gower and Geoffrey Chaucer. For postmedieval readers, the mixed contents and uncertain structure of the *De nugis* have produced two critical approaches, which might be described as anecdotalist and metacritical, respectively. Each approach espouses a distinct literary aesthetic for locating Map's book within our broader understanding of literary forms and traditions. Each responds to Map's authorship and writing by accentuating the qualities that two successive cultural moments in our own modernity value as strong markers of literary craft and consciousness.

Traditionally, the *De nugis* is read as the work of a gifted anecdotalist. Thomas Wright in the *editio princeps* describes Map thus: "Walter Mapes was evidently a man not only of much learning and extensive reading, but of great taste for lighter literature. His mind appears to have been stored with legends and anecdotes, and he was universally admired for his ready wit and humour."[10] Twentieth-century criticism continued in the direction of Wright's appraisal. M. R. James concluded that the work was jotted down "as the fancy struck the author."[11] James Hinton finds Map "not restrained by a definite plan" of composition and lacking the narrative artist's "ability to construct" stories beyond a single episode or incident.[12] Lewis Thorpe calls the *De nugis* "an interesting work, but incomplete, uneven, without shape or order."[13] C. N. L. Brooke extends the medieval appreciation of Map as a wit and describes his book as "the commonplace-book of a great after-dinner speaker."[14] A. G. Rigg says, "Map is primarily a raconteur and a humorist." Rigg also reveals the literary

---

9. The genre, tradition, and composition of the *De nugis curialium* are recurring issues in the scholarship, and the list of forms I give here is a conflation of the descriptions offered in modern criticism.

10. Map, *Gualteri Mapes De Nugis Curialium Distinctiones Quinque*, ed. Wright, viii.

11. Idem, *De Nugis Curialium*, ed. James, xxiv.

12. Hinton, "Walter Map's *De Nugis Curialium*," 131. Bennett, "Walter Map's Sadius and Galo," 34–56, argues against the aesthetic dismissal of Map as a narrative artist but does not address the question of his larger structural control over the *De nugis*. Rigg, *History of Anglo-Latin Literature*, 88, suggests a measure of overall unity within each Distinctio.

13. Thorpe, "Walter Map," 6.

14. Brooke, xlv, who also quotes Gerald of Wales's report that Map sees himself as a vernacular master of words rather than writing (xxii). Bates, "Walter Map," 862, contends that Gerald mentions Map to glorify himself. Map also cites anecdotes as examples of his wit (e.g., 5.6). See Thorpe, "Walter Map," 7–9, for Bothewald's *Invectio* (written between 1197 and 1210) directed against Map for his metrical and prose "derisoria" written in youth and old age, and for later medieval references to Map's "jocunda."

aesthetic that has informed most attempts to interpret the *De nugis*. He opens his review of the revised edition of M. R. James's standard text and translation with revealing comparisons: "Walter Map had the taste for the bizarre and the macabre of a Poe, the black humour of an Evelyn Waugh, and the style of a P. G. Wodehouse." This list is slightly expanded in a subsequent appreciation: "As modern analogues for Map I have proposed Wodehouse, Waugh, Poe, Stevenson, and the shaggy dog story. This improbable mixture suggests something of Map's spirit."[15] Map the anecdotalist is the narrative craftsman of the short story and the novel of manners and social comedy. With Poe and Stevenson no less than Wodehouse and Waugh, he is a modernist.

The metacritical approach to the *De nugis* gives particular weight to Map's self-reflexive comments about authorship. G. T. Shepherd says of the *De nugis*, "Though *nugae* are its matter it is also a book about stories and about their status." For Shepherd, the book poses an aesthetic question whose apparent contradiction reflects both Map's wit and the literary ambitions of his age: can *nugae* be taken seriously?[16] Robert Levine formulates a related set of issues in discussing Map's rhetorical pose of authorial humility. Map's *diminutio*, he contends, is a means for affirming faith in his text. In addition, Map's text covers troubling, unresolved materials beneath its surface of wit and self-deprecation: "Under the mask of triviality, Walter offers playfully bitter misogyny, satire and complaint, with deliberately grotesque fantasies of impotence, castration, necrophilia, and decapitation."[17] The most fully theorized response to Map's autocommentary is Siân Echard's study of metafiction. Echard argues that the metafictional framework of the *De nugis* provides a rationale and even a structural principle for the work.[18] For Echard, metafiction aligns the book with the rhetorical and conceptual strategies of parody and with an aesthetic that features multiple voicing and a prominent role for the reader. Self-conscious and ambivalent, Map is a postmodernist.

As this summary suggests, both approaches recontextualize Map in order to understand his fascinating and puzzling book. To a striking degree, both draw attention to the same textual evidence. The metafictional approach has a strong debt to the anecdotalist reading: the writerly qualities and wit of Map the modernist are also the literary codes laid bare and disrupted by postmodern Map. Furthermore, both approaches share the conviction that something important in literary history is truly at stake in the *De nugis*. For Map functions as an author simultaneously within and against a sophisticated literary sphere that had its own official discourse of secular and religious chronicles,

---

15. Rigg, *History of Anglo-Latin Literature*; and idem, rev. of *De nugis curialium*, 177.
16. Shepherd, "Emancipation of Story," 53.
17. Levine, "How to Read Walter Map," 95 and 105.
18. Echard, "Map's Metafiction," 292.

vernacular translations from the classics, hagiography, romances, and moral and political didacticism.[19] Those forms carried an authority that is the necessary condition of Map's book and at times the oblique target of its parody—for example, in the contrast with John of Salisbury's *Policraticus* and similar works of princely instruction.[20] Map uses and manipulates his context in ways that serve an aesthetic end sustained by court writing but insistently distinct from it. At certain junctures, the effect of writing from the margins challenges the ideology of English historical continuity promoted by official historiography.[21] His book thus offers an important witness to literary culture in the High Middle Ages and to the inscription of agency and subjectivity within a defining social and political context. As Egbert Türk reminds us, the court Map inhabited for some thirty years was an object of external ideological conflict as well as internal strife, as royal government asserted its independence from ecclesiastical tutelage.[22] R. Howard Bloch points out that courtiers' struggles for recognition are the equivalent of political contests for territory and that they lend themselves particularly to representation.[23]

The broad literary project informing the *De nugis* is the assertion of authorship within the framework of courtly culture. Such authorship rests on a calculated positioning of the writer's role, a distinct location of writing, and the hermeneutic power of reading. Under the guise of recording anecdotes and other notable materials, his book claims for Map the shifting roles and pleasures of authorial performance. It cultivates marginalized literary discourse as a separate space of imagination and even as a vehicle of modernity. Though ostensibly a private gathering of writings, the *De nugis* makes readership and reception parts of a dialectic of textual and cultural meaning. Finally, the book contains within itself tales that mirror the problem of constructing an inward sphere of writing and literary imagination. Map explores these issues in a work that he claims to have written hurriedly, composing sections on separate sheets under the pressure of time and circumstance: "Hunc in curia regis Henrici libellum raptim annotaui scedulis" (4.2) [This little book I have jotted down by snatches at the court of King Henry].[24] His mode of composition consequently produces a theory of authorship that is dispersed,

---

19. On Henry II's court as literary center, see Bezzola, *Les origines et la formation*, 3:3–207, and Crane, "Anglo-Norman Cultures in England," 41–43.

20. Brooke, xxxii–xxxv. Echard, "Map's Metafiction," 299, suggests that Map's ambivalence about the court echoes John of Salisbury's protests to Thomas Becket, the dedicatee of the *Policraticus*.

21. Robert R. Edwards, "Notes toward the Angevin Uncanny," 87–107.

22. Türk, *Nugae curialium*, xv.

23. Bloch, "Wolf in the Dog," 71.

24. I quote the text and translation from James, rev. ed; citations refer to the Distinctio and chapter.

allusive, and thematic. But Map's thoughts on these issues echo each other, and we can trace their patterns across his text and in his framework of writing.

"NUDUS PUGIL ET INERMIS": MAP'S COUNTER-AUTHORSHIP

Map's comments on authorship are well catalogued in the scholarship but perhaps underappreciated in their rhetorical and conceptual resonance.[25] Modern critics generally take them as discursive statements about writing rather than parts of Map's imaginative text. To be sure, Map portrays himself as an unwilling author, alienated from his task and from an immediate community of readers. He relies on the humility topos to claim his unfitness for the task that Geoffrey has evidently given him, protesting that Geoffrey has asked "hominem ydiotam et imperitum scribere" (1.10) [You are asking an inexperienced and unskilled man to write]. He renews this protest slightly later: "In pluribus est timor meus: me macies accusabit sciencie, me lingue dampnabit infancia, me contempnet quia uiuo modernitas" (1.12) [For myself, I have many fears: want of knowledge will accuse me, inaptness of speech will condemn me, the present generation will look down upon me because I am still living]. At the end of his satiric attack on the Cistercians, he admits, though with ulterior motives, "etiam ydiota sum" [I am an imbecile] and "ineptum me fateor et insulsum poetam" (1.25) [I confess myself a foolish and dull poet]. In the "Dissuasio Valerii," Map's style serves as the exact mirror of his authorial failures: "Sic impericia cordis mei uicium oracionis exprimit" (4.3) [So it is that the faults of my style reflect my want of skill]. Later, even his modest subject matter ostensibly overmasters him: "Hec forte friuola sunt et magnis inepta paginis, sed meis satis apta sunt scedulis, michique uidentur stilo meo maiora" (5.5) [These matters are perhaps trifles and unfit for great books, but for my sheets they are suitable enough, and to me they even seem too high for my pen].

Within these conventional tropes, however, Map sets out a form of authorship radically defined by negation. He seems to claim the transparent role of transcriber: "Meum autem inde propositum est nichil noui cudere, nichil

---

25. Webster, "Walter Map's French Things," 272–74, identifies the chief passages where Map discusses his authorship as a form of poetic or philosophical discourse, which Webster takes as meaning simply to compose. See also Brooke, xxxiv, for a review of the passages. Echard, "Map's Metafiction," 298 and 302, rightly points out that Map adopts several voices, such as the self-parody of the desperate householder. One might argue that the "Dissuasio Valerii" is a distinct rhetorical voice as well.

falsitatis inferre; sed quecunque scio ex uisu uel credo ex auditu pro uiribus explicare" (1.12) [My own purpose in the matter is to invent nothing new, and introduce nothing untrue, but to narrate as well as I can what, having seen, I know, or what, having heard, I believe].[26] His language contrasts his writing with false coinage (*cudere*) and bad reasoning (*inferre*) so that Map claims, in effect, to stand beyond the fabrications of discourse, innocent of any intention except his good faith. Similarly, in his concession of imbecility, ineptness, and dullness, he insists on a difference—he is not a "falsigrafum" (1.25), a "writer of lies," as James translates the phrase, but one who executes an authentic, unforged, transparent text.[27] Map's inscription locates him in a domain of writing apart from the juridical responsibility that produces meaning: "non enim mentitur qui recitat, sed qui fingit" (1.25) [for he does not lie who repeats a tale, but he who makes it]. In the "Dissuasio Valerii," he ostensibly sets aside rhetorical ornament ("purpurissum oratoris aut cerussam") and offers instead unadorned writing: "scribentis uotum et pagine ueritatem accepta" (4.3) [be content with the good will of the writer and the honesty of the written page].

In the passages usually cited as conventional, Map dismantles the normal expectations of authorship. To Geoffrey he asserts not just his own inadequacy but the artfully contrived impossibility of the task given him (1.10). Geoffrey would make Map courtly, though not witty ("curialem ... non dico facetum"), a child who by definition cannot speak yet who speaks nonetheless ("puer sum et loqui nescio—sed dico"), an unwilling philosophizer of the court to which he is at once bound and exiled ("religatum et ad hanc relegatum"). A courtier without wit has, of course, no social or political efficacy. Map belies his professed inadequacy in anecdotes about his deflating the mythology of St. Bernard's miracles (1.24) or the ambitions of Geoffrey Plantagenet (5.6). His play on *loqui/dico* recalls Augustine's famous etymological derivation of infant from *infans*: "infans, qui non farer" [an infant, who cannot speak].[28] The play on *religatum/relegatum* registers the ambivalence that Map expresses variously elsewhere: "In hac ego miserabili et curiosa languesco curia, meis abrenuncians voluntatibus, ut placeam aliis" (4.13) [In this pitiable and care-ridden court I languish, renouncing my own pleasure to please others].[29]

---

26. James's translation of this passage does not convey the sense of minting and forging in the verb *cudere* or of inference and conclusion in *inferre*. Brooke, xxiv, and Hinton, "Walter Map's *De Nugis Curialium*," 127–28, construe Map's use of *philosophari* and *poetari* as synonyms meaning literary composition.

27. In Boethius's translation of Aristotle's *Topica* and *De sophisticis elenchis* and in John of Salisbury's *Metalogicon*, "falsigrafum" refers to bad reasoning in geometry and logic.

28. Augustine, *Confessionum libri XIII* [1.8.13], ed. Skutella, 7.

29. *Religatum/relegatum* echoes the etymology of *religio* given by Cicero in *De natura deorum* 2.72 and cited by Isidore of Seville, *Etymologiae* 10.234, but rejected polemically by Lac-

In another passage, complaining that he is asked to write in the midst of discord ("inter has precipis poetari discordias"), Map consciously restructures the story of Balaam and the ass as a parallel to his authorial task.[30] His patron has used Balaam's spurs, he says, to drive him to writing about the court: "At ualde timeo ne michi per insipienciam cedat in contrarium asine, et tibi in contrarium Balaam, ut dum me loqui compellis incipiam rudere, sicut illa pro ruditu locuta est, fecerisque de homine asinum, quem debueras facere poetam" (1.12) [I am much afraid that my stupidity will cause our parts—mine of the ass, and yours of Balaam—to be reversed, so that when you try to make me speak I shall begin to bray—as the other spoke instead of braying—and you will have made an ass out of a man whom you wanted to make into a poet]. At one level, the confused references in Map's illustration fully demonstrate the "insipienciam" that he ascribes to himself: in the biblical story (Numbers 22: 21–35), God, not Balaam, gives the animal the powers to see the angel blocking Balaam's path and to tell him that her unexampled actions are a portent whose meaning the angel, not the ass, explains. At another level, though, Map does not confuse the comparison so much as relocate its meaning. The message Geoffrey wants Map to convey is not divine injunction but an account of noise ("discordias") that signifies the court, "nostra procellosa"—a phrase that recalls the stormy fellowship of human life that Augustine links to language as the articulation of human desires.[31] In this sense, the reversal of roles and the failure of articulate speech fit the task.[32] Map can faithfully report the strife of court life only by speaking as an ass: "Fiam tamen asinus pro te, quia iubes" (1.12) [Well, an ass I will be, since you wish it].

The theory that Map suggests by his comments might be called counter-authorship. By that I mean a form of authorial self-definition that exists in virtue of its differences from official literary roles, the higher genres of literary discourse, and the sociopolitical imaginary that those roles and genres sustain.[33] Counter-authorship is a program of committed alterity, incompleteness, and subordination. It operates by contrast to dominant formations in

---

tantius, *Diuinae Institutiones* 4.28.3.

30. What I argue about Map's authorship at a conceptual level is closely related to what Margaret Sinex calls his echoic irony, a practice in which the second element in a pair of terms both echoes and interprets the content of the first term; see Sinex, "Echoic Irony," 277.

31. Augustine, *Confessions* 1.8.13: "uitae humanae procellosam societatem."

32. John of Salisbury, *Policraticus* (7.19) uses the figure of the braying ass in a disquisition on ecclesiastical ambition and makes the biblical episode a figure of interpretation—the spirit that hides in the letter. Lucken, "Eloge de l'Ane," 110, takes the braying of the ass as a sign of truth emanating not from a divine source but from the world.

33. The discussion of counter-authorship has its roots in Johnson, "Problem of the Counter-Classical Sensibility," 123–51.

literary culture, yet it depends on them in order to function. Hence Map's powerful ambivalence toward his commission to write the book: "a corde meo uiolenter extorsi, domini mei preceptis obsequi conatus" (4.2) [(I) have wrung (this little book) by force out of my heart, in the attempt to obey my lord's orders]. In his resistance, Map anticipates the ambivalence that Chaucer continually registers as a ground of writing; in his deference, he previews a characteristic gesture of Chaucer's self-designated successors, Thomas Hoccleve and John Lydgate. Map's counter-authorship treats the writer's role as a form of subjectivity and inwardness, the equivalent of interior faith carefully preserved "in cordis archana puritate" [in the hidden purity of the heart] so that outward events in the social sphere do not change the interior man ("non permutent extrinseci casus interiorem hominem" [4.13]). At the same time that the author claims a subjectivity situated within writing, his writing and authorship nonetheless have a public circulation. The *De nugis* is premised on the aesthetic contradiction that a private book is at the same time commissioned by a lord and read by others, including the objects of his satiric attacks.

The beginning of the *De nugis* illustrates how counter-authorship works as a practice of composition. Map quotes Saint Augustine on time in order to frame a partial analogy of hell and the court. The expressive power of the analogy consists precisely in its partiality: the court is not identical to hell by genus but only by its common properties. Map soon recognizes that he digresses from this topic to a lament on human degeneracy ("quo iam deuenit?"). Digression, he realizes, is an essential feature of his literary practice: "Sic incudunt semper aliqua que licet non multum ad rem, tamen differi nolunt, nec refert, dum non atrum desinant in piscem, et rem poscit apte quod instat" (1.1) [Such topics are always liable to emerge, perhaps not much to the purpose, yet refusing to be put aside; nor is it a very serious matter so long as they do not end in a black fish's tail, and the intrusive subject is one which fitly demands treatment]. On this view, writers find their topic within discourse, in the act of composition. As Map stipulates with his allusion to Horace's *Ars Poetica* ("atrum / desinat in piscem" [3–4]) and with the adverb *apte*, authorship balances imaginative freedom and discovery with a craft and literary decorum (later, he will imagine the collapse of literary decorum in 4.2). But the emphasis here falls clearly on those topics that insist on being put into language. The *De nugis* subsequently enacts this concept at the beginning of Distinctio 2, where Map announces that he will defer two moral tales in order to begin the *miracula* of holy men and phantasms.

At the start of Distinctio 3, Map offers an image of ludic performance for what counter-authorship entails. His writing, he says, is the alternative to philosophy and theology. Designed for recreation and sport, the compositional topics are intentionally trifling ("innolibiles et exsangues inepcias" [3.1]). Their triviality, however, is public and visible, acted out as a form of self-representation. Map chooses the metaphor of theater and spectacle to convey a kind of authorship that offers not merely the antidote to high matters ("seria") but the playful negation of them: "teatrum et arenam incolo nudus pugil et inermis" (3.1) [it is the theatre and the arena that I haunt, a naked unarmed fighter].[34] He cultivates the sphere of performance that medieval culture treats as a source of depravity in Tertullian's *De spectaculis* and moral confusion in Augustine's *Confessions*. Map's theatricality may be closer still to the agonistic theater imagined by the authoritative, if frequently wrong, encyclopedist Isidore of Seville. For Isidore, the theater is an image of the present world as well as an allegorical brothel where prostitutes set upon the apparently defenseless spectators. He derives *theatrum* from *spectaculum* and emphasizes that the theater is a place of doubled spectatorship: "quod in eo populus stans desuper atque spectans ludos scenicos contemplaretur" [it is so called because in it the people standing above and watching the scenes being played are themselves observed].[35] The telling detail here is that Map as author stands at the center of this theatrical spectacle. He presents himself as the protagonist and combatant singularly unsuited for the encounter he has devised. He thus evokes an image of ritualized struggle and stylized conflict in order to position his authorship as the object of collective observation and a source, as Tertullian and Augustine insist, for inciting desires through representation.[36]

In the epilogue placed before the "Dissuasio Valerii" but written a decade later, Map develops this image of defenseless, agonistic spectacle. He is banished from the court that formerly held him, and he now enjoys the intoxicating but hopeless experience of freedom: "lucrum inestimabile nunc primo uidens quod a curia liber sum, unde relegatus quiete noua percipio quam misere fuerim ibi religatus" (4.2) [(I) realize (for the first time) the inestimable gain of being freed from the court; banished from it I see in my unwonted quiet how hard were the bands that held me there]. The ironic peace ("quies")

---

34. The pairing of *inermis* and *nudus* is cited from Lucretius onward (*De rerum natura* 5.1289). Cicero, *De finibus bonorum et malorum* 1.7.22, uses it to mean "unprepared, not well versed."

35. Isidore of Seville, *Etymologiae* 15.2.34 and 18.42.1. Boethius, whose commentary on Porphyry is the source for Map's discussion of the genus of Hell (1.1), describes theater as a part of spectacle in order to illustrate the proper ties shared by objects having a common substance: "ut est theatrum uel spectaculum aliquod, quod spectantibus omnibus commune est"; see Boethius, *In porphyrii Isogogem Porphyrii commenta* [1.10], ed. Schepss and Brandt, 162.

36. Map contrasts his uncertain position with the security and repose conferred by retirement on ecclesiastical writers like Gilbert Foliot, Bartholomew of Exeter, and Baldwin of Worcester (1.12). At the end of the "Dissuasio Valerii," Map makes Gilbert a figure of heroic resistance who continues to write despite offended readers and the onset of blindness (4.5).

he enjoys is apocalyptic, for it is a liberation from the court that occurs in the collapse after Henry's death, which leaves no appeal to justice in the public sphere and, as a corollary, no standards applicable to literary craftsmanship. Map imagines himself in a social and literary posthistory that reproduces but intensifies the discord that his patron Geoffrey thrusts him into. He defines this as "nichil humanitatis"—a condition in which moral and aesthetic collapse parallel and mirror each other. In a context of no constraint ("Quidlibet ut libet agimus"), he turns to writing that stands beyond vatic poetry and traditional craft in the realm of self-inaugurating authorship: "Ideo tutus et inermis aggredior quod trepidabam" (4.2) [Therefore I can approach the task I used to fear, in confidence and unarmed]. The substitution here of *tutus* for *nudus pugil* marks a step beyond the ludic violence of theater and spectacle. Authorship, Map implies, is all that is left after moral and literary judgments have lost their cultural coherence.

Map makes a similar point after the "Dissuasio Valerii," where his authorship is a potential point of contention in the reception of his tract against marriage. He says that the classical names of the author and recipient given in the title are a strategy of concealment designed to protect the book from dismissal as a modern work: "Sin autem, abiecissent illam, ut me" (4.5) [Had I not done so, my book, like myself, would have been thrown aside]. His ruse, Map reports, confers pleasure and safety: "Hoc solo glorior, quia ab inuidia tutus sum" (4.5) [My only satisfaction is that I am safe from envy]. Concealment, like collapse, offers an ambivalent freedom from historical contingency. Indeed, Map enjoys the spectacle of misidentification and disguise he has orchestrated, as he surveys the reception of the pseudoauthor he has sent out into public to hold his place.[37] Counter-authorship moves, then, within theatrical spectacle, posthistory, and the erasure of the writer behind his text. Map claims a place for writing founded on the performance of subjectivity and protected by marginality.

"FRIUOLA NARRACIO": THE MARGINS OF DISCOURSE

Map's subject matter—his inventional *materia*—is the aesthetic correlate of counter-authorship. His curial satire, for instance, depends on an exquisitely balanced comparison that does not identify the court with hell but merely claims that the two share common properties: the court is and is not hell. His

---

37. Schullian, "Valerius Maximus," 516, notes that scribes who copied the "Dissuasio" attributed it to Valerius Maximus.

treatment of folklore, *fantasmata,* apparitions, and prodigies, as Alberto Vàrvaro and Gilda Caiti-Russo point out, reflects a significant cultural shift in the High Middle Ages when popular stories reenter literary discourse as sources for invention, critical reflection, and wonder.[38] The narratives that incorporate romance motifs draw him close, as his contemporary Hue de Rotelande suggests, to blurring fiction and lies.[39] Map complains of the *materia copiosa* in Geoffrey's commission to him (1.12), and he admits to a malicious attack on the monastic orders: "michi de malicia carmen est" (1.25) [my song is of mischief]. When he comments on his writings, though, the emphasis falls preponderantly on his anecdotal materials. For these he has a critical lexicon of apparent diminution and dismissal: *fatua et friuola narracio* (3.2), *incidencia* (4.2), *friuola et inepta* (5.5). These gestures are always located, however, in the ways the stories may appear to others. Map nowhere terms his writing *nugae*, though some contemporaries did so.[40]

In a broad sense, Map's subject matter fits within the generic expectations of advice literature. Thus, while Map protests his inabilities, he can nonetheless assert the traditional efficacy of his materials as *dulce et utile*—"recitacio placeat et ad mores tendat instruccio" (1.12) [that the reading of it may amuse, and its teaching tend to moral improvement].[41] At the beginning of Distinctio 3, he sees the same objectives in the anecdotes he has been directed to collect: "Scribere iubes posteris exempla quibus uel iocunditas excitetur uel edificetur ethica" (3.1) [You bid me record examples (stories) for posterity such as may serve either to excite merriment or edify morals]. The dual aims of pleasure and profit also inform the writing of history and fiction, despite their differing truth claims. Both modes of discourse produce the moral lessons of choosing virtue and eschewing vice: "Nam historia, que ueritate nititur, et fabula, que ficta contexit, et bonos fine florenti beant, ut ametur benignitas, et fedo malos dampnant interitu, uolentes inuisam reddere maliciam" (1.31) [For history, which is founded on truth, and story, which weaves together fiction, both of them make the good happy by a flourishing end, that goodness may be loved, and condemn the wicked to a dismal death, wishing to make malice hateful]. Vàrvaro claims that the distinction between history and fable is not pertinent for Map and merely reflects different degrees of elaboration.[42] Map makes it clear that history and fiction share the same alternating structure of

---

38. Vàrvaro, *Apparizioni fantastiche,* 15–19; and Caiti-Russo, "Situation actuelle," 127.

39. Cartlidge, "Masters in the Art of Lying?" 1–16.

40. Levine, "How to Read Walter Map," 92, quoting Thorpe, "Walter Map," 9, who argues against the manuscript title of the *De nugis* and observes that Map's contemporary Bothewold twice refers to Map's "nugae."

41. The two tales Map defers at the beginning of Distinctio 2 are consciously not useful or pleasurable: "que non solum non delectant sed tediosa sunt" (2.1).

42. Vàrvaro, *Apparizioni fantastiche,* 27–32, 48; cf. Caiti-Russo, "Situation actuelle," 132.

adversity and prosperity so that one functions semiotically as the substitute for the other: "quatinus utraque semper habita pre oculis neutri fiat propter alteram obliuio" (1.31) [so both being ever before our eyes, neither may be forgotten for the other]. Their alternation, he insists, shares the specific common ground of writing—one following the other "in scripturis," a phrase that M. R. James translates as "in the records" and Frederick Tupper and Marbury Ogle render as "in narratives."[43]

The phrase "in scripturis" may provide a further clue to what writing entails in Map's literary context. Near the end of the *De nugis,* Map offers an idealized account of Henry I's domestic governance, which contrasts pointedly with the contemporary court, though Map tactfully limits his criticism of Henry II. The basis of Henry I's governance is writing: "Scriptas habebat domus et familie sue consuetudines, quas ipse statuerat" (5.5) [He had the customs of his house and household, as ordained by himself, kept in writing].[44] Henry's records serve the practical purpose of regulating provisions and expenditures and of maintaining stable allowances, which thereby avoid the discord and confusion inherent in other courts. At the same time, these authorized records establish the textualization of the court. The social and political spheres are made intelligible and subsequently governed not just by policy and craft but also through representation. The Golden Age that Map ascribes to Henry's court is thus produced by social reality originating in language, specifically in description. Wise kingship may remain the ultimate source of this felicity, but it works through writing.[45]

Against this background of textualized social practice, Map takes on a subsidiary commission, which is directed to a particular form of rhetorical invention: "dicta scilicet et facta que nondum littere tradita sunt" (1.12) [it is just the sayings and doing which have not yet been committed to writing]. Map's technical vocabulary shows that his subject matter is *materia illibata,* new materials not yet treated by other writers, and it discloses the ambition of bringing these topics within literary discourse.[46] His phrasing also recalls

---

43. Map, *Master Walter Map's Book,* trans. Tupper and Ogle, 78; cf. idem, *Contes des courtisans,* trans. Perez, 83: "dans les écrits."

44. Map subsequently describes Henry's publication of his itinerary (5.6) as a means of bringing order: "Nichil inprouisus aut inprouidus aut properanter agebat" [Nothing was done without preparation, or without previous arrangement, or in a hurry].

45. The playful respite from business and serious reading that Map takes as his own space of writing in 3.1 has its source in the order of Henry I's court: "eratque scola uirtutum et sapiencie curia regis illius ante meridiem, post, comitatis et reuerende leticie" (5.5) [and this king's court was in the forenoon a school of virtues and of wisdom, and in the afternoon one of hilarity and decent mirth].

46. Douglas Kelly's studies of invention remain fundamental to understanding the means for composing in high literary culture in the Middle Ages: "Scope of the Treatment," 261–78, and "Theory of Composition," 117–48.

Valerius Maximus's collection of materials for rhetorical invention, the *Facta et dicta memorabilia*. Valerius seeks to preserve the information of cultural memory within exemplary discourse, but Map gives a particular coloring to what he includes from the deeds and sayings of the Angevin court. His writing focuses on "conspeccius miraculum," things that have produced wonder and marvel as well as the wisdom of cultural memory. *Miraculum* includes a mixture of materials, particularly the *friuola* that balance exemplary narrative and expand its resources and potential scope.

Map broadens this view of writing by asserting the value of modernity as a source for exemplarity. By modernity, Map intends his own century. The "notabilia" that have occurred within it are the objects of immediate memory and possible witness (1.30). These two elements underwrite his claim to narrate what he has seen or what he believes to be true. Repeatedly in the *De nugis*, Map invokes the topos of the Golden Age not merely to condemn the present age but to argue as well for its importance as a source for reflection and moral instruction. The most systematic expression of the latter theme comes at the beginning of Distinctio 5, where he connects the cultural authority of the past to writing. If the poets have preserved the deeds of the ancients within cultural memory, modern writers have condemned their own age to oblivion by their fondness for controversy: "sic ingenua temporis huius strenuitas enormiter extinguitur, et lucerna non defectu materie sopitur, sed succumbunt artifices, et a nostris nulla est autoritas" (5.1) [thus the generous valour of this age is outrageously quenched and the lamp burns dim, not from lack of material, but because the craftsmen are supine and our writers have no influence]. Popular poetry—the "scola mimorum" celebrating Charlemagne and his dynasty—cannot perform the cultural work that Map envisions, which he expresses in the verb *impaginare*, to commit to writing and so to make intelligible in the same way that the social imaginary of Henry I's records make governance intelligible.[47]

Map's understanding of the *materia* produces both comic paradox and a serious literary claim. The modern penchant for dispute rather than writing creates just the kind of marvel that is Map's topic: "Miraculum illustre! Mortui uiuunt, uiui pro eis sepeliuntur!" (5.1) [A notable wonder! The dead live, and the living are buried in their stead!]. Amplifying the irony, Map goes on to insist that the moderns possess the same vices as the ancients even if they lack the virtues to make them notable. The larger point behind these turns of wit, however, is that modernity proves capable of the same exemplarity that

---

47. Tupper, *Master Walter Map's Book*, 255, translates *impaginare* as "to put upon a page" and Perez, *Contes des courtisans*, 243, as "le mettre en page." Otter, *Inventiones*, 128, argues that for Map and others the textuality of historical writing entails uncertainties about reference.

antiquity offers. On a stylistic level, Map contends that modernity fully suits the didactic function of middle style, which is to praise and blame. On a moral plane, it supports the complete interpretive work of scrutiny and reflection: "Pictam hic nempe inuenies cum suis honestatem fauoribus in modernis et cum suis turpitudinem odiosis flagiciis. Hanc tibi uitandam proponimus pro ueneficiis, illam eligendam pro beneficiis; neutri subducas oculum nisi uise penitus et agnite" (5.1) [For here you will find portrayed honour in modern men with its comeliness, and baseness with its hateful crimes. This we hold up to you to be shunned for its banes, the other to be chosen for its boons: withdraw not your eye from either unless you have thoroughly viewed it and taken it in]. In the rest of Distinctio 5, he gives his own demonstration of what a full and attentive review of modern examples might yield. Reading the record from Cnut to the present today, he contrasts the kingly generosity in Henry II and Louis VII with the covetousness of Earl Godwine. Map, as scholars note, commits a number of historical errors in his account of twelfth-century politics, but his authorial gesture is to make modernity a topic of complex scrutiny and reflection by bringing it into writing. Thus, Godwine's covetousness is balanced by the sheer appeal of his intelligence in rewriting Cnut's letter in order to make himself king of the Danes. The exemplary qualities of King Apollonides, prudence and forbearance, overcome Map's personal distaste for the man.

MAP'S READERS

The fiction of the *De nugis*, like the terms of Map's authorship and writing, turns on contradiction. On the one hand, the book is a private compilation, composed hurriedly, intermittently, and somewhat reluctantly, of modern *notabilia* worthy of attention and capable of bearing moral significance. On the other, it is commissioned by an addressee, who may be fictitious, and read by others, who in some cases are certainly not. It might be argued that the monks who have discovered the book and call Map a religious persecutor ("me religionis persecutorem dicunt" [1.25]) read a portion of Distinctio 1 that circulated independently. So, too, might have the original addressee and later readers of the "Dissuasio Valerii," who have put Map's tract against marriage into textual and cultural circulation: "Scimus hanc placuisse multis, auide rapitur, transcribitur intente, plena iocunditate legitur" (4.5) [This production I know has caught the fancy of many; it is greedily seized upon, eagerly copied, and read with vast amusement]. Traugott Lawler notes of the "Dissuasio": "It expects annotation; it uses the tradition of annotation; and it annotates itself."[48] Thorpe contends that the materials of the *De nugis* were simply too amusing to remain private and must have circulated among a coterie.[49] Within the text, Map gestures repeatedly to the imagined readers of his text as if they were indeed real. Some of the gestures are used as transitional devices from one narrative to another.[50] Others contain a hortatory moralization available to any reader willing to follow the bitter paths of righteousness from *friuola* (3.2), to see the lessons of denying lust (3.5) and covetousness (4.15), or to ponder the complex spirit of Godwine (4.3) and the exemplary serenity of Louis the Fat in the face of adversity (5.5).

In other respects, the tropes of reading prove critically important to Map's theory of authorship. Readers are a complement to the decentered counter-authorship expounded in the *De nugis* and to the materials that Map invents. The structure of adversity and prosperity in history and fiction, for example, is reproduced within reading, which involves a moral and social hygiene carried out by the reader himself: "se medico temperamento moderentur, ne unquam modum superet eleuacio uel fractura" (1.31) [men may regulate themselves by a medical mixture, that neither rise nor ruin may predominate overmuch].[51] Such regulation, Map hastens to add, is limited to temporal matters, not divine charity. It is the regime of the court subject. In a moral and political sense, it is a counsel of prudence, as one looks toward the future. One anticipates the future, however, with affect, and so readers operate by controlling hope and fear and following a mean not just of public self-presentation but also of internal discipline. Like the author protected by his defenselessness ("inermis"), the reader is a subject protected by his inwardness, the *interior homo* untransformed by exterior change.

The reader Map imagines moves knowingly among the topics of history and fiction. At the end of the story of Sadius and Galo, which shares a number of features with chivalric romance, Map distinguishes competent readers from those who misjudge the significance of his work ("Fatua forsitan hec uidebitur et friuola narracio") and thereby risk becoming the topic of it themselves (3.2).[52] The former are well intentioned and incisive ("benignis et argutis"),

---

48. Lawler, "Medieval Annotation," 96. Lawler goes on to propose that the last two-thirds of the "Dissuasio" is Map's authorial annotation of the first third (97).

49. Thorpe, "Walter Map," 14–16.

50. 1.11: "Libetne nuper actis aurem dare parumper?"; cf. 4.3: "libetne tamen nuper actis aurem dare parumper?" or 4.13: "Quas excusaciones quomodo Salius uitauerit, audite."

51. Map offers a parallel conceit to the hygiene of reading in the hard but healing hand of the surgeon (4.4).

52. Bennett, "Walter Map's Sadius and Galo," catalogues the generic resemblances between the tale and romance, particularly Arthurian romance.

and they recognize the mixed composition of Map's *friuola*: "scientes quod abscinthium et thimum argumentosa degustet apis, ut electos ex amaris et dulcibus conferat in thesaurum sapiencie fauos, ex friuolis his, et a Deo sibi data gracia colligens quantinus eligat et diligat amaras iusticie uias" (3.2) [for we know that the busy bee tastes both wormwood and thyme that it may gather into the treasure-house of wisdom the honeycomb it has collected both from bitter and from sweet, yes, and from such frivolities as it gathers too, by God's grace given to it, to the end it may choose and love the bitter paths of righteousness].

Map returns to the image of the bee at a similar position in the story of Parius and Lausus, which is the inverse parallel of the story of loyalty and trust in Sadius and Galo. Echard contends that Map's repetition makes a sharper division between good and bad readers.[53] Here the image expresses the active construction of literary meaning. Map compares the bee and the reader in their shared capacity to extract and carry away something from their mixture of sources. Reading is not just a matter of persuasion, as in the commonplaces of praise and blame, but a form of attention and intellectual labor: "Instat enim et adheret litere, nec habet aliquam inuisam nisi peruisam, aut neclectam nisi perlectam" (3.3) [For he pores upon the letter and clings to it, holds no word disapproved till perused, none overlooked till looked over]. Map's rhetorical contrasts in this passage (*instat/adheret, inuisam/peruisam, neclectam/perlectam*) trace a movement forward toward understanding—from approach to attachment, from rejection to attention, from disregard to thorough reading. The second element in each pair defines the task; taken together, they describe a process of acquiring, mastering, and scrutinizing the text. Map repeats the idea in urging the value of reading about moderns: "Legenda enim tibi est omnis pagina quam uideris et examinanada, nec sit ulla neclecta nisi perlecta" (5.1) [For you should read and scrutinize every page you see, and not one should be disused without being perused].

In Map's formulation, the onus of meaning falls explicitly on the reader rather than the author. The reader must penetrate the text to find meaning. Map describes this labor of sustained, invasive reading as a heroic enterprise rewarded at length by conquest: "sepeque repulsus dum inprobe luctatur euincere quod iuuet aut prosit, in nouas et meliores incidit argucias quam penes se auctor habuerit" (3.3) [yet in his persistent struggles to extract some-

---

53. Echard, "Map's Metafiction," 312. The bad readers—the "impii"—described here, in echoes of Psalm 1:4 and Revelation 22:11, recur in Map's imagined reception of the "Dissuasio Valerii": "oderunt enim antequam audierint, uilipendent antequam appendant, inuident priusquam uideant" (4.2) [for they hate before they have heard, scoff before they scrutinise, envy before they view].

thing helpful or pleasant, he stumbles upon new refinements, better than the author's own]. The contest to reach meaning yields the pleasant and useful effects of Horace's literary decorum. But Map envisions a further possibility in discoveries produced by the effort. These unlooked-for subtleties (*nouae argutiae*) are generated by hermeneutics, and they reflect a power in reading that corresponds to the digressive authorial freedom that Map claims in writing. His contemporary, Marie de France, develops a similar line of reasoning in adapting Priscian's model of glossing the letter so that the reader adds a supplement ("surplus") of meaning ("de lur sen") to a text.[54]

Map's account sets up a proportion at the center of literary understanding: readers are to the discovery of meaning as writers are to the recording of history and fiction. At the end of Distinctio 2, Map sets his role explicitly in relation to his reader in the metaphors of forestry and hunting. He places the raw materials gathered from decentered writing—"Siluam uobis et materiam, non dico fabularum sed faminum appono" (2.32)—before his readers for them to transform into the finished objects of cultural circulation and currency: "Singuli lectores appositam ruditatem exculpant, ut eorum industria bona facie prodeat in publicum" (2.32) [Every reader must cut into shape the rough material that is here served up to him, that thanks to their pains it may go forth into the world with a fair outside]. His terms are fully consistent with those used at the end of the Parius and Lausus story. The reader's work, his "industria," is the means that transforms what the writer has found for him into something new and potentially better. The *bona facies* of his labor is the aesthetic analogue of the *argutiae,* the complex and brilliant insights, discovered by the triumphant reader in the other passage. In his second metaphor, Map stresses the transformative power of reading: "Venator uester sum; feras uobis affero, fercula faciatis" (2.32) [I bring you the game, it is for you to make dainty dishes out of it]. Map's *venator* is not the huntsman of Ovidian elegy, who traps and holds his prey because he has, in theory, been able to discipline himself. Rather, the hunting metaphor is a counterpart to the solitary, inward work that Map sees in invention. His work reaches completion in the reader's transformation of the raw and wild materials ("feras") into the finished products of culture ("fercula"). But even here, as Rigg suggests, the work of interpretation may be as vexed as that of writing.[55]

---

54. Marie de France, *Les Lais,* ed. Rychner, 2; *Lais,* trans. Burgess and Busby, 41.
55. Rigg, "Anglo-Latin,"127: "What is doubly ironic in Map is that he insists that his tales have morals and the reader must read them diligently and attentively, but the tales often defy moral analysis." In this respect, Map anticipates the hermeneutic impasse of Chaucer's Nun's Priest's Tale, which exploits St. Paul's claim that all that is written is written to teach (Romans 15:4).

ALLEGORIES OF AUTHORSHIP

Map's self-reflexive commentary in the *De nugis* posits a theory of authorship based on a consciously decentered writer, materials from the margins of literary discourse, and reading that complements writing in the production of meaning. Though his work is ostensibly commissioned, Map claims a place outside patronage in an imaginative sphere that is simultaneously inward and performative. He draws on episodes and topics found elsewhere but privileges this material because it represents what court culture rejects and dismisses. His *materia* offers new possibilities for writerly invention not because the content is innovative but because it has not been deemed worthy of writing. The idealized reader Map imagines for his book is not a passive collector of moralizations drawn from exempla but the active creator of meaning, sometimes unforeseen meaning. In this sense, he is the figure who realizes what the writer has begun with his authorial gestures. Taken together, these features suggest a radical form of authorship within twelfth-century literary culture. That is, Map commits himself to writing as a way of defining and exercising agency inside the ambivalence of his historical context, the court to which he is simultaneously bound and exiled.

Map's authorship places him outside the epideictic role of other writers at Henry's court, on the margins of official discursive forms, and at the mercy of the reader who can match his wit, irony, play, and insight. If Map theorizes authorship in this way, it follows that he might incorporate as well his own interrogation of the imaginative space that he claims for writing. Three stories from the *De nugis* seem particularly to explore the consequences of Map's authorial invention. The episode of the knight Waleran is a monitory example for Map's court persona. The story of Sceva and Ollo illustrates the imaginative power to construct identity and social reality from rhetorical invention. The tale of Eudo examines the sinister possibility that *nugae* embody a narrative logic that even their authors cannot escape. All three tales resituate the means of Map's theorizing—his themes, images, and language—within narratives whose literary artifice outweighs the interpretive machinery of exemplarity.

Waleran's story appears among the anecdotes recounting Louis VII's acts of justice and kindness. Though unlettered, Waleran is known for his wit at court, and he displays his talents by composing a satirical poem in French against the king's most powerful ministers and twice shaming a noble, if dissolute, woman in the king's family who complains that Waleran has written "obscena carmina" (5.5) about her and the king. The complainants receive their vengeance when Waleran is proscribed, his holdings are destroyed, and he flees to Henry II's court in England. Waleran regains Louis's favor through a stratagem, arranged with Henry, in which the disheveled and disgraced knight, looking like the poorest man in the kingdom, is driven away as if he were a beggar. Because of his disposition, Louis is moved to compassion, and he sets in motion Waleran's restitution and reconciliation.

Waleran is a figure for Map's verbal wit and the role of a satiric poet-jester.[56] His satirical poems attack the predations of well-placed courtiers who have abused the trust placed in them by their king in order to enrich themselves. When Louis tells Waleran that he can bear the "onprobria" allegedly directed to him but not to a kinswoman, a member of his family ("unum membrorum meorum"), Waleran plays on the connotations of member: "Hoc herniosus es membro" (5.5) [A very sick member]. Map notes that Waleran's French answer is wittier: "De ce membre es tu magrinez" (5.5) [You are lessened by this member].[57] Waleran then makes a joke out of the woman's insistence that three prostitutes be ordered to scourge him for the laughter his wordplay has produced: she needs to find, he remarks, only two more. The last incident is recounted only in Latin, but the first two are recorded in both Latin and French, and they depend on French as their mode of transmission and social efficacy. Map's introduction of the vernacular, as elsewhere in the *De nugis,* is a gesture toward the margins of discourse from which he invents his topics.

The scene of dramatized abasement that Waleran arranges with Henry in order to secure reconciliation with Louis is the same kind of spectacle that Map imagines for himself as an author. Waleran's filthy, impoverished appearance, which attracts Louis's notice, is the equivalent of Map's "nudus pugil." The staged violence of his being helplessly dragged off occurs in the theatrical space that is the site of Map's defenseless ("inermis") writing. Beforehand, Waleran has advised Henry of the spectacle he is about to see ("nostro rege premunito"), and so he, like Map, is safe in his performance. The end of the episode both praises Louis and indulges the satirist's fantasy of exercising power and settling scores. Louis recognizes that the penalty given Waleran arose from a social and political misreading of language: "corrigendus erat uerbo pro uerbis, non fustigandus ac proscribendus" (5.5) [for a word he should have been chastened by words, not cudgelled and proscribed]. Walter, Waleran's chief persecutor among the royal ministers, restores and in fact overcompensates Waleran to head off any future disputes, while the king reconciles the knight with his other antagonists.

---

56. Levine, "How to Read Walter Map," 96.

57. James offers a modern French translation: "De ce membre tu es megrimé" (447). The background for Waleran's comment is the list of disqualifications for the priesthood enumerated in Leviticus 21:17.

In the story of Sceva and Ollo, Map explores another facet of what his authorial theory entails. Like the anecdote about Waleran, the story is premised on disaffection, in this case the neglected friendship of two merchants who rise to prosperity together, separate, and establish their households in different cities. The narrative theme that shapes the story is division, first of the mercantile partnership that made their success and then of the emotional ties they pledged to maintain after parting. When Sceva feels rebuffed on his visit to Olla, who is leaving for a fair, he exacts a calculated vengeance and indulges a rage that is given no other rationale or expression. Sceva insinuates himself into Olla's house, seduces his wife, and conspires with her, the household, Olla's neighbors, the prince, the sheriff, and the judges to refuse Olla entrance back into his house and to set himself up as Olla. The comic scene that takes place as Olla demands admission from his servants at the gate to his house rewrites Plautus's *Amphitryon* as a casuistic debate over being and knowledge.[58] Olla asserts his identity to his servant Nicholas: "Serue mi, numquid non ego sum?" (4.16) [My man, am I not I?]. Nicholas takes the rhetorical question literally and therefore comically: "Scio quod tu es tu, et tu ipse hoc nescis?" [I know you are you; are you in any doubt of it yourself?]. He wonders only how the Olla he refuses to recognize can know so much about Olla's household: "a quocunque sint edocta uel recordata, nomina bene retines" [from whoever you got them or remembered them, you have the names pat].

In the slippage between what he is and what he talks about, Olla plays on Map's opening *dubitatio* about hell and the court: "in curia sum, et de curia loquor, et nescio, Deus scit, quid sit curia" (1.1) [in the court I exist and of the court I speak, but what the court is, God knows, I know not]. Furthermore, Sceva perversely demonstrates the readerly power to establish meaning in Map's texts. Map does not fully collapse fiction and reality in the story. Sceva's plan is described as a good trick (*bonus dolus,* reversing the judicial term *dolus malus*, "willful deceit"), and he is described as the "preceptor fraudis" [manager of the intrigue] instructing everyone on what is needed to maintain his fiction ("commenta" [4.16]). In the end, Baratus, one of his servants, acknowledges Olla's identity and admits the truth of Sceva's ruse: "Domine, nos rei ueritatem scimus." But Sceva has meanwhile acted as Map demands of his reader. His elegant and subtle joke ("faceta derisio"), devised after he observes and appraises Olla's household ("omnia secreta domus . . . edoctus"), corresponds to authorial invention and the *nouae et meliores argutiae* of Map's attentive, invasive, and thorough reader.

---

58. Vàrvaro, *Apparizioni fantastiche,* 166–67, reviews the sources and analogues from Plautus through the Italian novella of the Quattrocento.

Sceva in fact carries out the possibility that Map leaves open to these readers, for he goes beyond what he discovers in a shepherd's chance account of Olla's holdings in land and property ("statum Ollonis"). Olla is literally and juridically the *auctor* of his household. He insists to Nicholas, the man he has promoted to watchman of the yard, "has domos feci, et omnia que in eis sunt mea sunt" (4.16) [I built this house, and everything in it is mine]. Sceva, by contrast, is the reader who has created better refinements (*meliores argucias*). He first pays for a feast to gain the loyalty of the household, bribes the officials, and then squanders Olla's holdings. Olla's servants and neighbors prefer the impostor's prodigality to Olla's thrift and austerity. At the end of the story, Sceva has so overmastered Olla that he leads Olla bound to court as a trespasser. Shamed by the prospect of the judges' derision, Olla accepts the better fiction of Sceva's devising and resigns any claims against him: "abiurat Sceue calumpniam." The false charges (*calumpniae*) he foreswears are ironically the truth of his identity and domestic authorship.

The inner logic of narrative, exploited in the Sceva and Olla story to express vicarious comic aggression, takes on a sinister form in Map's story of Eudo, who reenacts the parable of the prodigal son to horrifying and tragic effect in a pact with the devil. Eudo squanders his inheritance but eventually acknowledges his abasement. His recognition occurs in a moment of dissociation ("ex incertitudine sui deportatur ab ipso flagiciosus animus" [4.6]) in which a demon appears to him. Eudo knows that he has encountered a demon "in uera uisione" and realizes that he is the prey ("preda"). The demon assuages his anxiety by promising three warnings to prompt repentance before Eudo's death, and he describes his inventive powers by contrast with those of malevolent demons: "Ridiculis fateor et ludificacionibus apti, prestigia struimus, fingimus imaginaciones, fantasmata facimus, ut ueritate conteca uana ridiculaque simultas appareat. Omne quod ad risum est possumus, nichil quod ad lacrimas" (4.6) [Skilled in comical tricks and delusions, we do, I confess, cast glamour, contrive hallucinations, cause apparitions so as to veil reality and produce a false and absurd appearance. We can do anything that makes for laughter, but nothing that makes for tears].

The comic demons acquire knowledge, craft (*astucia*), and the capacity to judge and anticipate events; these they pass along to their subjects, who exercise ludic power in the arts of war and governance. An inset exemplum of the demon Morpheus and the monk he leads into sin without penalty illustrates that these powers create a sustained interim of play, for the monk escapes all punishment for his excesses in the story's mock-comic resolution. The demon thus interprets his text as if it were one of Map's exemplary anecdotes, confirmed as it is by first-person witness and presented as a notable, if frivolous, story: "Hec Morpheum fecisse scias, et me fratrem eius, qui talibus et tam urbanis frequenter usi lusibus" (4.6) [This, I tell you, Morpheus did, and I am his brother, and we often indulge in such amusing jests]. Abjuring the hunt for souls, the demons are the seemingly unarmed authors of play: "Inter uiuos ludicris exercitamur, aut serio iocundo" (4.6) [Among the living we practise laughable tricks or make earnest jest]. Once Eudo accepts the bargain, he begins a perverse reformation ("astutus et audax") as a brigand, regaining worldly possession while giving himself up to unregulated depravity. The warnings given by his demonic master Olga bring temporary repentance, followed by a return to sin. Map sketches a wonderfully parodic scene of moral instruction in which Olga urges penance as a guarantee of God's power and a prudent measure lest the limitations of the demon's foresight accidentally bring their agreement into disrepute.

The crucial feature of Map's story is not, however, the legalism of Eudo's pact with the devil or the moral lesson that the habit of sin subtly erodes the freedom of the will by creating a second, alien nature within one's character—a perverse *habitus*. The story shows, rather, that the logic of narrative produces the constraint of writing that Map seeks to escape by decentering authorship, inventing material outside higher genres, and investing his readers with the authority to interpret and go beyond his story. Eudo repents after the death of his son and his own symbolic funeral on a bed of ashes. He obtains forgiveness from those he has injured, and they accompany him to petition the bishop of Beauvais for absolution, which will complete the sacrament of penance. Like Waleran, Eudo performs repentance with wretched clothing, a transformed body, and a sympathetic audience seeking full reconciliation. A skilled rhetorician ("persuasor efficacissimus") and abject figure of contrition, Eudo aligns the spectacle and reality of penance. Map insists on the truth of his intention: "ille uera contricione . . . uero tam uero corde, tam ueris lacrimis" (4.6) [he, in true contrition . . . with such sincerity of heart, such genuine tears].

What Eudo encounters in the bishop, whose absolution he has betrayed repeatedly before, is the reader who refuses to believe the spectacle and accept the witness of those who have made peace with Eudo. Map's language echoes and reverses the terms of idealized reading. The bishop refuses the labor of thorough and attentive reading: "Negat episcopus et pernegat, et totus in contradiccione persistit" (4.6) [The bishop refused and went on refusing and continued in complete denial]. He does not penetrate the text like Map's incisive, heroic reader but instead makes himself the surface that cannot be opened or entered: "Claudit ab eo uiscera ne misereatur eius, firmatque sibi cor ne medeatur infirmo; statuit obnixe ne deludatur amplius, et totus obdurescit in calibem" (4.6) [He shut up his bowels of mercy against him and hardened his heart, not to heal the sick; firmly resolved not to be tricked again, he hardened himself wholly into iron]. The bishop thus reverses the contrasts and the forward movement toward meaning that Map outlines earlier (3.3). He dismisses Eudo's contrition (*inuisam/neclectam*) because he does not see it thoroughly (*peruisam/perlectam*).

In only one ironic sense does the bishop follow Map's decorum of reading. He is preparing to burn a sorceress when Eudo and the others approach him to seek forgiveness. The bishop improvidently sets a test for Eudo's intentions that is also retribution for his sins: "Infligo tibi pro peccatis, ut hunc orgum insilias" (4.6) [I lay upon you for your sins that you leap into that fire]. The bishop's stipulation is the *noua argutia* of Map's story, the subtlety that is simultaneously cunning and incisive. Eudo has already expressed contrition and made a full confession to the bishop, including this time a disclosure of his subjugation to Olga and other "secreta pessima." He has not been trapped in the traditional literalism of the devil's pact, but he accepts the literalism of the bishop's penance by leaping into the fire. Eudo's self-immolation pushes the story to the conceptual limits of Map's theorizing about authorship and writing. Map questions Eudo's zeal and condemns the bishop's obduracy, but he cannot unwrite the logic of his story.

Map's stories offer a valuable perspective on his theorizing, for they not only illustrate its chief components but also reveal the complex position of authorship as a position in the social sphere. Waleran's wit divides into the *dicta* that furnish court amusement and the *facta* of authorial performance, which secure his restoration and reconciliation. His restoration discloses, however, both the desire to frighten his enemies and a willingness to join them symbolically in their excess and avarice. Sceva's fictive identity as Olla is a *dolus,* at once a trick and a deceit, sustained by social consensus and ratified by Olla's abandonment of any claim against it. Sceva's authorial triumph stands against the realization that all other social bonds—those between friends, man and wife, master and servants, householder and neighbors, citizen and magistrates—have meanwhile collapsed. Eudo's story locates authorship and inventive power in the demonic, both in Eudo's parodic reform as a brigand and in the inverted Marian tale of the lascivious monk. It is only when Eudo reenters the social sphere, seeking to rejoin a community of believers, that he falls victim to the slippery literalism of language and promises. In these stories, Map not only satirizes the social domain but also unveils the contradictions within the imaginative space claimed by authorship. He discovers in writing the paradox of binding and exile that authorship works to escape.

CHAPTER 2

Marie de France

Signature and Invention

MARIE DE FRANCE, the most accomplished woman writer in medieval England, exists only in her function as an author. Though scholars have proposed various identifications for Marie, she remains an authorial signature made present through the self-inscriptions she leaves in her works and in the testimony of contemporary and later writers.[1] In line with the traditions of medieval literary culture and in contrast to Walter Map's effort not to be recognized as the actual author of the "Dissuasio Valerii," Marie presents herself as a named author connected to a body of writing.[2] In the prologues and epilogues attached to her works, she appropriates the conventions of authorship to describe herself as a compiler and translator moving between marginal and dominant, vernacular and classical traditions. In the Prologue to the *Lais*, she describes a process of invention that holds for both her secular and religious materials: "M'entremis des lais assembler, / Par rime faire e reconter" (Prologue 47–48) [I set myself to assemble lays, to compose and to relate them in

---

1. Bloch, *Anonymous Marie de France*, makes the strongest case that Marie's isolation from any biographical context is a condition of her constituting a founding moment of literature.
2. Marie's assertion of authorship contrasts, too, with that of her contemporary, the nun of Barking Abbey (possibly Clemence of Barking), who refuses to identify herself in the prose epilogue to her life of Saint Edward; quoted in Wogan-Browne et al., *Vernacular Literary Theory*, 24.

rhyme].³ The extrinsic features of authorship developed in these paratexts are complemented and significantly extended, however, by negotiations of authorship within Marie's poems. It is in her narratives, I shall argue, that she exercises agency to revise her received materials from popular and learned sources and to create a hybrid classicism in which she operates as a counterpart and conscious alternative to a Latin *auctor*. The most sustained project of revision occurs in her reinvention in the *Lais* of Ovid's erotodidactic project from the *Ars amatoria* and *Remedia amoris*. Marie's "Lanval" and "Le Fresne" have Middle English translations that carry her revisions forward, and the *Lais* are translated into Old Norse in the thirteenth century as the *Strengleikar*.⁴ Her transformation and relocation of the Ovidian project as well as the narratives anticipate the efforts that English writers will make in the later Middle Ages and Renaissance.

The most discussed and problematic example of Marie's naming herself as the author of her works appears in the epilogue to her *Fables*: "Marie ai num, si sui de France" (4) [Marie is my name; I am from France].⁵ Marie's identification of herself as French—"si sui de France"—has become the test for any effort to identify her within the aristocratic, ecclesiastical, and royal milieux of twelfth-century England. As identities are proposed, the meaning of "France" varies—does it refer to her region of birth, family, residence, or a cultural identity based on continental rather than insular French? Whatever the intent in this passage, the self-naming in the *Fables* reflects a consistent practice of identification in Marie's other works, a claim of authorship based on her ability to gather materials and render them "en romanz." In the *Lais*, "Guigemar" opens with Marie's address to her audience, which is putatively male and aristocratic: "Oëz, seigneurs, ke dit Marie" (3) [Hear, my lords, the words of Marie]. In the epilogue to the *Espurgatoire Seint Patriz* (2297), she identifies herself as a translator: "Jo, Marie, ai mis, en memoire, / le livre de l'Espurgatoire / en Romanz" (2297–99) [I, Marie, have put the Book of Purgatory into French as a record].⁶ At the end of *La vie Seint Audree*, a poem now increasingly attributed to her, Marie inscribes herself as the author of a written text, a poem that must circulate in a context of reading and interpretation: "Ici escris mon nom Marie" (4919) [Here I write my name Marie].

---

3. Marie de France, *Les Lais*, ed. Rychner, 2; *Lais*, trans. Burgess and Busby, 41. See the Epilogue to the *Fables* ("m'entremis de cest livre faire" [11]) and the Prologue to the *Espurgatoire Seint Patriz* ("pur ceo m'en sui ore entremis" [10]).

4. *Strengleikar*, ed. Cook and Tveitane. This collection adds the translator's comments to Marie's Prologue, omits Marie's mention of Priscian as an authority for exegetical reading, and argues that the vernacular is an aid to reading and understanding; it translates all of Marie's lais except "Eliduc" and adds ten other pieces.

5. Marie de France, Fables *of Marie de France*, trans. Martin, 252.

6. Marie de France, *Saint Patrick's Purgatory*, trans. Curley, 170–71.

The witnesses to these assertions of authorship are a cultural elite in Angevin England that serves as the audience, too, of Map and other Latin writers and of vernacular writers such as Wace, Hue de Rotelande, and Benoît de Sainte-Maure.[7] Marie's contemporary Denis Piramus testifies to her popularity in circles of aristocratic men ("Cunte, barun e chivaler") as well as women: "Les lais solent as dames pleire" (46) [The *Lais* usually please courtly women], who find their wishes expressed in the stories.[8] The complete political structure—"Li rei, li prince e li curtur / Cunte, barun e vavassur" (50–51), which reconstitutes the conditions of English literary culture in the twelfth century—Denis adds, can displace its worldly experience of sorrow and distress by means of imaginative works that include stories, songs, fables, and "bon diz qui sunt delitables" (52). At the same time that he places Marie in this context of literary production, Denis contrasts his historical writing with Marie's fictions and dismisses the truth value of her lais: "Ke ne sunt pas del tut verais" (38) [Which are not all true].[9] At the beginning of the lai of "Guigemar," which serves in effect as a second Prologue, Marie suggests that the poems have had enough success to incite envy: "Cil ki de sun bien unt envie / Sovent en dïent vileinie: / Sun pris li volent abeissier" (9–11) [People who are envious of their abilities frequently speak insultingly of them in order to damage this reputation]. In the Epilogue to the *Fables,* she repeats the suggestion: "Puet cel estre, cil clerc plusur / Prendreient sur els mun labur: / ne vueil que nuls sur lui le die" (5–7) [It may be that many writers will claim my work as their own, but I want no one else to attribute it to himself]. If Map's counter-authorship looks forward to Chaucer's performative ambivalence about his position as a writer, Marie's self-naming and assertion of authorship forecast the alternate gesture of claiming authorship directly made by Chaucer's contemporary and interlocutor, John Gower.

"BONE MATEIRE" AND THE FRAMES OF AUTHORSHIP

Denis Piramus's reservation about the truth of Marie's *Lais* brings into focus a fundamental question of her authorship—how does the revisionary *materia* of her poems align with the institutional conventions of writing, which regulate meaning and use? The *Lais* are the boundary case because of their origin in Breton oral tradition, as are the marvels, apparitions, and prodigies that Map

---

7. Rossi, *Marie de France,* 117–49.
8. Piramus, *La vie seint Edmund le rei,* ed. Kjellman.
9. Later references to Marie's *Fables* appear in the thirteenth-century *Couronnement de Renart* and the *Évangile aux femmes* attributed to Marie de Champagne; see Rossi, *Marie de France,* 144–49.

takes from folklore in the *De nugis curialium*.¹⁰ But the question persists in her other works. The *Fables,* comprising a book entitled *Esope* (*Ysopet*), have migrated as wisdom literature from Greek to Latin and then to King Alfred's English before Marie translates them "proprement" (19)—that is, accurately, suitably, and appropriately for the source she seeks to reproduce and appropriate. *L'Espurgatoire seint Patriz* recounts journeys to the Otherworld from Henry of Saltrey's *Tractatus de Purgatorio Sancti Patricii* "si cum li livre le nus dit" (4) [Just as the book tells us about them]. The *Tractatus* is widely translated in European vernaculars, but Marie's version is distinctive in shifting the focus from a Cistercian monastic context to a lay, courtly framework represented by the knight-pilgrim Owen.¹¹ *La vie seinte Audree,* if it is by Marie, translates the life of St. Etheldreda from the *Liber Eliensis* and brings the story again from a monastic institutional context to something closer to a hagiographical romance for lay readers.¹²

Marie's prologues and epilogues are the devices that consciously frame her authorship as an exercise of revision and recontextualization. Across her works, they comprise a discursive field with several distinctive features. Proverbs typically open her poems and state an ethical principle whose fulfillment can be realized in the social sphere of reading. Beginning with a proverb is both a narrative tactic and a gesture toward poetics and contemporary rhetorical doctrine.¹³ Naming herself, Marie challenges contemporary court writers who might seek to appropriate her work; her claims to authorship mark literary ownership and a juridical claim to possession and responsibility for her "labur" (Epilogue to the *Fables* 4). Her repeated intention of writing "pur remembrance" (*Lais* 35, Epilogue to *Fables* 3, *Audree* 4625) challenges the commonplace that medieval writers are anonymous representatives of mankind as a whole. Marie preserves not just the stories of adventure but her authorship of the stories as objects of cultural memory.¹⁴ In the epilogues to the *Fables* and *Audree,* she states the aim of being remembered as an author as a general principle applicable to all writers: "cil uevre mal ki sei ublie" (*Fables* 8) [He who lets himself fall into oblivion does a poor job] and "Mut par est fol ki se

---

10. Robert R. Edwards, "Notes toward the Angevin Uncanny," 87–107.
11. Marie de France, *Saint Patrick's Purgatory,* 24.
12. McCash, "*La vie seinte Audree,*" 759–63.
13. Murphy, *Rhetoric in the Middle Ages,* 167–68, notes that twelfth-century grammarians focus on beginnings and endings. Opening with a proverb is a feature of treatises from Matthew of Vendôme's *Ars Versificatoria* (ca. 1175) through Geoffrey of Vinsauf's *Poetria Nova* (1208–13) and John of Garland's *Parisiana Poetria* (ca. 1234). Among Marie's contemporaries, Hue de Rotelande uses the device in his *Ipomedon.*
14. Whalen, *Marie de France,* makes the strongest argument for memory as a structural element at multiple levels in Marie's work.

oblie" (*Audree* 4623) [One is indeed foolish who forgets himself].¹⁵ Marie's authorship is also a negotiation of gender and agency, for she claims a place in a sphere of masculine literary and disciplinary authority, translating materials that speak to the moral and spiritual values of aristocratic life, which encompasses men and women as audiences and writers ("Hummë u femme de grant pris" ["Guigemar" 8]). Those who would appropriate her work, she says in the *Fables*, are men defending their occupational control and prerogative over letters ("cil clerc" [Epilogue 5]). Across her works, Marie's patrons and audiences serve as not only an authorizing source for writing but also as the terminus. Her aims as an author are realized when her book is finished and delivered to them as a performative gesture, as in the presentation to Henry II in the *Lais*, Count William at the end of the *Fables*, or the "pruzdum" (9) who requested the *Espurgatoire*.

In the Prologue that begins the *Lais*, Marie makes it clear that her own cultural grounding is in Latin—which is to say, written—literary culture. The *Lais* depend fundamentally on established traditions of writing, reading, and commentary. Marie takes on the project of composing the *Lais* as an alternative to translating "aukune bone estoire" (Prologue 29) from Latin to French. She thus shifts her topic from *res gesta*, such as Denis Piramus privileges, to *aventure*, as preserved in the vernacular. Moving from a dominant historical form to a marginal genre, writing itself becomes *aventure*. Marie's approach to the stories remains, however, the same as it would be for a Latin text. As such, it complicates the distinction it ostensibly makes. She follows the model of the ancients who, according to Priscian, composed their works "oscurement" so that later readers can gloss them and provide the supplement ("surplus") that completes their meaning within a community of schooled readers: "K'i peüssent gloser la lettre / E de lur sen le surplus mettre" (15–16) [(those who) could provide a gloss for the text and put the finishing touches to their meaning].¹⁶ This "surplus," as R. Howard Bloch points out, directs the tales toward the future, not the originary past, toward an audience of readers moved by their own desires, at the same time that it presents reading—glossing the literal body of *aventure* and supplying something beyond what it possesses—as both hermeneutic and erotic.¹⁷ The interpretive "surplus" is the act of invention that generates writing and authorship.

Marie makes a bold literary claim here, easily as ambitious as Dante's assertion over a century later in the *De vulgari eloquentia* that Romance literatures

---

15. Marie de France, *Life of Saint Audrey*, ed. and trans. McCash and Barban, 246–47.

16. Whalen, "Prologues and Epilogues," 1–30; and idem, *Marie de France*, 35–60. Zanoni, "'Ceo Testimoine Precïens,'" 407–15, suggests that the school exercises of Priscian's *Praeexercitamina* may be intended rather than his *Institutiones*.

17. Bloch, *Anonymous Marie de France*, 42–48.

have a coherent and independent poetic tradition. At a theoretical level, she argues that vernacular stories function within the compositional and interpretive procedures of Latin culture and that they carry the same exemplary and allegorical value as Latin texts. Like Latin texts, they can bear the attention and scrutiny of moral reflection, which is the possibility for meaning that they hold out for their readers to supply. As Robert W. Hanning points out, such an audience is a constitutive element of Marie's authorship.[18] In practice, Marie's location of vernacular stories within literary tradition reveals a perhaps still bolder conception, which reflects her particular historical and cultural moment. When she turns to classical sources for expressions, themes, and incidents in the *Lais*, she borrows frequently from the *romans d'antiquité*—the Old French redactions of the stories of Thebes, Troy, and Rome that view classical Latin epics through the lens of courtly culture.[19]

Marie's citation and evocation of these texts suggests a new kind of hybrid classicizing behind authorship in mid-twelfth-century Angevin literary and cultural life. The *Roman d'Eneas* and *Roman de Thèbes* represent the Theban and imperial Roman stories as authoritatively as do Vergil and Statius. Wace's *Brut*, another source for Marie, stands in for any "bone estoire" or Latin chronicle of the Anglo-French national story of Trojan origins, a preoccupation of Angevin writing and patronage.[20] Latin literary culture, in other words, already includes the vernacular among its narrative models. *Translatio studii* (the migration of learning and cultural authority) moves apace with *translatio imperii* (the descent of power and political legitimation).

In the Prologue to the *Fables*, this movement serves as a validation of Marie's authorship. As in the *Accessus ad auctores*, Marie provides the background to her work by describing an origin for her source. She credits "li ancïen pere" (11) with writing down good proverbs warranted by recognized authorities ("li philosophe" [2]), and she cites the example of Romulus's letter to his son recommending the practical wisdom of guarding against deception. Aesop, Marie says, anticipates his master's intentions and dispositions; accordingly, he translates fables from Greek to Latin for him, adding meaning ("sun sens" [22] and "philosophie" [24]) that becomes the point of the tales ("tuz li fes" [26]). Commentators point out that Aesop is traditionally an author rather than translator of the fables. Marie's apparent mistake obliquely defines the authorship she claims. Aesop writes for his imperial master, just as Marie writes for her courtly lord, "ki flurs est de chevalerie, / d'enseignement,

---

18. Hanning, "Courtly Contexts," 44; idem, "Talking Wounded," 144.
19. Hoepffner, "Marie de France et l'*Eneas*," 272–308; Richards, "Les Rapports," 45–55; and Burgess, *Lais of Marie de France*, 4–6.
20. Crane, "Anglo-Norman Cultures in England," 41–43.

de curteisie" (Prologue 31–32) [who is the flower of chivalry, of learning, and of courtliness]. Translating Aesop, she reproduces his authorship. As she indicates in the Epilogue, this inaugurating gesture remains valid even if she has used the English translation she ascribes to King Alfred as an intermediary in a genealogy of authorship. As we shall see in later chapters, the genealogy of authorship becomes a crucial topic for English vernacular writers in the later Middle Ages.

In the *Espurgatoire* and *Vie de seinte Audree*, the procedures remain constant as the *materia* shifts to religious topics. Marie begins the *Espurgatoire* by stating her intent as a translator: "vueil en Romanz metre en escrit" (3) [I wish to put into writing in French]. Her aims are memorial, and the occasion for her writing comes from a commission from "Uns prozdum" (9), who is also the "Beals pere" (16) directing her work and the witness to a reverse invention as she reveals her work: "jo voldrai aovrir / ceste escripture e descovrir" (29–30) [I want to open up this writing / For you, and reveal its contents]. Throughout her translation of the *Tractatus*, Marie asserts its textuality. Gregory and Augustine are the authorities who provide models for the topical "essamples" collected to record journeys through Saint Patrick's Purgatory. Owen's account of his journey, the longest narrative section, adapts the romance convention of a knight's giving a deposition after his *aventure*: "Puis reconta ço que il vit, / e il le mistrent en escrit" (1911–12) [Then he recounted what he had seen, / And they set it down in writing]. The motif is repeated when he later returns from Jerusalem: "Tut en ordre li a cunté / de sa vie la verité" (1921–22) [He recounted to the king, / In proper order, the true course of his life]. The Prologue of *Audree* states Marie's *intentio auctoris* of honoring Audrey as queen and saint, and it initially divides the material into lineage and life before adding the miracles that accrue to Audrey. The last miracle, which centers on the veracity of an English life of the saint ("En engleis est la vie escrite" [4549]), is an emblem of Marie's authorship, for it balances the written record of her source ("Si com en latin l'ay trové" [4609]) with the testimony of oral witness ("les miracles ay oÿ" [4610]).

"LE LIVRE OVIDE"

The theories of authorship evoked in Marie's prologues and epilogues have a sustained practical application in the *Lais*, where Marie rewrites Ovidian elegy into the vernacular *materia* of the Breton lais. Scholars generally approach Marie's classicism as a source for specific borrowings, for material gathered discretely from other texts and then inserted into the narrative skein of her stories of *aventure*. Her classical sources constitute the official history and dynastic procession of Thebes, Troy, Rome, and Arthurian England. They consequently lend cultural authority and dignity to her retelling of localized, parochial stories from both sides of the Channel. In Ovid's erotodidactic poems, however, Marie finds a topic and conceptual frame for invention and authorship rather than rhetorical adornment and learned allusion. This use of Ovid as a literary project differs from narrative parallels that have been widely cited: "Les Deus Amanz," "Laüstic," and Ovid's tale of Piramus and Thisbe; "Laüstic" and the Philomela story; or, more broadly, the Narcissus story as a model for narratives on the power of beauty.[21] Ovid's *Ars amatoria* and *Remedia amoris* furnish a way for Marie to imagine the workings of love and desire within the sphere of baronial culture and to present herself as Ovid's authorial successor in a literary *translatio*.

In "Guigemar," Marie introduces Ovid's erotic teaching as part of an elaborate architectural description. The aging lord of the city to which the wounded Guigemar is carried by a mysterious ship protects the chastity of his young wife by placing her in a green marble enclosure situated beneath the donjon of his castle. The enclosure has a single, guarded entry and contains inside it a room where the lord has put his wife, accompanied only by his niece. The key to the gate of the enclosure is held by a castrated old priest who says mass in the chapel at the entrance to the room and serves meals to the wife. The sexual imagery of the phallic donjon looming over the enclosure translates immediately into the symbolism of male power seeking to contain and dominate female sexuality. It is an assertion of control that also reveals the anxiety at the heart of Ovidian and baronial power. For there is a mordant irony in an impotent old man acting as unlikely gate keeper, spiritual warden, and domestic staff in place of a vigilant and jealous old husband, driven now by envy rather than lust. The *senex amans* has accidentally and comically produced a version of himself as the support staff in his wife's love story. The most striking detail of Marie's description, however, is her account of the paintings that adorn the inside of the room:

> La chaumbre ert peinte tut entur;
> Venus, la deuesse d'amur,
> Fu tres bien mise en la peinture;
> Les traiz mustrout e la nature
> Cument hom deit amur tenir

---

21. Segre, "Piramo e Tisbe," 2:845–53; Cargo, "Marie de France's *Le Laustic*," 162–66; and Gertz, "Echoes and Reflections," 372–96.

E lealment e bien servir.
Le livre Ovide, ou il enseine
Comment chascuns s'amur estreine,
En un fu ardant le gettout,
E tuz iceus escumengout
Ki jamais cel livre lirreient
Ne sun enseignement fereint.
La fu la dame enclose e mise.
(233–45)

The walls of the chamber were covered in paintings in which Venus, the goddess of love, was skillfully depicted together with the nature and obligations of love; how it should be observed with loyalty and good service. In the painting Venus was shown as casting into a blazing fire the book in which Ovid teaches the art of controlling love and as excommunicating all those who read this book or adopted its teachings. In this room the lady was imprisoned.

Though Rychner and other commentators confidently gloss "Le livre Ovide" as the *Remedia amoris,* the literal and figurative meaning of Marie's citation of Ovid remains a topic of some critical debate and uncertainty.[22] Herman Braet points out that a case can be made for identifying the Ovidian book as either the *Ars amatoria* or the *Remedia amoris.*[23] Hanning sees a more comprehensive reference: "Not just the *Remedia amoris* but the whole Ovidian system (*Ars* and *Remedia* alike), which seeks to control the force and course of love by artfulness and strategy, stands condemned by Venus and by Marie, for whom the goddess here stands surrogate."[24] He suggests elsewhere that Marie displaces Ovid and offers a "vernacular discourse of desire" in which writing gains its authority from pain and provides truthtelling from the margins.[25] SunHee Kim Gertz, tracing the oscillations between metaphor and literalization in Marie and Ovid, finds a "dissonant relation" between the description of the mural and the rest of the *lai.*[26]

Read as a visual program with a coherent message, Marie's *ekphrasis* at once evokes and modifies Ovid's love treatises. In the *Ars amatoria* and *Remedia amoris,* Ovid sets out an erotic project with four distinct phases: find-

---

22. Marie de France, *Les Lais,* ed. Rychner, 244.
23. Braet, "Note sur Marie de France," 21–25.
24. Hanning, "Courtly Contexts," 45.
25. Hanning, "Talking Wounded," 141–42.
26. Gertz, "Echoes and Reflections," 382.

ing, capturing, keeping, and abandoning a lover when she becomes tedious or troublesome. The medieval *accessus* describes the first three phases as the method of exposition in the *Ars amatoria*: "Modus istius operis talis est, ostendere quomodo ipsa puella possit inueniri, inuenta exorari, exorata retineri" [The method of this work is as follows: to show how a girlfriend herself can be found; how she can be won by entreaty; and once won by entreaty, how she can be kept].[27] Ovid's metaphor for the first two phases is hunting. The visual details in "Guigemar" show that Marie's concern is with the third phase—how a woman can be retained after she has been induced to take a lover ("exorata retineri"). The paintings reveal the nature of love and demonstrate how a man can extend and protract the duration of his love affair: "Cument hom deit amur tenir" (237). The burning of Ovid's book on controlling love ("Comment chascuns s'amur estreine" [240]) effectively cancels out the final stage of the Ovidian program contained in the *Remedia amoris* and incidentally demolishes a book whose writing Cupid fully sanctions in a scene in Ovid's poem (*Remedia amoris* 40: "Et mihi 'propositum perfice' dixit 'opus'").

The wife is immured, then, within a visual program whose topic is the maintenance of love after hunting and capture but before pleasure, satisfaction, and fulfillment erode. Marie has transformed the erotic project from servicing Ovidian appetite against the decaying arc of gratification to sustaining courtly devotion ("lealment e bien servir" [238]). M. L. Stapleton thus argues that Marie "domesticates" Ovid, divesting him of deceit and cynicism.[28] Certainly, the emphasis on fidelity in love is expressed consummately later in the tale in the two knots that only Guigemar and his lady can untie and elsewhere in permutations of the phrase *amer lëalment*.[29] Marie exploits the belatedness of authorship by recontextualizing Ovidian conventions and finding equivalents to the thematic complexities that the conventions generate.

In the painted room in "Guigemar," Marie's transformation of eros is expressed in the contrast between the husband's obsessive desire to control his wife by layers of containment ("La fu la dame enclose e mise" [245]) and the devoted lover's task of drawing out and extending the duration of love within those walls and constraints. As Gertz notes, one point of critical debate is whether and how the paintings on the wall bear out the intentions of the husband who presumably authorized their execution in the chamber.[30] Do they represent what he hopes for himself or fears from his wife? Stapleton argues that we must separate the prescription about preserving love faithfully

---

27. I cite the text from *Accessus ad auctores*, ed. and trans. Wheeler, 48–49, which preserves the ordering of the manuscript.
28. Stapleton, "Venus Vituperator," 294.
29. Burgess, *Lais of Marie de France*, 147–58.
30. Gertz, "Echoes and Reflections," 382.

from its mode of representation.[31] To focus on the husband's intentions as a defining source for meaning is to ignore the "surplus" that Marie makes an element of reading in her prologue to the *Lais* and the condition of desire in her writing.[32] It is the lover hovering in the future, the concrete embodiment of husbandly anxiety and wifely desire, who will interpret and perform the scene painted on the walls of the wife's chamber.

"MUT FU DELITUSE LA VIE"

The *ekphrasis* in "Guigemar" serves as a poetic emblem for one of the central concerns in the *Lais*—the fragile interim of pleasure that lovers cooperate on constructing for themselves. By canceling the *Remedia*, Marie truncates the four-step Ovidian project to direct the narrative focus to the problem of erotic dilation, to the interval of stolen pleasure unfolding in a joint venture of ingenuity and dedicated, clandestine betrayal. Her topic, put another way, is the enjoyment and maintenance of pleasure operating against time and contingency. In "Guigemar" (537) and "Milun" (277), Marie uses the word *vie* to demarcate this erotic interval within the larger narrative. In "Eliduc," the fixed *terme* of his military service overseas to the king of Exeter corresponds to his first erotic interval with Guilliadun (550, 689). Erotic *otium* is the space of invention where Marie intervenes to amplify her materials. Inside and outside the text, desire and authorship run in parallel.

In the *Ars amatoria*, Ovid points out that this phase of protracted enjoyment, as opposed to discovering and capturing erotic prey, depends essentially on ingenuity: "Arte mea capta est, arte tenenda mea est. / Nec minor est virtus, quam quaerere, parta tueri: / Casus inest illic; hoc erit artis opus" (2.12–14) [by my art you gained her, by my art she must be kept. Nor is there less prowess in guarding what is won than in seeking; in that there is chance, but this task demands skill]. *Ars*, as Ovid uses the term in his didactic poems, means craft and technique; its source lies in practice and experience (*usus*) rather than vatic inspiration. Such craft, says Ovid, is Protean, adapting itself and improvising as needed in order to remain pleasing. It is ongoing invention. It depends, too, on *cultus*—the manufacture of an attractive appearance and personal habits—and especially on self-mastery. For modern critics, this can amount to a mechanization of the lover, who remakes the self into an artifact.[33] In Book 3, Ovid extends the principle of self-fashioning to women as well: "Maius opus mores composuisse suos" (3.370; cf. *Remedia* 53–54) [more

---

31. Stapleton, "*Venus Vituperator*," 293.
32. Fitz, "Prologue to the *Lais*," 563.
33. Downing, "Anti-Pygmalion," 235.

important is it to control one's own behaviour]. The greatest threat for the Ovidian lover, male or female, is not rivals or the obstacles provided by a husband or guardian—substantial though they are—but the surfacing of desire, which destroys the twin illusions of technical control and self-mastery, the bases of virtuoso artistry.

Ovid's poetic aim in these teachings is frankly satiric. His broad topic is *concessa furta* (*Ars amatoria* 1.33)—a sanctioned form of carnal indulgence, sexual theft, and betrayal that carries no consequence because it is directed toward women who supposedly have no interest in virtue or chastity. Ovid belies his satiric pose, however, at several points. Desire can snare the *praeceptor amoris* as well as his disciples. "Sed facile haeremus" (3.543) [But we are easily caught], he admits near the end of the *Ars amatoria*. Moreover, the predatory craft of gratification can momentarily reveal unexpected sympathies and ethical values. Early in Book 2, Ovid sets himself the task of containing Cupid; and he exhorts lovers to cultivate wit as well as beauty (2.112), to make a soul that abides the disappearance of the confected self (2.119), and to develop tact and persistence. Later, he proposes an ethics of mutuality between lovers. Imagining the scene of consummation, Ovid stresses equality, reciprocity, and fulfillment: "Quod iuvet, ex aequo femina virque ferant. / Odi concubitus, qui non utrumque resolvunt" (*Ars* 2.682–83) [Let both man and woman feel what delights them equally. I hate embraces which leave not each outworn]. In Book 3, he makes the same point in precisely the same language: "ex aequo res iuvet illa duos" (3.794) [let that act delight both alike]. Marie's erotic couples—collaborators and dedicated conspirators in love—are the active social form analogous to Ovid's pair of lovers, collapsed in mutual pleasure. Both pairings find the "surplus" that Marie takes as intrinsic to writing and reading.

Marie's poetic invention of Ovid builds on the point of greatest vulnerability for the teacher and students of love. The emergence of desire as a force beneath appetite and gratification threatens to disable Ovidian erotodidaxis, but desire is already the starting point for Marie's lovers. Though pleasure and jouissance lead Equitan to chivalry ("Equitan" [15–16]), he falls in love with the seneschal's wife without seeing her: "Sanz veüe la coveita" (41). So, too, does Milun's beloved, moved as she is by mention of his name. Marie thus poses the question implicit but largely suppressed in the *Ars amatoria*: how do lovers maintain and protract an erotic interim based on desire rather than appetite and simple gratification? This is a distinguishing feature through which Marie exercises authorial agency. The Ovidian lover draws out his liaison by subterfuge and manipulation and finds a momentary resolution in the equity of sexual exhaustion. Marie explores an interval of erotic reciprocity that varies in time yet remains strikingly constant in structure and intensity. "Chievrefoil" recounts a brief meeting of Tristan and Isolde in the forest that encompasses satisfaction, intimacy, and pleasure: "Entre eus meinent joie mut grant. / A li parlat tut a leisir / E ele li dit sun pleisir" (94–96) [They shared great joy together. He spoke freely to her and she told him of her desire]. The faery mistress of "Lanval" promises a succession of these encounters:

> Quant vus vodrez od mei parler,
> Ja ne savrez cel liu penser
> U nuls puïst aveir s'amie
> Sanz repreoce e sanz vileinie,
> Que jeo ne vus seie en present
> A fere tut vostre talent.
> (163–68)

Whenever you wish to speak with me, you will not be able to think of a place where a man may enjoy his love without reproach or wickedness, that I shall not be there with you to do your bidding.

Separated from external shame and internalized censorship ("Sanz repreoce e sanz vileinie"), the imaginary site of erotic plenitude anchors the fantasy of a libidinal object fully available and compliant to the lover's demands: "present / A fere tut vostre talent." Structurally and thematically, Marie sets this presence against the denials and omissions of favor at Arthur's court, which Lanval gladly abandons for Avalon at the end of his tale.

Some of Marie's stories portray the interval of pleasure as real but unreachable. The couple of "Deus Amanz," ostensibly bound in a committed love for each other ("s'entreamerent lëaument" [72]), perishes in their effort to meet the letter but circumvent the constraints imposed by the lady's father, who decrees that anyone seeking his daughter must be able to carry her up the high mountain outside the city of Pitres. What fails them in a practical sense is "mesure" (189), the self-possession and internalized discipline of the Ovidian lover (*modus*), for the lover in Marie's tale resists drinking the potion that will assure success in his trial. The lady of "Chaitivel" proves a better Ovidian lover than her suitors, playing all four of them against each other but then losing three to the chance slaughter of a tournament designed to show their prowess. The survivor faces the prospect of endless service without pleasure. He is granted the company of his mistress but no comfort: "Si n'en puis nule joie aveir / Ne de baisier ne d'acoler / Ne d'autre bien fors de parler" (220–22) [I cannot experience the joy of a kiss or an embrace or of any pleasure other than conversation].

"Deus Amanz" and "Chaitivel" are stories of predicament, in which narrative action is contained by the governing fictional premise (an impossible task or choice), and their stasis reveals a key element of Marie's portrayal of desire. The conditions imposed by the father on his daughter's suitors in "Deus Amanz" scarcely conceal his incestuous desire, as is the case of the story of Apollonius of Tyre. His unwillingness to suffer the loss of her comfort and proximity ("Pres de li esteit nuit et jur" [30]) provokes widespread censure: "Plusur a mal li aturnerent, / Li suen meïsme le blamerent" (33–34) [Many people reproached him for this, and even his own people blamed him]. In some measure, the daughter seems to accept and ratify his desire. When she rejects her lover's plea to flee with him, her sympathies lie with her father, and she imagines his response to her flight as that of a rejected lover:

> Si jo m'en vois ensemble od vus,
> Mis pere avreit e doel e ire,
> Ne vivreit mie sanz martire.
> Certes tant l'eim e si l'ai chier,
> Jeo nel vodreie curucier.
> (96–100)

> But if I went away with you, my father would be sad and distressed and his life would be an endless torment. Truly, I love him so much and hold him so dear that I would not wish to grieve him.

The surviving lover of "Chaitivel," whose wound may be a sign of castration, faces the kind of predicament posed by a *demande d'amour*: is it better for a lover to face rivals with the prospect of consummation, or to have no rivals yet no chance of pleasure?[34] Moreover, his lady's continued deferral after chance has produced a single result—the removal of all rivals—represents a flight from desire and from the interim of pleasure that other lovers seek in Marie's tales. These tales of predicament forestall the lovers' consummation precisely because the couple's erotic attachments are uncertain and contested from within. It is a critical commonplace that Marie's lovers must be committed to each other, even in a problematic case like "Equitan," where a lord wrongly desires his vassal's wife. But as "Deus Amanz" and "Chaitivel" dem-

---

34. Bloch, *Anonymous Marie de France*, 93.

onstrate, reciprocity demands in turn a commitment to desire (hence "Equitan" as a monitory example, a critique not just of lordship blinded by lust but of desire as the condition of unforeseeable reversal).

In stories where Marie goes beyond predicaments to create a richly imagined and potentially unstable fictional world, the dilation of eros finds a complex and highly nuanced treatment of the Ovidian interim. For Guigemar, this period begins with treatment for the wound ("la plaie" [113]) to his thigh, caused by the ricocheted arrow during his hunt in the forests of Brittany. The external symbolic wound ("Sa plaie" [370]) healed by the lady in her chamber becomes the indwelling metaphorical wound of love ("Amur est plaie dedenz cors" [483]). When he discloses his love, Guigemar asks the lady not to act like a manipulative Ovidian lover or the conflicted lady of "Chaitivel." His request centers on the ethics of managing the erotic interim:

Femme jolive de mestier
Se deit lunc tens faire preier
Pur sei cherir, que cil ne quit
Que ele eit usé cel deduit.
(515–18)

A woman who is always fickle likes to extend courtship in order to enhance her own esteem and so that the man will not realize that she has experienced the pleasure of love.

Burgess finds in this passage a prescription for loyal service in love.[35] Hanning sees it as an example of Marie's using love casuistry against itself.[36] The Ovidian background shows how closely Marie links temporality and desire. Ovid recommends that women use delay as a tactic for control, consolidation, and amusement: "Quod datur ex facili, longum male nutrit amorem: / Miscenda est laetis rara repulsa iocis" (*Ars amatoria* 3.579–80) [What is easily given ill fosters an enduring love; let an occasional repulse vary your merry sport]. Delay (*mora*) hovers between two forms in Ovidian doctrine— *tuta* (safe) and *brevis* (short-lived). The *praeceptor* advises slow lovemaking to his male disciple: "Crede mihi, non est veneris properanda voluptas, / Sed sensim tarda prolicienda mora" (2.717–18) [Believe me, love's bliss must not be hastened, but gradually lured on by slow delay]. He counsels women to time their public entrances to their greatest advantage, adducing a proverb with larger applications to the management of eros: "maxima lena mora est"

---

35. Burgess, *Lais of Marie de France*, 135–36.
36. Hanning, "Courtly Contexts," 51.

(3.752) [a great procuress is delay]. Guigemar condemns the mystification of such tactics; they are, he says, a means for leveraging esteem while obscuring desire. He argues instead for the lady to act on her pleasure: "Ainz l'amerat, s'en avrat joie" (523) [She should rather love him and enjoy his love]. Revealing desire produces the erotic "surplus" (533) of "Guigemar." What follows from that disclosure is a year-and-a-half interlude, replete with sensual pleasure: "Mut fu delituse la vie" (537).

The acknowledgment of desire, such as Guigemar urges, is the precipitating event of the parallel story "Yonec," where the aging husband isolates his wife within a paved chamber in his tower, attended by his sister. Here the patriarchal anxieties over lineage, inheritance, and cuckoldry in "Guigemar" and other tales are made explicit. The lady laments the isolation forced on her by her husband. The remedy she seeks lies in *aventure* as a social and discursive form, for she turns to stories like her own as they are memorialized within aristocratic culture:

> Chevalier trovoent puceles
> A lur talent, gentes e beles,
> E dames truvoent amanz
> Beaus e curteis, pruz e vaillanz,
> Si que blasmees n'en esteient
> Ne nul fors eles nes veeient.
> (95–100)

Knights discovered maidens to their liking, noble and fair, and ladies found handsome and courtly lovers, worthy and valiant men. There was no fear of reproach and they alone could see them.

This story she acknowledges as the object of her wish and will ("ma volenté [104]). It is a textualized model of erotic subjectivity, which Marie reinscribes into romance tradition. Muldumarec, the princely lover who immediately arrives in the form of a hawk, reports that he has already desired her but could not come to her until she has made her self-disclosure, until she has read and applied the story. Once the lady is reassured of her lover's belief in God, which adds no apparent scruple of conscience about adultery, the couple commits itself to the erotic plenitude of laughter, play, and intimacy ("unt asez ris e jué / E de lur priveté parlé" [193–94]). This period, Marie makes clear, is a dimension of time enclosed on itself: "E nuit e jur e tost e tart / Ele l'ad tut a sun pleisir" (222–23) [Night and day, early or late, he was hers whenever she wanted]. The phrase *avoir tut a sun pleisir* echoes the promise of erotic repletion given by the faery mistress in "Lanval": "present / A fere tut vostre talent" (167–68). As in "Equitan," this period is punctuated and given shape only by the comings and goings of the lady's husband, even though discovery and vengeance wait in the background.

In "Milun," Marie reformulates the periodicity of erotic fulfillment from "Lanval" into an incremental narrative structure. Milun and the lady who summons him as her lover enjoy their first interval of pleasure in her garden and bedchamber: "La justouent lur parlement / Milun e ele bien suvent" (51–52) [Milun and she frequently arranged a meeting]. This period ends with her pregnancy, the sending away of the child to Milun's sister, and the lady's subsequent arranged marriage to a local nobleman, as Milun leaves for paid service as a warrior. His return begins a second interval, in which the lady's husband replaces the father as the obstacle to pleasure, just as Meriaduc serves as a rival but unwanted suitor to replace the jealous husband in "Guigemar." The swan who serves as a messenger between Milun and the lady is the sole mechanism for sustaining a twenty-year love affair (277–88). Marie makes the swan a figure for the ingenuity of Ovidian erotic craft: "Nuls ne poet estre si destreiz / Ne si tenuz estreitement / Que il ne truisse liu sovent" (286–88) [No one can be so imprisoned or so tightly guarded that he cannot find a way out from time to time]. The starvation and feeding of the bird as it shuttles between the lovers carrying messages symbolizes the epicycles of separation and plenitude. The final interval begins as their son, who has unknowingly proved the chivalric equal of his father by unhorsing him at a tournament, prepares to kill the lady's husband, and a sealed message arrives announcing the husband's death. The son's betrothal of his mother to his father—done on his own authority ("Sanz cunseil de tute autre gent" [526])—fulfills his Oedipal desires and circumvents the anxieties of that desire by restoring the man he has mastered as his mother's partner. Reunited and freed from obstacles, Milun and the lady resume their roles as an erotic couple: "En grant bien e en grant duçur / Vesquirent puis e nuit e jur" (529–30) [Thereafter they lived night and day in happiness and tenderness]. They live the life of pleasure in south Wales that Lanval finds by removing himself from Arthur's court to Avalon.

In portraying the interval of erotic plenitude for her lovers, Marie borrows and transforms structural devices from Ovid. The husbands and guardians—*vafer maritus* and *vigil custos* (3.611–12)—who stand as obstacles to the lover in the *Ars amatoria* have their counterparts in the *senex amans* of "Guigemar" and "Yonec," the seneschal of "Equitan," the violent husband of "Laüstic," the incestuous father of "Deus Amanz," the husband who replaces the father in "Milun," King Mark in the Tristan episode of "Chievrefoil," the retainers ("chevalier fiufé") of "Le Fresne," and even Guildeluëc, the wife of Eliduc. These figures simultaneously block the lover's satisfaction and bring the pressures of time and contingency that give definition to the lovers' erotic interlude. Lovers outwit these obstacles and communicate through intermediaries who function like the maids and go-betweens who must be cultivated in the *Ars amatoria*. In the *Lais*, they are not, however, as in Ovid, potential objects of seduction themselves. The old husband's niece in "Guigemar," assigned as a companion to the captive lady, becomes a collaborator in the love plot in a way that redounds to her credit and stature: "Mut ert curteise e deboneire" (464). The abbess who raises Le Fresne abets her concubinage with Gurun. The chamberlain in "Eliduc" negotiates Guilliadun's cautious approach to her lover. The nightingale in "Laüstic" and the swan in "Milun" are devices for arranging the lover's encounters.

In the *Ars amatoria*, the space for finding and capturing a lover is the Roman cityscape, but the site of desire and pleasure is the bedchamber (*thalamus*). The Ovidian teacher proclaims, "Conveniunt thalami furtis et ianua nostris" (2.617) [Chambers and a locked door beseem our secret doings]. The obstacle of a barred door, he advises later, can be a stimulus to desire: "Adde forem, et duro dicat tibi ianitor ore / 'Non potes,' exclusum te quoque tanget amor" (3.587–88) [Add but a door, and let a doorkeeper say to you with stubborn mouth, 'You cannot'; once shut out, you too, sir, will be touched by love]. The bedchamber is a stronghold under siege by the recruits and veterans ("vetus miles") of the *militia Veneris* (3.559–74) whose tactics differ while their objective remains the same. Access to the chamber is thus a metaphor for access to the lover's body, and admission to the private space is a form of sexual penetration. Submerged under Ovid's pretext of harmless pleasure and displaced from the teacher's consciousness is the additional sense that entry to the chamber is also trespass on another man's household—by extension, a hostile occupation of the central domain of patriarchy. It is here that Marie, imagining a baronial rather than cosmopolitan, imperial world, rejects Ovid's governing premise: "Nos venerem tutam concessaque furta canemus, / Inque meo nullum carmine crimen erit" (*Ars* 1.33–34) [Of safe love-making do I sing, and permitted secrecy, and in my verse shall be no wrong-doing]. For her the erotic interim is framed not just by obstacles (all potentially comic in Ovid) but by violence within a militarized society, always potentially at war among and within its patriarchal households.

In the *Lais*, Marie exploits the Ovidian equation of bed, body, and property for its nuances as well as its basic structure. Guigemar is brought into the lady's chamber to be healed, and it is there that the wound in his thigh becomes the hidden wound of love. Equitan and his lover are discovered on the seneschal's bed, as he bursts into his chamber to discover his wife's betrayal and the means she has prepared to murder him. Le Fresne recovers her identity and her lover in Gurun's bedchamber, where she presides over the preparations for consummation that become, by chance disclosure and happy substitution, her own marriage. Lanval's lady has a portable chamber in the richly appointed pavilion where he first encounters her. The lady's bedroom window opens on her lover's house in "Laüstic," granting him a visual display of his otherwise unattainable lover. The garden where Milun meets his lady is next to her bedchamber. Eliduc and Guilliadun disclose their love to each other in the bedroom that he enters with the king's encouragement, interrupting her chess lesson with another knight but securing access to her person in the most intimate space of the castle.

Marie's most striking use of the Ovidian *thalamus* occurs in "Yonec." Muldumarec, the shape-shifting lover who appears immediately after the lady's self-disclosure of desire, enters by a narrow window ("Par mi une estreite fenestre" [107]) that represents both her jealous husband's constraint and the sexual organs he seeks to protect and employ to assure himself of an heir, without success. The first interlude with the lover restores the lady's beauty, fuels her desire, and gives her a new appreciation of solitude: "Sun ami voelt suvent veeir / E de lui sun delit aveir" (219–20) [She wanted to see her beloved often and to take her pleasure with him]. The old woman charged with guarding her, herself widowed and barren like the castrated priest of "Guigemar," remarks that the lady now remains alone more willingly than before (239–40). In this way, the chamber is transformed from a site of privation, where the lady is removed from society and conversation by a sterile marriage. The lover provides a "surplus" to its desolation, and this supplement is pleasure, sociability, intimacy, and progeny.

When the husband discovers the cause of his wife's restoration, he acts to prevent her body from penetration by rendering the space of her chamber lethal. The *engin* he prepares, a counterpart to an author's invention, is both a deadly trap and a clever assertion of his right of seigneurial possession:

> Broches de fer fist granz furgier
> E acerer le chief devant:
> Suz ciel n'ad rasur plus trenchant!
> Quant il les ot apparailliees
> E de tutes parz enfurchiees,
> Sur la fenestre les ad mises,
> Bien serreies e bien asises,
> Par unt li chevaliers passot,

Quant a la dame repeirot.
(286–94)

He had large iron spikes forged and the tips more sharply pointed than any razor. When he had prepared and cut barbs in them, he set them on the window, close together and well-positioned, in the place through which the knight passed whenever he came to see the lady.

This fortified barrier does not simply defend the aperture that grants the lover entry to the lady and her body, nor does it make the passage inaccessible or forbidding. It is an aggressive, inverted phallic display designed to inflict a wound ("sa plaie" [334]) on the trespasser in vengeance for his transgression of household, property, and patriarchal ambitions. The symbolic aim of the sharply-honed spikes is to castrate the lover, to reverse the sequence of wounds in "Guigemar" and to make Muldumarec as impotent as the lover in "Chaitivel." Muldumarec impales himself on the barrier, seemingly unaware of the trap, but enters the room and seats himself on the bed. His flow of blood on the sheets ("tuit li drap furent sanglent" [316]) represents his insemination of the wife, just as her tracking him by the trail of his blood back to his ornate chamber symbolizes the eventual succession of their son Yonec as lord of the city, after he beheads the lady's husband at the site of his father's tomb.

IMPOSSIBLE DESIRE

In her most richly plotted *Lais,* Marie transforms the Ovidian interim of pleasure into some form of stable consolidation, often marriage or restitution. Guigemar destroys Meriaduc's castle, kills his rival, and goes off with his lover to a place beyond threat: "A grant joie s'amie en meine: / Ore ad trespassee sa peine" (881–82) [With great joy he took away his beloved. Now his tribulations were over]. The love triangle of Gurun, Le Fresne, and La Codre is resolved by La Codre's marriage to another man when she returns with her parents to her country. Lanval and his faery mistress retire to Avalon. Milun and his lover are married by their son. Where erotic transformation fails, restitution prevails. Bisclavret, the werewolf betrayed by his wife out of fear, is restored to his land and possessions, while his wife goes off with the knight who had since married her. Yonec buries his mother at his father's tomb and becomes lord of Muldumarec's city before returning to the fief in Caerwent held by the stepfather he has murdered. The narrative mechanism that produces these transformations is disclosure. Disclosure forces the narrative crisis that brings *aventure* to resolution, thence to public memory and literary form. The ending of "Le Fresne" plots the dual trajectories of closure and disclosure from fiction to writing and authorial performance: "Quant l'aventure fu seüe, / Coment ele esteit avenue, / Le lai del *Freisne* en unt trové" (515–17) [When the truth of this adventure was known, they composed the lay of *Le Fresne*].

Marie writes other tales, however, that significantly resist the transformation of desire within narrative fiction and readerly understanding. "Deus Amanz" leaves its two dead lovers in a sepulchre on the mountain as a memorial to unconsummated desire. "Chaitivel" oscillates between two names (the other is "Les Quatre Deuls") to show the undecidability of its underlying love question. Both names signify thwarted desire, and the answer to the *demande* posed by the story is that neither tragic rivalry nor barren possession is preferable. "Chievrefoil" promises a future reconciliation between Tristan and King Mark, but its tradition tells us that the "acordement" (98) promised during their encounter is a device for deferred consummation. In "Eliaduc" and "Laüstic," Marie goes beyond desire as stasis to examine the Ovidian interim in perhaps its most radical terms.

"Eliduc" in fact begins with the stable erotic interim that is the point of closure for Marie's stories of couples who overcome obstacles to achieve sustained fulfillment at the end of their *aventure*. In her opening summary of the tale, Marie locates Eliduc and Guildeluëc exactly at the point where nothing more can be told in "Guigemar," "Lanval," and "Milun": "Ensemble furent lungement, / Mut s'entreamerent lëaument" (11–12) [They lived together for a long time and loved each other with great loyalty]. The element that intervenes in their happiness is external in the opening summary ("soudees" [14; paid military service]) and internal in the narrative ("l'envie del bien de lui" [41]), yet in both cases it calls into question whether the erotic interim can be sustained within social structures based on a network of implicit allegiance and feudal loyalties: "amur de seignur n'est pas fiez" (63) [a lord's love is no fief]. Eliduc's conflicted loyalty to his wife and mistress duplicates the competing claims that his Breton lord and English employer hold over his services. In Marie's invention, terms like *fiance, fei,* and *leauté* apply equally to political allegiance and love.[37]

Though Eliduc's military service structures time and contingency, the poem's narrative concentrates on a series of erotic intervals. When Guilliadun falls in love with Eliduc, her chamberlain assures her that she can operate within the period of Eliduc's contracted service to her father: "Asez purrez aveir leisir / De mustrer lui vostre pleisir" (453–54) [Thus you will have enough

---

37. Burgess, *Lais of Marie de France,* 152–57.

opportunity to show him your desire]. She accepts those limits in her ensuing interview with Eliduc (532–36), and there follows an interim of pleasure notable for its absence or suppression of sexual appetite:

> Mes n'ot entre eus nule folie,
> Joliveté ne vileinie;
> De douneier e de parler
> E de lur beaus aveirs doner
> Esteit tute la druërie
> Par amur en lur cumpainie.
> (575–80)

There was no foolishness between them, nor fickleness, nor wickedness, as their love consisted entirely of courting and talking, and exchanging fair gifts when they were together.

Marie sets this restraint and sublimation against the desire that her characters so intensely experience. The circulation of words and gifts displaces but stands for sexuality. Sandra Pierson Prior observes that at the start of these exchanges Guilliadun becomes "the desiring Ovidian female," while Eliduc's feelings are those of "the desired object rather than of the desiring subject."[38] A second interval—Eliduc's temporary return to Brittany to aid his lord—repeats the first. Limited again by a promised term of service, Eliduc rejoins his wife and retainers but remains alienated from their joy and isolated within his concealed desire: "Mut se cuntient sutivement" (717) [He behaved most secretively]. When Guildeluëc discovers Guilliadun after another return journey, she recognizes "la verité" (1017) of his withdrawal in a scene where she views Guilladun's body, ironically adopting the lover's gaze and cataloguing the features it beholds (1010–16). Motivated "tant par pitié, tant par amur" (1027), Guildeluëc removes herself as an obstacle, taking the nun's veil and founding a religious community with thirty other women.

Guildeluëc's removal permits the kind of unforeseen closure we see at the end of "Milun," where the husband suddenly dies so that the son can marry his parents. This device returns the story to the erotic consolidation with which it began, though with a different couple. Eliduc and Guilladun marry and resume the life of apparent plenitude in a conscious echo of the restored couple in "Milun": "Ensemble vesquirent meint jur, / Mut ot entre eus parfite amur" (1149–50; cf. "Milun" 530) [They lived together for many a day and the love between them was perfect]. Unlike "Milun," however, in

---

38. Prior, "'Kar des dames,'" 129.

"Eliduc" this new form of erotic interval, secured by trial, suffering, and generous resignation, is as untenable as the first. The life of plenitude that Eliduc and Guilliadun lead centers on charity and good works, which lead to religious conversion. In most modern readings of the poem, this final step demonstrates a movement from earthly to spiritual love.[39] Guildeluëc receives Guilladun as a sister in her community; the two pray for "lur ami" (1171), the shared husband turned patron who prays for them in return. The "bone fei" that Eliduc first pledges Guildeluëc when he leaves Brittany for England (84) presumably finds its proper object in their collaborative enterprise—a spiritual *amicitia* of rivalry in devotion and prayer: "Mut se pena chescuns pur sei / De Deu amer par bone fei / E mut par firent bele fin" (1177–79) [Each one strove to love God in good faith and they came to a good end]. Placed in the final, emphatic position in the sequence of *Lais* in British Library, MS Harley 978, the mid-thirteenth-century English manuscript that offers the only medieval disposition of the full collection, "Eliduc" seemingly gives Marie's last word on the Ovidian project of amplifying pleasure.

But if "Eliduc" follows a trajectory toward spiritual transcendence (*mut bele fin*), its narrative closure leaves open an interpretive "surplus" for Marie's readers. Marie says at the beginning that the poem used to be called *Elidus* but is now called *Guildeluëc ha Guilliadun* (21–28); at the end, she says that the Bretons made a lai "de l'aventure de ces treis" (1181). The stable point among the shifting titles is Marie's intervention as an author. The shifts in the title point as well toward the undecidability of the *matiere*. Is "Eliduc" about a knight who finds salvation after securing worldly pleasure? Is it about two women who eschew rivalry and become spiritual sisters? Is it about a love triangle transformed by something other than removing the obstacle or devising a double marriage? The *aventure* that all three share comes at the end to mean separation as well as reconciliation. Lodged in their monastic houses and communicating through messengers, the characters inhabit a sanctified version of the chambers holding unhappy wives elsewhere in the *Lais*. Their exchange of messages is a benevolent form of the "druërie" that sustains lovers and perhaps forms a link with Marie's religious writings.

The shift from worldly contentment in the Ovidian interval to spiritual transcendence marks the paradox of desire in "Eliduc"—its simultaneous impossibility and persistence. Throughout the poem, the erotic intervals cannot be sustained within the social structures where Marie locates human action, will, and gratification. Eliduc and Guildeluëc lose their happiness to envy and court rivalry. Eliduc and Guilladun cannot consummate their love

---

39. Nelson, "Eliduc's Salvation," 37–42; Robertson, "Love and the Other World," 167–76.

during Eliduc's service to the King of Exeter. When they are legitimized as a couple, charity ("Granz aumoines e granz biens" [1151]) replaces eros in their "parfite amur."[40] When they undergo conversion, they reenact their courtship, safely beyond the threat of pleasure and consummation, its intimacy now fully contained in language.

"Eliduc" ends, then, with sublimation, not reconciliation, and its closure is perhaps more apparent than real. The husband and his two wives commit themselves to prayer as a form of exchange, a means of continuing transactions. The late conversion of Eliduc and Guilladun shows that Guildeluëc has failed or miscalculated in her gesture of resigning marriage for the nun's veil so that Eliduc can take his lover ("Elidus ad s'amie prise" [1145]). The problem of the poem is not to find the right couple but to find an arrangement for all three. This they discover in the exchange of messages, whose topic is the exposure of female emotion and affect ("Pur saveir cument lur estot, / Cum chescune se cunfortot" [1175–76]). Separated by agreement rather than jealous husbands, politics, or social constraints, Eliduc and his wives devise what we might call a spiritual Ovidianism. The messengers he sends to Guildeluëc and Guilladun continually pose the lover's demand that his beloved reveal herself fully to him.

The demand for such disclosure is what constitutes the Ovidian interim of "Laüstic." Marie adapts the Piramus and Thisbe story for her fictional premise and evokes the story of Philomela at the point of narrative crisis. Yet the differences from Ovid's mythographic narratives are as important as the parallels. "Laüstic" is the story of adults, not children thwarted by their fathers; and it goes to the heart of baronial culture, not Semiramis's lascivious and incestuous Babylon, by showing the contradiction of a social order centered simultaneously on rivalry and identity. St. Malo, Marie's locale for the story, enjoys its reputation "Pur la bunté des deus baruns" (11) [Because of the fine qualities of the two men]. Their "deus forz maisuns" (10) opening onto each other, with no barrier except a wall, are the social core of the city. The wife whom one of the noblemen marries is the obstacle who disrupts their chivalric identification with one another and generates their rivalry. She accedes to her neighbor's desire precisely because of the qualities that he implicitly shares with her husband: "grant bien" (25), reputation ("Tant pur le bien qu'ele en oï" [27]), and proximity. (The only difference that emerges between the men is the husband's later cruelty in strangling the nightingale.)

As this roster of qualities suggests, desire operates in "Laüstic" through language. The Ovidian interim made possible by the architecture of the houses

---

40. Mickel, "Reconsideration of the *Lais*," 64.

is a traffic in signs and performance conducted through the lovers' prudence and ingenuity. Conversation and gifts move across the wall and enter through the window of the lady's bedchamber, much as Muldumarec penetrates the window of his lover's room in "Yonec." Nothing impedes the lovers' display for each other in their facing windows: "Nuls nes poeit de ceo garder / Qu'a la fenestre n'i venissent / E iloec ne s'entreveïssent" (54–56) [No one could prevent their coming to the window and seeing each other there]. Marie makes it clear that all these signs are linguistic substitutes for erotic consummation:

N'unt gueres rien ki lur despleise,
Mut esteient amdui a eise,
Fors tant k'il ne poent venir
Del tut ensemble a lur pleisir.
(45–48)

There was scarcely anything to displease them, and they were both very content except for the fact that they could not meet and take their pleasure with each other.

What she also demonstrates is that symbolic exchange not only replaces but comes to constitute desire. As Michelle Freeman points out, the lady finds an alternative to the role of the *mal mariée* under conditions not for lovemaking "*but for dialogue.*"[41] The interim for maintaining the love affair ("Lungement se sunt entreamé" [57]), as Paul Zumthor observes, is the sole marker of time in the poem.[42] It lasts until the lady exceeds the moderation (*modum*) of Ovidian craft and uses the nightingale as a pretext for their meetings. Asked by her husband why she rises in the night, she indirectly but fatefully speaks her dissatisfaction, the distance between him and the joy she finds in her nightly meetings: "Il nen ad joië en cest mund / Ke n'ot le laüstic chanter" (84–85) [Anyone who does not hear the song of the nightingale knows none of the joys of this world].

The husband's capture and killing of the nightingale is the transgression (*vileinie*) that differentiates him morally and socially from his baronial double and reorders the economy of desire in "Laüstic." Thomas A. Shippey proposes that the nightingale stands for the "ideal love" sought by the lovers.[43] Emanuel J. Mickel Jr. glosses the dead bird subsequently carried by the lover as the

---

41. Freeman, "Marie de France's Poetics of Silence," 868.
42. Zumthor, *Essai de poétique médiévale*, 389.
43. Shippey, "Listening to the Nightingale," 51.

"agonizing memory of his lost love."[44] The wife describes the nightingale to her husband as desire that stands beyond him: "mut me semble grant deduit; / Tant m'i delit e tant le voil / Que jeo ne puis dormir de l'oil" (88–90) [it brings me great pleasure. I take such delight in it and desire it so much that I can get no sleep at all]. When the husband breaks the nightingale's neck and splatters its blood on her tunic in an oblique echo of "Yonec," the crisis for the lady is hermeneutic. Deprived of her pretext for nightly display, she wonders how her lover will interpret her absence at the window. Her problem, in other words, is to control the interpretive "surplus" of possible meanings, which Marie makes a condition of writing: "Il quidera ke jeo me feigne" (131) [He will think I am faint-hearted (or: dissimulating or: that I have abandoned him]. She solves her problem by generating her own authorial surplus. The dead bird is transformed into a funerary artifact, wrapped in a rich silk cloth embroidered with gold and writing. To assure the right reading of this overwrought sign, she sends with it a messenger as glossator to explain her intended meaning ("sun message" [143]) to her lover, who nonetheless adds his own surplus to what the messenger says and shows ("tut li ad dit e mustré" [145]).

The dead bird, as Bloch remarks, is sent to the lover as a poetic envoi that marks the impossibility of desire.[45] Without the pretext of the nightingale's song, the erotic exchanges between the wife and lover are no longer possible, and the Ovidian interim closes down under violence to the symbol of love lyric. The lavish reliquary that the lover orders to be made for the bird represents, however, a double, even contradictory, meaning. At one level, the entombment equates death and desire, for the nightingale is not just placed inside the reliquary but the casket is sealed ("Puis fist la chasse enseeler" [155]), as the final act in the lovers' erotic exchanges. At another level, this fixing of desire is what allows desire to persist. The lover always carries the reliquary with him, as a memorial presence. Though sealed (*enseelee*), what the object represents cannot be concealed: "Cele aventure fu cuntee, / Ne pot estre lunges celee" (157–58) [This adventure was related and could not long be concealed]. In ordering the reliquary, the lover has shown that, unlike the husband (116), he is not "vileins" (148), and the object that contains impossible desire makes sure that desire persists in the lai preserving the *aventure*.

The reliquary of "Laüstic" inevitably recalls the marble tomb of "Deus Amanz." But the lovers of "Laüstic" do not have the unreachable desire of the young couple who possess the means but not the wisdom to overcome the obstacle placed in their way. The more revealing comparison is with "Eliduc." In "Eliduc," the Ovidian interval seemingly transforms into religious conver-

---

44. Mickel, "Reconsideration of the *Lais*," 56.
45. Bloch, *Anonymous Marie de France*, 73.

sion. Similar interpretations have been made for "Laüstic," arguing that the reliquary retains its religious symbolism and that entombing the dead bird amounts to a transubstantiation of earthly love into "an ideal spiritual bond."[46] Whether spiritual, idealized, memorial, or morbid, love in "Laüstic" remains desire only partially transformed. The dead bird is not a metaphor but a metonymy for the lovers' Ovidian interval, the symbol of sustained pleasures arbitrarily brought into the economy of signs and performance when the wife improvises an excuse for her nightly displays. It is preserved in the vessel ordered by the lover, just as the three converts in "Eliduc" are situated in the houses and rules they create for themselves. Though the lady sends her message, the lover's continual possession of the reliquary ("Tuz jurs l'ad fete od lui porter" [156]) acts out Eliduc's demand that the women separated from him continue to reveal themselves by telling how they feel.

Marie engages "Le livre Ovide" imaginatively at the phase of the Ovidian project that demands the greatest craft and artfulness. In her rewriting of the *Ars amatoria*, keeping love is neither a domestic nor harmless enterprise. Though the Ovidian interim in her stories remains somehow beyond moral condemnation, it still belies Ovid's claims to commit no trespass (*nullum crimen*) and to celebrate love without penalties (*venus tuta*). Resituated in a context of baronial power, the erotic interval is all about consequences. Only in the fantasy of "Lanval" does Marie approach something like the licensed intrigues (*concessa furta*) that Ovid claims to extoll. At the same time that she represents the Ovidian interim under time and contingency, Marie also discovers that the transformations of desire to marriage, restitution, and mourning offer provisional answers to its urgent demands. "Eliduc" and "Laüstic" suggest that in Marie's fictive realm the fixing of desire only masks its continuing circulation.

In the *Lais* and her other poems, Marie stands as a distinctive figure for the invention of authorship in post-Conquest England and particularly for the evolving relation of the vernacular to Latin literary culture. She mobilizes the dominant commonplaces to establish herself as a revisionary author in a vernacular tradition seemingly subordinate yet firmly located in and speaking to contexts of social and political power. Marie's authorial signature is a continual feature of her works, as is the naming of individual pieces. Her insistence on authorship carries forward, however, to her claims over a corpus of writing—fiction as well as religious and didactic writing, all of them narratives that provoke reflection. Her repeated intention is to preserve such narratives "en memoire." Her means for doing so is to create a text—"metre en escrit"—

---

46. Tudor, "Religious Symbolism," 1–3; Cottrell, "*La Lai du Laustic*," 504.

that circulates within cultural memory. Marie styles herself as the compiler, composer, and translator of official and recovered sources. Her achievement depends not simply on reproducing the materials but on recontextualizing them within practices of writing by finding equivalents to their defining aesthetic features. In this way, the signature she leaves on her works is the trace of both her authorship and her invention.

PART 2

Authorship Direct and Oblique

CHAPTER 3

John Gower

Scriptor, Compositor, Auctor

JOHN GOWER is arguably the paradigmatic author in late medieval England.[1] His work lays claim to the literary terrain of the period, ranging over the three principal languages of composition—Latin, French, and Middle English—and addressing the moral and political concerns of the age as a voice of poetic wisdom.[2] Gower differs significantly from his contemporaries, however, by the extent to which he foregrounds the external marks of authorship. All his major works and many others besides are carefully framed by a textual apparatus derived from the academic traditions of biblical and pedagogical commentary but largely emanating from Gower himself. The apparatus provides

---

1. Throughout this chapter, Gower's works are quoted from *Complete Works of John Gower*, ed. Macaulay. I have also drawn from Peck, ed., *John Gower: Confessio Amantis*; Carlson, ed. and Rigg, trans., *John Gower: Poems on Contemporary Events*; Yeager, ed. and trans., *John Gower: The Minor Latin Works*, with *In Praise of Peace*, ed. Livingston; and Yeager, ed. and trans., *John Gower: The French Balades*. Translations for the *Mirour de l'Omme* are taken from *Mirour de l'omme*, trans. Wilson and Van Baak and for the *Vox Clamantis* and *Cronica Tripertita* from *Major Latin Works of John Gower*, trans. Stockton. The translations for the minor Latin poems and French balades are Yeager's. In citing lines, I have used the following abbreviations: CA = *Confessio Amantis*, CB = *Cinkante Balades*, CT = *Cronica Tripertita*, MO = *Mirour de l'Omme*, VC = *Vox Clamantis*.

2. Minnis, "John Gower, Sapiens in Ethics and Politics," 207–29; idem, *Medieval Theory of Authorship*, 177–90. Aers, "Reflections on Gower," 185–201, argues, by contrast, that Gower does not acknowledge the contradictions within his ethical and political positions.

interpretive commentary on the text, signals the analytical divisions of Gower's *materia,* and reveals the articulation of its parts within a conceptual and formal unity. In this way, Gower situates his poems explicitly within medieval literary culture and writerly practice, and he structures reading across a variety of audiences, fictional and historical. At a formal and technical level, he aligns his work with the *modus tractandi*—the multiple forms of discourse that medieval commentators found in the Bible and classical texts. At the same time, his writing employs the *modus tractatus,* the organizing principle thought by commentators to inform a particular text and make it an intelligible object of knowledge.[3]

Gower's authorship is a focal point within his major and minor works, and it serves as both a condition of writing and a source of literary meaning. Over the course of his career, his poems actively negotiate the position not just of a poet creating his works but also of a writer located within literary traditions and discursive communities (secular, clerical, and political). In this respect, they can be usefully seen as works of what Rita Copeland terms "secondary translation"—the products of rhetorical invention and poetic imitation building from Latin and vernacular academic traditions.[4] Gower's authorship develops, too, through the paratexts written to accompany the major works. These take the form of colophons and independent compositions and thus augment the textual apparatus of commentary and gloss as well as passages of self-commentary. Gower clearly saw his major poems as an integral literary canon. He went on to complete a second body of work—a minor canon comprising a second poetic *cursus*—that reprises the major works and offers commentary on them. Authorship takes a public, commemorative shape in Gower's tomb in Southwark Cathedral, where his effigy lies recumbent, the head resting on three substantial books with parallel Latin titles—*Vox Clamantis, Speculum Meditantis,* and *Confessio Amantis*—under an epitaph of his own composition. The success of this authorial self-fashioning in later periods is evident from the late Middle Ages and Early Modern period. Gower is included with Chaucer and Lydgate in a triumvirate of English national poets, and he appears as a representative of a national poetic tradition in Renaissance theater, civic spectacle, literary polemic, and popular narrative.[5] In Shakespeare's *Pericles,* perhaps the most notable witness to this reception, "ancient Gower" is a canonical poetic voice imitated in his characteristic meter—in

---

3. Minnis, "Literary Theory," 133–45; idem, *Medieval Theory of Authorship,* 118–59.

4. Copeland, *Rhetoric, Hermeneutics, and Translation,* 7–8 and 202–20. Minnis, *Translations of Authority,* 11, suggests that medieval Latin functioned as "the great medieval European vernacular" and ascribes the absence of Middle English hermeneutics to the threat of Lollardy (17–37).

5. Fisher, *John Gower,* 1–36; Cooper, "'This worthy olde writer,'" 99–113.

short, an author with a distinctive style. The Early Modern recognition of Gower's authorship carried the price, however, of reducing the scope of his achievement. His French and Latin poems exercised little influence in succeeding periods.

Throughout his literary career, Gower presents himself as a moralist speaking to private conduct and the social order.[6] He maps the considerable overlap between ethics and politics, as set out by learned commentaries on Aristotle and made available in vernacular translation with the rise of late medieval civic and court culture by figures like Brunetto Latini and Nicholas Oresme. Ethics and politics coalesce in addressing monarchs and men of power, Gower's primary audience before he redirects the later recensions of the *Confessio Amantis* to England as a nation. It is an abiding critical principle of modern interpretation that Gower has a coherent literary project: "Gower's three major poems are one continuous work."[7] This continuity is supported by Gower's themes of virtue and responsibility, individual governance and social justice, and the common profit as a political ideal. When Chaucer directed *Troilus and Criseyde* to "moral Gower" (5.1856) in the mid-1380s, he recognized a quality that Gower himself strove to present in his foundational French and Latin poems, the *Mirour de l'Omme* and the *Vox Clamantis*, respectively.

In most reckonings, Gower figures as a poet who writes as a moralist. On this view, his poetic achievements must be gauged within a medieval literary system that conventionally subordinated poetry to ethics (*ethice supponitur*). To be sure, in the late medieval period, ethics came to encompass a more complex reflection than a system of virtues and vices or a set of spiritual imperatives, though the technical vocabulary and formal arrangements remained stable.[8] For Gower's modern readers, technical accomplishment and some measure of narrative skill are ostensibly what remain when doctrine has been subtracted from his poems. In many respects, however, the opposite

---

6. Political readings of Gower are given initial formulation in Coffman, "John Gower in his Most Significant Role," 52–61; and idem, "John Gower, Mentor for Royalty," 953–64. Middleton, "Idea of Public Poetry," 94–114, situates Gower with other writers of the period. Peck, *Kingship and Common Profit*, xix–xxv, and idem, "Politics and Psychology," 215–38, stresses the reciprocity of moral and political governance.

7. Fisher, *John Gower*, 135. By contrast, Nicholson, *Love and Ethics*, 4, contends that despite the borrowings from the *Mirour* and the *Vox*, the *Confessio* is a fundamentally different poem.

8. Giles of Rome, *De regimine principum* asserts the importance of figurative representation and particularity ("ipsa acta singularia") for moral deliberation; quoted in Copeland, *Rhetoric, Hermeneutics, and Translation*, 212. Buridan, *Quaestiones in decem libros Ethicorum Aristotelis ad Nicomachum*, 3 (Book 1, quaestio 1), affirms that virtue consists in human action and so falls outside *scientia*. For modern adaptations of medieval ethical discussion, see Nicholson, *Love and Ethics*, 58, 68; and Mitchell, *Ethics and Exemplary Narrative*.

formulation holds true and gives a more complete understanding of his work: Gower functions as a moralist precisely by being an author. He claims the identity of "sapiens" in ethics and politics through imitation as much as invention. To develop his themes, Gower, like his contemporaries, must appropriate forms of authorship already established within tradition. Moreover, the moral and political doctrine—the *materia* of his writing—which Gower expounds as complete and coherent, as rooted in first principles and providential creation, is on closer inspection contingent and contested. Gower confidently offers a description of moral being and the social sphere. But his accounts represent not settled arrangements so much as the desire for a convincing and ratified description of the social order; even at their most insistent, they are demands for forms of feeling, conduct, action, and belief—in short, a social imaginary. Their sources lie within writing and literary culture. Seen as a whole, then, Gower's poetic career reflects a sustained and continually renewed performance of authorship in the service of ethical and political reflection.[9] Authorship is the necessary condition of "moral Gower."

MIROUR DE L'OMME

The fictional moment in which Gower first presented himself as an author probably occurred in the missing stanzas that originally opened his earliest major poem, the *Mirour de l'Omme* (1376–79).[10] In the one surviving textual witness (Cambridge University Library Additional MS 3035), the *Mirour* is accompanied by a table of contents that divides the poem into ten sections, concentrating mostly on the social estates. The divisions sort oddly, however, with the actual structure (*modus tractatus*) of the work. Like the *Vox Clamantis* and *Confessio Amantis,* the poem seems to have developed in conception as Gower wrote. An allegorical narrative recounts the efforts of the Devil, Sin, Death, and the World to subvert mankind's salvation. From this narrative, there follow the other major structural divisions of the *Mirour*: an allegory of vices and virtues, a denunciation of contemporary ills in the social estates, and a redemptive meditation on the life of Christ and the Virgin Mary. The poem

---

9. Mahoney observes that the presentation miniatures of fifteenth-century manuscripts of the *Confessio* offer "not a record of an actual event, but a performance of the presentation"; see Mahoney, "Gower's Two Prologues," 36; cf. idem, "Courtly Presentation," 97–160.

10. Yeager, "Gower's French Audience," 111–37, argues for a later date for completion of the *Mirour,* after Gower took up residence at the Austin priory of St. Mary Overes in Southwark in 1378, with a corresponding shift from the original aristocratic audience to a clerical audience.

is a composite, with no single source, but draws heavily on penitential and devotional traditions, biblical and classical exempla, and meditative sources.[11]

Though Gower's originary moment is lost to us, the extant text of the *Mirour* begins with the kind of authorial self-definition likely contained in Gower's original exordium: "Mais quiq' en voet fuïr les mals, / Entende et tiegne mes consals, / Que je luy dirray en avant" (MO 10–12) [But whoever wishes to flee evils, let him listen to and keep my counsels, which I shall give him hereafter]. Gower assumes the role of moral and spiritual guide that he will write into other poems. As the passage suggests, the advice that he confidently promises to deliver is literal and direct, seemingly uninflected by the slippage of meaning within figurative language. He describes it as the very opposite of imaginative and inventive fiction: "Ce n'est pas chose controvée / Dont pense affaire ma ditée" (MO 13–14) [It is no imaginary matter my poem intends to treat]. From the outset, he intends to speak truthfully—"Ainz vuill conter tout voirement" (MO 15)—about the daughters of Sin, who are the vices sired in a double incestuous genealogy with the Devil and Death and thereafter sent into the world as the Seven Deadly Sins to thwart mankind's salvation.

For all these claims to literal and direct truth, Gower establishes from the beginning a complex relation between counsel and authorship. If personal and public morality are the theme and content of his writing in the *Mirour* and elsewhere, Gower nonetheless conditions moral teaching and understanding on the workings of authorship. The *Mirour*'s initial framing of its topic employs a lexicon of poetic fiction and authorial guidance. The "chose controvée" ("imaginary matter") that he rejects as the defining condition of imaginative representation reappears in descriptions of vices such as Vaine Gloire (1220), Avantance (1955), Sompnolence (5193), Supplantacioun (3292), and Foledelit (9227), subspecies of the vices that operate by illusion and deceit. But Poverte, too, he says, transforms ("fait controver") experience to make one serve, love, and fear God (15852–55). Gower calls his work a *ditée*; the term means a composition, imaginative work, poem, song, and, in a technical sense, a moral treatise, narrative, or expository work.[12] The didactic and devotional content in his work cannot be separated cleanly from its medium

---

11. Olsson, "Cardinal Virtues," 113–48, argues for the importance of penitential sources, especially the discussion of the Seven Deadly Sins, while Bestul, "Gower's *Mirour de l'Omme*," 307–28, sees a private, devotional element in the contemplation of the lives of the Virgin and Christ. Kittredge, 254–55, reviewing Macaulay's edition, divided the poem into three parts: cause (vices and virtues), circumstances (social estates), and remedy (appeal to Christ and the Virgin).

12. Godefroy, *Dictionnaire de l'ancienne langue française*, s.v. ditie; *Dictionnaire du Moyen Français*, version 2010, s.v. dité (ATILF CNRS—Nancy Université. http://www.atilf.fr/dmf).

of literary expression. He uses *conter* to refer to a structured, formal account and to a narrative of the enticements of sin. To relate his poetic *matiere* in complete truth ("conter tout voirement") dignifies a means of expression that always carries the potential of deceit and falsification.

Gower does not stand, then, outside his authorial predicament of being a moral rigorist with a fallible instrument for understanding and persuasion.[13] Nor is he removed from what he teaches. Instead, he turns from the beginning of the *Mirour* to exploit the expressive and conceptual power of language. His ethical position is that the world quickly passes like a dream into nothing: "Trestout come songe passeroit / En nient" (MO 28–29). Love of the world is constrained to return to nothing: "l'amour seculer / En nient au fin doit retorner" (MO 31–32). Thus, as a corollary of rendering a truthful account of sin, Gower must undertake the paradoxical effort of devising a poetics of nothing, which he phrases in the same terms as speaking truthfully: "Un poy du nient je vuill conter" (MO 34). The sources for the idea that sin has no being are biblical and exegetical, but the rhetorical antithesis of recounting "tout voirement" and "un poy du nient" is Gower's own figure.[14]

Gower develops the conceit of recounting nothing in his treatments of vice in the allegorical narrative and of sin in the social order. The hypocrite, like the Pharisees in Matthew 23:27, resembles a sepulcher with beautiful images on the exterior and corrupting flesh inside (MO 1117–28). Presumpcioun, like a tiger deceived by the hunter who steals her cubs and leaves only their images in mirrors to delay pursuit, thinks to possess what has already been lost to the devil (MO 1570–72). Gower likens prayer without devotion to exposed leaves on a barren bush or a messenger without letters or instructions: "Ove vuide main le fist mander, / Dont vuid reverte a sa maisoun" (MO 10427–28) [With empty hand he was sent forth, so that empty he returns to his house]. Echoing Ecclesiastes 2:1, he reproves the vanity of human deeds, which pass like a dream and turn possession into loss: "Sicomme la chose q'est foreine" (MO 11711) [like an alien thing]. In an extended metaphor, he compares the worldly ambitions of bishops to a beehive, a beautiful house with dark corners and holes, constructed from wax and doomed to lose the treasure of labor: "Car toute chose est frele et nient / Du quoy le siecle se revelle" (MO 19436–37) [For everything in which the world rejoices is frail and nothing].[15] His long apos-

---

13. Wetherbee, "John Gower," 593.

14. Macaulay, *Complete Works*, 1:394, cites John 1:3 ("sine ipso factum est nihil quod factum est") as the source and emphasizes Augustine and Gregory. See also Lombard, *Sententiae* 1. Dist 46.3.10 and 2. Dist 35.2.1; and Aquinas, *Quaestiones disputatae de malo*, 1.1. Sed contra 3. Perhaps the most compelling account of sin as nothing is Augustine's episode of the pear tree in *Confessions* 2.4.9–2.10.18.

15. Pliny, *Natural History* 11.4, on bees with respect to labor and communal organization.

trophe to Fortune, as he turns his attention to emperors holding the highest secular office, teaches the lessons of change, illusion, and loss: "Tu es le songe qant l'en dort, / Qe tous biens par semblante apport, / Mais riens y laist de l'avantage" (MO 22090-92) [You are the dream when one sleeps that brings the appearance of all good things but leaves nothing of value].[16] Addressing the estate of knights and men-at-arms, he claims it is no estate at all ("Ce n'est pas en estat de nient" [MO 23595]) but exists only as a practice of honor and social duty. Gower gives a positive formulation to the conceit in the spiritual example of contemplatives, half dead to the world and desiring death (MO 10645-47). In the world, prudent men do not grieve for the illusory good ("rien present") and thereby solve the logical and linguistic predicament of living in freedom: "Et qui du riens se fait doloir / Ne porra vivre tristement" (MO 15285-86) [And he who grieves at nothing cannot live sadly].

Gower's authorial claim to speak "tout voirement" at the beginning of the *Mirour* depends structurally and symbolically on a turn away from song, which he associates broadly with popular and courtly lyric. Yvresce is a source for songs and inspires a promiscuous mix of Latin and the vernacular in the usage of laymen (MO 8149-51). Foldelit leads young girls to excessive adornment and dance accompanied by song: "En chantant a leur chançonettes / Que tout sont fait du fol amour" (MO 92850-56) [Singing their little songs that all deal with wanton love]. Gower repeats the point in an exhortation to maintain virginity: "Riens valt dancer a la carole / Dont puis covient euer en plour" (MO 16940-41) [It is useless to go dancing a carole and then to be cast down in tears]. He explicitly likens Sin to the Sirens singing with their sweet, sonorous voices ("leur doulces vois halteines" [MO 9950]) and cites Ulysses's escape from them as an example of the productive use of fear (MO 10909-20). Insincere prayer, he says, is like a discordant note in song (MO 10390-92). Vain men display their failings, to evident approval, in song and social play (MO 11692-94).

If such warnings about song and poetry are conventional morality, they nonetheless serve Gower as a defining contrast to the project of the *Mirour* and his subsequent works. At the end of a section that traces the responsibility for evil to individuals (a theme resumed powerfully at the beginning of the *Confessio Amantis*), Gower admits to wantonness and vain joy in his youth. As Matthew W. Irvin points out, "Gower identifies himself not as the distant author of advice, but an agent of advice who must also receive it."[17] The literary form of his early moral abandonment is lyric poetry and song: "Et les fols ditz d'amours fesoie, / Dont en chantant je carolloie" (MO 27340-41) [and (I)

---

16. Cf. *Vox* 2.2.
17. Irvin, *Poetic Voices of John Gower*, 28.

composed foolish love ditties, which I danced about singing]. Lyric composition is introduced specifically in order to be cancelled out as a form of writing that stands before authorship and before the assumption of the moralist's role. Gower mentions it, much as Chaucer does in his career summaries in the *Legend of Good Women* and the "Retraction" at the end of the *Canterbury Tales,* to contrast his main authorial project with a preliminary and undifferentiated mass of song.[18] The lyric forms of youth are also a cultural practice that includes not just dance but also fashion and display—a form of social performance that must be replaced with authorship performed through literary sources and intertexts to effect moral understanding and social action.

Gower goes on to contrast the abandoned lyric with a new and different song, "Un autre chançon" (MO 27347), which is distinguished by a narrative arc moving from sorrow to joy. In the allegorical narrative of the *Mirour,* three minstrels (Ben pensement, Bon fait, and Bon dit) play for the seven virtues as they go to marry the figure Resoun and help defend mankind (MO 10123–28). The poet describes his subsequent account of the daughters sired by Resoun on the virtues as a "chauncoun flourie" (MO 10176), an amplified, ornamented, and multibranched description of the penitential system. Bonnegarde, the first daughter born from Chasteté, guards her tongue to avoid speaking or singing of lechery (MO 16630). In their political governance, worldly kings, says Gower later in the poem, are obliged to act like harp players who bring musical chords into harmony (MO 22897–920). Harmony in this instance means mutual good deeds between king and people, tempered by a concord of power and obedience (MO 22909–20). The mirror of such governance, "comme dist l'auctour" (MO 22873), is King David, who furnishes six exemplary points for imitation—as shepherd, harper, knight, prophet, penitent, and king.

As the example of David suggests, Gower's moral and social project involves the orchestration of multiple poetic voices as *modi tractandi.* The *Mirour* begins with a first-person claim to authority for offering counsel. Gower underwrites his claim throughout the poem with gestures of warrant and citation—"je lis" and "je truis escript"—that refer at times to specific textual authorities but, more important, confirm that the principles he espouses are authorized within written tradition. As he moves through the vices, virtues, and social estates, the hortatory and expository power of the first-person voice intensifies. Addressing the properties of Sin, the speaker sees himself as the victim of the monstrous beast with seven heads and ten horns (Apocalypse 13:1), swollen by the monster's venom: "Trop sui de son venym enflé"

---

18. Chaucer's equivalent to Gower's "fols ditz d'amours" are "many a song and many a lecherous lay" (*Canterbury Tales* X.1087).

(MO 9924). He adopts the voice of preacher and expositor in his peroration to the discussion of Franchise, the virtue of generosity that opposes Avarice: "pour ce vous dy / Faison franchise envers autruy / Sicomme vers nous dieus le fesoit" (MO 16210–12) [Therefore I say to you let us show generosity to others as God did to us]. The authorial voice, asserting the conceptual order of his materials, imposes itself on the poem by way of recapitulation at the end of the account of the vices: "Ore est a trere en remembrance / Comme je par ordre en la romance / Vous ai du point en ponte conté" (MO 18373–75) [Now one should recall how I have told you the story in order, from point to point]. It emerges distinctly in the final section of the poem to mark the separate narrative units in the double life of Christ and the Virgin.

Gower's device is, on the one hand, a practical signpost that reveals the conceptual structure of his exposition, a verbal rubric that identifies discreet sections of discourse. On the other, it is a direct statement of authorial invention and disposition, anatomizing the plan and arrangement of the work in the rhetorical and commentary traditions. Moreover, as Gower turns to the theme of redemption in the final part of the *Mirour*, the first-person voice becomes an exemplary "I" that stands for those addressed at the beginning of the poem as sinners who want to flee evil and are now offered counsel. Seeking a source for sin in the world, he traces it to himself as a pattern of malfeasance and a locus of responsibility common to public and private readers of the poem: "Je suy certain que plus que moy / Nuls ad mesfait envers son dieu" (MO 27293–94).

Preaching and prophecy offer Gower two important models of authorship, which combine the aims of teaching, exposition, warning, revelation, and exhortation within a multiform *modus tractandi*. Gower organizes his treatment of Fear, for example, around four questions put to sinners in the penitential narrative and to devotional readers in their private reflection: "U es," "Quoy fais," "Dont viens," and "U vas" (MO 11353–520). He addresses merchants on the principles of lawful exchange and circulation, while expounding the principles of his office. Preaching against vices, he says, corrects evil men in the same act that praises the good: "car le blamer / Des mals as bons est le priser" (MO 25216–17). By contrast, preachers who fail their own standards shift moral responsibility away from themselves, as Gower insists in a triple repetition of *vile*: "N'est pas honneste, ainçois est vile / Maniere, qant prechour revile / Ce dont est mesmes a viler" (MO 27253–55) [It is not an honorable manner but rather a vile one when a preacher reviles that for which he is himself to be blamed].

Prophecy is one of Gower's most powerful authorial modes in the *Mirour*; it becomes a dominant form in the *Vox* and other works and a source for spiritual, moral, and social reform in the *Confessio*. In the *Mirour*, Gower directly cites all the major prophets and most of the minor prophets as well as figures like Moses, Elijah, and Elisha. Prophecy encompasses the forms of discourse that St. Paul enumerates in 1 Corinthians 14:6: "Quid vobis prodero nisi si vobis loquar aut in revelatione aut scientia aut prophetia aut in doctrina?" [What shall I profit you, unless I speak to you either in revelation or in knowledge or in prophecy or in doctrine?]. Biblical commentators in the Middle Ages associated these forms with fourfold scriptural exegesis—revelation with allegory, knowledge with tropology, prophecy with anagogy, and doctrine with literal, historical meaning.[19] David offers the assurance of revelation: "Ce qu'il disoit ne fuist pas fable" (MO 22935) [What he said was not fable]. Prophecy teaches the tropological lesson of double love ("soi soi amant" [MO 13743]) directed toward God and one's neighbors, to which Gower will add marriage in a later formulation. Isaiah's anagogic prophecy about judges (1:23) is borne out by present corruption in their estate (MO 24769–72). Nobles whose predations bring misery are unknowingly part of a historical pattern of rise and decline orchestrated by God (MO 23590–92). The master figure attached to prophecy is apostrophe. Gower uses it across the structural divisions of the *Mirour*, addressing sinners and the social estates directly with instruction and reproving allegorical figures such as Fortune.

Preaching and prophecy ground authorship in the apparently settled doctrine of literal and figurative instruction; they speak the desire to make political governance "estable" (MO 22943), to put it beyond contingency and mutability. Gower employs a potentially more ambivalent form of authorship by invoking the warrant of the "vois commune," the voice of the people. The *vox populi* is a political commonplace in Livy, Cicero, and Lucan.[20] The proverb "vox populi vox dei" dates from the early Middle Ages. Gower cites the biblical example of Josaphat's battle against the Syrians (2 Chronicles 20) when God hears the voice of the people praying together (MO 10309–20). He repeats the proverb as a moral truism in his treatment of praise as a species of charity: "Au vois commune est acordant / La vois de dieu" (MO 12725–26). Most of his appeals occur, though, in his discussion of the social estates. He begins with clergy and the Roman curia, writing not on his own but recording the complaints of all Christians: "ainz est ensi / De toute cristiene gent / Murmur, compleinte, vois et cry" (MO 18446–48) [(it) is rather the murmur, complaint, voice, and cry of all Christian folk]. The voice of the people ("Sicomme dist la commune vois" [MO 22248]) holds that contemporary kings fail their

---

19. Robert R. Edwards, "Gower's Poetics of the Literal," 69.
20. Livy, *Ab urbe condita*, 3.56.7; Cicero, "De prouinciis consularibus oratio," 2.4; Lucan, *Pharsalia*, 1.268.

essential duties to love and serve God, maintain the Church, and safeguard laws. The machinery of justice is a particular source of complaint. By popular consensus ("Sicome la vois commune conte" [MO 24938]), sheriffs are oppressive. The people register "lour plaintes et lour cris" (MO 25162) at the corruption of lawyers, judges, sheriffs, investigators, and bailiffs within the legal system. "La commune vois" denounces, too, the workings of Fraud among merchants, such as jewelers (MO 25575) and tradesmen, especially victualers (MO 26126, 26182).

What the *vox populi* allows Gower is a simultaneous assertion and disavowal of prophetic authorship in the public sphere. Common opinion, not his personal knowledge, is the source for claims against bishops: "Car ce n'est pas de mon savoir / D'escrire ou dire ascunement" (MO 19059-60). The sexual conduct and simony of parish priests are reported from other sources: "N'en say la cause aparcevoir, / Si l'autre gent ne me disoiont" (MO 20351-52) [I really would not know the cause of this if other people had not told me]. In an ecclesiastical fabliau close to Chaucer's Shipman's Tale, priests assume the marital duties of husbands and manage an exchange of clothes for sex with foolish wives; such stories, Gower says with a broad irony, are widely retailed but of uncertain credibility: "Ne sai si fable ou verités" (MO 20376), fiction or history. The worldliness of friars is likewise a topic of general knowledge, not personal accusation: "N'ert pas de moy ce que je dis, / Mais a ce que l'en vait parlant" (MO 21183-84). The example of David's knighthood and social prophecy has been lost, according to general consensus ("om dist" [MO 22973]). Gower writes in these passages as a spokesman for authorized complaint, for prophetic denunciation legitimized by social consensus within the estates. As in the *Vox Clamantis* and *Confessio Amantis*, Gower draws on "contemporary language about government" and on theories of political representation that stress unanimity and speaking on behalf of all.[21] At the same time, however, the means of moral and political reform are murmur and clamor, rumor and ill fame—the raucous sounds of social forces that will figure prominently in the dream vision of the *Vox Clamantis*, where they are sources of political division and terror.

The modes of authorship derived from preaching, prophecy, and the "vois commune" depend radically on Gower's textuality. Textuality means in this instance both specific canonical sources and the enabling gesture of citation.[22] Gower draws repeatedly from the Bible and from classical writers and the

---

21. Ferster, "O Political Gower," 38-39, 42-45; idem, *Fictions of Advice*, 125-26, 129-32.

22. The argument for the textual artifice of authority in the *Confessio* made by Yeager, "English, Latin, and the Text as 'Other,'" 251-67, applies equally to Gower's other poems. Scanlon, *Narrative, Authority, and Power*, 37-54, insists at a theoretical level on the dependence of

Church Fathers for doctrine and illustrative examples. His errors in citing biblical authorities or medieval texts like the pseudo-Ovidian "Pamphilus de amore" (MO 14450) do not diminish the performative effect. Seneca and Cicero are Gower's most prominent authorities on morality. The one modern authority he cites, Hélinant de Froidmont, provides a model and stanzaic form for the *Mirour* as well as a key passage on Death (MO 11401–12), quoted by Fear.[23] Fear represents not just the countering virtue to the vice of Vainglory but also the most powerful and sustained source for inwardness and reflection within the *Mirour*'s moral psychology. Another modern, cited obliquely, is Geoffrey Chaucer, whose *Troilus and Criseyde* is evoked by mention of the principal characters and perhaps even a reference to the reading scene within Chaucer's poem (2.99–112): "U qu'il oït chanter la geste / De Troÿlus et de la belle / Creseide" (MO 5253–55).

Quite apart from the topicality, Gower presents himself as a writer who draws examples from a full range of textual authorities as a compiler. In his self-delusion, an arrogant man, says Gower, overestimates himself by comparing his strength to Samson's, his beauty to Absalom's, and his chivalric prowess to that of Lancelot and Bors (MO 1465–73). In his discussion of matrimony, a topic with a formidable array of commentary and exegesis, Gower recognizes the potential for misguided instruction from *auctoritates*. He hesitates before offering misogynistic commonplaces attributed to Aristotle, Cato, and Seneca, but nonetheless affirms the efficacy of authorized examples: "l'umaine vie / falt enfourmer d'essamplerie" (MO 17622–23) [human life has to be taught by examples]. Gower's textuality presumes a compendium of sources retrieved according to topics. The lives of the "saintz pieres" (MO 18253) offer a reading lesson to pursue the Aspre vie (Hard Life) of denial and mortification that counters wantonness. The book of Nature furnishes an example of a bishop's duty in the figure of the great fish whose mouth provides refuge to smaller species until a storm passes (MO 19909–20).

The most revealing intertext for the *Mirour* is the *Roman de la Rose*.[24] Gower makes particular use of the scenes early in the *Rose* in which the lover, aided by Bel Acueil, first approaches the rose. The rose is guarded by Danger, Honte, Malbouche, and Paour; the same personnel subsequently guard the

---

authority on textuality in medieval culture (37–54) and on Gower's awareness of the complexities of poetic language in the service of doctrine (245–97).

23. Yeager, *John Gower's Poetic*, 80–83.

24. Ibid., 79, 84. Yeager has observed: "Nothing is truly borrowed from the *Roman* into the *Mirour*, but its allegory stands conspicuously behind Gower's characters Reson, Paour, and Foldelit, forcing us to recall the *Roman* as their source." He suggests, too, that Gower attempts to rehabilitate the love language of the *Rose* by using it against itself (79).

gates of the castle built to enclose the rose. In Gower's poem, Danger, the personification of resistance who frustrates the attempts by Guillaume de Lorris's lover to possess the rose, is added by Orguil to the entourage of her fifth daughter, Inobedience. There he reveals the radical willfulness and individual isolation of disobedience: "Unques Danger fuist ne serra / Amé, qu'il unques nul ama" (MO 2311-12) [Danger was never loved and will never be loved, for he never loved anyone]. Danger is used elsewhere in the *Mirour* in an abstract sense to describe expected limits and constraints on lust (MO 9223), vainglory (MO 11087), possession (MO 15887), and drink (MO 22786).

Malebouche, whose purpose is to defame lovers in the *Rose*, is the chamberlain of Detraccioun, the first daughter of Envy; his malice takes over Envy's section of Gower's poem (MO 2677-3024) and continues into the related account of Joye d'autry mal, who takes pleasure in tales of others' misfortune (MO 3205-28); he reappears in the disorder of religious houses (MO 21142-44). Gower positions praise of others as the first daughter of Charity and the remedy for Detraccioun, and in so doing, he redirects to proper ends the deceitful honor shown Malebouche by the lover in the *Rose* (RR 10285-306). Honte (Shame), who likewise thwarts the lover in the *Rose*, is paired by Gower with Vergoigne (Modesty) in a subtle account of moral psychology that renegotiates the original alliance of shame and fear in Guillaume's story. In the *Mirour*, Honte and Vergoigne are stalked by Malapert, whose aim is scandal and disclosure (MO 1681-89), but they also represent the affective and rational qualities of Humilité, which counter Avantance (Boasting; MO 11900-64). In the poem's redemption narrative, shame, along with fear, is not just a personified attribute but a psychological obstacle experienced directly in the narrator's fitful progress toward repentance (MO 27397-402).

Fals semblant, who murders Malebouche and opens the way into the castle in the *Rose*, furthers Envie in Gower's poem by perverting reason and language (MO 3469-696). Gower counters him by the figure of Bonne Entencioun, the power of the will directed by charity over the arts of thought and language. He resituates the courtly values of Franchise and Largesce, who first appear among the dancers in the God of Love's carol in the *Rose* (1127-228). Franchise becomes a spiritual value, "a l'alme necessaire" (MO 15183); her daughters represent proper moral action within institutions and the social sphere: "Elle ad cink files du bon aire, / Q'envers le siecle et saintuaire / Se gardont sanz vilain enprise" (MO 15187-89) [(She) has five noble daughters, who conduct themselves without any baseness toward the world or the church]. Largesce offers a way of living with riches tempered by humility and social conscience. As Gower says, his poem is a guide for a just man, "ly droiturer" (MO 15919), not a perfect one.

Besides allegorical figures, Gower redirects narrative elements from the *Rose* to the ends of moral instruction and social action. La Vielle's vindictive instruction in erotic deception in the *Rose*, famously refashioned by Chaucer's Wife of Bath, is the material used in Gower's reproval of the adulterous wife (MO 8809–80) who follows the old women's instructions to deceive her husband. In Jean de Meun, the principle La Vielle expounds to Bel Aceuil through an elaborate play on grammatical and physical gender is that Nature has made all men for all women and all women for all men: "Toutes pour touz et touz por toutes, / Chascune por chascun commune / Et commun chascun por chascune" (RR 13875–77). Desire thus infuses the human world, and it stands before cultural and social differences, the strictures of positive law. In Gower's treatment, the doctrine is relocated to its proper level in the hierarchy of being; it moves from the domain of the human, which includes reason, to the animal, which contains sensation. Thus, horses in a meadow are fit mates for each other regardless of their color and markings (MO 17377–88), which Gower enumerates with a comparable play on grammatical gender that both acknowledges and corrects Jean de Meun: Nature "n'ad fait morell pour morelle, / Ainz la griselle pour morell, / Et la morelle pour grisell" (MO 17381–83) [(Nature) has not made the black horse for the black mare alone, but rather the grey mare for the black horse, and the black mare for the grey horse]. The lesson he draws is the opposite of La Vielle's: marriage is a state open to all without sin or cancellation. Gower's textuality, then, extends beyond the appropriation of sources and the conscious performance of citation to include a reinscription of vernacular authority. The *Rose*, like Gower's penitential and devotional sources, serves as a compendium of materials that he can direct toward the practice of moral reform and salvation for both an exemplary, first-person author and those who can read the counsel of his example.

VOX CLAMANTIS

Like the *Mirour*, Gower's *Vox Clamantis* (1377–81) is a composite work that employs authorship in the service of moral instruction and political order. It largely functions through retrospect and hermeneutics. Gower successively revised and readapted the *Vox* to contexts as historical forces created decisive moments in late medieval English political life. As originally conceived, the poem focuses broadly on contemporary evils; it proceeds through the traditional social estates of clergy, knighthood, and peasants, adding lawgivers and monarchs to its social vision; it ends with the iconic image of Nebuchadnezzar's ruined statue, which prompts warnings against the Seven Deadly

Sins and the need for justice in a corrupt age. These topics rehearse much of the doctrine that comprises the *materia* of the *Mirour*. They return as well to Gower's earlier thematic concerns with Fortune and individual moral responsibility for political ills, and they reappear in the Prologus to the *Confessio*.

Gower subsequently frames this material (Books 2–7) with two additions that can stand as individual works but give the *Vox* a different shape and a specific historical grounding. Responding to the trauma of the Rising of 1381, he adds a separate book, a "Visio Anglie," to the beginning of the poem (Book 1), using multiple conventions of the dream vision to describe the twofold metamorphosis of peasants into domestic animals and then into beasts who capture the city and drive off the higher social orders.[25] Within the dream frame, the appetite of the rebels is poised uneasily against Gower's own claims to power and representation.[26] The noble and aristocratic refugees, the poet-narrator among them, seek refuge in a ship resembling the Tower of London, which seems to founder; but the storm abates and directs the ship to the island of Britain, where a heavenly voice enjoins the poet to record his dream. In the scene of intercession, Gower lays bare his appropriation of authorial theory, for the divine Author and primary efficient cause of writing commissions the human author as a second efficient cause.

At the end of the original poem, Gower adds a second work, the *Cronica Tripertita*, which describes Richard II's political setbacks at the hands of the Lords Appellant and the Merciless Parliament of 1387, his revenge on his enemies in 1397 (cunningly planned, Gower suggests), and his overthrow in 1399. The *Cronica* incorporates the parliamentary Record and Deposition that formally removed Richard from kingship on 30 September 1399 and turns to other sources and the poet's invention, including literary allusion, where the Record is silent.[27] The three sections of the *Cronica* reflect its ideological investments in Lancastrian usurpation and legitimization as well as Gower's participation in textualizing Henry's accession. Though states of the text can be distinguished for the *Vox*, Gower's additions to the original estates satire seek to create the impression that the *Vox* is a single unified work describing a period of moral and social disintegration stabilized in the end by the accession of a just king.[28] The rubric introducing the composite work—"Incipit Cronica

---

25. Fisher, *John Gower*, 171.

26. Galloway, "Reassessing Gower's Dream-Visions," 292. For the *Vox* as depicting the conflict of differing kinds of knowledge in the social orders, see idem, "Gower in His Most Learned Role," 327–47.

27. Carlson, "Parliamentary Source," 100.

28. Oxford, Bodleian Library, MS Laud 719 contains a text of the *Vox* that omits the metamorphoses of the peasants into beasts (VC 1.165–2150; Macaulay, *Complete Works*, 4:lxviii) so that the dream vision leads to the social commentary of Books 2–7. Stow, "Richard II in John

que *Vox Clamantis* dicitur"—effaces the generic differences of its component parts (dream vision, estates satire, and historiography) within a *modus tractatus* devised from retrospect. The three "laureate poems" that follow the *Cronica* praise Henry IV as a divinely sanctioned monarch who rescues his country and people from oppression, and they offer the princely advice on governance that Henry's predecessor had ignored.[29]

The *Vox* parallels the *Mirour* as a work of moral counsel and social theory but moves toward higher political stakes as its plan of composition evolves. Gower's performance of authorship tracks this development not by redefining his role within new literary categories but by amplifying dimensions that had earlier been claimed, such as the didactic and prophetic modes of addressing individual sinners and admonishing the social orders. One aspect of authorship missing in the *Mirour* but present in the *Vox* is the warrant conferred by patronage. In the dedicatory epistle, old and blind Gower sends his poem to Thomas Arundel, archbishop of Canterbury, who is figured as the Phoebus shedding light on Gower's writing. Gower's poem in turn magnifies Arundel's brightness: "Hoc magis ad lumen tibi scriptum dono volumen" (VC Epistola, line 14) [I present you with this volume as a source of light].

The *Vox* opens with a prose introduction (*accessus*) that brings the common features of textual commentary on authors to bear on the poem. Under the title *Vox Clamantis*, the introduction explains the author's intention, which is to describe the peasants' rebellion. The author is a *compositor*, an arranger or designer. His material is the double transformation of the "rustici," who abandon their true nature and attack freemen and nobles. Such material requires the dream vision ("per sompnium") and lamentation ("flebile carmen" [VC Prol 1.33]) as its modes of discourse. The work divides into seven parts, which are enumerated in a subsequent description of the books and chapters comprising the poem. In these divisions, the author shows the causes of events that are dramatically out of scale and outside normal rules ("enormia"). In several manuscripts, a drawing of an archer gives a visual figure for Gower's authorial role; the accompanying Latin verses explain that he sends arrows into the world to wound those living badly. The verse prologue that intro-

---

Gower's *Confessio Amantis*," 3–31, examines revisions in Book 6 of the *Vox* that reflect Gower's changing attitude toward Richard's rule; cf. *Major Latin Works*, trans. Stockton, 13.

29. The "laureate group" of shorter Latin poems praising Henry IV ("Rex celi Deus," "O recolende," and "H. aquile pullus") follows the *Cronica Tripertita* in the four earliest manuscripts, which are contemporary with Gower and contain his corrections (Macaulay, *Complete Works*, 4:lx). The advice offered in the first of them is borrowed from *Vox* 6.18, directed to the youthful Richard: "O iuuenile decus, laus Regia, flos puerorum" (VC 6.18.1197*) [O youthful glory, royal honor, flower of youths]; see Yeager, *John Gower: The Minor Latin Works*, 74; Macaulay, *Complete Works*, 4:416, 3:554.

duces Book 1 shares with the *Confessio* (Prol 1–11) an opening theme that the writings of the past convey examples of the future: "Scripture veteris capiunt exempla futuri" (VC Prol 1.1). It cites the biblical precedents of Daniel and Joseph for the meaning of dreams, which function as memorable signs of future things ("Signa rei certe commemoranda" [VC Prol 1.16]). Gower introduces the *nomen auctoris* in a linguistic puzzle that constructs his name as "John Gower" out of hidden fragments and draws, moreover, on associations with John the Baptist, the "vox clamantis in deserto," and John the author of the Book of Apocalypse.

The tensions that underlie Gower's multiple forms of authorship in the *Mirour* acquire a particular resonance in Book 1 of the *Vox*. His vision invokes the Macrobian principle (*Commentum in Somnium Scipionis* 1.3) that some forms of dream convey meaning.[30] This principle had its most influential vernacular expression at the opening of the *Rose*, which carefully elaborates the contradiction that dreams are true because some dreams prove to be true; contemporaries like Chaucer exploited the ambiguity to locate writing as an imaginative space between empty images and prophetic truth.[31] Gower's phrasing in defense of dreams is Ovidian: "Sompnia pondus habent, hic est quod mira reuoluam" (VC 1.181) [Dreams have significance; hence it is that I shall unfold these marvels]. His source is the episode in the *Metamorphoses*, in which Byblis is driven by an overpowering desire for her brother Caunus, which is made vivid in her dreams. She argues, "Quid mihi significant ergo mea visa? quod autem / somnia pondus habent? an habent et somnia pondus?" (*Metamorphoses* 9.495–96) [What then do my visions mean to me? What weight do dreams carry? Do dreams have weight?]. Though Gower cites Ovid in the *Vox* with a frequency that gives the poem the quality of a cento, two features link the dream vision to its textual source.[32] The first is the extremity and fury of Byblis's desire, which serves as an index of the ferocity of the rebels in Gower's vision. The second is the cancellation of family bonds and social roles that Byblis must undertake to pursue desire, just as the rebels seek to upend hierarchy and the established arrangements of class and power.

---

30. At roughly the same time, Chaucer was demonstrating the contradictions of Macrobian dream lore in the Proem to his *House of Fame*.

31. Robert R. Edwards, *Dream of Chaucer*, 162–63. Rigg, "Anglo-Latin," 140, finds "the themes of Ricardian vernacular poetry" in the *Vox*—the validity of dreams, the garden setting, and devices for narrative transition.

32. See Macaulay, *Complete Works*, 4:369–405, for Gower's textual sources for the *Vox*, supplemented by Carlson and Rigg, *John Gower: Poems on Contemporary Events*, 174–245, for Book 1 ("Visio Anglie"). Yeager, *John Gower's Poetic*, 48–61, discusses Gower as a writer of cento, who decontextualizes his borrowings and uses his source materials at the level of the line and smaller syntactic units.

Gower's use of his source is an exercise in figural reading: unnatural sexual desire within a family is an adumbration of unnatural demands for dominion in society, politics, and culture.

Gower recounts his dream, as the rubric to chapter 16 describes him, "quasi in propria persona." He will return to something like this formulation in the first book of the *Confessio*. Here he moves beyond the authorial voice of counselor and penitent in the *Mirour*. He is a first-person narrator bearing witness to his own account and thereby moving toward testimony and exemplarity, while retaining the affective link of lamentation and complaint ("Hic plangit secundum visionem"), moved by his identification with freemen and nobles displaced and exiled by the rebels. His mode of lamentation is especially apt for the equation he draws between the fall of Troy and the sacking of London, New Troy. The destruction of Troy, as Gower remarks (VC 1.983–1000), has partial counterparts in the fall of other great cities, notably Thebes, Carthage, and Rome. But Troy offers the most powerful model for both ruin and authorship. The rebels take a city lacking walls and heroic defenders. The murder of archbishop Simon Sudbury is described symbolically ("quasi per figuram") as the death of the priest who served the Palladium protecting the city. Sudbury's murder also evokes memories of Thomas Becket's death, ordered by an angry king, though the cause here is the mob's fury: "Disparilis causa manet et mors vna duobus" (VC 1.1061) [The cause is dissimilar, yet there was one death for the two]. Within the narrative of the medieval Troy story, the scene stands in place of the episode of Priam's death at the hands of Pyrrhus, obscuring the threat against the king's person. In crafting his figural account, Gower fashions himself as a Troy poet, joining the company of *auctores* who "bere up Troye," as Chaucer describes them (*House of Fame* 1464–72). But his mode of writing differs significantly from chronicle historians and epic poets. Gower locates himself among the writers of imagined elegies such as "Pergama flere volo" and "Viribus arte minis," who look to the Troy story as a source for poetic invention and imitation. Like Chaucer in *Troilus and Criseyde* (5.540–53), he adds a biblical echo in seeing New Troy as the desolate widow ("que vidue lenguida more" [VC 1.880]) of Jeremiah's Lamentations.[33]

Gower's dream furnishes an internal warrant for authorship that applies not just to the vision but to the rest of the poem. The rubric situates Gower in a dream state ("vt si ipse mentaliter sompniando" [VC Book 1, ch. 20]) as the allegorical ship reaches England and the heavenly voice ("vox celica" [VC 1.2019]) directs him to writing: "Quicquid in hoc sompno visus et auris habent, / Scribere festines, nam sompnia sepe futurum / Indicium reddunt"

---

33. Robert R. Edwards, "Desolate Palace," 394–416.

(VC 1.2048–50) [I advise you to hasten to write down whatever you have seen and heard in this dream . . . for dreams often furnish an indication of the future]. The echo of "exempla futuri" from the Prologue makes it clear that Gower's commission is to write in a prophetic voice, which both forecasts events to come and admonishes a community, people, and nation.[34] Extending the claims of prophecy from the *Mirour*, Gower takes the allegorical dream narrative as the literal historical ground, and he recasts the instructional material of the original poem as a corrective—the integrated moral, social, and political remedy—that responds to the catastrophe he describes. (It follows, implicitly, that the *Cronica* sketches a monitory history of what ensues when prophetic instruction is ignored.) Gower ends his dream account by transforming memory into writing ("scribens memoranda notabit" [VC 1.2135]) while he remains shaken by his experience. This condition he addresses in a triple iteration of its nature and properties, "O vigiles sompni" (VC 1.2141, 2143, 2145) [O wakeful sleep]. It presents true events ("somnpia vera"), lessons for moral agents in the future ("exemplum quisque futurus habent"), and interpretive difficulty: "quorum sentencia scriptis / Ammodo difficilis est recitanda meis" (VC 1.2145–46) [whose difficult meaning my writings must now tell]. The dreamwork consciously exhibits the external conditions of literary discourse—its truth claims, application, and semiotic, even stylistic qualities. Gower serves as the translator of his dream into textuality: the significance of the dream, though difficult because of its allegorical figures, has to be presented publicly henceforth in his writings. His authorship proceeds from the invention and inscription of his own *materia*.

The main poem reframed by the addition of Gower's horrific dream vision carries traces of its own literary *accessus* and a somewhat more contained sense of authorship than is claimed in Book 1.[35] Gower appeals for inspiration to the Christian God rather than the muses or pagan deities. His work's value lies in the matter, not the man ("Rem non personam" [VC Prol 2.13]). His literary style is "stillatus" (Prol 2.19), tenuous but also cumulative, as if conveying its meaning drop by drop. Gower sees his office as that of a ready messenger ("instructus nuntius" [VC Prol 2.76]). The circumstance of his writing is his visions, but he admits to drawing on old authorities to strengthen his writing with other examples. He explains the *nomen libri* by projecting the biblical image of the voice crying within a contemporary context ("scripta noui verba doloris" [VC Prol 2.84]) to produce a written account of present events.

---

34. Fisher, *John Gower*, 184–85, argues that the universal voice of Old Testament prophets distinguishes medieval complaint from classical satire.
35. Minnis, *Medieval Theory of Authorship*, 171–77.

The prophetic voice introduced in the *Mirour* and deployed in the successive openings of the *Vox* provides a sustained model of authorship elsewhere in the poem. Gower prefaces his discussion of the clergy by saying that he does not reprove individuals but cries out ("increpo") against their faults: "Non ego personas culpabo, set increpo culpas, / Quas in personis cernimus esse reas" (VC Prol 3.9–10; cf. 7.1457–60). His writings denounce publicly ("mea scripta notant" [VC 4.246]) those monks more attracted to the world than to Christ. Gower moves from the conceit of public address to textual form in two passages that imitate the letters of exhortation and instruction that might be sent to judges (VC 6.309–418) and to the king (VC 6.581–1200).[36] His closing chapter combines the authorial function of compiling with the revelatory power of prophecy: "Hos ego compegi versus, quos fuderat in me / Spiritus in sompnis" (VC 7.1443–44) [I have compiled these verses, which a spirit uttered within me during my sleep]. Here Gower's textuality serves the prophetic voice by recording it as a text to be received: "Hec set vt auctor ego non scripsi metra libello, / Que tamen audiui trado legenda tibi" (VC 7.1445–46) [But I, as an author, have not set down these lines in a book; rather, I am passing on what things I heard for you to read]. As he makes clear at the beginning of Book 1, what has to be read ("legenda") is difficult, and it requires the work of interpretation. His authorial role is not to create the difficulty but to transmit it: "Que sompno cepi, vigilans mea scripta peregi" (VC 7.1461) [While awake, I have set down these my writings which I received during sleep]. As his choice of the verb *peragere* suggests, he has described or related his material and at the same time carried the transmission of the materials through to completion. He functions, as in the dream vision of Book 1, as an instrumental cause of writing, a human counterpart to the divine Author.

One crucial feature of Gower's authorship remains, however, fundamentally unresolved, or at least desperately balanced. As in the *Mirour*, the voice of the people is a source of both disorder and legitimation. In the dream vision, the first band of mutated rebels he sees are asses whose uncontrolled braying ("sua sternutacio" [VC 1.189]) terrifies citizens. The wild boar from Kent makes a grating sound ("rauco . . . stridore" [VC 1.327]). Fields shake from barking dogs (VC 1.380) whose noise ("strepitus" [VC 1.429]) reaches Satan's ears and makes hell rejoice at the sound. Birds, whose song initially greets the poet-narrator in an "alter paradisus" (VC 1.79), upset their natural hierarchies to produce horrible sounds (VC 1.543, 553). In the rebel assembly, Wat Tyler, in the figure of the jay, silences them and asserts his dominion over

---

36. Carlson and Rigg, *John Gower: Poems on Contemporary Events*, 5–6, suggest that the "Epistola ad regem" was likely an independent piece added to the *Vox*.

them with his "Vox fera" (VC 1.687). John Ball serves as their prophet.³⁷ As the rebellion takes form, its symbol of discord and division is noise: "Sepius exclamant monstrorum vocibus altis, / Atque modis variis dant variare tonos" (VC 1.797–98) [Time and time again they cried out with the deep voices of monsters and they kept making various noises in various ways]. In a remarkable piece of amplification (VC 1.799–830), Gower rehearses the cacophony produced by each group of beasts, a *vox terribilis* of "rudis clangor, sonus altus, fedaque rixa" (VC 1.815) [the loud din, the wild clangor, the savage brawling]; it echoes off rocks, and transforms into terrifying rumor among the nobles and into terror itself at the name of the strident jay.³⁸

Set against the raw noise of rebellion is the authorizing and legitimating sound of the voice of the commons. The faults Gower makes public are reported by the "plebis / Vox" (VC Prol 3.11–12); he speaks as the crowd speaks ("Vt loquitur vulgus loquor" [VC Prol 3.13]; "Que michi vox populi contulit, illa loquar" [VC Prol 4.20]). He chastises the clergy with popular and divine sanction: "Vox populi cum voce dei concordat" (VC 3.1267) [The voice of the people agrees with the voice of God]. His critique of mendicants likewise proceeds from the "vox populi" (VC 4.710). His complaint as a prophet and moralist against unjust lawgivers is identical to that of the people: "Hoc ego quod plebis vox clamat clamo" (VC 6.15) [I cry out what the voice of the people cries out]. He repeats the point, though with a measure of qualification, in closing the *Vox* and describing his authority for writing: "Quod scripsi plebis vox est, set et ista videbis, / Quo clamat populus, est ibi sepe deus" (VC 7.1469–70) [What I have set down is the voice of the people, you will also see that where the people call out, God is often there].

Gower resolves the tension between the raucous noise of rebellion and the legitimate voice of the people within the three-part structure of the *Cronica Tripertita*. At the beginning, he distinguishes the work of man (to seek peace) from the work of hell (to disturb peace) and the work done in Christ (to depose proud men from the throne and raise the humble). As the distinctions suggest, the structure is at once circular and linear; it achieves a historical and political equilibrium both by restoring a lost communal project and by decisively removing the means of division. The explicit linking of the *Vox* to the *Cronica* identifies Gower as the "scriptor" who intends to clarify the roles of Thomas Duke of Gloucester, Richard Earl of Arundel, and Thomas Earl of

---

37. Compare Ball's "alta scola" ("deepest learning" [VC 1.794]) with the "scola lata" that is claimed for Gower's poetry in the Latin poem "Eneidos Bucolis."

38. Gower's phrasing for the echo of rumor off the rocks ("saxa sonant" [1.817]) employs epic diction: *Aeneid* 12.587; *Pharsalia* 6.670; Silvius Italicus's *Punica* 4.370, 655; Albertus Stadensis's *Troilus* 3.407; and *Georgics* 4.47.

Warwick in the first phase. The marginal gloss at the beginning of the first part of the *Cronica* calls him a "compositor" (CT 1.1 gloss), and the gloss at the end of the first part clarifies his function: "Hic in fine compositor gesta dictorum trium pocerum laudabiliter commendans, pro eis apud altissimum deuocius exorat" (CT 1.214 gloss) [In conclusion the compiler commends the deeds of the three aforesaid nobles with praise. He prays devoutly to the Almighty in their behalf].

Gower composes his poem from the materials of history (*res gesta*), praising the principal historical actors of the episode while praying for their salvation. He is the author, in other words, of a moralized history apportioning praise and blame. In the second part, the force of this history registers on the "compositor" as an exemplary figure overcome by the sorrow of events: "Vix mea penna sonat hec que michi Cronica donat" (CT 2.4).[39] In the third part, he anticipates the hope of future glory and a poetic function of praise (CT 3.5). As the pattern of history reaches completion, the *Vox* retrospectively becomes a "speculum generale" (CT 3.283), a mirror to all. Henry's election to succeed Richard is objectified by popular acclaim ("vniuerso populi in eius laudem conclamante" [CT 3.284, gloss]), one common basis for Lancastrian efforts to legitimate Henry's usurpation. The people in one person clamor for retribution for Gloucester's death (CT 3.370–71). Their love and complaint ("communis amor popularis et vndique clamor" [CT 3.373]) are received as law by a beneficent king. Gower's prophetic authorship, like the sources of popular dissonance and aristocratic division, disappears in the monarch's appropriation and imagined consolidation of all opposition.

CONFESSIO AMANTIS

In the *Confessio Amantis* (first recension 1390, second and third recensions ca. 1393), Gower makes his most ambitious claim to authorship. The ambition lies in his effort to align Latin and vernacular traditions, which had interpenetrated the *Mirour* and *Vox*, with a poetic structure at once didactic and imaginative. Gower composes introductory Latin verses that mark structural divisions in the prologues and elsewhere in the work, and he appends marginal glosses throughout to provide interpretation and identify the speakers in the confessional dialogue between Genius and Amans. The Latin materials

---

39. Macaulay's base manuscript and most other witnesses read *penna*, but the variant *lingua* is consistent with Gower's prophetic voice; Stockton adopts *lingua* in his translation (*Major Latin Works*, 299, 476).

are a program integrated with the English but distinct from it.[40] The material layout of Gower's poem in the earliest manuscripts strives to give it the external appearance of a canonical text within high literary culture.[41] As in the *Mirour* and *Vox*, Gower draws on multiple modes of discourse, particularly exposition, exemplum, and exhortation. He conceives the organizing principle of his work according to a "middel weie" combining "Somwhat of lust, somwhat of lore" (Prol 17, 19). The Latin penitential tradition of the Seven Deadly Sins is joined to the topic of worldly love, apparently for the first time, and provides a narrative frame for Amans, the fictional character assumed by the author, to confess his sins against love and receive guidance from Genius, Venus's priest.[42] Love, understood as ethical and affective, serves as well as a metaphor for politics, in particular governance and statecraft. The Prologus first treats the threat of division in a social sphere where "love is falle into discord" (Prol 121) and then moves to the wonder and misfortunes of lovers. The confessional pattern for examining love is subsequently interrupted in Book 7, which presents a mirror for rulers drawn from the Latin tradition of princely instruction.[43] Vernacular tradition furnishes an equally important resource for Gower's authorship. The lover as retrospective narrator has a predecessor in the *Rose*, as does the shifting identity from author to lover and back to author again, which marks Jean's earlier appropriation of Guillaume's narrative.[44] But Gower found still more promising models in the poetry of contemporaries like Guillaume de Machaut and Jean Froissart. Machaut offers the precedent of a vernacular writer who organizes and oversees his poems as a body of work with a coherent theme and material presence.[45] Both Machaut and Froissart place their retrospective lover-narrators outside the framework of a dream vision and focus on the drama of their frustrations and obstacles in pursuing love.

The relation of Latin and vernacular traditions is dynamic in the *Confessio*, and Gower carries forward into his poem the devices used to establish authorship in his earlier works. An extensive textual apparatus positions the work and provides a discursive space to perform authorship. Gower both presents himself as an *auctor* and represents authorship through other figures in the

---

40. Pearsall, "Gower's Latin," 15–16.
41. Parkes, "Influence of the Concepts of Ordinatio and Compilatio," 35–70.
42. Burrow, "Portrayal of Amans," 5–24.
43. Fisher, *John Gower*, 198; Peck, *Kingship and Common Profit*, 140; and Copeland, *Rhetoric, Hermeneutics, and Translation*, 211, argue that Book 7 serves as a guide to the organization of the *Confessio*.
44. Butterfield, "Articulating the Author," 84.
45. Nicholson, *Love and Ethics*, 3–40; Butterfield, "Articulating the Author"; Burrow, "Portrayal of Amans."

vision, confessional frame, and exemplary narratives of the poem. A number of his narratives offer poetic emblems of authorship—elements within the text that reflect on the nature of writing. At the end of the *Confessio,* Gower consolidates his career in what seems a double *recusatio,* a withdrawal from love, as Amans recognizes himself as an old man unfit for Venus's service, and from authorship, as Venus give him a new commission consistent with poetic retirement. This finely calibrated moment of closure proves instead an occasion for refusal and for defining a second authorial canon.

Gower introduces the *Confessio* with the apparatus of two prologues. The formal Prologus is an extrinsic prologue, which identifies the discipline to which a work belongs, while the opening of Book 1 introduces the text with an intrinsic prologue.[46] In addition, Gower composes introductory Latin verses that mark structural divisions in the prologues and elsewhere in the work, and he appends marginal glosses throughout to provide interpretation and identify the speakers in the confessional dialogue between Genius and Amans. The first prologue serves as a preface to the work as a whole. The initial topos of the introductory verse is poetic modesty, but Gower's underlying gesture is Ovidian and even nationalistic, though the medium of expression is Latin: "minimus ipse minora canam" (CA Prol Latin verse 1.2) [I, least of all, sing things all the lesser]. The turn toward less lofty subjects (*minora*) is Ovid's self-inaugurating claim and his *recusatio* at the opening of the *Amores,* which opens up for Ovid a critical perspective on the major genres and corresponding subjects of the classical canon. Through his Latin elegiac verse, Gower states his intention of composing English verse: "Anglica Carmente metra iuuante loquar" (CA Prol Latin verse 1.4). He does so under a dual sanction, using the language of Hengist, which is the idiom of Britain ("canit Insula Bruti"), and invoking the power of Carmen, who brought Latin writing to Italy.[47] As the allusions suggest, Gower's opening is contingent and belated. He announces his English project through Latin in the elegiac verse associated with Ovid but revived earlier for the *Vox.* He evokes mythological sources for both languages that are not fixed points of origin but evidence of cultural change, idioms of place (England, Italy) that have driven out earlier languages by conquest. Gower's media of expression carry with them a political history and imperial design that apply to both classical and vernacular languages. Their relation is not regulatory or stabilizing—the authority of Latin does not police the unruly vernacular—but unstable, for the Latin verses and glosses

---

46. Minnis, *Medieval Theory of Authorship,* 177.
47. Echard, "With Carmen's Help," 10.

are themselves multiple forms of Latin that call into question and frequently subvert textual control.[48]

The English verse following the Latin introduction in the Prologus continues these authorial themes of contingency and belatedness. Books and writing stand as placeholders and intermediaries for lost authors and poetic material: "Of hem that writen ous tofore / The bokes duelle, and we therfore / Ben tawht of that was write tho" (CA Prol 1–3). The commonplace is *ars longa, vita brevis,* but Gower turns it to a different purpose than does Chaucer, for whom "the craft so long to lerne" is love (*Parliament of Fowls* 1). In Gower's formulation, books stand in ("duelle") for authors who remain beyond recovery, and they serve as the means for knowing their teachings as embodied in writing. Poetic imitation provides access to authors and doctrine for moderns who "wryte of newe som matiere, / Essampled of these olde wyse" (CA Prol 6–7). As happens so often in Gower and Chaucer, simple language conveys enormous subtlety—in this case, the impossible demand at the heart of imitation, which is to write an original copy. To write "of newe som matiere" is to write "new, for the first time" and to write received materials "anew, afresh, again" (MED, s.v. *neue* [n.]). Such writing is by definition poetic imitation; it is "essampled" in the dual sense of setting a precedent or exemplifying (MED, s.v. *exaumplen* [b], citing this passage). In other words, it is constrained in its contents (as example) and in its mode of presentation (as precedent). The sources for imitation likewise divide for Gower between authors and the works that stand for them in time: "These olde wyse" refers to "these wise men of olde" and to old books.[49]

The mode of discourse that Gower chooses for summoning former authors and their writing is equally contingent: "I wolde go the middel weie / And wryte a bok between the tweie, / Somewhat of lust, somewhat of lore" (CA Prol 17–19). He repeats the idea at the end of the *Confessio,* confirming that he undertook "in englesch forto make a book / Which stant betwene ernest and game" (CA 8.3108–9); in the earlier, Ricardian version, some part is written "as for to lawhe and forto pleye" and some to be "wisdom to the wise": "So that somdel for good prise and eek somdel for lust and game" (CA 8.3057*, 3059*, 3060–61*). The underlying formula is the Horatian principle that literary works both please and teach. Gower seems to hedge his investment in the

---

48. Ibid., 26: "It is the *failure* of the Latin to explain or repair the problems of the vernacular which is crucial to an understanding of the role of Latin in Gower's poem"; cf. idem, "Gower's 'bokes of Latin,'" 123–56; Wetherbee, "Latin Structure," 7–35; idem, "Classical and Boethian Tradition," 181–96.

49. Macaulay, *Complete Works,* 2:457, cites the "Traitié selonc les auctours pour essampler les amantz marietz" (15.1.4): "Pour essampler les autres du present"; Peck, *John Gower: Confessio Amantis,* 1:43, glosses, "wise [men/books]."

hope that some readers will be drawn to some part of the work. The "middel weie" is, however, more than an accommodation among topics, a reference to style, or a strategy to maximize readers. Gower provides his own gloss on the phrase in a discussion of the virtue of Largesse, which stands between avarice and prodigality. Genius advises Amans, "Halt evere forth the middel weie" (CA 5.7691). The allusion is to the Aristotelian mean, which is a zone of moral action plotted between the excess and deficit of a particular virtue and calculated according to the inclinations of character. There is no single defining point on the spectrum. An author on the "middel weie," like someone pursuing virtue, operates within a range of contingencies. His actions are made intelligible by the models embodied in his forebears.

The authorizing moment in the extrinsic prologue divides sharply in the Ricardian (first recension) and Lancastrian (later recensions) versions of the *Confessio*, though marginal glosses in both versions identify "Iohannes Gower" as the writer of the book (CA Prol 22, Prol 34*). Gower's final cause as an author in the Ricardian version is to make a book "for king Richardes sake" (CA Prol 23), and in the Lancastrian version, the book is "for Engelondes sake" (CA Prol 24). The Ricardian version contains a narrative of patronage, as in the *Vox*, in which Gower encounters the monarch's barge on the Thames, joins Richard, and receives a commission to write "some newe thing" (CA Prol 51*), which will fall under the king's scrutiny: "That he himself it mighte loke / After the forme of my writynge" (CA Prol 52–53*). Richard's commission immediately places Gower in a courtly world of potential blame and "jangling" (CA Prol 69*), in which instruction and pleasure are prudent aims for writing. The tactic that sustains them is compilation. In the marginal gloss accompanying the passage, Gower uses the image of the honeycomb (*favus*) traditionally associated, as in Walter Map, with gathering and memory to describe the method and sources of compilation: "tanquam fauum ex variis floribus recollectum, presentem libellum ex variis cronicis, historiis, poetarum philosophorumque dictis . . . studiossime compilauit" (CA Prol 41* gloss) [he zealously compiled the present little book, like a honeycomb gathered from various flowers, from various chronicles, histories, and sayings of the poets and philosophers].[50] As classical and Christian authors remark, one feature of the honeycomb is growth and multiplication.[51]

The Lancastrian version has its own authorizing narrative, in the extrinsic prologue, though it is submerged. England requires a book because of social and political division, the loss of a Golden Age of virtue that was cotermi-

---

50. See Olsson, *John Gower and the Structures of Conversion*, 5–11, for discussion of the image. Carruthers, *Book of Memory*, 37–39, discusses the image in mnemotechnics.

51. Lewis and Short, *Latin Dictionary*, s.v. *favus*.

nous with a reverence for books and writing. Against this background, Gower situates himself as an author of retrospect and recuperation. He proposes to write a book about a renewing world, "After the world that whilom tok / Long tyme in olde daies passed" (CA Prol 54–55). The plan he sets out at the end of the opening section differs from the earlier description and from the work he actually produces. Gower says that he writes about worldly fortune for the wise; he will end with the wonder and misfortune of love, and direct his work to powerful men who must negotiate virtue and vice, chief among them his new dedicatee, Henry of Lancaster.

The intrinsic prologue that begins Book 1 of the *Confessio* claims a turn "to treten upon othre thinges" (CA 1.8), new materials "noght so strange" (CA 1.10) as the doctrinal teachings of the *Mirour* and *Vox* or as extraordinary as Book 1 of the *Vox*. Gower's poetic *materia* is the overpowering force of love within animate nature: "loves lawe is out of reule" (CA 1.18). The marginal gloss to the passage incorporates salient features of the academic prologue, such as the conceptual order of the work, the author's intention, the name of the work, and the *materia*:

> Postquam in Prologum tractatum hactenus existit, qualiter hodierne condicionis diuisio caritatis dileccionem superauit, intendit auctor ad presens suum libellum, cuius nomen Confessio amantis nuncupatur, componere de illo amore, a quo non solum humanum genus, sed eciam cuncta animancia naturaliter subiciuntur. Et quia nonnulli amantes ultra quam expedit desiderii passionibus crebro stimulantur, materia libri per totum super hiis specialius diffunditur. (Marginal gloss at CA 1.8)

> After he has set forth to this point the treatment in the Prologue of how the division of today's condition has overcome the love of charity, the author presently intends to compose his little book, whose name is "The Confession of a Lover," concerning that love by which not only the human species but indeed every living thing is naturally subjected. And since some lovers are often goaded by the passions of desire beyond what is appropriate, the matter of the book throughout is set forth for these especially.

The gloss identifies Gower as an author performing the tasks that go along with rhetorical and poetic invention in a didactic poem. But as he takes up "my matiere" (CA 1.95), Gower draws first on a vernacular *modus tractandi*, the retrospective narrative frame of the love vision. He goes beyond his French models, moreover, by coordinating the roles of author, poet, narrator, and lover.⁵² The crucial step, which has gone largely unremarked, is Gower's subtle reversal here of the conventional relation between author and lover.

Gower's marginal note explains that the author has fashioned himself in the persona of Amans to write about the various passions that lovers undergo: "Hic quasi in persona aliorum, quos amor alligat, fingens se auctor esse Amantem, varias eorum passiones variis huius libri distinccionibus per singula scribere proponit" (marginal gloss at CA 1.59) [Here the author, fashioning himself to be the Lover as if in the role of those others whom love binds, proposes to write about their various passions one by one in the various sections of this book]. The most revealing phrase in this passage is "fingens se auctor esse Amantem," for the expectation associated with the love vision is that the lover becomes a poet, if not an author, by retelling his dream vision.⁵³ Gower reverses this expectation by taking it for granted that he is an *auctor*, so that it is the role of lover that has to be fashioned and feigned. He posits authorship as the foundational identity and the lover as a fiction built upon it.

Gower's exemplary position as author and lover involves not just illustrating doctrine but negotiating moral contingency. The traditional lesson is to avoid the moral perils of sensual love. Gower's invention of his material sets, however, a complicated moral and literary problem. His subject matter is the compelling force of love over sentient creatures ("cuncta animancia"), who find themselves constrained by appetite and desire yet obliged ethically to act in accordance with reason and proper moral action. His mode of instruction, as the second Latin verse of Book 1 makes clear, is the lessons of radical ambiguity: "Vt discant alii, docet experiencia facti, / Rebus in ambiguis que sit habenda via" (CA Book 1, Latin verse ii.3–4) [Experience of the deed teaches so that others might learn what path should be held amidst uncertain circumstances]. The road that matters is the one that traverses ambiguity. This path Gower calls the "Devius ordo" (ii.5), the twisting progress that moves off the main and direct route of first principles into the terrain of contingency and experience. In Gower's metaphor, Amans as guide (*dux*) provides examples to those following behind him, while the author records and exhibits to the world the disastrous events (*casus*) of Amans's erotic career. He thereby writes the text that must be read and interpreted in order to effect transformation.

The textual apparatus in the prologues and elsewhere thus places Gower inside and outside his poem, as simultaneously a character and author.⁵⁴

---

52. In Jean's portion of the *Rose*, the God of Love indirectly identifies Guillaume as Amant: "Guillaume de Lorris / Cui Jalousie, sa contraire" (10526–27); *Le Roman de la Rose*, ed. Poirion.

53. Irvin, *Poetic Voices of John Gower*, 82–83, argues that the note distinguishes poet and lover, and sets out prudent advice undermined by the text, which collapses the two voices.

54. Meecham-Jones, "Prologue: The Poet as Subject," 17.

Gower composed the introductory Latin verses and the marginal glosses that appear alongside (and occasionally inside, in later manuscripts) his vernacular text. The glosses, particularly those attached to Genius's narrative *exempla*, generally follow a model that first identifies the topic (*hic tractat*) and then summarizes the narrative (*et narrat*). The material layout of the text, both in Gower's planned *ordinatio* and in the forms that scribes may have given independently in the course of transmission, presents an author functioning in multiple modes—as a poetic voice in the Latin verse, a commentator glossing his work and describing its narrative elements, and a narrator and teacher employing characters to convey his stories and teachings. The effect of Gower's apparatus is to propose and then dislocate hierarchies of description and meaning. The Latin verse frequently exploits the ambiguities of language and syntax. The Latin prose summaries in the *Confessio* hover uncertainly between controlling accounts of the vernacular narratives or sketches that the vernacular amplifies and redefines. Similarly, the dialogue frame of Amans's confession to Genius both evokes and mimics authoritative models such as Boethius's *Consolation of Philosophy*.[55]

Gower's authorial role finds important restatements in Genius and Amans. Just as Gower's major poems develop in scope and connection, so Genius has to expand his range of topics beyond "my spekynges / Of love, but of othre thinges, / That touchen to the cause of vice" (CA 1.239–41). In Book 7, he recounts Aristotle's teachings to Alexander, mindful that "it is noght to the matiere / Of love" (CA 7.7–8). At the end of his instruction of Amans, he acknowledges that his office as confessor has outweighed his allegiance to Venus: "I seide I wolde of myn office / To vertu more than to vice / Encline, and teche thee mi lore" (CA 8.2081–83). For his part, Amans admits that he has produced the kind of lyric poetry (CA 1.2726–35) that Gower earlier dismissed in the *Mirour*. But he asks directly, too, for Genius to function as an exemplary writer. At the start of Book 4, he exchanges the tales that have delayed his suit of his lady for "som goodly tale" (CA 4.70) to avoid sloth. Finding a contradiction in Genius's account of the stealthy theft of love, he prays Genius to tell "a tale lich to the matiere / Wherof I myhte ensample take" (CA 5.6800–801) and thus avoid the sin of covetise. Under the sin of gluttony, he admits that his ear "is fedd of redinge of romance / Of Ydoine and of Adamas" (CA 6.878–79) and other tales that resemble his predicament.

Except for the opening dream of Nebuchadnezzar and the frame tale of the *Confessio* itself, Gower's narratives are related through Genius, and they offer self-reflexive commentary on the kind of writing that Gower's author-

---

55. Wetherbee, "Classical and Boethian Traditions," 6.

ship supposes. It is a commonplace of modern criticism that Genius's moralizing reading stretches the narrative logic of his exempla. At various points in the *Confessio*, however, his fictions demonstrate the narrative and hermeneutic stakes of exemplary writing. In the tale of Albinus and Rosemund (CA 1.2459–646), the polished skull of Gurmond, Rosemund's father, transformed to a drinking vessel and presented to his daughter, represents the literal truth that artifice and elaboration cannot refine away.[56] Canace's letter to Machaire (CA 3.143–336) revises the opening image in its source, Ovid's *Heroides*, to make visible the toll exacted by melancholy. In Ovid, Canace presents a scribal image of herself holding a pen in one hand and the sword sent to her by her father in the other, with a papyrus unrolled on her lap to receive both blood and ink (*Heroides* 11.5–6); in Gower's version, the child of her incestuous love with her brother replaces the writing surface: "In my barm ther lith to wepe / Thi child and myn, which sobbeth faste" (CA 3.302–3). With this change, the narrative adds a further echo to the image. The child pictured in Canace's lap is also Canace herself, who has earlier pleaded, "Ha mercy! Father, thenk I am / Thi child, and of thi blod I cam" (CA 3.225–26). Later, the statue of Araxarathen and the sepulcher of Iphis, her suicidal lover (CA 4.3631–84), likewise create a tableau in Venus's temple at Salamis that warns of despair yet reveals the tragic connection of desire and death.

Elsewhere the *Confessio* recounts a number of stories that conventionally stand as emblems of poetic art, such as the transformation of Pygmalion's "colde ymage" (CA 4.422) of Galatea to flesh and bone; the threefold imitation of Ceix by figure, voice, and form (CA 4.3034–55); and Philomena's woven silk text of "lettres and ymagerie" (CA 5.5771) recounting Tereus's violence against her. The Ceix and Alceone story is prefaced by the argument from vernacular tradition, used earlier in the *Vox*, that dreams "fulofte sothe thinges / Betokne" (CA 4.2923–24). An image of Gower's own position as an author on the edge of power emerges in his account of the Roman triumph. The "Ribald" (CA 7.2383) who sits with the Emperor in his chariot speaks the plain truth of transient glory as the Emperor enjoys the triple honor of conquest. Gower's instruction of princes in the *Confessio* may have a wider scope than the Ribald's warning, but it proceeds from the same recognition that power ultimately stands victim to change.

The ending of the *Confessio* separates the roles of author and lover that Gower joined in Book 1 as the governing fiction of his poem. The *Confessio*, like Chaucer's *Troilus*, moves through a sequence of provisional endings.[57] In

---

56. Robert R. Edwards, "Gower's Poetics of the Literal," 59–73.
57. Nicholson, *Love and Ethics*, 378–94; Burrow, "Sinning against Love," 228.

the frame tale, Amans is aggrieved when Genius gives his final advice, in a close echo of Chaucer's *Troilus* (5.1842–48): "Tak love where it mai noght faile" (CA 8.2096). His letter of supplication to Venus and Cupid seeks redress from love's maladies yet brings the ironic remedy of Gower's dismissal from the company of lovers as an old man unfit for service. As Amans recedes, Gower stages something like a scene of authorial recovery within the frame tale. He answers when Venus asks him to name himself: "'Ma dame,' I seide, 'John Gower'" (CA 8.2321). His naming is emphasized dramatically and made part of an ongoing recovery of identity in the Lancastrian version of the poem. (In witnesses from the first and second recensions of the poem, a balanced structure is evident, for Gower had identified himself in Book 1, when Venus first appears to him and asks who he is: "Ma dame I sayde Iohn Gowere" [CA 1.161 variant].) He swoons at the discovery that his career as a lover is over and has an internal vision in which Cupid and companies of "gentil folk" (CA 8.2457) led by Youthe and Elde attend him. Both groups are the protagonists of classical myth and medieval romance, with four exemplary wives (Penelope, Lucrece, Alceste, and Alcione) prominent among them. More than exemplary figures, they are the topical material of authorial imitation and invention, a gathering of narratives organized around two dominant topics:

> The moste matiere of her speche
> Was al of knyhthod and of Armes,
> And what it is to ligge in armes
> With love, whanne it is achieved.
> (CA 8.2296–99)

When Cupid removes his dart and Venus anoints him with a healing salve, Gower sees his true image in a mirror. It is this authorial John Gower whom Venus addresses in the dismissal scene, giving him a rosary of black beads with the legend *Por reposer* inscribed in gold and a new project—to seek and pray for peace. In doing so, she directs him to an authorship already established by the *Mirour* and the *Vox*: "But go ther vertu moral duelleth, / Wher ben thi bokes, as men telleth, / Whiche of long time thou has write" (CA 2925–27). The phrasing here echoes that of the envoy at the end of *Troilus*, where Chaucer prepares to shift his book to a new generic register: "Go, litel bok, go, litel myn tragedye, / Ther God thi makere yet, er that he dye, / So sende myght to make in som comedye!" (5.1786–88). Gower's works are a locus of "vertu moral." They have found an influential audience of readers and commentators, "men" who can affirm their value. Written "of long time," they are themselves venerable *auctoritates* worthy of imitation and the products of protracted labor. At the end of the *Confessio*, then, Gower establishes himself as the full measure of an author.

GOWER'S PARATEXTS

Gower's works are frequently accompanied and framed by paratexts that seek to establish his position as an author within literary tradition. The quatrain "Quam cinxere," an epistle ostensibly sent "a quodam philosopho" [by a certain philosopher] but likely written by Gower himself, celebrates the completion of the *Confessio*. The piece offers a threefold definition of Gower as "Carminis Athleta, satirus . . . siue Poeta" [champion of song, satirist, or poet]. The terms anatomize authorship in the contested territory of morals and politics, and they reprise the image from the *Vox* of the poet as an archer sending arrows into the world to wound those living wrongly. The poem preserves as well the tensions built elsewhere into Gower's authorial juxtapositions of Latin and vernacular writing. England "laude repleta" [full of praise] sings Gower's happy songs ("tua carmina leta"), but the syntax leaves uncertain whether it is England or Gower's poems that are full of praise. Similarly, the poem's wish for Gower to receive complete praise, a glory without limit ("quo gloria stat sine meta"), refers equally to secular fame and spiritual salvation.

The colophon "Quia vnusquisque" again presumably written by Gower though appearing in various positions among manuscripts of the *Confessio* and *Vox*, brings his works and poetic languages together in a virtuoso reckoning of authorship. The piece credits Gower with having produced three books for the purpose of bringing instruction to the attention of others ("doctrine causa compositos ad aliorum noticiam") and describes the *Mirour*, *Vox*, and *Confessio* in their order of composition. Gower borrows here from the framework of the commentary tradition to report titles and specify the material of the works, the divisions of the material, the mode of treatment, and the utility. To be sure, his description of his corpus in "Quia unusquisque" is highly selective in its inclusions and emphases.[58] Accordingly, the *Mirour* is a poem on virtues and vices as well as social estates, though it clearly evolved in the process of composition to include other material, notably the lives of Christ and the Virgin. The *Vox* is described in the colophon from the retrospect of Richard II's fall but omits mention of the dream vision of Book 1. The *Confes-*

---

58. Pearsall, "Gower's Latin," 24, regards the colophon not as a commentary on the *Confessio* but an authorial misrepresentation of it.

sio is cast first as a poem about the succession of kingdoms (Nebuchadnezzar's dream in the Prologus) and princely instruction (Book 7) but then mostly about love and the foolish passions of lovers, along the lines of school commentaries on Ovid's elegiac poems. The aim of Gower's colophon, however, is not to give a full descriptive account but to insist on the coherence of his canon, hence his authorial project. Gower is an ethical poet addressing the moral, social, and political order and instructing both princes and lovers on self-governance. The critical importance lies not just in the themes of Gower's authorship but in the systemization. Gower frames a reading of his corpus through the analytical and descriptive categories that confer the literary dignity of authorship. In the process, he makes his corpus an object of commentary, a virtual requirement of authorship.

The Latin poem "Eneidos Bucolis," which follows Gower's colophon in five manuscripts of the *Confessio Amantis*, directly applies these conventions to Gower. The poem is credited to "a certain Philosopher" [quidam Philosophus] writing on the imagined occasion of Gower's completing three books. It is located, in effect, at the fictional—and provisional—moment of consolidating his poetic canon into a major corpus of works. As with "Quam cinxere" and "Quia vnusquisque," Gower is the likely author.[59] Whether friend and associate or convenient fiction, the speaker makes the bold move of equating Gower's three little books (*libelli*) with the three books (*libri*) that won Vergil honor over other poets and secured him praise as an author in the school curriculum.

> Hiis tribus ille libris prefertur honore poetis,
>   Romaque precipuis laudibus instat eis.
> Gower, sicque tuis tribus est dotata libellis
>   Anglia, morigeris quo tua scripta seris.
> ("Eneidos Bucolis" 3–6)

On account of these three books he (Vergil) is preferred in honor over all poets, and Rome bestows upon them its chief praises. Thus, too, O Gower, with your three little books is England endowed, where you accommodate your writings to serious things.

---

59. Macaulay surmised that the philosopher might be Ralph Strode, the co-dedicatee with "moral Gower" of Chaucer's *Troilus and Criseyde* (*Complete Works*, 4:419); Yeager has suggested that Gower himself might have penned these lines of commendation and commemoration as part of a campaign of authorial self-presentation (*John Gower: The Minor Latin Works*, 83–86).

The poem does not press specific correspondences between Gower's corpus and Vergil's by matching up particular works or genres, though Gower may have seen his poems as "a kind of triple epic" in comparison to the *Aeneid*.[60]

The poem aims to exploit the contrasts that the numerical correspondence secures. Rome praises Vergil, but England is enriched ("dotata") by Gower's turn to serious topics. Vergil writes in one language so that distinguished Italians will reflect on his poems ("sua metra . . . sint recolenda"), whereas Gower writes in French, Latin, and English in order to achieve a wider learning ("scola lata") among men. Vergil astounds Roman ears with vanities, while Gower's writing proves illustrious ("fulget") for Christians and secures him not just worldly fame but praise in heaven. These contrasts propose that Gower surpasses Vergil because he is a national and Christian poet. "Eneidos Bucolis" is as much concerned with *translatio*—the relocation of ascribed cultural values—as it is with praise, commendation, or self-promotion. It sets out a proportion rather than a simple equation: Vergil is to a city (Rome) and a region (Italy) as Gower is to a nation (England) and a spiritual community (Christendom). As an author, Gower surpasses Vergil by having literary and salvation history on his side.[61]

The model behind the contrast of Gower with Vergil is the *cursus honorum*, the sequence of works progressing from lower to higher genres. The *cursus* was ascribed to Vergil, and it served as a paradigm for authorship and the phases within a literary career. In the *Amores* (1.15.25–26), Ovid traces Vergil's progression from bucolics to georgics to epic, while recognizing the political stakes for Augustan empire in achieving fame at the end of the sequence: "Tityrus et segetes Aeneiaque arma legentur, / Roma triumphati dum caput orbis erit" [The shepherd Tityrus and crops and the arms of Aeneas will be read as long as Rome is the ruler of a conquered world].[62] He seems to echo the provisional four-line proem to the *Aeneid*, later removed by Vergil's literary executors, which tracked the poet's progress through genres:

> Ille ego qui quondam gracili modulatus avena
> carmen et egressus silvis vicina coegi
> ut quamvis avido parerent arva colono,
> gratum opus agricolis, at nunc horrentia Martis
> arma virumque cano.

---

60. Kuczynski, "Gower's Virgil," 164.
61. For an earlier discussion of "Eneidos Bucolis," see Robert R. Edwards, "Authorship, Imitation, and Refusal in Late-Medieval England," 57–59.
62. Cheney, "Introduction: 'Jog on, jog on,'" 9.

I am he who once tuned my song on a slender reed, then, leaving the woodland, constrained the neighbouring fields to serve the husbandmen, however grasping—a work welcome to farmers: but now of Mar's bristling arms and the man I sing.[63]

The same progress through genres appears in the epitaph composed by Vergil for his tomb: "cecini pascua rures duces" [I have sung pastures, fields, and princes].[64] Propertius (2.34) likewise surveys Vergil's career, paying deference to the *Aeneid* while "deforming" the *Eclogues* to resemble his own writings.[65] In the prologue to Servius's commentary on the *Eclogues,* Vergil is said to have followed the natural order for writing poetry by observing this sequence of composition: "et dicit Donatus, quod etiam in poetae memoravimus vita, in scribendis carminibus naturalem ordinem secutum esse Vergilium: primo enim pastoralis fuit in montibus vita, post agriculturae amor, inde bellorum cura successit" [Donatus says that Vergil followed natural order in writing his poems, which we likewise mention in the life of the poet: first there was the pastoral life in the mountains, then love of agriculture, from which the pain of wars followed].[66]

The life of Vergil attributed to Suetonius ("De poetis") adds a fourth step to this progression, which may give us a framework for locating Gower's later writing. Vergil, says Suetonius, intended to spend three years polishing the *Aeneid* and then devote the remainder of his life to philosophical contemplation: "Anno aetatis quinquagesimo secundo inpositurus 'Aeneidi' summam manum statuit in Graeciam et in Asiam secedere triennioque continuo nihil amplius quam emendare, ut reliqua vita tantum philosophiae vacaret" [At the age of fifty two, planning to give final polish to the 'Aeneid,' he decided to withdraw to Greece and Asia Minor and do nothing other than correct the poem for three full years, so that the rest of his life might be devoted completely to philosophy].[67] Donatus ("Life of Virgil" sec. 35) included the Suetonian biography in his commentary on Vergil, and it became a feature of the medieval and Renaissance transmission of Vergil's works, including, for example, Petrarch's manuscript.[68]

---

63. *Aeneid* 1a–1, *Virgil,* trans. Fairclough, 1:240–41.
64. Cheney, "Introduction: 'Jog on, jog on,'" 10.
65. Cairns, "Varius and Vergil," 313–14.
66. Servius, *In Vergilii Bucolica et Georgica Commentarii,* ed. Thilo, 3–4.
67. Suetonius, "Vita Virgilii," 2:476; for a possible echo of *Georgics* 2.475–82, see Paratore, *Virgilio,* 289.
68. Brugnoli and Stok, *Vitae vergilianae antiquae.* For the history of Donatus's "Life of Virgil," see Stok, "Virgil between the Middle Ages and the Renaissance," 15–22. Petrarch's Vergil is Milan, Biblioteca Ambrosiana, MS S.P.Arm.10, Scat. 27; see Enenkel, "Modelling the Human-

Gower's paratexts suggest that his conscious self-fashioning has a specific model and structure in the *cursus,* which is designed to produce a result: Gower is a vernacular classical author with an established canon of works sustained by commentary and a context of reception, even if those are fabricated by the author himself. The *Confessio* marks the consolidation of that canon, at least from the retrospect that Gower was prepared to impose on his body of work in the mid-to-late 1390s. Moreover, it takes him precisely to the point at which, in the Suetonian model, he could be expected to move from writing to philosophical retreat. Such a step is implied in the inscription *Por reposer* and Venus's instruction to seek and pray for peace, a Christian equivalent to the philosopher's contemplation. That Gower refuses to complete the model represents a crucial feature of his career and an index to his commitments as a moralist, social theorist, and writer. It shows, too, that "Gower ethicus" depends fundamentally on Gower as an author.

GOWER'S SECOND CURSUS

Gower's paratexts establish the canon of his major works and thereby allow him to position a corresponding canon of minor works. Ovid may swerve from the dominant position of the Vergilian canon by becoming a counter-imperial elegiac poet, but Gower defines his minor canon by contrast to his own work. The three languages successively marked out in the colophon "Quia vnusquisque" are replicated in the cycle of later works: *In Praise of Peace,* the *Traitié pour essampler les amantz marietz* and *Cinkante Balades,* and a group of shorter Latin poems, including the "laureate poems" praising Henry IV. This minor canon finds a material embodiment in the Trentham manuscript (British Library, MS Additional 59495), which contains most of the work, uniquely *In Praise of Peace* and the *Cinkante Balades.*

In Praise of Peace takes up the commission that Venus gives Gower at the end of the *Confessio.* It does so not in the abstract but by addressing the monarch as the agent most capable of acting decisively in the interests of peace. Scholars differ on the historical context that might bear most directly on the poem, but it was most likely written in the period 1399–1400. The poem rehearses the standard claims to Lancastrian legitimacy (descent, election, and conquest) and warns of the transience of earthly glory, while addressing Henry as a figure of restoration and recovery. Henry encouraged such a char-

---

ist," 16. Boccaccio, *Genealogie deorum gentilium* [14.4], ed. Romano, 694, contrasts the peace of poetic retirement with the ongoing turbulence and litigation of lawyers: "Poete in secessu carmina sua canunt" [Poets sings their own songs in retirement].

acterization by political strategies such as his "chalange," in which conquest ostensibly served to recover a realm "in poynt to ben undoo for defaute of governance and undoying of the good lawes."[69] Gower situates the poem as a functional analogue to the *Confessio* and a realization of the moral and political lessons discussed in the earlier 1390s. He opens, as in the *Confessio*, with prefatory Latin verses and writes the body of the poem in the rhyme royal stanzas that appear toward the end of the *Confessio* in Amans's Supplication to Venus (8.2217–300). At the conclusion, as in the *Confessio*, he identifies himself in the first person: "I, Gower" (374). Yet he pointedly reverses Venus's dismissal of him from her and her court. He sends his "lettre" to Henry "as Y which evere unto my lives ende / wol praie for the stat of thi persone / In worschipe of thi sceptre and of thi throne" (376–78).

Editors and commentators have noted that Gower recurs to themes and exempla from the *Confessio*, particularly the treatment of Wrath in Book 3 and the instructions for princes in Book 7. Solomon, Alexander, and Constantine link the two works closely, if ambiguously, as figures of kingship. Equally important are the transpositions that Gower introduces. Henry's accession is "the glade fortune" of rightful governance, yet Gower insists on the primacy of choice and human agency, as in the Prologus to the *Confessio*: "The man is overal / His oghne cause of wel and wo" (*Confessio* Prol 546–47). Division, the calamity that threatens the kingdom and the very structure of civil society in the *Confessio* (Prol 968–1052), is replaced—or at least made concrete—by the threat of war. Gower sets out a fairly complicated position on war to a monarch whose claims to kingship rested partially on conquest and whose sovereignty by law and custom allows recourse to violence. In some measure, he seems to contradict his earlier stance about war with the Saracens.[70] His main claim, however, remains clear, especially in the chronical history of successive empires briefly rehearsed in the poem: "The fortune of the werre is evere unknowe" (290). It is a lesson that John Lydgate will make prominent in his retellings of Trojan and Theban history.

Gower never defines peace in this poem, but he gives it a structure that revises the moral and political formulation of the *Confessio*. Both the Ricardian and Lancastrian versions of the *Confessio* end with an affirmation of charity (8.3162–72, 3098–114*) as the ground of morality and politics. *In Praise of Peace* argues instead that peace is foundational. Christ's "testament" (177), says Gower, bequeaths peace "which is the foundement / of charite" (179–80); and charity in turn stabilizes peace, maintains love, and justifies laws. The cause for this change may lie in Gower's partial redefinition of authorship through

---

69. Quoted from Grady, "Lancastrian Gower," 556.
70. Livingston, "In Praise of Peace," *John Gower: The Minor Latin Works*, 127.

the poem. His purpose has shifted from the instructional objectives of the *Confessio* and the prophetic voice that suffuses all his major works, though key points remain, such as the equation of self-governance and political governance. Here Gower's aim is persuasion and practical deliberation. He is, as the poem's explicit says, an *orator,* and he addresses not just his own king but "othre princes Cristene alle" (380), including Charles VI of France, who remained on fragile terms in the early years of Henry's reign.[71] Gower may have faced the same turbulent political landscape that he experienced before with Richard, but his rhetorical objective has shifted subtly but significantly. His poem does not tutor a prince so much as argue policy and tactics for a new, if troubled, political order that, at a minimum, wants to be seen to receive counsel, if not actually follow it.[72]

Gower's French balades offer another kind of complement to his major canon. The dating of the *Traitié* and the *Cinkante Balades* is by no means certain, though the most recent scholarship argues for composition in the earlier 1390s.[73] The rubric in Fairfax 3 presents the *Traitié* as a complement to the *Confessio*:

> Puisqu'il ad dit ci devant en Englois par voie d'essample la sotie de cellui qui par amours aime par especial, dirra ore apres in François a tout le monde en general un traitié selonc les auctours pour essampler les amantz marietz, au fin q'ils la foi de lour seintes espousailes pourront par fine loialté guarder, et al honour de dieu salvement tenir.

> Since he has written just before in English by way of example of the foolishness of those who particularly love in a courtly fashion, now he will deliver a treatise in French to everyone in general according to the authors in order to exemplify married lovers, in order that they might keep the promise of their holy vows through perfect loyalty and firmly hold to the honor of God.

Much depends, of course, on whether one reads *puisque* as temporal or causal, but the construction *puisque/ore* clearly marks a sequence: then English, now French.[74] The *Traitié,* on most views, sums up the major themes of the *Confes-*

---

71. Sobecki, "*Ecce patet tensus,*" 932–46, argues that Gower's counsel is directed not to domestic governance but urging peace with France.

72. Pearsall, "Hoccleve's *Regement of Princes,*" 386.

73. Yeager, *John Gower: The French Balades,* 10 (not later than 1390 for the *Traitié*) and 53 (1391–93 for the *Cinkante Balades*).

74. Glasgow, Hunterian Museum, T.2.17 has an alternative form of the rubric, describing Gower's treatise on marriage and its aim of supporting wedding vows, which probably served as a model heading when the *Traitié* does not appear with the *Confessio* (Macaulay, *Complete*

sio.⁷⁵ It derives its doctrine and examples from *auctores,* appends Latin prose commentary, and shares its *exempla* with the narratives of the *Confessio,* ranging across classical, biblical, and medieval vernacular sources. Moreover, as in the *Confessio,* Gower signs the work as its author, in the double sense of its creator and the source to which it can be traced: "Al universitee de tout le monde / Johan Gower ceste Balade envoie" (XVIII.22–23).⁷⁶

Gower's treatment of *exempla* shared with the *Confessio* abbreviates the narratives in the interests of illustration, most often by suppressing the complications in the middle of the stories.⁷⁷ The account of Albinus's downfall (CA 1.2459–647), for example, omits the grotesque detail of turning Gormond's skull into a drinking vessel and commanding his daughter to drink from it. The story of Philomena (CA 5.5551–6047) cancels out her mutilation by Tereus and her weaving a text to communicate her sufferings to Procne. Similarly, the epic machinery of Jupiter's casks of good and evil lead to the unexpected lesson of observing the mean: "Parentre deux falt q'om se modifie" (15.13) [One has to adapt between the two]. Gower's abbreviation represents, however, more than the citational gestures of exemplary writing. The narrative digests in the balades follow directly from Gower's focus on marriage, whose primacy Genius explains in the *Confessio* as "honeste love": "Thilke love is wel at ese / Which set is upon mariage" (CA 4.1476–77). The *Traitié* advances the claim that marriage finally resolves the overpowering force of *Naturatus amor* (*Confessio* Book 1, Latin verse 1.1) and the wandering desire of love *par amors.*

The *Cinkante Balades* continues this program of extending and revising the project of Gower's major canon. The text may have developed through earlier forms. If so, it is reframed in a Lancastrian context that simultaneously marks Gower's position as an author. As in the *Traitié*, though on a far more modest scale, marginal glosses identify the subject matter of the poems. Gower again names himself and claims the role of orator, but this time in direct address as a royal subject to his monarch: "Vostre oratour et vostre

---

Works, 1:lxxxiv). Butterfield, "French Culture," 119, notes that the transition from English to French here reverses expectations so that English is the language of courtly love and French the language of married love.

75. Fisher, *John Gower,* 83, sees the *Traitié* as an addendum; and Yeager, *John Gower: The French Balades,* 156, as a coda.

76. Robert de Quixley's fifteenth-century English translation of the *Traitié* omits this authorial signature. Gower names himself in the shorter Latin poems "De lucis scrutinio" (101) and "Est amor" ("vetus annorum Gower" 26). He is identified in a marginal note in one manuscript of "De lucis scrutinio" ("Nota quod Iohannes Gower auctor huius libri") and in the initial rubrics to "Est amor" and "O deus immense."

77. Hume, "Why Did Gower Write the *Traitié*?" 266, argues, "As well as flattening out the diverse morals of the *Confessio,* the *Traitié* fails to suggest the colour or interest of the *Confessio* stories."

humble vassal, / Vostre Gower, q'est trestout soubgitz" (Dedication I.15–16). The triple use of "vostre" delineates and connects these elements under a comprehensive subordination. The work he offers Henry in these roles is a new and different service ("Vous frai service autre que je ne fis" [Dedication I.18]), combining poetic performance through the balades with the moral performance of virtue. After the Latin verses in praise of Henry V, Gower broadens his address to include Henry's court: "Por desporter vo noble Court roial / Jeo frai balade" (Dedication II.27–28). Recent scholarship suggests, however, that Gower's poetic stakes extend still further. The *Cinkante Balade* can be read in the context of poetic production generated in the early 1390s by the literary fashion of *Le Livre de Cent Balades,* the collection begun by Jean de Saint-Pierre and expanded to include contributions from the upper echelon of noble and aristocratic French poets.[78] Moreover, lyric forms and not just narrative and didactic works may have provided Gower a means to secure authorship in a framework of exchange that was at once insular and continental.[79]

As part of a minor canon, the *Cinkante Balades* allows Gower to renegotiate and reimagine aspects of his major works—in other words, to continue the work of poetic invention and authorial self-imitation. The speaker of Balade 37, for example, plays with language and imagery from the *Rose* much more closely than Amans ever does in his confession. He addresses his lady as the rose and teases out the topographical comparison of the garden and her body, both of which exclude him: "L'urtie truis, si jeo la Rose quiere" (CB 37.24) [I find the nettle, if I ask for the Rose]. As in the major works and the *Traitié,* Gower evokes classical, biblical, and medieval figures as illustrations and examples, and generally follows a model of universal history that integrates periods and cultures under a unified chronology. One interesting modification of this pattern occurs in Balade 43, in which the classical heroes represent erotic treachery, while medieval heroes from romances supposedly exemplify lovers who maintain loyalty, at least to their desire, if not always to their lords: "De Lancelot si fuissetz remembré, / Et de Tristans, com il se contenoit, / Generides, Florent, Partonopé" (43.17–19) [Let it be remembered thus about Lancelot, / And about Tristan, how he behaved himself, / Generides, Florent, Partonope]. The *Cinkante Balade* also allows rhetorical developments precluded in the narrative and penitential frame of Amans's confession. A woman speaks back in a group of poems near the end of the collection (CB 41–44 and 46) to both the male speaker and the broader tradition of French male poets.[80] She complains of betrayal and reverses gender roles in order

---

78. Yeager, "John Gower's Audience," 81–105.
79. Butterfield, *Familiar Enemy,* 234–65.
80. Barbaccia, "Woman's Response," 236.

to extol a lover's virtue and the fame it enjoys. Perhaps most important, she acknowledges the anxiety, self-consciousness, and desire that stand behind the resistance thwarting lovers like Amans. Gower's balade provides the other side of a lover's conversation that never occurs in the *Confessio*.

Gower's balades confirm the claim made in the *Traitié* and his other works for the primacy of marriage within bonds of affection and natural appetite. They go further, in one case (CB 49), to elevate marriage as the third of the great commandments after love of God and one's neighbor (Matthew 22:37–39, Luke 12:29–31), the "double love" propounded in the *Mirour* (13743). These three points map the full range of good love, and Gower claims to have given a complete definition: "De bon amour, pour prendre avisement, / Jeo vous ai dit la forme et la matiere" (CB 49.22–23) [Of proper love, for consideration, I have told you the form and the matter]. In the last poem, probably added to the original collection, Gower tropes two works from the major canon. As in the *Mirour*, the balades carry their themes forward to the Virgin "en qui gist ma creance" (CB 51.8) [in whom lies my belief]. At the same time, Gower writes to celebrate the unity and end of divisions that the *Confessio* had urged: "O gentile Engleterre, a toi j'ecrits, / Pour remembrer ta joie q'est novelle" (CB 51.25–26) [Oh gentle England, I write for you, / For remembrance of your new joy]. He leaves, however, a finely balanced ambiguity. Is Engleterre the nation or the monarch, and is the newfound joy national recovery or regal triumph?

John Gower's dual roles as moralist and public poet are basic to an understanding of his work and its place in late medieval English literary culture. Authorship adds a much-needed third term to this understanding. Gower is a revisionary poet, bidding to write himself into literary tradition.[81] His corpus of major works is paradoxically stabilized and mobile. All of them evolve in conception. The *Mirour* moves from penitential and devotional writing to estates satire to the redemptive lives of Christ and the Virgin. The *Vox* adds the dream vision of the Rising and the *Cronica Tripertita*. The three recensions of the *Confessio* stand at the beginning, not the end, of a process of resituating Gower's poem. This process is by turns authorial and scribal, for Gower's active repositioning of his works has a counterpart in the transmission and reception of the texts.[82] Against this background, Gower's later works offer an important perspective. His second cursus represents a continuing engagement with the major canon. It marks out a space of literary invention and models the response and commentary that a canonical author requires. His

---

81. For the *Vox*, see Carlson, "Rhyme Distribution Chronology," 15–55, and Carlson and Rigg, *John Gower: Poems on Contemporary Events*, 6; for the *Confessio*, Nicholson, "Gower's Revisions," 123–43, and idem, "Poet and Scribe," 130–42.

82. Echard, "Last Words," 99–126.

minor canon presents the work that speaks to power at close quarters. At the same time, it speaks to and about itself as an established literary corpus. Gower makes multiple attempts at a *recusatio* and poetic retirement, a gesture of self-cancellation that he ultimately refuses. His final position is the one revealed in the late poem "Quicquid homo scribat," extant in three versions and placed after the *Cronica Tripertita*. Across the differing states of the text, Gower makes his valediction by asserting the undiminished will to write, even in the face of limitations: "Ultra posse nichil, quamvis michi velle remansit" [I can do nothing beyond what is possible, though my will has remained].[83] In the prose commentary accompanying two versions of the poem, Gower portrays himself as the author of "varia carmina, que ad legendum necessaria sunt" [a series of poems of essential reading] who has come to the end of writing in death ("Scriboque finali carmine vado mori" in the Cotton, Harley, and Glasgow texts). The All Souls version of the poem prepares instead for another kind of writing that stands beyond the contingency of Gower's historical moment and the monument of his poetic corpus: "Scriboque mentali carmine verba Dei" [And in a poem of my imagination I write the words concerning God]. As the scene and means of writing shift, Gower positions himself finally as the scribe of the divine Author.

---

83. Yeager, *John Gower: The Minor Latin Works*, 46–47.

CHAPTER 4

Geoffrey Chaucer

Imitation and Refusal

GEOFFREY CHAUCER'S work reflects a sustained engagement with the question and problems of authorship. Early and late, in his poetry and prose, the conventions of medieval authorship serve as both an external framework for writing and an internal source for literary meaning. On most readings, Chaucer is a writer of artful ambiguity and indeterminacy who declines the title of poet and presents himself instead as an artisanal *maker*; he is a craftsman of verse whose powers of invention are ostensibly subordinated and directed to service for something else—in this case, an imagined audience or readers rather than a patron. Ambiguity and indeterminacy lie at the heart of an established critical tradition that sees in Chaucer's work a crucial meditation on the place of poetry and fiction in human understanding. He is a pattern for Sir Philip Sidney's sixteenth-century description of a poet as a writer who "nothing affirmeth, and therefore never lieth."[1] This tradition depends largely on abstracting Chaucer from his literary and cultural contexts in order to focus on his poetics as an independent system and on his writing as what Sidney calls "a good invention" or "an imaginative ground-plot of a profitable invention" free from contingency. Authorship restores a substantial measure, though not all, of Chaucer's aesthetic ambivalence to relevant historical contexts. While the status of poetry and fiction is a theoretical concern, author-

---

1. Sidney, *Defence of Poesie* [1579/1595], ed. Duncan-Jones, 235.

ship is a practical matter, for it brings Chaucer's writing into the domain of social, political, and cultural authority. It is there that ambiguity and indeterminacy are not resolved but negotiated. In this chapter, I argue that the negotiation proceeds reciprocally through imitation and refusal. Imitation is the mechanism of authorship, situating a writer in relation to tradition, established canons, and literary forebears (real, imagined, and even fictitious). Refusal is the mechanism of agency—a sphere of action and rethinking—made possible by and within imitation.

Scholars have persuasively demonstrated how Chaucer engages the formal machinery of authorship prominently in his later writing. Alastair Minnis points out that Chaucer adapts the vocabulary of the commentary tradition and exploits the rhetorical and performative capacities of being a compiler who rehearses his sources and orders the structural patterns of his work. A striking innovation occurs in the *Canterbury Tales* where Chaucer in effect compiles a work using his fictional characters as the *auctores* who provide the *materia* for arrangement.[2] Authorial conventions also stand behind the stated aims for writing that Chaucer presents as an analogue to the *causa finalis* adduced for texts by the commentary tradition—"sentence and solace" (I.306) and the Pauline dictum (Romans 15:4) that all that is written is written for our profit (VII.3441, X.1083).[3] For Rita Copeland, the Prologues of the *Legend of Good Women* are a major site for Chaucer's authorship. The Prologues function as the *accessus* to the legends that are subsequently rehearsed in Chaucer's poem, and they affirm, with varying emphases, the place of the vernacular within academic traditions of exegesis. Copeland proposes that Chaucer becomes not just a compiler but an *auctor* in the Prologues. The narrative fiction of his heresy and apostasy explains the *intentio auctoris* along the lines of commentaries on Ovid, especially on the *Heroides*. His auto-exegesis "confers full authorial status on the vernacular translator" of classical materials.[4] Stephanie Trigg's review of the authorial positions open to Chaucer draws its major example from a third text—the Retraction at the end of the *Tales* that ambiguously carries his authorial signature and evidently reverses the ethical values ascribed to his works in the Prologues to the *Legend* and the Man of Law's listing of Chaucer's Ovidian corpus.[5] We shall return to the *Legend* and the *Tales* as crucial sites for Chaucer's invention of authorship. But they reflect

---

2. Minnis, *Medieval Theory of Authorship*, 203. Gower's return to the *materia* of his earlier writings at the end of the *Confessio Amantis* offers a parallel to Chaucer's finding authority in his fictional characters.

3. Chaucer's works are quoted from *Riverside Chaucer*, ed. Benson.

4. Copeland, *Rhetoric, Hermeneutics, and Translation*, 192.

5. Trigg, *Congenial Souls*, 69.

only part of Chaucer's engagement with authorship. The engagement begins with Chaucer's earliest works, and it is in those works that Chaucer's contemporaries first recognized him as an author.

CONTEMPORARY RECEPTION

For his fourteenth-century contemporaries, Chaucer is a named writer and a writer worth naming: by mid-career, he had produced a recognized body of work with ambitious claims to literary and cultural authority, executed in distinctive modes of poetic composition and style and able to be reproduced by other writers.[6] In the mid-1380s, Thomas Usk fashions Chaucer a poet and author on the model of Boethius, and he draws on Chaucer's *Boece, House of Fame,* and *Troilus and Criseyde* to compose the *Testament of Love.* Usk echoes Chaucer's language and phrasing, and the allegorical figure of Love calls Chaucer "myne owne trewe servaunt the noble philosophical poete in Englissh."[7] Love's description is a double attribution: Chaucer parallels Troilus as a servant, hence a courtly poetic amateur, while Chaucer's poem—"a treatise that he made of my servant Troylus"—is the textual authority Usk cites for treating Boethian *materia* such as the origin of evil and divine foreknowledge. In the same period as Usk, Sir John Clanvowe borrows Chaucer's characteristic locutions and constructs his *Boke of Cupide* along the lines of Chaucer's dream visions. He invites comparison with the *Parliament of Fowls* by using Chaucer's device of narrative deferral for a debate on love and incorporating a final lyric. His topic and formal techniques show Clanvowe to be both a reader, a member of the putative Chaucer circle, and an imitator in closely aligned literary and social contexts of courtly production.[8] Both Usk's *Testament* and Clanvowe's poem were long ascribed to Chaucer, and the persistence of these misattributions is one measure of Chaucer's capacity to be imagined as an author.[9]

---

6. For Trigg, the difference between the "Geffrey" named in the *House of Fame* (729) and the "Chaucer" named in the Man of Law's Prologue (II.47) reflects the difference between a narrator operating in his own fiction and an author to whom works are ascribed (62–63).

7. Usk, *Testament of Love,* ed. Shoaf, 15–16.

8. Patterson, "Court Politics," 7–41. Staley, *Languages of Power,* 18–21, locates Clanvowe's poem in a later court context than does Patterson.

9. Gust, *Constructing Chaucer*; Carlson, "Chaucer's Boethius," 29–70. The unique textual source for Usk's *Testament* is William Thynne's edition of Chaucer's *Workes* (1532). Clanvowe's poem is preserved in Chaucer manuscripts, including the Oxford Group, and the Findern MS, which contains Chaucer excerpts and shorter poems, excerpts from Gower's *Confessio Amantis,* and Thomas Hoccleve's translation of Christine de Pisan's *L'Epitre au Dieu d'Amours*; it

At the start of the next decade, in the Ricardian recension of his *Confessio Amantis,* John Gower has Venus describe Chaucer from largely the same vantage point. Venus sends her greeting to Chaucer as "mi disciple and mi poete" (8.2942*) and identifies him as her favored youthful writer of "Ditees" and "songes glade" (8.2945*) suitable for the stylized erotics of court entertainment. Now "upon his latere age" she sets him the culminating task ("an ende of alle his werk" 8.2953*) to write "his testament of love" (8.2955*) much as Gower has completed his capstone work in the *Confessio,* his "schrifte above" (8.2956*). This final task is commissioned not in Chaucer's capacities as disciple and poet but as "myn owne clerk" (8.2954*), producing a text to be preserved as a document ("So that mi Court it mai recorde" 8.2957*).[10] Whether or not this "testament of love" refers obliquely to Usk's *Testament,* as Anne Middleton has proposed, it participates in the narrative fiction commonly applied in romance, under which a chivalric adventure is not complete until the story is recited and recorded in documentary form for a courtly archive.[11] Alternatively, Gower's Venus may be referring to an anticipated (or imagined) completion of the *Legend of Good Women.* In either case, the fiction clearly calls for Chaucer to deliver a work equivalent to the *Confessio,* for which Gower early on reveals himself as the *auctor* (gloss at 1.59).

The most prominent contemporary witness to Chaucer's authorship is a French ballade by Eustache Deschamps, dated most recently to 1391, which was conveyed by Sir Lewis Clifford with a selection of Deschamps's poems that the poet pretends to dismiss as his school-boy writings ("les euvres d'escolier").[12] Traditionally, Deschamps's poem has been read as an extended compliment to Chaucer as the English translator of the *Roman de la Rose,* a theme asserted in the refrain "Grant translateur, noble Geffroy Chaucier." Recent interpretations of the poem stress, however, Deschamps's fascination with names, including his own, and his play with puns and verbal slippage. Ardis Butterfield argues that the poem will not allow meaning to reside in a single language so that translation, of the kind that Chaucer effects in his *Romaunt of the Rose,* is a continual and reciprocal effort to establish intelligibility.[13] Critics recognize as well that there is a political edge to the literary relations that Deschamps establishes. David Wallace proposes, "The ballade might be considered a spirited act of reverse or returned colonization" in which the classical *auctores*

---

is printed in Thynne's *Workes* and in subsequent Chaucer editions by John Stow (1561) and Thomas Speght (1598 and 1602).

10. In the *Confessio Amantis,* the great clerk most often identified is Ovid; see 1.2274, 2.2297, 3.736, 5.140, 5.5570, 8.2266.

11. Middleton, "Thomas Usk's 'Perdurable Letters,'" 63–116.

12. Text in Jenkins, "Deschamps' Ballade," 268–78. I follow Butterfield, *Familiar Enemy,* 145, in rendering "les euvres d'escolir" as juvenalia, though one might see them, too, as exercises.

13. Butterfield, *Familiar Enemy,* 150–51.

associated with Chaucer at the outset of Deschamps's poem (Socrates in philosophy, Seneca in morals, Aulus Gellius in practical matters, and Ovid in poetry) are merely honorific, while the real poetic business is restricted to translating the *Rose* into English.[14]

Deschamps offers a seemingly appreciative judgment of Chaucer's formal achievement ("En bon anglès le livre translatas"), though no evidence exists to suggest that he read Middle English works. He imagines himself as only a nettle in the metaphorical garden that Chaucer has planted in England from French seeds—an inferior strain but a hardy stock and persistent reminder of an origin that cannot be fully effaced. The praise and rhetorical self-deprecation do nothing, however, to change the fact that Chaucer is belated and subordinate with respect to the *Rose* and to French literary culture. On this view, he is a subaltern who has made good on the colonial investment of literary and social capital on the margins of a cultural empire. Belatedness and subordination, Deschamps implies, constitute Chaucer's authorship. The fictive poetic orchard that Chaucer constructs as a writer depends on the plants he asks for in a chain of substitution organized by ambition: "De ceuls qui font pour eulx auctorisier" [from those who compose to acquire authority for themselves as writers]. Chaucer as "grant translateur" serves an enterprise that recognizes and appropriates his poetic agency to its own prestige and authority. Stephanie Downes suggests that by naming Chaucer Deschamps places him in the company of contemporary French poets whom he also names in his works (Guillaume de Machaut, Oton de Granson, Christine de Pizan).[15] Deschamps's final request that Chaucer write back ("de rescripre te prie") is an invitation both to participate in a tradition of vernacular authorship and to submit to the authority of its French model.[16] Critics have also taken Deschamps's refrain in a broader sense than he intended, and they argue that translation lies at the root of Chaucer's corpus.[17]

AUTHORIAL CATALOGUES

The view of Chaucer's authorship that emerges from the testimony of his contemporaries has a counterpart in Chaucer's own descriptions of his work.

---

14. Wallace, "Chaucer and Deschamps," 186.
15. Downes, "After Deschamps," 123. See also Wimsatt, *Chaucer and His French Contemporaries*, 251–54; and Calin, "Deschamps's 'Ballade to Chaucer,'" 73–83.
16. See Wimsatt, *Chaucer and His French Contemporaries*, 254–62, for discussion of what Deschamps might have sent to Chaucer and inspired by way of response.
17. Ellis, "Translation," 443–58; Machan, "Chaucer as Translator," 55–67; and Olson, "Geoffrey Chaucer," 566–88.

These accounts establish one necessary condition of authorship within medieval literary culture—the link between a named writer and a corpus of writings organized by the titles of works. They also exploit as a literary theme another necessary condition—the persuasive, evidentiary, and socially acknowledged authority of the corpus. It is between these two conditions that Chaucer invents a form of authorship that becomes a signature. Within his literary fictions, Chaucer directly claims the former, setting out a canon of works, most of them generated through forms of poetic imitation and attached to some version of his name. At the same time, his framing of these claims undermines the discursive and citational authority attached to an *auctor* or *auctoritee*. This gesture of refusal, as we shall see, constitutes an effort to cancel the directly instrumental uses of his works, as in the ambivalent references to the Wife of Bath in the Clerk's Tale and the Envoy to Bukton. The scholarship traditionally identifies three passages as containing these authorial catalogues, all from mid-career onward. They are preceded, in our usual understanding of the chronology of Chaucer's works, by another passage, which both confirms the contemporary descriptions of Chaucer's authorship and anticipates continuing features of the three major descriptions of his canon. Moreover, all these passages link poetics to hermeneutics. What Chaucer creates through imitation is presented in contexts that show how his work is to be interpreted and understood.

In Book 2 of the *House of Fame,* as the poet-narrator Geffrey (728) begins his ascent toward Fame's palace, the eagle sent by Jupiter to reward his service to Venus and Cupid describes Chaucer's writings. His account, much like Gower's a decade later, focuses on lyric composition. Chaucer has, the eagle says, selflessly dedicated himself "to make bookys, songes, dytees / In ryme or elles in cadence" (622–23). In this formulation, the "bookys" (presumably the early narrative dream visions) are continuous with the production of songs and "dytees"—works of stylized court entertainment. As later in the Prologues to the *Legend* and in *Troilus,* Chaucer's efforts are directed to Love's servants. The surface conceit, carried forward to the other works, is that Chaucer produces works for a game in which he is unable and profoundly ill-suited to participate. Still, beneath the joke lies a recognition of the singular isolation of writing. The eagle recounts what Chaucer's authorship entails: "Thou wolt make / A-nyght ful ofte thyn hed to ake / In thy studye, so thou writest" (631–33). His form of writing—"ever mo of love enditest" (634)—is not poetic creation as such but an imitation of the forms produced by courtly amateurs. Chaucer has made the polite literature of entertainment an object of writing, a *materia* as removed from his experience as that of classical authors. The cost of his writing—the "labour and devocion" (666) supposedly recompensed by Jupiter—is isolation. He produces his works in an aesthetic act removed from the dynamic, lived element of "tydinges" (644) that might connect him to "Loves folk" (645), other creatures, strangers in distant lands, and even "thy verray neyghebores / That duellen almost at thy dores" (649–50). He exchanges the account books of the Wool Custom for "another book" (657). Chaucer the reader is as immured in a textual world as is Chaucer the once-removed courtly writer.

In the Prologues to the *Legend,* the scope of authorship expands from imitating courtly compositions to presenting a full canon of translation and poetic making. Queen Alceste enumerates the titles of Chaucer's works in her defense of him against Cupid's charges of heresy and apostasy, which are based, Cupid says, on his translating the *Rose* and composing *Troilus and Criseyde*.[18] Her defense surveys an ambitious body of work in order to refute Cupid's narrow charges and his reductive literary appraisal of the writing.

> He made the book that hight the House of Fame,
> And eke the Deeth of Blaunche the Duchesse,
> And the Parlement of Foules, as I gesse,
> And al the love of Palamon and Arcite
> Of Thebes thogh the storye ys knowen lyte;
> And many an ympne for your halydayes,
> That highten balades, roundels, virelayes;
> And, for to speke of other holynesse [besynesse G 412],
> He hath in prose translate Boece,
> [And Of the Wreched Engendrynge of Manykynde,
> As man may in Pope Innocent yfynde; G 414–15]
> And maad the lyf also of Seynt Cecile.
> He made also, goon ys a gret while,
> Origenes upon the Maudeleyne.
> Hym oughte now to have the lesse peyne;
> He hath maad many a lay and many a thing.
> (F 414–30)

In the F Prologue (usually dated 1386) and the G Prologue (dated after 1394), the only substantive variation occurs in the replacement of "holynesse" by "besynesse" and the addition of a couplet on Pope Innocent III's *De misera conditionis humane*; both are indicated by square brackets in the passage quoted above. The canon ascribed to Chaucer in the poem remains strikingly

---

18. Robert R. Edwards, "Faithful Translations," 138–39. Chaucer does not identify *Troilus and Criseyde* as a translation.

uniform in its content and language. It is a body of work firmly established and evidently corrected by the addition of Innocent's treatise, which does not survive as a translation or adaptation by Chaucer.

Alceste's account divides Chaucer's writing into four parts. The supposedly offending translations of the *Rose* and the *Filostrato* are a group separated from other narratives, predominantly dream visions, that serve love, from the lyric compositions that Chaucer's contemporaries identified with him, and from philosophical and religious works translated from Latin. Her survey of the corpus is thus both a listing of titles and a taxonomy of the sort applied to the works and careers of classical *auctores* (the Vergilian *cursus* of pastoral-georgic-epic is the paradigm and Gower's colophon "Quia vnusquisque" the clearest example of adapting it to the vernacular). If we construe the passage literally, simply reading through the transparent fiction of a poetic defense located in a narrative dream vision, we find Chaucer assembling the body of his previous work and enumerating the titles in his next work. If we attend to the fiction and read the integument as an obstacle and filter, it becomes clear that Alceste's account serves a hermeneutic function; it invites us to recognize Chaucer's writing as an authorial corpus with a structure and a range of topics and modes of composition. In this respect, it responds to the eagle's description of Chaucer as a courtly poet in the *House of Fame* and suggests that he has found new matter in reading "another book" (HF 657) at night in the isolation of his house.

The Prologues, as critics emphasize, serve as *accessus* to the *Legend* and thereby confer literary authority on the work and authorship on its composer. The *intentio auctoris* is expressed in the narrator's insistence on his "entente" (F 471, G 461) as a translator, maker, and compiler, which he distinguishes from "what so myn auctour mente" (F 470, G 460). Copeland suggests that the narrative frame of Cupid's indictment and Alceste's defense underwrites authorial intent as an explanation (*causa*) of how the *Legend* came to be written.[19] The *materia* at the root of Cupid's indictment is the literary discourse of women's virtue, which is the "matere" of the legends that follow—"wommen trewe in lvyng al hire lyve" (F 438, G 428) and "goode wymmen, maydenes and wyves, / That weren trewe in lvyng al hire lyves / And . . . false men that hem bytraien" (F 484–86, G 476–78). At the end of the F Prologue, Cupid prescribes his *modus agendi*: "Suffiseth me thou make in this manere: / That thou reherce of al hir lyf the grete, / After thise olde auctours lysten for to trete" (F 573–75). Chaucer is thus enjoined to adapt the techniques of abbreviation ("Sey shortly" F 577) within a practice of imitating textual authorities.

---

19. Copeland, *Rhetoric, Hermeneutics and Translation*, 187–90.

Throughout the Prologues, the *causa finalis* or *utilitas* of Chaucer's writing, though Cupid initially disputes it, has been "to forthren trouthe in love and yt cheryce, / And to ben war fro falsnesse and fro vice / By swich ensample" (F 472–74, G 462–64).

Besides adapting the framework and techniques of exegesis, Chaucer exploits the imaginative possibilities of authorship within the commentary and pedagogical traditions. Cupid is a notoriously mistaken interpreter. If he read Chaucer's translation of the *Rose* in Fragment A of the *Romaunt of the Rose,* he mistook Guillaume de Lorris's courtly fantasy of desire for Jean de Meun's reduction of desire to appetite; at a minimum, he admits what he seeks to deny, for the tenor of his complaints about Chaucer's translating the *Rose* "in pleyn text" (F 328, G 254) is that the text exposes the inherent folly of love. He reads *Troilus and Criseyde* as an attack on the fidelity of women, while Chaucer's source, Boccaccio's *Filostrato,* offers an explicit, if disingenuous, means of understanding Criseida. The Proemio written by Boccaccio's narrator-poet as an introduction explains that passages portraying the beauty, habits, and praiseworthy traits of Criseida refer to Filomena, the fictional dedicatee and recipient of the work; their purpose is to spark desire in her.[20] Troilus's sorrow, the narrator's laments, and Criseida's are the only allegorical components; the rest, he says, is simply an old story. In a passage in the G Prologue, the longest specimen of Chaucerian revision, Cupid amplifies his point about women's virtue by appealing to cultural memory and the textual record: "Was there no good matere in thy mynde, / Ne in alle thy bokes ne coudest thow nat fynde / Som story of wemen that were goode and trewe?" (G 270–72). The narrator-poet's library ("sixty bokes of olde and newe / . . . alle ful of storyes grete" [G 273–74]), he says, preserves the textual record, the archive of virtuous women transmitted by Greek and Roman writers. Moreover, there is full poetic and interpretive agreement on women's virtue across the entire domain of writing: "Ek al the world of autours maystow here, / Cristene and hethene, trete of swich matere" (G 308–9).

Cupid's energetic misreading of the *Rose* and *Troilus* is paralleled by Alceste's partial explanations of Chaucer's intent. She portrays him as a poetic maker who, by turns, does not understand his "matere," writes according to the commission of a powerful patron, or repents "outrely of this" (F 368). The G Prologue adds the further observation that he is a prolific and heretofore reliable author: "For he hath write many a bok er this. / He ne hath not don so grevously amys / To translate that olde clerkes wryte" (G 348–50). When the

---

20. Boccaccio, *Il Filostrato,* ed. Branca, 2:8: "quante volte le bellezze e costumi, e qualunque altra cosa laudevole in donna, di Criseida scritta troverete, tante di voi esser parlato potrete intendere."

narrator subsequently undertakes his own defense, dissociating his "entente" from what the authors of the source texts meant, he makes the conventional case that his works advance virtue and dissuade vice. Alceste cancels his apologia, however, by completing the rhyme of the narrator's "my menynge" with her regal instruction, "Lat be thyn arguynge" (F 474–75, G 464–65). Alceste's silencing is a practical device to complete the framing fiction by which Chaucer will subsequently compose legends of good women and unfaithful men as penance for his translations. It does not resolve the debate over authorial intent. What the forced closure reveals instead is that Chaucer's authorship resides within an essentially contested hermeneutic.

The hermeneutic frame is a defining feature of the introduction to the Man of Law's Tale, which portrays Chaucer as an Ovidian poet and the Man of Law as an enthusiastic, if sometimes careless, reader of his works. The Man of Law's initial complaint extends Cupid's indictment in the *Legend* to the impact of Chaucer's corpus, and it resituates the rhetorical tropes of the Prologues. Chaucer remains, as Alceste earlier suggested, a comically inept writer, though in technical execution rather than thematic understanding of his material: "He kan but lewedly / On metres and on rymyng craftily" (II.47–48). His writing has monopolized composition so that "no thrifty tale" (II.46) has not been already told by him "of olde tyme" (II.50). He thus assumes a reverse image of the poetic maker in the *Legend* who gleans what he can in the field of invention after the courtly "lovers that kan make of sentement" (F Prol 69) have finished their poetic harvest. Chaucer's current standing as a narrative monopolist is widely recognized, "as knoweth many a man" (II.50). His corpus has the totalizing effect on narrative that Cupid earlier asserts for "al the world of autours": "And if he have noght seyd hem, leve brother, / In o book, he hath seyd hem in another: (II.51–52). In this ironic portrait, Chaucer not only overgoes Ovid's *Heroides* in stories about lovers; he also seems to foreclose authorial invention and imitation altogether.

The catalogue recounted by the Man of Law connects the Ceyx and Alcyone story from the *Book of the Duchess* with the *Legend*. The *Legend*, he says, is a "large volume" (II.60), hence a work commanding authority, and it bears a title: "the Seintes Legende of Cupide" (II.61). The contents he describes are notoriously disparate from the nine tales transmitted in extant manuscripts of the *Legend*, and the tales that overlap differ in several prominent details. Whatever the accuracy of his account, the Man of Law insists that an element of pathos suffuses the legends. For the most part, he associates stark visual images (e.g., the wounds of Lucrece and Thisbe, Aeneas's sword for Dido, the tree from which Phyllis hangs herself) with the stories as mnemonic devices. In his account, pathos marks an authorial decorum. The Man of Law's observation that Chaucer would not write "swiche unkynde abhomynacions" (II.88) as the Canacee or Apollonius stories delineates Chaucer from Gower, perhaps even as a moral poet. In context, the refusal encompasses both Chaucer as an author and the Man of Law as a narrator: "I wol noon reherce, if that I may" (II.89). The catalogue shows at the end a multilevel, self-ironic staging of belatedness. Chaucer's character, forestalled by Chaucer's output, can only follow him as an author and offer inferior goods: "I come after hym with hawebake" (II.95). The tale he tells from the paltry remains available to him is the Tale of Custance, which Gower offers as an example of Envy (*Confessio Amantis* 2.587–1598), the unacknowledged motive of authorial emulation.

Chaucer's Retraction contains the final catalogue of his works and a self-presentation that takes Chaucer seriously as the author responsible for a literary corpus. The status of the Retraction within the narrative frame of the *Canterbury Tales* and the textual tradition of the *Tales* is a topic of critical and scholarly debate.[21] The rubric linking the Retraction to the Parson's Tale—"Herre taketh the makere of this book his leve"—signals an authorial exposition, even if the subsequent reference to "this litel tretys" (X.1081), a phrase shared with the Tale of Melibee (VII.957, 965), creates ambiguity: is the "tretys" the Parson's Tale or the *Tales* as a whole? Chaucer clearly draws formally and thematically on the tradition of the writer's retraction derived by Augustine and ecclesiastical writers from late classical models.[22] The retraction served the primary aims of correcting, reviewing, and cataloguing an author's work—in other words, getting it right with respect to both doctrine and a corpus. The immediate context of the Parson's Tale may give Chaucer's Retraction a penitential cast closer to the modern sense of withdrawing or disavowing earlier work. As in the Prologues to the *Legend,* Chaucer separates reception from authorial "entente" (X.1082).[23] Pleasure in the *Tales,* he says, owes to Christ and displeasure to the "defaute of myn unkonnynge" (X.1082). The *intentio auctoris* ("my wyl") aligns with the Pauline principle (Romans 15:4) used earlier by the Nun's Priest (VII.3441–42), who expands its application from scripture to all discourse: "Al that is writen is writen for oure doctrine" (X.1083). The machin-

---

21. Earlier views on Chaucer's authorship of the Retraction, the relation of the Parson's Tale and Retraction to the *Canterbury Tales,* and the speaker implied by the text (Chaucer or the Parson) are summarized in Benson, *Riverside Chaucer,* 965; Cooper, *Canterbury Tales,* 410–12; and Obermeier, *History and Anatomy of Auctorial Self-Criticism,* 210–20. Partridge, "'The Makere of this Boke,'" 106–53, reviews the manuscript evidence in light of these debates, the presence that Chaucer seeks to establish in his self-referential gestures, and the textual culture of late medieval France and England.

22. McGerr, "Retraction and Memory," 97–113. The analogues to Chaucer's Retraction are richly illustrated in Obermeier, "Chaucer's Retraction," 2:775–808.

23. Fumo, "God of Love," 157–75.

ery that Chaucer puts in place to introduce his catalogue is at once authoritative in its genre and subtly contested by its context and earlier use in the *Tales*.

Chaucer's catalogue follows convention by dividing his corpus into works of "worldly vanitees" and those of philosophical and doctrinal value.[24] The taxonomy used in the Prologues to the *Legend* lies behind the structure and enumeration of the Retraction. Thus, "my translacions and enditynges of worldly vanitees" (X.1085), the expanded list of courtly works (including the *Legend* and the lost "book of the Leoun" possibly redacted from Machaut or Jean Froissart), and an unnamed portion of the *Canterbury Tales* ("thilke that sownen into synne" X.1086) correspond broadly to the translations of the *Rose* (not listed specifically) and the *Filostrato* and to the dream narratives enumerated by Alceste. The lyric compositions written for Cupid in the *Legend* become "many a song and many a lecherous lay" (X.1089), poems originally serving the observance of Love's "halydayes" (F 422) now acknowledged for their error and disavowed. The *Boece* and what Alceste earlier calls "other holynesse" (F 424; "besynesse" G 412) is the part of the corpus that stands after Chaucer's moral and spiritual appraisal. He foregrounds the translation of Boethius and "othere bookes of legendes of seintes, and omelies, and moralitee, and devocioun" (X.1088). In the Retraction, Chaucer compiles and orders not his sources but his own works in a revised *ordinatio* that combines the role of author with that of penitent. The proxy voice of Alceste from courtly culture seemingly gives way to that of the Parson. What later and especially modern readers take as Chaucer's greatest achievements are works of imitation, and his final gesture, however we interpret it, is to refuse those works in favor of didactic and religious writing.

AUCTOURS AND AUCTORITEE

As the catalogues suggest, Chaucer positions himself within and against the institution of authorship throughout his career. In the *Book of the Duchess,* the book of "romaunce" (48) commanded by the narrator-dreamer is a compilation of fables written by clerks and "other poetes" (54); it is thus the product of *auctores*, though he does not name them as such. *Auctor* and *auctoritee* enter his poetic lexicon with the *House of Fame* and *Parliament of Fowls*. These two works clearly register his encounter with the literary and cultural power of classicism and vernacular writing in Trecento Italy. The terms assume a special prominence in works of his middle and later career. *Auctor* and *auctoritee*

---

24. Obermeier, "Chaucer's Retraction," 2:782–802.

retain their lexical value from medieval literary culture. An *auctor* is a source or point of origin and a named writer with a body of work that is doctrinally correct and deserving of respect and credence. *Auctoritee* refers narrowly to a passage of text that supplies support in an argument and more broadly to a work that conveys doctrine or an author with correct views.[25] Chaucer employs these standard lexical meanings and develops a rich semantic usage for the terms. God is the primary *auctor* in the *Boece* (1.p6.88 and 3.m6.11), while Christ is "the auctour of matrimoyne" in the Parson's Tale (X.882). In the imagined pagan world of *Troilus*, Jupiter is the deity addressed as "auctour of nature" (3.1016); but in the Boethian *Canticus Troili*, God "auctour is of kynde" (3.1765).[26] *Auctour* designates a source or point of origin for institutions and cultural forms. In the *Boece* (3.p510), it places God as the legitimating source for political power in earthly realms. It identifies the courtly lady of the balade "Womanly Noblesse" as a source for social conduct, the "Auctour of norture" (27) for lovers as subjects.

Chaucer uses *auctour* to name Macrobius in his translation of the *Rose* (Rom 7, reproducing Guillaume de Lorris's error in supposing that Macrobius wrote the *Somnium Scipionis*), Petrarch in the Clerk's Tale (IV.1141), and probably Cicero or Valerius Maximus in the Nun's Priest's Tale (VII.2984). *Auctour* is used for direct citation, as in references to Vergil (1139, 1228) and Ovid (1352) in Dido's story from the *Legend*. Moreover, citation becomes a literary effect. Chaucer exploits the rhetorical gesture of citation to posit a settled understanding based on textual authorities that are not present or may not be even in substantial agreement. The revision he works into the trope of knowledge through texts in the G Prologue to the *Legend* foregrounds an understanding of stories through "the naked text in English" (G 86) conveyed by "autours": "leveth hem if yow leste" (G 88), he proposes. As we have seen in the narrator's apologia for his translations later in the *Legend*, the original authors of the *Rose* and *Filostrato* reduce to "myn auctour" (F 470, G 460), and the debate on women's virtue has a single resolution to be found in "al the world of autours" (G 308). The same device of citing an authorial consensus appears, too, in the old woman's speech on gentility, poverty, and age in the Wife of Bath's Tale (III.1212) and in the Nun's Priest's displacement of misogyny onto authors and Chauntecleer: "Rede auctours, where they trete of swich mateere" (VII.3263).

Auctour serves, then, to assert a source for discourse that stands apart from the lexical definition of a known writer who deserves credence; it func-

---

25. *MED*, s.v. "auctor" and "auctorite."
26. Chaucer's source for the *Canticus Troili*, Boethius's *Consolation of Philosophy*, 2.m8, does not name a deity.

tions, additionally and provocatively, as a source that appeals to belief by citation alone. In the *Boece*, Lady Philosophy explains the double peril of fame in the public life of governance and moral virtue that Boethius has chosen. Writers, she warns, omit and forget virtuous men, and then perish themselves: "The whiche writynges long and dirk eelde doth awey, bothe hem and ek hir auctours" (2.p7.92). In the Manciple's Tale, the juridical sense of *auctor* as a source that bears responsibility for what is said is complicated when the Manciple paradoxically does what his source (in this instance, his mother) warns against: "Be noon auctour newe / Of tidynges" (IX.359–60). Earlier, in the *House of Fame*, the narrator famously claims authorial responsibility to recount Dido's complaint as it appears in his dream: "Non other auctour alegge I" (314). We shall examine below the fullest elaboration of *auctour* as a named writer, origin, citation, and source for discourse in Chaucer's creation of Lollius, the fictitious source for *Troilus and Criseyde*.

Chaucer's use of *Auctoritee* parallels that of *auctour* in several respects. *Auctoritee* refers to specific authors such as Plato in the *Boece* (1.p4.40), Solomon in the Merchant's Tale (IV.2276), and Publilius Syrus, the writer of maxims, in the Tale of Melibee (VII.1470), a work constructed of authors. Moreover, it is used to create the effect of citation, evoking writers of cultural and probative standing without actually naming them. In his dispute with Pertolete over dreams in the Nun's Priest's Tale (VII.2975), Chauntecleer counters her appeal to Cato: "Men may in olde bookes rede / Of many a man moore of auctorite / Than evere Caton was" (VII.2974–76). The Friar urges the Wife of Bath to abandon such "auctoritees" (III.1276) in their exchange after she has used them so effectively in her prologue and tale. Justinus regards January's views on marriage in the Merchant's Tale as so patently wrong that "He wolde noon auctoritee allegge" (IV.1658) to refute them. *Auctoritee* as an established principle underwritten by textual tradition and social consensus sets up the rhetorical comparisons with proof and experience that appear in the Prologues to the *Legend*, the tale of Phyllis in the *Legend* (2394), the opening of Theseus's First Mover speech in the Knight's Tale (I.3000), the Wife of Bath's famous exordium in her Prologue (III.1), and the old woman's speech in the Wife's tale (III.1208). In all these instances, the radically singular knowledge of particulars is placed in relation to the universals attested in an authoritative textual tradition.

In the Melibee, Prudence cites Cicero on the efficacy of the "auctoritee of persons" (VII.1165), by which she means models of moral virtue suitable for imitation by a ruler. The dominant use of *auctoritee* is associated, however, with power, prestige, status, and prerogative. In the *Boece*, *auctoritee* refers to the power of God (4.p1.49) and the "imperial auctorite" (1.p1.80) of Lady

Philosophy. Boethius uses it to describe the power of his political office and administration (1.4.62–63 with gloss). The Parson's teaching on the sin of pride identifies "contumacie" as opposition against "everich auctoritee or power" (X.402) that exercises rightful sovereignty. Drawing on canon law, he denies civil status ("auctoritee" [X.931]) to a wife offering legal testimony without the leave of her husband. The Pardoner, by contrast, asserts the power of a forged authority for his bulls (VI.387); and Almachius, the pagan magistrate judging Cecilia in the Second Nun's Tale, wrongly asserts "bothe power and auctoritee" (VIII.487) over the life and death of his subjects.

The political claims of power to confer legitimacy and proper standing, which these examples evoke, shade into personal prerogative, which other narratives disclose and critique as acts of willful indulgence. Old January foolishly chooses his wife "of his owene auctoritee" (IV.1597), and Prudence counsels Melibee against vengeance taken "as of youre propre auctoritee" (VII.1385). Calkas, who turns the arts of divination to private ends in *Troilus and Criseyde* is "a lord of gret auctorite" (1.65) at the start of the poem. The thematic balance to misguided prerogative appears in the kinds of agency that also operate as *auctoritee*. The cuckoo who joins with others of the lower orders to interrupt the "cursede pletynge" (495) of the aristocratic birds in *The Parliament of Fowls* acts, he says, "of myn owene autorite, / For comune spede" (506–7). The "man of gret auctorite" (2158) who appears in the noise and chaos of the Wicker House at the end of the *House of Fame* ostensibly brings order, but his entrance may equally be designed to show the impossibility of authoritative statements in an imagined world where truth and falsehood are compounded and tidings are indistinguishable from true statements. The point in this poem, early in Chaucer's engagement with the institutional power of language and writing and going forward throughout his work, is that authorship operates as a social force; that force becomes visible in discursive and narrative contexts as authority; and authority simultaneously asserts and belies its own power.

AUTHORSHIP AND VERNACULAR IMITATION

Chaucer begins his public career as an author through successive acts of imitation and resistance, the latter often in the form of replacing authority. It is likely that his earliest writings are shorter poems in the lyric *formes fixes*, as in the French poems intriguingly attributed to "Ch" in an anthology composed of works from Machaut, Deschamps, Froissart, Nicole de Margival, Jean de le Mote, Oton de Granson, and anonymous poets.[27] Granson is the one French poet whom Chaucer names ("Graunson, flour of hem that make in Fraunce" [82]) in "The Complaint of Venus," which adapts three of Granson's balades.[28] The adaptation of Granson, variously dated from the mid-1380s to early 1390s, is a reminder that Chaucer's engagement with French poetry continues throughout his career. These connections support a project that Helen Cooper identifies as "a cosmopolitan production" that chooses an English vernacular medium for French and later Italian models.[29] In the dream visions that comprise Chaucer's early narrative poems, the cosmopolitan features show, too, in his initially anchoring the poem in a redaction of a classical text. These treatments of the *auctores* may have stood independently at some point as exercises in imitation; their function in the dream visions is to establish a theme whose meaning is subsequently resituated within courtly forms of understanding. If Chaucer gains standing as an author by strategies of translation and rewriting, he renegotiates the authority of literary production within a vernacular language and context of reception.

In the standard chronology of Chaucer's works, the *Book of the Duchess* is his inaugural narrative. The poem has an important social context in its commemoration of the death of Blanche of Lancaster; its focus on the grieving Man in Black offers homage to John of Gaunt and implicitly acknowledges Gaunt's patronage and sponsorship. Equally important, there is a public and literary dimension in Chaucer's visible imitation of prevailing courtly writers. The opening self-portrait of a melancholic narrator-poet adapts the first lines of Froissart's *Paradis d'amour*, a poem written for Queen Philippa in the early 1360s. The exchange with the Man in Black has a model, too, in Froissart's *Dit dou bleu chevalier* (1364), a poem also conscious of its place in Froissart's canon.[30] Chaucer's borrowings from Machaut give him *materia* to rework—Ovid's tale of Ceyx and Alcyone as redacted in the *Dit de la Fonteinne amoureuse* (composed for Jean, duc de Berry, John of Gaunt's hostage at the Savoy), the narrative conceit of overhearing the knight's complaint from the *Jugement dou Roy de Navarre*, and the themes elaborated in the knight's complaint from the *Remede de Fortune*. Foregrounding Froissart and then turning to Machaut is a complex authorial gesture made before a sophisticated Anglo-French audience.[31] It reflects the compositional practice of compilation using vernacular,

---

27. Wimsatt, *Chaucer and the Poems of "Ch."*
28. Two witnesses have a rubric that identifies Chaucer as a translator (Benson, *Riverside Chaucer*, 1187).
29. Cooper, "Chaucer's Poetics," 33.
30. Pickens, "History and Narration," 119.
31. Wimsatt, *Chaucer and His French Contemporaries*, 209, proposes that Froissart "showed Chaucer what Machaut had to offer."

courtly materials rather than biblical or classical authors. It is an unveiling of Machaut as the author who stands behind Froissart as a model of literary discourse and an author who curates his corpus of works. At the same time, it is a figure for Chaucer's succession of Froissart as a court writer after Froissart's return to Hainault, following Philippa's death in 1369. Chaucer fills the literary space left open for a court poet to translate and partially reshape French poetic conventions and cultural presence.

The *Book of the Duchess* matches the performative gestures of court authorship with internal poetic emblems and a logic of replacement. The "romaunce" brought to the narrator to displace his melancholy is a compilation shaped by authorial intent. Its material is the lives of kings and queens, read through the interpretive frame of a Golden Age, "while men loved the lawe of kinde" (56). Ovid's tale of conjugal love and devotion is located within courtly conventions in Chaucer's immediate sources and subsequently made a standard of natural devotion in his hermeneutic revision of the Ceyx and Alcyone story.[32] Moreover, the reanimation of Ceyx's body is explicitly an act of imitation. Juno specifies, "Do the body speke ryght soo, / Ryght as hyt was wonded to doo / The whiles that hit was alyve" (149–51). The seemingly revived Ceyx stands as a figure for poetic creation and for Chaucer's reanimating the story itself. Another emblem appears in the narrator's awakening into his own dream, which he claims is beyond biblical or classical interpretation. He falls asleep on and effectively into his book, waking up in a room whose walls are covered with scenes from the Troy story and the *Roman de la Rose*. This composite sequence of illustrations brings together the foundational narratives of the courtly sphere, for Troy gives an origin and defining pattern to chivalry, while the *Rose* serves as a compendium of erotic play and conduct. Through the carefully marked sections of the poem, which correspond to Chaucer's *forma tractatus*, we can see authorship emerge in a pattern of substitutions. The redacted Ovidian story in the book of romance is overwritten by the Man in Black's narrative; that narrative, reaching an artificial end rather than a resolution, is overwritten in turn by the narrator's story of composing the poem that memorializes it. The classical story that elicits authorial pity and compassion from "I, that made this book" (96) is thereby balanced structurally by returning to a starting point for imitation, as the narrator awakens holding the book of romance and resolves "to put this sweven in ryme" (1332).

Vernacular imitation, as the *Book of the Duchess* suggests, is a twin negotiation between classical sources and vernacular redactions on the one hand and within vernacular traditions on the other. Chaucer's practice as a compiler and translator is to rewrite his literary sources through poetic invention, yet

---

32. Robert R. Edwards, *Dream of Chaucer*, 74–82.

the works he produces repeatedly deny the authority derived from imitating those sources. This authority, as I have argued, lies in the social and cultural contexts of literary production and reception; it is based in the institutional uses of writing to establish dominant understandings of works. In the *House of Fame*, a poem rightly identified as an *ars poetica*, these issues inform and connect Chaucer's revisions of Vergil and Ovid, his encounter with the canon of *auctores*, and the courtly milieu that Chaucer finally envisions for the poem.

Chaucer opens his poem by returning to the interpretation of dreams, which stand as symbols for poetic texts. In the *Book of the Duchess*, the narrator claims that his dream of the Man in Black is "so ynly swete . . . / So wonderful" (276–77) that it exceeds the capacity of Joseph or Macrobius to explain it. In the *House of Fame*, he begins with the hermeneutic categories of Macrobius's dream lore, rehearsing the taxonomy of true and false dreams, expanding their number from five to six, and asserting their indeterminacy. The problem of deciding the significance of dreams, he says, is a matter of locating causes that cannot be identified—"But why the cause is, noght wot I" (52). Chaucer's rehearsal of Macrobius's dreamlore deprives it of explanatory power. It appropriates the most influential dream authority from Late Antiquity to relocate the significance of dreams (and by extension, literary works) to the realm of effects, not causes—that is, to the contingency of hermeneutics rather than the determinate intent of poetics.

In the first part of the dream, the glass temple containing Vergil's *Aeneid* is the site for both authorial imitation and the refusal occasioned by hermeneutics. Venus presides over the temple and so directs the theme of Vergil's poem from empire to erotics and shifts the gender of its protagonist from male to female. The narrator finds the opening lines a fixed text "writen on a table of bras" (143) and translated into English. The sequence of visual images that he then describes recounts the events of the *Aeneid*, focusing principally on the episode of Aeneas and Dido in Book 4. Chaucer rewrites Vergil's poem through Ovid's authorship and his own. In a sense, Ovid's authorship is already his own—a counter-classical sensibility that makes visible the underlying tensions within representation.[33] In Dido's fictitious letter of complaint to Aeneas, *Heroides* 7 recasts the heroic determinism of Aeneas's historical mission as elegiac betrayal and loss. But even before he cites Ovid, Chaucer absorbs his revisionary approach. The narrator repudiates Aeneas as a "traytour" (267) simulating a faithful lover: "What harm doth apparence, / Whan hit is fals in existence!" (265–66). The doubleness he describes recurs in the faithless male lovers of the *Legend*; it opens up a critique of the power of imi-

---

33. Johnson, "Problem of the Counter-Classical Sensibility," 123–51.

tation, reversing earlier examples such as the reanimation of Ceyx's corpse in the *Book of the Duchess,* where appearance and being happen to coincide. At the end of the episode, he returns to a roster of faithless lovers drawn from the *Heroides* but contextualized, in the case of Demophon and Theseus, by the narratives that the *Legend* later describes. Between these points, the narrator cites Vergil and Ovid as sources for Dido's death and final speech: "Rede Virgile in Eneydos / Or the Epistle of Ovyde" (378–89). More important, he asserts his own authorship for Dido's extended reflection on unfaithful lovers (300–60). The radical claim is that his dream alone stands as the source for quoting Dido's lament: "Noon other auctour alegge I" (314). Vergil and Ovid record what Dido says later in the *Aeneid.* Asserting his own authorship as the source responsible for words, he imitates his fictional character as an Ovidian alternative, a woman whose "name" (346) loses the capacity to limit the meanings attached to it and lies open to the inventive and distorting power of fame, as happens, too, with Criseyde. If Chaucer sympathizes with Dido in her Ovidian guise, as he does here and in the *Legend,* he nonetheless participates in the continuing publication of her downfall.

The contested nature of authorship and authority is a topic of scrutiny throughout the poem's description of the "hous and site" (1114) of Fame. Poets and clerks are the conservators of fame, yet the reputation they supposedly secure for illustrious men and women remains contingent and vulnerable to change in Chaucer's poem. The names engraved in the rock of ice supporting Fame's palace melt away or remain distinct depending on their chance placement in the sun or shade. Minstrels, performers, and heralds create a soundscape of noise. Fortune capriciously bestows fame through Clere Laude and Sklaundre, even to those who do not wish it. The most stable element is the canon of authors placed on pillars who represent Jewish history, Thebes and the youth of Achilles (the *Statius maior* and *Statius minor* for medieval readers), the Troy story in its classical and medieval versions, Vergil, Ovid, Lucan and other "clerkes / That writen of Romes myghty werkes" (1503–4), Claudian, and "hem that writen olde gestes" (1515). Of these, Claudian is mentioned for his mythographic epic and not his court and political poems, and Ovid is "Venus clerk" (1487), the poet of elegies. The other works enumerated are public poems, focused on epic heroism and historical deeds.

Chaucer emphasizes that the authors "bear up" the fame of their topics. They not only memorialize but fix and sustain the cultural understanding of the *materia*—what we know and accept about "Jewes gestes" (1434), Thebes, Troy, "Pius Eneas" (1485), Caesar, and Pompey. The fracture of canonical authority occurs, fittingly enough, in the central narrative. The Troy story is collective and competitive. Homer, Dares and Dictys, the fictional Lollius,

Guido delle Colonne, and Geoffrey of Monmouth bear up the fame of Troy.[34] The Trojan authors differ, however, in their means of composition (*forma tractandi*) and their allegiances. Homer's poetic invention and his favoring the Greeks stand against the chronicle history derived from Dares and Dictys and carried forward to Guido. By adding Lollius to the chronicle tradition, Chaucer suggests that he recognizes it not as an alternative to Homer's poetic lies but as a fiction of authorship, a pattern of citation based on counterfeit authors. John Lydgate, as we shall see, will exploit this fiction to create a simulation of Chaucerian authorship.

The fractures within classical authority that become visible among the writers of the Troy story are vastly amplified in the Wicker House that serves as the final "hous and site" of the poem. The "Domus Dedaly" (1920) is a frenetic place of "tydinges" and circulation. The substance of rumor, like its sources, is secondary to its value in exchange. If the narrator sees "fals and soth compouned" (2108) in a single tiding that escapes the whirling cage, the final scene of the poem is the comic piling up of men bearing love tidings. These men, as the narrator realizes, possess no certain knowledge; their purpose is to augment rumor. They are the symbolic representatives of courtiers, whose driving motive is to be part of the circulation.[35] It is this imperative that introduces the enigmatic "man of gret auctorite" (2158) whose entrance ends the poem. His arrival immediately poses the question of how a man of authority might distinguish the truth and falsehood compounded in tidings inside a structure where language itself is the source of continual invention and transformation. With that question comes a second: how might such a distinction operate as it returns to the social world of the court, where interpretation and exchange stand over the referential power of signs?

The *Parliament of Fowls* opens with a scene of reading that prepares for imitation. Old books, the narrator asserts, yield "al this newe science that men lere" (25). As in the *Book of the Duchess* and the *House of Fame*, the poem proceeds through a redacted classical text into a second scene with recognizably literary features, thence to its central narrative focus. The anchor text for the *Parliament* is the *Somnium Scipionis,* the concluding portion of Cicero's *De re publica* and the only substantial portion of Cicero's work known to medieval writers. The *Somnium* circulated in Late Antiquity and the Middle Ages with Macrobius's Neoplatonic commentary. It stands as a paradigmatic text that elicits interpretation and formal commentary and thereby claims authorship.

---

34. Cooper, "Four Last Things," 39–66.
35. Cartlidge, "Narrative and Gossip," 224–26, proposes that "tydinges" as gossip designates not a form of discourse with truth claims but a particular social relationship among familiars and intimates.

Chaucer provides an *accessus* to the *Somnium,* identifying the title, author, and *ordinatio* of the work, "Chapitres sevene" (32), which seem to correspond more to topics than a formal division into chapters or the six books of Cicero's work. The utility of the *Somnium* resides in the ethical principle of "commune profyt, wel ithewed" (47) [endowed with virtues] and in the metaphysical order that links personal morality and political duty to the disposition and workings of the universe. Common profit emerges as the dominant theme of Chaucer's epitome of Cicero, as it does in Gower, but modern commentators emphasize the discontinuities between Cicero's theories and medieval theology, particularly on the question of the soul's salvation.[36]

Africanus, like the eagle of the *House of Fame,* presents the dreamer's vision in the next section as compensation for service, in this case for reading "myn olde bok totorn" (110). The visionary experience moves through landscapes signifying the preeminent authors of the vernacular tradition—Dante's gates of Hell (*Inferno* 3), the garden of the *Rose,* and the temple of Venus from Boccaccio's *Teseida* (7.50–66). The gate gives a contradictory message of welcome to "grace" (129) and "good aventure" (131) as well as a warning—"Th'eschewing is only the remedye" (140). The message perfectly expresses the ambiguity attached to Ovidian elegy in the commentary tradition. Africanus emphasizes that he offers *materia* for composition: "If thow haddest connynge for t'endite, / I shal the shewe mater of to wryte" (167–68). The materials are the set-piece description of the *locus amoenus,* the *ekphrasis* of Venus's temple that recurs in the Knight's Tale, and Nature's gathering of birds on Saint Valentine's day. In each of them, the subordination of love and desire to providential designs and common profit proves illusory. The power of Cicero's formulation to regulate an understanding of love and desire falls short in all these locales, perhaps most notably in Nature's parliament, where the cuckoo bids to act on his own authority for "common spede" (507) to move the choosing of mates along.

"OLDE STORIES":
AUTHORSHIP AND WRITING ANTIQUITY

In the dream visions, classical texts serve as the initial sources for Chaucer to imitate thematically in the narrative action that becomes the eventual focus of his poem. Thus Ceyx and Alcyone is a model for the themes of loss and enduring affection, Dido's story forecasts the workings of rumor within chi-

---

36. Discussion in Robert R. Edwards, *Dream of Chaucer,* 130–37.

valric and courtly culture, and Scipio's dream provides a rationale for desire within a providential divine order. These early poems differ from works that appear in the middle of Chaucer's career, which register the influence of Trecento writers, for whom classical authors and texts are sources of appropriation and use. What Chaucer learns from Dante, Petrarch, and Boccaccio is not simply that antiquity is an instructive thematic parallel but that the classical past can be engaged as an imagined domain in itself, different from medieval modernity, with specific historical pressures and moral coherence.[37] At a minimum, antiquity offers lessons in ethics and wisdom through the figure of the virtuous pagan. But Chaucer goes further, though the details of his vision of antiquity have been variously characterized as humanist, scholastic, or something else altogether. A. C. Spearing proposes that Chaucer "attempted with remarkable success to re-imagine a classical pagan culture in its own terms—a culture interesting for its difference from his own, and yet imaginable as part of a universal human culture, in which pagan and Christian are one."[38] Minnis argues for a historically constrained representation of the pagan past that shows "how they thought and behaved in their historical time and place" as those were construed within medieval culture. Chaucer, says Minnis, "applied the authentic finish, as it were the period veneer, to artifacts which were to a large extent of his own making."[39] John V. Fleming finds in *Troilus and Criseyde* a "deep classicism," by which he means the effort "to imagine and to reconstruct a spiritually foreign ancient culture" in its literary, social, and religious features ("hire olde usage" [1.150]).[40] Whatever the suppositions, to construct such an imagined domain through imitation and invention and to see its limits as well as its achievements critically is to become an *auctor*. For Chaucer, the writer who best represents this ambition is Boccaccio, who promotes himself as the missing Italian epic poet that Dante identifies in *De vulgari eloquentia* and who imagines antiquity not just as a collection of narratives but a form of living.[41] Boccaccio's *Teseida* and *Filostrato* are the texts that Chaucer uses for his own inscription as a vernacular classical author. The *Filocolo*, which he used chiefly if not exclusively through the sequence of "Ques-

---

37. Minnis, *Chaucer and Pagan Antiquity*, 7–30.
38. Spearing, *Medieval to Renaissance*, 86.
39. Minnis, *Chaucer and Pagan Antiquity*, 6, 22, 25.
40. Fleming, *Classical Imitation and Interpretation*, xiii.
41. Dante leaves open the position of an Italian poet writing on epic materials in *De vulgari eloquentia* 2.2: "Arma vero nullum latium adhuc invenio poetasse." For Boccaccio's amplified claim to this position, see Robert R. Edwards, *Chaucer and Boccaccio*, 21–23. McGregor, *Image of Antiquity*, argues that Boccaccio wants to reimagine classical antiquity in its most capacious cultural terms.

tioni d'amore," provides an intriguing model for the transition from pagan antiquity to early Christianity.[42]

The unfinished experiment *Anelida and Arcite* illustrates the difference between the thematic use of classical narratives as overtures in the dream visions and the authorial project of writing antiquity. Chaucer puts in place the machinery for imitating a classical work at the start of *Anelida*.[43] He adapts Boccaccio's invocation to Mars (*Teseida* 1.3.1–2) and announces an epic argument that serves, too, as the *intentio auctoris*: "in Englyssh to endyte / This olde storie, in Latyn which I fynde / Of quene Anelida and fals Arcite" (9–11). His intent of preserving a "noble storie" (13) from the consuming effects of time produces what Lee Patterson calls a "disordered mnemonics"—"a form of consciousness that remembers everything yet understands nothing" as it repeats the past.[44] This repetition occurs, moreover, in a space of invention claimed by Chaucer as a writer in a Statian tradition of literary succession. The epigram introducing his narrative is taken from Statius's *Thebaid* (12.519–20) and shared with the Knight's Tale. It celebrates Theseus's triumphal entry into Athens with his Amazon captives and marks the place in Statius's poem where Creon's tyrannical rule in Thebes begins after the deaths of Eteocles and Polynices, the defeat of the Argives, Jocasta's suicide, and Oedipus's banishment. Chaucer inscribes himself in this space as a belated author: "First folowe I Stace, and after him Corinne" (21). He opens his story with a translation of the Statian epigram to portray a scene of triumph in Theseus's entrance into Athens but turns quickly to the aftermath of the Theban war, expressed in the imagery of Thebes's desolation and barrenness. Statius, as in the *House of Fame*, bears up the fame of Thebes and sets the narrative in a city ruled by a tyrant who monopolizes power by gathering the aristocracy within Thebes and effectively transforming a political network of alliances into a court, a forced association of "frendes" (68) shaped by Creon's political will.

In the coerced sociability of Creon's Thebes, Anelida's singular devotion and "stidfastnesse" (81) fall victim to Arcite's "doubleness" and his "newfanglenesse" (141). Doubleness is the defining feature of Theban history, while faithlessness is the moral and social correlate. Anelida's complaint after Arcite's betrayal is generally regarded as a lyric response to the epic narrative frame. Chaucer specifies that the complaint is a written text: "Of her owne hond she gan hit write" (211). Feminine complaint is given a formalized, closed structure

---

42. Wallace, *Chaucer and the Early Writings of Boccaccio*, 39–60.
43. A. S. G. Edwards, "Unity and Authenticity of *Anelida and Arcite*," 177–88, argues for reading the two parts of the poem as separate works.
44. Patterson, *Chaucer and the Subject of History*, 65.

by a chiasmic arrangement of stanzas. Here Chaucer presumably follows the female Theban poet Corinna and so enacts his double model of authorship—male and female, epic and elegiac. As he follows Corinna, Anelida follows an Ovidian model. Beyond the dramatic situation of addressing an absent lover through a written text, the poem incorporates reminiscences of the *Heroides*, most notably the figure of the dying white swan (Ovid's "albus olor" [*Heroides* 7.4]) that begins Dido's letter to Aeneas but closes Anelida's stanza of conclusion, just as it will end Dido's complaint in the *Legend of Good Women* (1355–57). In *Anelida*, Chaucer rewrites Thebes so that the recursive appetite for power in Statius is transposed to the obsessive demand of erotic novelty and change. If Statius's poem shows the damage and sterility of naked power ("nuda potestas" [*Thebaid* 1.150]), *Anelida* registers the cost of erotic circulation in a city that holds its subjects captive under tyranny, immured within the walls and soon to be besieged outside them.

The Knight's Tale, whether it is "the love of Palamon and Arcite / Of Thebes" mentioned in the *Legend* (F Prol 417–18) or a later version elaborated for the *Canterbury Tales*, shares the same inventional space as *Anelida* and offers a closely worked revision of Boccaccio's *Teseida*. The *Teseida* incorporates the tradition of the *roman antique* to create a vernacular analogue to classical epic.[45] Boccaccio follows the disposition of classical epic into twelve books, adds his own glosses to the poem, and enacts the roles of *autore*, poet, and lover.[46] Structurally, the epic material surrounds both a narrative of desire and an imagined world of social performance and stylized display; this world functions in the feasts and play that Arcita laments losing as he dies at the end of the poem and then repudiates in his soul's ascent after death (a scene that does not carry over to the Knight's Tale). Chaucer's revisions generally emphasize the symmetry and balance of scenes and clarify the Boethian grounding of the poem.[47] They also add the pressure of history in ways that complicate and resist the certainties of narrative closure, which are represented by the joyful wedding night of Emilia and Palemone. Patterson has argued that a historical understanding of Chaucer's poem involves not a formal and thematic conflict between order and chaos but the contradictions within a chivalric idea of order, where chivalry constitutes a particular form of consciousness read back into an imagined classical framework.[48] The actions and social practices described within that framework bear the impress of radical contingency.

---

45. Anderson, *Before the Knight's Tale*; Barbara Nolan, *Chaucer and the Tradition of the Roman Antique*.

46. Barbara Nolan, *Chaucer and the Tradition of the Roman Antique*, 160–63.

47. Robert R. Edwards, *Chaucer and Boccaccio*, 31–43.

48. Patterson, *Chaucer and the Subject of History*, 168. Patterson's critique of the dominant reading of the poem, which derives from Muscatine, *Chaucer and the French Tradition*, 181,

Chaucer imitates Boccaccio and Boccaccio's authorship by intensifying the pressures that bear on agents and their actions in the poem. Theseus's triumphal entry into Athens carries the evidence of his earlier doubleness and newfangleness as a lover in the emblem of the Minotaur on his banner, which is also an index of his betrayal of Ariadne. The Theban princes pulled out of the heap of corpses after the battle with Creon are political, dynastic, chivalric, and erotic doubles. Their extraction by the "pilours" (I.1007) scavenging on the battlefield and their immediate legibility to Theseus's heralds who read their chivalric devices form a clever conceit for the poet's work of reinscription. Displaced from the wreckage of Theban chivalry and violence, they are translated to a new story, where rivalry is expressed—in a reversal of *Anelida* and Ovid's *Heroides*—by the stasis of male complaint, first in Palamon's speech bewailing Fortune and then in Arcite's bleak rejoinder that love overrides all positive law and custom. The tower holding the two prisoners, whom Theseus gives no hope of ransom, is the counterpart to Creon's tyrannical closed city, and it presents royal will as political prudence. The judicial duel devised and subsequently modified by Theseus convokes all the chivalric world, whose violence and ceremonies operate under Theseus's governance. The duel is settled, however, by the unforeseen chance and remote causes that governance seeks to control and drive from consciousness as a possibility. Theseus's consolatory speech, like the ceremonies of heroic fellowship and sociability that he oversees even as Arcite is dying, shows the limits of Chaucer's imagined antiquity and its ways of living. At one level, the forces of Amazonian and Theban violence have been brought under the rational control of Athenian power in the mandated marriage of Emily and Palamon. At another, Theseus is shown not to resolve contradictions—to "make of sorwes two / O parfit joye, lastynge everemo" (I.3071–72)—but to impose arrangements and assert closure.

Troilus and Criseyde represents Chaucer's most ambitious imitation of a classical genre and his most inventive solution to the problem of securing authorship. Both issues present a surface of apparent agreement complicated by deep-lying uncertainty. Chaucer calls his poem a "tragedye" (5.1786). In most commentary, tragedy is associated with a character's fall from prosperity to catastrophe.[49] The philosophical and thematic rationale for the definition is given in the gloss that Chaucer adapts from Nicholas Trevet and adds to Lady Philosophy's remarks on the "unwar strook [that] overturneth the realmes of greet nobleye": "Tragedye is to seyn a dite of a prosperite for a tyme, that endeth in wrecchidnesse" (*Boece* 2.pr2.70–72). The Monk seems to repeat the definition in the headlink to his tale: tragedy is a "certeyn storye," preserved

---

ascribes a formal resolution where Muscatine proposes a continuing dialectic.
49. Summary in Windeatt, *Troilus and Criseyde*, 154–61.

for our recollection in written texts "of hym that stood in greet prosperitee, / And is yfallen out of heigh degree / Into myserie, and endeth wretchedly" (VII.1973, 1975–77). Patterson observes, however, that in the passage from the *Consolation of Philosophy* Lady Philosophy is ventriloquizing Fortune, who appeals to emotion and imagination rather than reason.[50] In both passages, the genus of tragedy is narrative ("a dite" [Trevet: "carmen"] or "certeyn storie"), which Patterson equates with classical epic or the *carmen heroicum*. On this view, the tragedy of Troilus is not a simple turn from good to bad Fortune but a heroic narrative that ends in catastrophe. Similarly, "myn auctour called Lollius" (1.394) seems to warrant a Troy story as the writer whose name is attached to a literary source; he thus situates the poem as deriving from respectable authority and operating within a recognized literary genealogy. Chaucer creates instead a fiction of authorship that proves useful to both his own aims and to those of his successors.

One distinguishing feature of Chaucer's portrayal of antiquity is his insistence on the difference between his poem and the epic framework it seems to evoke and imitate. As soon as he introduces his material and sets his narrative in motion with Calkas's defection to the Greeks, the narrator-poet turns sharply from the subject of Troy's destruction: "But the Troian gestes, as they felle, / In Omer, or in Dares, or in Dite, / Whoso that kan may rede hem as they write" (1.145–47). When Pandarus first enters Criseyde's household in Book 2, he encounters a scene of reading directly relevant to Troy's destiny— "the geste / Of the siege of Thebes" (2.83–84)—and spectacularly misconstrues the topic ("Is it of love?" [2.97]), though he quickly trumps the description of the vernacular version in the *Roman de Thèbes* given by the women by alluding to the presumably authoritative Latin version in Statius's *Thebaid*. At the end of the poem, as Troilus approaches his death, the narrator comments that Troilus's deeds of epic fury against the Greeks can be read "in thise olde bookes" (5.1753), but he separates his writing from this epic context: "And if I hadde ytaken for to write / The armes of this ilke worthi man, / Than wolde ich of his batailles endite" (5.1765–67). The phrasing—"The armes of this ilke worthi man"—enticingly parallels his earlier translation of Vergil's epic proposition for Aeneas's story: "I wol now synge, yif I kan, / The armes and also the man" (HF 143–44). Yet Chaucer insists that his *materia* lies off to the side of heroic action: "His worthi dedes, whoso list hem heere, / Rede Dares, he can telle hem alle ifeere" (5.1770–71).

Troilus and Criseyde, then, is presented as a classical poem that shifts its topic from epic to eros. Chaucer's *recusatio* has literary precedent from Cal-

---

50. Patterson, "Genre and Source," 211.

limachus onward, but the most influential proximate source is Ovid's *Amores* (1.1, 2.1, and 3.1), which defers epic material for an erotic theme and substitutes the elegiac couplet for hexameter as its formal medium. The refusal of epic material allows Chaucer to focus on what transpires specifically within the frame of epic in a besieged city whose fate has already been determined by two rapes—the ravishing of Hesione from Lamedon's Troy and then Paris's carrying off of Helen to Priam's Troy. The poem addresses an imagined, external audience ("Ye lovers, that bathen in gladnesse" [1.22]) that is presumably identical with the social world inside the fictional Troy. In one sense, the poem's love theme is a complement to the epic frame, adding romance material and reminders of its origins in Boccaccio's adaptation of the vernacular *cantare*. In another, eros occasions the unwriting of epic, for the world of classical heroism that Chaucer and his contemporaries knew from the chronicle tradition of Troy is strikingly vulnerable to desire, as is seen most prominently in the deaths of Hector and Achilles, who seek objects that cannot answer their love (the spoils of armor and the Trojan princess Polyxena, respectively). In *Troilus and Criseyde*, Chaucer invents Ovidian elegy within a framework of epic and chronicle history. Ovidian erotics may constitute a realm of subversive play or an implicit moralism, as Fleming insists.[51] In either case, it casts Troy as a city constituted by affect and emotional bonds. Troilus first appears in a male affinity of warriors at the feast of the Palladium. Pandarus offers his service to Troilus as a friend and balances that role against his familial bond with Criseyde. Criseyde's household is first shown as a gathering of women linked to each other as readers, and women come to her as friends (4.681) after the exchange for Antenor is decided. Pandarus describes Troy as a city governed by friendship to Criseyde ("Swych love of frendes regneth al this town" [2.379]) and as a city full of eligible ladies to Troilus (4.401). The internal space of the city is a network of sites charged with affect and desire: temples, domestic settings such as Deiphebus's house, and the places associated with Criseyde that Troilus visits as he navigates the city in her absence.

Chaucer's creation of Lollius is the enabling fiction for both an eroticized Troy story and the claims of authorship. Lollius is commonly explained as a misreading or textual corruption of two lines from Horace (*Epistles* 1.2.1–2), which address his friend Publius Lollius Maximus. Chaucer identifies Lollius earlier, however, in the *House of Fame* (1468), where he is listed with Homer, Dares, Dictys, Guido delle Colonne, and Geoffrey of Monmouth as an author in the tradition of the Troy story. In a limited sense, Lollius is a

---

51. Fleming, *Classical Imitation and Interpretation*, 62–63.

screen that obscures Boccaccio as the source for Chaucer's poem; in a larger view, he serves to position Chaucer's poem in relation to authority. Winthrop Wetherbee sees him as an emblem of incomplete or ambiguous versions of the classical material.[52] Fleming regards him as a pseudoantique authority who is "already a part of the tradition in which he worked" and who thereby opens the possibility of redirecting Boccaccio's aims in the *Filostrato* toward a moral purpose such as Horace states in his original assessment of Homer.[53] The narrator-poet of *Troilus* names Lollius twice as his author. In both cases, his confident citation belies his misrepresentation. In the first, he claims to translate "naught only the sentence, / As writ myn auctour Lollius" (1.393–94) but also "every word" (1.397). The text he renders as the "Canticus Troili" is Petrarch's sonnet 132, "S'amor non è," which he mistranslates at several points and expands to three rhyme royal stanzas.[54] In the second case, Troilus finds the brooch he gave to Criseyde as a token on her departure to the Greek camp, "as telleth Lollius" (5.1653). The reference to Lollius is Chaucer's addition, and it marks the point at which Troilus realizes that "his lady nas no lenger on to triste" (5.1666).

Between these two points, Chaucer's references to "myn auctour" are in every instance an addition to Boccaccio. The narrator-poet excuses himself for his failings in ways that anticipate his defense in the Prologues to the *Legend*: "For as myn auctour seyde, so sey I" (2.18). He ostensibly follows his author at the beginning of Book 1 (2.49) and in Criseyde's reasoning about Troilus as a potential lover (2.700). Later, he asserts, "Nought list myn auctour fully to declare / What that she thought" (3.575–76) when Pandarus falsely assures Criseyde that Troilus is out of town. References to "myn auctour" (3.1196, 1325) bracket the consummation scene at the end of Book 3 (3.1817). The final citation serves only to diminish Lollius as the source for the story ascribed to him: "How longe it was bytwene / That she forsok hym for this Diomede, / Ther is non auctour telleth it, I wene" (5.1086–88). In the gestures that evoke him throughout the poem, Lollius serves to assert an authorial presence that Chaucer has to efface in the end as pagan antiquity's way of living proves untenable.

This ambivalence pervades the classical stories recounted in the *Legend*. Cupid in the G Prologue asserts that "al the world of autours" (308) agrees systematically on the virtue of women. The *forma tractandi* that expresses this agreement in the *Legend* is Ovidian epistolary elegy transposed into exemplary narrative. In the single letters of the *Heroides*, Ovid attributes authorship

---

52. Wetherbee, *Chaucer and the Poets*, 25.
53. Fleming, *Classical Imitation and Interpretation*, 192.
54. Benson, *Riverside Chaucer*, 1028.

to women and thus opens up the possibility and means for a radical rewriting of antiquity, focused on the position of women subjects and offering a critique of male heroism and its discursive forms.[55] Chaucer exploits this possibility formally by providing incipits and explicits to mark the individual legends that presumably carry out the dual commission by Cupid and Alceste in the Prologues; he compiles the narratives in a thematic legendary (what the Man of Law calls "the Seintes Legende of Cupide" [II.61]) and completes the narrative with a complaint. In this last step, he has followed the sequence and *forma tractatus* but reversed the emphases of *Anelida*. Chaucer turns to the *Heroides* as a source for the stories of Phyllis and Hypermnestra, Dido, Ariadne, and Hypsipyle. In addition, he applies his structure to the stories of Thisbe, Ariadne, Hypsipyle, Philomela, and perhaps Medea from the *Metamorphoses*; Lucrece from the *Fasti*; Cleopatra from Vincent of Beauvais; and Medea and possibly Hypsipyle from Guido delle Colonne.[56]

In the structure that Chaucer devises for the legends, the narrator-poet visibly performs the role of an author. In the legend of Cleopatra, he abbreviates a description of her wedding to Antony and the celebrations: "Forthy to th'effect thanne wol I skyppe, / And al the remenaunt, I wol lete it slippe" (622–23). He also adds a description of the naval battle. Neither event is found in Vincent's entry for Antony and Cleopatra in the *Speculum Historiale* (6.53). Chaucer recasts Cleopatra as Antony's faithful wife, not the woman whose advances are spurned by Augustus after Antony's death, and he has her commission a shrine for Antony's body above the serpents' pit where she dies. Her complaint represents Cleopatra as a faithful wife who maintains her "covenaunt" with Antony (683, 693). The narrator-poet asserts, "This is storyal soth, it is no fable" (702). In Pyramus and Thisbe, he cites Ovid as his source— "Naso seyth thus" (725)—but follows the same pattern by adding and expanding, particularly in amplifying Thisbe's pathos, and redirecting the focus of the tale to Pyramus: "Of trewe men I funde but fewe mo / In alle my bokes, save this Piramus" (917–18).

As in the *House of Fame*, Dido's story provides an occasion for significant authorial revision. The narrator-poet invokes "Virgil Mantoan" (924) as the "lanterne" (926) he follows. He thus answers the question that Cato poses to Dante and Vergil as they emerge from Hell—who was your guide and your lantern? (*Purgatorio* 1.43). The answer to Cato's question, for Dante's medieval and Early Modern readers, was that divine illumination or reason guided their ascent. Chaucer applies the figure to a classical author and stresses following

---

55. Hagedorn, *Abandoned Women*, 21–46.
56. Minnis, *Shorter Poems*, 348–49.

rather than guidance. But his gesture of deference to Vergil is immediately an appropriation: "In thyn Eneyde and Naso wol I take / The tenor, and the grete effectes make" (928–29). The authority of Dido's story is double (epic and elegiac), and doubleness serves as *materia* for invention. Authorial intention here—"the grete effectes make"—is consistent with the authority claimed over Dido's words of complaint in the *House of Fame*: "Non other auctour alegge I" (314). The epic project of the *Aeneid* thus gives way because "it acordeth nat to my matere" (955). Instead, "of hym and of Dido / Shal be my tale" (956–57).

Chaucer's imitation of the story entails, then, a partial erasure of Vergil, a cancellation that leaves him visible. "I coude folwe, word for word, Virgile, / But it wolde lasten al to longe while" (1002–3), the narrator-poet says of Aeneas's encounter with Venus. Aeneas's invisibility as he views Dido's Carthage hovers between the implausible ("I can nat seyn if that it be possible" [1020]) and the ambiguously affirmed: "Thus seyth the bok, withouten any les" (1022). Later, "oure autour telleth us" (1139) of Cupid's substitution for Ascanius, but the narrator demurs, "as of that scripture, / Be as be may, I take of it no cure" (1144–45). The "effect" of Chaucer's invention, "the fruyt of al, / Whi I have told this story, and telle shal" (1160–61), is Dido's erotic obsession; and the moralizing that ensues after the mutual betrothal in the cave frames Aeneas's behavior as a false courtliness, equivalent to Arcite's "doubleness" and "newfangleness" in *Anelida* and to the consuming appetite that will be ascribed to Jason later in the *Legend*. The details Chaucer subsequently adds to the episode, including the pregnancy that Dido claims, move the story toward its Ovidian counterpart. Chaucer shifts "myn auctour" (1352) from Vergil to Ovid and quotes the opening of *Heroides* 7, as Dido begins her complaint. His final citation affirms the primacy of his reconception of the materials: "But who wol al this letter have in mynde, / Rede Ovyde, and in hym he shal it fynde" (1366–67). In Ovid, the rest of Dido's letter moves between Aeneas's betrayal of her love and the political issues of war, conquest, statecraft, and empire that affect both Aeneas and Dido: the erotic, in its consequences, is the political. In Chaucer's version, desire and politics remain subordinated to the stasis of exemplary complaint.

The overlay of authorities, as Dido's legend demonstrates, creates the space of invention for a belated and resistant author. In the legend of Hypsipyle, Chaucer turns to Guido delle Colonne and the chronicle tradition of Troy and supplements Guido's authority with mention of the *Argonautica* of Valerius Flaccus; but the central action, as Jason and Hercules arrive at Lemnos, is "nat rehersed of Guido, / Yit seyth Ovyde in his Epistels so" (1464–65). The elegiac challenge to epic is staged again at the end as Chaucer rehearses part of Hypsipyle's complaint from *Heroides* 6. Between those citations, however, he inserts the theme of mediated desire, as Hercules's praise of Jason inspires Hypsipyle's love, while Hercules and Jason are men bound to each other in their "shrewed lees" (1545) of deceiving Hypsipyle. In the companion tale of Medea, Guido's heroic narrative is turned against itself. Jason's obsessive desire is likened to matter endlessly desiring form. In his *Historia*, Guido uses the simile to describe the cultural consensus on female desire: "Scimus enim mulieris animum semper virum appetere, sicut appetit materia semper formam" [For we know that the soul of woman always desires man, just as matter always desires form].[57] Shifting the comparison to Jason, Chaucer recasts Jason's boundless appetite "to don with gentil women his delyt" (1587) as feminine desire, a helpless demand. The shift has its full effect at the end when Chaucer translates a portion of Medea's letter (*Heroides* 12) that laments the attraction of Jason's appearance and beguiling manners, the characteristic features of the feminine subject, which have appeared earlier in the Dido legend. Beneath her complaint there also lies an alternative history that might have shaped antiquity otherwise. Had Jason perished in his quest for the Golden Fleece, Medea asserts, "Ful mikel untrouthe" (1677) would have perished with him; so, too, would the remote but determining causes of the Trojan War, which begin with Jason's voyage to Colchis.

The stabilizing claims of classical authority show their fractures elsewhere in Chaucer's imitations in the *Legend*. The story of Lucrece ostensibly claims a double source in Livy and Ovid and a sympathetic reader of Lucrece's wifehood and steadfastness in Augustine. But Livy plays no role, and Augustine roundly condemns Lucretia's suicide.[58] In addition, the political dimension supposedly suppressed in favor of extolling Lucrece's truth and fidelity returns obliquely in the display of her body as a rallying point for patriarchal revolt against the Tarquins and for the narrator-poet's moralizing denunciation of men's betrayal of women as "tirannye" (1883). In other legends, Chaucer signals his rewriting of antiquity by manipulating the "remenaunt" (623, 2383) of his Ovidian sources. He abbreviates Ariadne's complaint but supplements Ovid with further mythographic detail. In the Philomela and Procne story, the ending is suppressed to remove the sisters' vengeance and to focus on Tereus's infamy. Phyllis's letter to Demophon, which tracks betrayal over generations from Theseus to his son, is offered in a running, excerpted translation. The intimate life of antiquity, gendered feminine, is rendered visible but insistently partial and potential, waiting to be described fully.

---

57. Guido delle Colonne, *Historia Destructionis Troiae*, ed. Griffin, 17.
58. Augustine, *De civitate Dei* [1.19], ed. Dombart and Kalb.

In following the Ovidian critique of epic heroism, Chaucer also marks the limits of elegy at the boundary of affect and identification. The narrator-poet turns away from writing Dido's complaint to her sister because he has "So gret a route" (1345). Tereus's "foule storye" (2239) is a painful, textual venom for readers and writers. In Phyllis's story, he is "agroted herebyforn / To wryte of hem that ben in love forsworn" (2454–55). His final position within the imaginative and affective world of elegy depends on the self-legitimating agency of authorship: "Trusteth, as in love no man but me" (2561). The claim is not to trust him in loving but to trust him in writing about love. His role is to imitate Ovidian elegy but to transpose it as well, to make it exemplary and emblematic: "Men may ensaumple se" (2560).

"I SPEKE HIR WORDES PROPRELY": THE *CANTERBURY TALES*

At the end of the pilgrims' portraits in the General Prologue to the *Canterbury Tales*, Chaucer lays claim to radically different kinds of authorship and imitation from those in his earlier works. He speaks in a voice that runs through the *Tales* but emerges intermittently: a first-person "I" who narrates a perspectival account of an imaginary event in which he was both witness and participant yet speaks directly as an author. What is remarkable about this formulation is the invention of its object. Chaucer's persona is not a device for authenticating a fiction narrated through retrospect and recollection. The object is to imitate speakers in the transmission of their literary (and didactic) works. As Alistair Minnis points out, Chaucer takes his fictional characters as *auctores* whose works are gathered in a literary compilation. At issue, then, is style broadly understood as a distinguishing habit of expression that allows us to reach judgments about characters and what they say. Chaucer's formulation here is not a dramatic frame, though it complements the exchanges between characters in prologues and linking passages and across tales. Rather, it reflects theories of imitation developed in classical antiquity, in which choosing an ethical persona to imitate as a model of conduct is tied to choosing topics and a characteristic style of expression.

Chaucer introduces this formulation in the General Prologue as he resets and specifies his literary decorum after the occupational descriptions of the pilgrims. He aims to "pleynly speke in this mateere" (I.727), conveying words and behavior; and he asserts a consensus on his *modus tractandi* ("this ye knowen al so wel as I" [I.730]):

Whoso shal telle a tale after a man,
He moot reherce as ny as evere he kan
Everich a word, if it be in his charge,
Al speke he never so rudeliche and large,
Or ellis he moot telle his tale untrewe,
Or feyne thyng, or fynde wordes newe.
(I.731–36)

Commentary on this passage stresses the principle, made explicit a few lines later and ascribed to Plato (probably through Boethius's *Consolation of Philosophy*), that "the wordes moote be cosyn to the dede" (I.742). Minnis points out the influence of academic prologues in enumerating the components that go into an author's modes of discourse and treatment.[59] Less apparent but equally important is the kind of authorship that Chaucer envisions for himself and his characters. The key feature is expressed in the resonant phrase "telle a tale after a man." The primary meaning is to rehearse a story which has a previous author and so to become part of a narrative succession, to come after a previous speaker or writer. The rehearsal is necessarily a revision, but it is controlled theoretically by an imitation of the characteristic discursive style of the author, which incorporates intent. Both senses of "after a man"—succession and faithful imitation—establish the juridical dimension of authorship. To "telle a tale after a man" is to identify who is responsible for discourse and for what it represents. It is speaking their words "proprely" (I.729)—that is, in a way pertaining to someone individually, characteristically, strictly, accurately, and suitably.[60] Chaucer thus moves from authorship as a question of literary sources, as in the contested narratives of antiquity, to authorship as a judicial and moral burden for imaginative works. This burden he displaces from his immediate composition to its sources in his literary fiction.

The rest of the passage focuses on faithfully reproducing discourse that has its source and liability elsewhere. The close approximation to language—rehearsing "as ny as evere he kan / Everich a word"—warrants a good faith effort by the belated author. The qualification "if it be in his charge," within his power, sets a relative rather than absolute standard.[61] This standard allows transgressive and undisciplined language to be reproduced: "Al speke he never so rudeliche and large." The alternative to reproducing such language, when it appears, is the only condition under which Chaucer risks liability as an author.

---

59. Minnis, *Medieval Theory of Authorship*, 167.
60. *MED*, s.v. "propreli(e)" 1–5.
61. *MED*, s.v. "charge" 11a, cites this passage in the sense "to be in (one's) power."

Responsibility shifts to him should he represent an "untrewe" tale or fabricate the material ("feyne thyng") or invent "wordes newe" that do not correspond to the source. The concern arises again in the Prologue to the Miller's Tale, where the Miller "tolde his cherles tale in his manere" (I.3169). Authorship absolves the narrator-poet as it indicts the Miller and other fictional *auctores*: "I moot reherce / Hir tales alle, be they bettre or werse, / Or elles falsen som of my mateere" (I.3173–75). In this instance, the moral tenor is clear, and Chaucer speaks directly as an author: "The Millere is a cherl; ye knowe wel this" (I.3182). The dramatic link to the Melibee allows some slippage between "sentence" and "the same wordes . . . / As ye han herd" (VII.959–60), but the problem of decorum and telling "proprely a thyng" (IX.209) returns with more complexity in the Manciple's malicious pleasure in reporting "knavyssh speche" (IX.205) in the tale of Apollo and the crow.

The Wife of Bath's Prologue and Tale are remarkable inventions made possible by Chaucer's displacement of authorship to his characters. For most scholars, the Wife was the speaker originally intended for the Shipman's Tale, and so the cash nexus of the tale reflects her occupation and the economic agency it confers. Chaucer's revised plan is commonly explained as his discovery of the resources of his character. The Wife's Prologue has no link or dramatic context but begins with her voice as the defining frame: "Experience, though noon auctoritee / Were in this world, is right ynogh for me / To speke of wo that is in mariage" (III.1–3). In this signature passage, the Wife does not equate experience and authority. The syntax makes it clear that experience is seen as an adequate ground for sorrow in marriage, even if there were no authority to invoke; but there is, as she will demonstrate, authority in abundance to confirm experience. With her assertion of experience, the Wife claims a juridical sense of authorship as the source for speech that can be traced back to the one responsible for generating it. As her Prologue unfolds, she acts as both a commentator and compiler of textual authorities. More important, she fulfills the role of *auctor* by subordinating the authorities she quotes to her own line of argument and exposition. The heavy glossing in the Ellesmere manuscript from the opening of the Prologue to the point where the Pardoner interrupts (I.1–183) shows that Chaucer's scribal readers recognized her references and furnished citations.[62]

The Wife is a figure who drives debate about gender, identity, agency, and material conditions, but these issues arise from her control over authorities and her engagement with Latin and vernacular textual sources. Ovid's elegiac poetry offers a prefiguration for the Wife in the *vetula* who serves as a

---

62. Hanna and Lawler, "Wife of Bath's Prologue," 2:351–55.

go-between and sexual schemer. La Vieille from the *Roman de la Rose* is the proximate model for the Wife's capacity to embody and reverse antifeminist doctrine and themes. The authoritative sources that she resituates are Walter Map's *Dissuasio Valerii ad Rufinum*, the "Liber Aureolus" attributed to Theophrastus, and St. Jerome's *Adversus Jovinianum*. These are, on close inspection, a clerical satire circulating as a classical text, a work known only by citation and incorporation in Jerome's text, and a satirical polemic on marriage. The authorities that the Wife compiles are themselves works grounded as much in rhetorical contexts as doctrine. Meanwhile, as Minnis points out, the Wife holds an uncertain position within the Church, which granted women status as teachers, and she exercises an authority that both absorbs and restructures traditional rationales for her speaking.[63]

Authorship for the Wife implies the power to decide what accepted, foundational texts such as the Bible and particularly the Bible as filtered through Jerome mean in the domain of social relations and institutions.[64] Her initial efforts in the Prologue are to challenge and direct the language of textual interpretation to her own aims. Not by chance do the males who intervene in her "tale" represent the authorized forces of ecclesiastical, hence social order, whatever their moral failings. The Pardoner finds her "a noble prechour in this case" (III.165), but she repulses his effort to take over discussion by threatening to use authorized speech against him: "I shal telle ensamples mo than ten" (III.179). Even her apparent concession after his capitulation—"I speke after my fantasye" (III.190) and "myn entente nys but for to pleye" (III.192)—demonstrate her capacity to direct the mechanisms of interpretation and control to her ends. The Friar's complaint, "This is a long preamble of a tale" (III.831), results in his granting her "licence" (III.855) to continue her tale, which begins with an Arthurian setting imagined before its disenchantment and colonization by friars. Yet even after the tale's resolution, he insists that the Wife "lete auctoritees, on Goddes name, / To prechyng and to scoles of clergye" (III.1276–77).

The Wife is emphatically the author of her own narrative and the exemplary force of narrative. Her account of three old husbands features her striking adaptation of the Jealous Husband's imagined speech from the *Rose*, which redirects the original complaint against women in his imagined voice into a lesson for "wise wyves" (III.225) to exercise governance in their marriages. The climactic episode with Jankyn begins with his preaching and her resistance to the application of his examples: "I wolde nat of hym corrected be"

---

63. Minnis, *Fallible Authors*.
64. Miller, *Philosophical Chaucer*, 192, argues that Chaucer explores the myth of the subject and where the power of the myth comes from.

(III.661). His composite book of wicked wives, containing Map, Theophrastus, and Jerome and supplemented by other standard authors in the antifeminist dossier of authorities, is perhaps Chaucer's fullest expression of a literary text as cultural authority. It also marks a form of authorship that she cannot appropriate or repurpose to her intents but instead aligns with male authority through Jankyn.[65] She can damage the book by tearing out three pages, yet she cannot fully unbind it. What she does in her Tale is to supersede Jankyn's book. She provides a counter-narrative of beneficent female governance that parallels the accord she negotiates when Jankyn concedes sovereignty in marriage to her.

In her Tale, the Wife removes the dynastic concerns of Gower's Tale of Florent and its penitential framework in the *Confessio Amantis,* where it is an example extolling obedience over the sin of pride. As important as the story of the redeemed knight, worthy of redemption only because of his ceding mastery to his wife, is the interpretive weight that the Wife adds to the old woman's rebuttal of the knight's rejection of her for low birth, poverty, and age. Dante's *Convivio* anchors her argument about "gentillesse." The virtue of poverty, she says, is upheld by "Senec and othere clerkes" (III.1184). For age, "auctours shal I fynden, as I gesse" (III.1212)—on the face of it, an assertion of confidence rather than uncertainty. If the Wife is a figure who allows possibilities of imagining subjectivity and historical change, she negotiates those possibilities through a sophisticated practice of authorship.

The redirection of discourse that underlies the Wife's authorship is foregrounded in the Pardoner's performance and self-impersonation. The Host's call for the Pardoner to "telle us som myrthe or japes" (VI.319) immediately uncovers the anxiety that the Pardoner evokes and that remains his defining feature as a literary character. Within the frame of the pilgrimage, the "gentils" fear "ribaudye" (VI.321) and demand "som moral thyng, that we may leere / Som wit" (VI.325–26). The Pardoner, of course, gives them both, though obliquely: his tale is a jape (a story of cunning and deceit) and a device to deceive them as well as a moral example that uses wit to plot reversals in the action. Formally, he employs the resources of sermon techniques to state his biblical theme from 1 Timothy 6:10 ("Radix malorum est Cupiditas") and to make structural divisions in the "tavern sins" of gluttony, gaming, and swearing. The exemplary tale of the three rioters seeking Death shows its wit precisely in their finding the literal meaning of the allegorical personification they pursue. The sermon structure reappears in the sins enumerated in the Pardoner's apostrophe after their death to point the moral that signals the

---

65. See Hanna, "*Compilatio* and the Wife of Bath," 1–11.

close of the tale: "O glotonye, luxurie, and hasardrye! / Thou blasphemour of Crist with vileyne / And othes grete, of usage and of pride!" (VI.897–99).

Yet for all the craft he devotes to his tale, which is presented to the Canterbury pilgrims as a "moral tale" preached for his worldly profit (VI. 460–61), it is the public display of authorship that drives the episode. Chaucer speaks the words "proprely" that the Pardoner claims as both his property (the practical means that sustain his livelihood) and his characteristic style of expression (words consistent with his imagined character). As with the Wife, we can trace language back to a source that is the agent responsible for speech. And the Pardoner goes beyond the Wife by offering a simultaneous narrative and direct exposition of his craft. The Pardoner's account of his preaching is designed, of course, to beguile the pilgrims by showing them explicitly the "gaude" (VI.389) that he plans to use later when he offers relics, pardon, and absolution. Dramatic readings of the *Tales* identify his belief in his craft as the Pardoner's blind spot: "It is joye to se my bisynesse" (VI.399). The Host exposes it in his angry, violent, and obscene rejection of the trick. The moral ambiguity of his "bisynesse" is revealed by the Parson himself: "For though myself be a ful vicious man, / A moral tale yet I yow telle kan" (459–60).[66] The persuasive power of the Pardoner, by contrast, stems from his presence as an author. His Prologue lays out his *forma tractandi*: "an hauteyn speech" (VI.330), followed by documentary authority (bulls, letters patent), "after that thanne telle I forth my tales" (VI.341), spiced with some Latin "to saffron with my predicacioun" (VI.345), and finally the display of relics. Tales—"ensamples many oon / Of olde stories longe tyme agoon" (435–36)—are the *materia*, and the *intentio auctoris* is clear: "For myn entente is nat but for to wynne, / And nothyng for correccioun of synne" (VI.403–4). Reform and repentance, he insists, "is nat my principal entente" (VI.432). The enduring paradox of the Pardoner is that the authorship he asserts by intention, material, and technique finds its significance in the surplus of meaning that he creates—in the performance he does not understand fully and the exemplary tale that shows that the end state of *cupiditas* is not evil but death.

The Wife and the Pardoner are the boundary cases of authorship in the *Canterbury Tales*, figures who push the already fictional sources of narrative into a critical reflection on fiction-making itself. Elsewhere in the *Tales*, Chaucer turns to authors and authorities with greater and lesser stakes for literary culture. The Monk's Tale comes up short on the wager that Boccaccio's Latin humanism can be adapted to vernacular institutional knowledge, while Sir Thopas fails to do for tail rhyme romance what Boccaccio achieved for popu-

---

66. Minnis, *Fallible Authors*, 98–169, examines the theological and ecclesiastical backgrounds of corrupt clergy performing valid spiritual work.

lar narrative in his pseudoclassical epics. In the Clerk's Tale and the Manciple's Tale, the stakes of authorship are exceptionally high. The Clerk recounts a story for which literary *translatio* from one writer to another is always an accompanying issue. The Manciple retells an Ovidian story that serves as a parable about the cancellation of authorship.

In the Prologue to his tale, the Clerk answers the Host's demand for "som myrie tale" (IV.9) in plain style, available to everyone's understanding, by rehearsing the tale he learned "at Padowe of a worthy Clerk" (IV.27), whom he names as Francis Petrarch. The tale carries the authority of not just clerical culture and a named author but also of an author who is "the lauriat poete" (IV.31) in the process of becoming an ancient rather than a modern: "He is now deed and nayled in his cheste" (IV.29). As commentators remark, the Clerk's burial of Petrarch activates his retelling of the story, for his acknowledged source can be cited and reinvented. What the Clerk also does—less noted but equally important—is to reprise Chaucer's earlier aim to "telle a tale after a man" and to "speke hir wordes proprely." He ends the Prologue with a variant of Chaucer's principle of imitation: "To tellen of this worthy man / That taught me this tale" (IV.39–40). Telling of Petrarch means to retell his tale (and thus renew his fame), but it also means to tell in a manner characteristic of Petrarch. Thus, he reproduces the proem to Petrarch's Griselda story "with heigh stile" (IV.41), recognizing it as necessary to "conveyen his mateere" (IV.55) but observing the Host's injunction not to introduce high style into the story proper.

The Clerk's citation of Petrarch overwrites the source and transmission of the Griselda story in a chain of authorial rewriting and recontextualizing. Petrarch's Latin translation of the Griselda story in *Seniles* 17.3 brings the last tale of the *Decameron* (10.10) into the sphere of the Petrarchan Academy, which David Wallace describes as "a small, consciously exclusive, masculine group of initiates dedicated to the pursuit of Latin culture" and disciplined by access to Petrarch's letter.[67] His translation appears in the suite of final letters to Boccaccio comprising Book 17 of the *Seniles*. Its aim is to preserve the exemplary story by assuring its afterlife in Latin letters. Petrarch acknowledges his transformations of Boccaccio's vernacular (if distinctly elevated) style in a way proper to the original: "historiam tuam meis verbis explicui, [imo] alicubi aut paucis in ipsa naracione mutatis verbis aut additis, quod te non ferente modo sed facente fieri credidi [I have unfolded your story in my own way, freely changing or adding a few words throughout. I believed that you would not merely have accepted this strategy, but encouraged it]."[68] His rewriting,

---

67. Wallace, *Chaucerian Polity*, 264.
68. Text and translation from Farrell, "Clerk's Tale," 1:110–11.

praised and sought by many, amounts to a covering that may disfigure or adorn the work; but the author, he insists, remains Boccaccio. The meaning of the author's text, as the next letter demonstrates, is less stable than the work itself, for Petrarch reports the differing responses of two readers in his circle as well as his own definitive understanding of the story (*Seniles* 17.4).[69] His hermeneutic parable obscures the fact that Boccaccio anticipates the multiplicity of readings at the end of the story as Dioneo returns interpretation to the *brigata* and that Boccaccio's own readers responded directly themselves.[70]

Most scholars believe that Chaucer read Petrarch's Latin version of the Griselda story in a manuscript that contained the introductory remarks of *Seniles* 17.3, which at least indirectly identify Boccaccio's *Decameron* as the source text.[71] As Warren Ginsberg points out, the trope of remaking and reclothing the story conveys Petrarch's suggestion that Boccaccio also take another form, presumably that of a moralist: "In offering the Griselda to Boccacio, Petrarch offered him as well the opportunity to translate himself."[72] Yet it is Petrarch's rendering that serves as the source for translations into the Italian and French vernaculars from which Petrarch ostensibly rescues the story. The two most important translations are Philippe de Mézières's *Le Miroir des Dames Marieés* and an anonymous *Livre Griseldis*, which served as Chaucer's French source for access to the tale. The appearance of the Griselda story in *Le Livre du Chevalier de la Tour Landry* and *Le Ménagier de Paris* as well as in other manuscript contexts shows its diffusion and adaptability. The story is authorized for these uses because it has Petrarch as its proximate author and satisfies the expectation of orthodox doctrine, regardless of how much the allegorical and exemplary applications may generate debate inside and outside the text.

The Clerk's Tale incorporates a number of internal gestures toward authorship, particularly through Walter's control of events. He arranges for Griselde's "translation" from humble to courtly attire, it is his "entente" that devises the

---

69. Robert R. Edwards, *Chaucer and Boccaccio*, 128–52.

70. Clarke, *Chaucer and Italian Textuality*, 107–28, examines direct responses to Boccaccio's version in Italian manuscript culture, including the Manelli Codex contemporary with Chaucer, whose commentary imagines a defiant and resistant Griselda.

71. Farrell, "Clerk's Tale," 1:108–9: "Librum tuum, quem nostro materno eloquio, ut opinor, olim iuvenis ededisti, nescio quidem unde vel qualiter ad me delatum vidi" [I saw your book in our mother tongue, though I don't know how or when it came to me]. The general consensus, described by Cooper, "Frame," 1:7–13, holds that Chaucer knew or knew of the *Decameron*, despite the absence of clear verbal echoes. Harkins, "Chaucer's *Clerk's Tale*," argues for several points of verbal similarity shared by Chaucer and Boccaccio but not Petrarch or other intermediaries.

72. Ginsberg, *Chaucer's Italian Tradition*, 248. See also Schwebel, "Redressing Griselda," 274–99.

tests of her *trothe* and constancy, and he decides when he has reached the conclusion of his obsessive testing: "This is ynogh, Grisilde myn" (IV.1051). The reproof of the "stormy peple" (IV.995) who abandon Griselde for Walter's fictitious younger bride, Chaucer's addition to the text, carries the manuscript gloss "auctor." The larger authorial meaning of the tale resides, at least ostensibly, with Petrarch, who is invoked to confirm its significance as an example of constancy for readers to imitate in the face of adversity: "Therfor Petrak writeth / This storie, which with heigh stile he enditeth" (IV.1147–48). Yet the hermeneutic control that he exercises and documents in the *Seniles* does not extend to the Clerk in the same way that it does to his earlier coterie readers. The Clerk reprises Petrarch's admission that Griselda's patience is inimitable for contemporary women ("que michi vix imitabilis videtur"): "It were ful hard to fynde now-a-dayes / In al a toun Grisildis thre or two" (IV.1164–65).[73] But he shifts the interpretive framework to an imitation of the Wife of Bath. The stanzaic Envoy imagined for her buries Griselde as the Clerk had buried Petrarch at the outset of the tale: "Grisilde is deed, and eek hir pacience, / And bothe atones buryed in Ytaille" (IV.1177–78). In place of patience, obedience, and constancy, it exhorts the "maistrie" (IV.1172) that the Wife extolls, and it recalls the marital tactics of control that she explains in her Prologue. The resistance to Petrarch's authorship lies not simply within the Clerk's ambivalence as a narrator; it draws on the imaginative resources of Chaucer's fictions, which are available as authorities recognized and ready for citation.

The authorial concerns for telling "a tale after a man" and rehearsing words "properly" return with higher stakes in the Manciple's Tale. The Manciple's Prologue moots the issue of responsibility for one's speech as the Host advises the Manciple not to reprove the drunken Cook, who may at some later point disclose his sharp practices in handling finances at the Inns of Court. The tale that the Manciple tells in place of the Cook explores the consequences of authoring speech and narrative by retelling Ovid's story of Phoebus and the Crow. The tale is based on the *Metamorphoses* (2.531–632), though details and emphases are modified.[74] Its theme of reckless speech provides an occasion for the Manciple both to transgress and displace responsibility for what he says. He repeats the misogynistic commonplaces about women's appetites but claims a different referent and intent: "Alle thise ensamples speke I by thise men / That been untrewe, and nothyng by wommen" (IX.187–88). He offends

---

73. Text in Petrarch, *Lettres de la Vieillesse XVI–XVIII*, ed. Nota and trans. Boriaud and Laurens, 193. The passage is incorporated as a gloss in the Ellesmere manuscript.

74. For possible influences from the *Ovide moralisé*, Gower's *Confessio Amantis*, and Machaut's *Livre de Voir Dit*, see Cooper, *Canterbury Tales*, 385–88; and Wheatley, "Manciple's Tale," 2:749–73.

decorum by describing Coronis's lover as "hir lemman" (IX.204) and doubles the effect while claiming to correct himself: "Hir lemman? Certes, this is a knavyssh speche! / Foryeveth it me, and that I yow biseche" (IX.205–6). The principle he invokes is the same as the Platonic rationale used by Chaucer in the General Prologue, which he echoes distinctly: "The word moot nede accorde with the dede. / If men shal telle proprely a thyng, / The word moot cosyn be to the werkyng" (IX.208–10). His later assertion, "I am a man noght textueel" (IX.235), belies his interest and pleasure in the fluid shifts between words and their applications.

Phoebus's crow is the proxy who demonstrates what it means to be responsible for speaking "proprely." In Chaucer's version of Ovid's tale, the crow has the power not just of speech and song but of imitation: "And countrefete the speche of every man / He koude, whan he sholde telle a tale" (IX.134–35). He disastrously follows the principle of matching words and deeds as he tells Phoebus of Coronis's betrayal of him with her lover: "For on thy bed thy wyf I saugh hym swyve" (IX.256). The disguised pleasure of offense lies in both the coarse verb *swiven* (shared with the tales of the Cook, Miller, Reeve, and Merchant) and the crow's witness to Phoebus's disgrace. The impact of his witness is amplified "by sadde tokenes and by wordes bolde" (IX.258). "Tokenes" in this context refer to the details that the crow relates in order to provide proof and confirmation, but they suggest, too, the physical objects and actions that warrant his account.[75] The exemplary meaning that the Manciple derives from the tale conflates the authority of Solomon on keeping silence with the experience of "my dame" (IX.317), which is a tissue of authorities, cited or simply repeated. As with the Cook and the crow, borrowed speech provides a mechanism to imitate and disavow imitation. The Manciple's displacements return, finally, to the recognition that Geoffrey makes in the *House of Fame* when he refuses to give his name. The Manciple discovers, "He is his thral to whom that he hath sayd / A tale" (IX.357–58). Being an "auctour newe / Of tidynges" (IX.359–60) shifts the hazard of accurate representation from fitting words to things to reckoning the contingencies of reception. Speaking properly does not produce freedom from error but places liability on authors for how their tales might be read.

The Manciple's once-removed tale is the endpoint of authorship and narrative in the *Canterbury Tales*. It is the last fictional work on what becomes a one-way pilgrimage toward Canterbury. Here the prestige of authorship finally gives way to the risks of being heard and read. The chain of succession by which narratives move in reimagined form from one author to another uncovers its limiting condition in the readings it generates. For this reason,

---

75. *MED*, s.v. "token" 4a.

the Parson has the final word in several respects. He ends the play of storytelling, "Thou getest fable noon ytoold for me" (X.31). With the same gesture, he ends the *translatio* of authorship, while citing authorities of his own, by turning from the proper words of established sources and antecedent writers to authority itself, to the "vertuous sentence" (X.63) that regulates how proper words are to be understood.

PART 3

Constructing a Canon

CHAPTER 5

Simulating Authorship

Thomas Hoccleve and John Lydgate

LATE FOURTEENTH-CENTURY English writers left their successors remarkable innovations in literary topics, themes, and genre but few direct options for advancing their own claims to authorship in either imagined or actual literary communities. William Langland's powerful social vision arguably makes him England's first national poet, if by national poet we mean one who draws readers and responses beyond cultural, ecclesiastical, and political elites. Yet Langland's influence lies chiefly in the literature of controversy and dissent and in the uses that can be made of social criticism in succeeding generations.[1] His poem inspires a tradition of imitation that adapts lines and phrasing like school exercises in Latin composition, but his shifting, conflicted views on poetry and writing offer no ground for sustained reflections on literary authorship.[2] John Gower connects his works within an organized literary cor-

---

1. A. S. G. Edwards, "Early Reception of Chaucer and Langland," 1–22, traces the historical reception as aesthetic and writerly for Chaucer and ideological for Langland. For Langland's internal signatures and the replacement of Will by Piers Plowman in the poem's reception, see Middleton, "William Langland's 'Kynde Name,'" 15–82. On the social background of Langland's readers, see Hudson, "Epilogue: The Legacy of *Piers Plowman,*" 251–66. Spearing, *Medieval to Renaissance*, 230–34, finds Langland's influence in the satirical edge of John Skelton's poetry.

2. Scase, "Latin Composition Lessons," 40–47. Bowers, *Chaucer and Langland*, 55, observes, "Because Langland's name was not firmly attached to his works during his lifetime, he created almost insurmountable obstacles for later readers trying to determine his identity. Writers in the subsequent *Piers Plowman* tradition, who remained ignorant or deeply confused

pus and goes on to frame them retrospectively as a counterpart to the classical *cursus honorum*, but he retains a singular focus as a moralist, and his virtuoso accomplishment in writing major poems in three languages attracts no immediate followers. He is effectively the last great Anglo-Latin and Anglo-French poet. (The royal captive Charles d'Orléans might make a claim in the opposite direction as a Franco-English poet, composing a body of French and English lyrics that only partially overlap and even arranging for a Latin translation of his French works.[3])

Geoffrey Chaucer, like Gower, describes his work as an organized, articulated literary canon, and he presents the most ambitious engagement of any medieval English writer with both the classical tradition and late medieval classicizing vernaculars. But his disavowals and resistance create a form of authorship that remains finally unreproducible and only partly usable for later writers.[4] European models of authorship devised by Machaut, Froissart, Deschamps, and Christine de Pisan or Dante, Petrarch, and Boccaccio hold some possibilities for English writers.[5] Henry IV's effort to bring Christine to England, had it succeeded, might have established a formal institution of authorship aligned with the court and direct royal patronage at the start of the fifteenth century. Boccaccio is recognized as an *auctor* by English writers for his Latin works and their potential for supplying the materials of a vernacular classicism.[6] These continental models are transmitted largely, however, though not exclusively, through Gower and Chaucer. No medieval English author after Chaucer registers the transformative experience of encountering a poet like Dante.

Faced with this configuration of possibilities, writers in the early fifteenth century discover alternatives that simulate authorship. By that I mean they turn to their immediate vernacular forebears as an occasion rather than a determinate or directly available source for authorship. Previous writers, like literary patrons, serve in effect as inventional topics for authorship. Later writ-

---

over what name to attach to the work, usually made no attempts whatsoever at naming its author. Consequently, Langland provided no model for literary authorship, no impetus for the stable formation of a canon, no potential for family or institutional endorsement, and no fixed origin for deriving a literary posterity."

3. Butterfield, *Familiar Enemy*, 304–7; Coldiron, *Canon, Period, and the Poetry of Charles of Orleans*.

4. Spearing, *Medieval to Renaissance*, 99–110.

5. Butterfield, "Articulating the Author," 80–96, examines the relation of authorship to the presentational form of vernacular poetic anthologies.

6. Wright, *Boccaccio in England*, 3–43; Armstrong, *English Boccaccio*, 19–156, examines the material base for translations of Boccaccio's *De Casibus Virorum Illustrium* and *De Mulieribus Claris*.

ers portray them selectively and drastically recontextualize them; thereby, they devise equivalents that stand in for recognized poets. These surrogate versions of the poets permit invention through a strategy of imitation, typically couched in a rhetoric of deference and belatedness. The immediate aims of these later writers are pragmatic and tactical, situated within the imaginative structure of their own works. The outcome of simulated authorship, however, is the unplanned creation of secular canons and a literary history founded on a representation of authors designed to serve the interests and ambitions of their successors. This literary history produces a national tradition whose contours are defined well before the appearance of the celebrated "self-crowned laureates" of the Early Modern period.[7] In the afterword to this book, I turn to the literary issues that such a recognized but incidental tradition, one grounded in the concrete objectives of belated authors, might pose for our understanding of what medieval "authors" meant to Renaissance authors.

In their writings, Chaucer and Gower anticipate some of the strategies that will be used to recontextualize them as authors by their literary successors. The most important examples are Chaucer's address to "moral Gower" at the end of *Troilus and Criseyde* (5.1856) and Gower's portrayal of Chaucer at the end of the Ricardian recension of *Confessio Amantis*, in which Chaucer is identified as Venus's "owne clerke" (8.2954*), her disciple and poet "of ditees and of songes glade" (8.2945*). The figure of "moral Gower" overwrites the deep political and polemical investments of the *Mirour de l'omme* and *Vox clamantis*, just as Venus's clerk defines Chaucer narrowly as an erotic poet, seemingly removed from social or political commentary.[8] The works imitated by Chaucer's contemporaries Sir John Clanvowe and Thomas Usk are further evidence of a narrowing of Chaucer's range to courtly pieces. Later, the Boethian teaching of Chaucer's "Gentilesse" is incorporated wholesale into the "Moral Ballad" produced by Chaucer's associate Henry Scogan for the instruction of Henry IV's sons. John Lydgate creates versions of Gower and Chaucer even as he fashions himself the "monk of Burye" and joins them, from the mid-fifteenth century onward, to establish a foundational triumvirate of English authors. Lydgate enjoys the distinction of being a literary disciple who fosters his own disciples, among them East Anglian poets in the mid-fifteenth century and Stephen Hawes at the start of the sixteenth century.

It bears remembering, however, that what I am calling the simulation of authorship occurs even as late medieval and Early Modern writers recognize the power of imagination and poetic inventiveness that distinguish Gower and

---

7. Helgerson, *Self-Crowned Laureates*.

8. Carlson, *Chaucer's Jobs*, provocatively reads this narrowing as a domestication and disciplining of any subversive energies in Chaucer.

Chaucer in modern literary appreciations and histories. Lydgate sees Gower as a model for prophetic social address and political reflection as well as a source for narrative poems.[9] John Walton responds directly, if negatively, to Gower's use of the pagan gods in *Confessio Amantis,* and Andrew Barclay refuses to translate Gower's poem because of its love theme, regardless of its political and ethical aims.[10] Scots poets of the fifteenth and sixteenth centuries respond to the frame and narratives of the *Confessio.*[11] In Thomas Usk's *Testament of Love* (3.4.559–60), the allegorical figure Love terms Chaucer "myne owne trewe seruaunt the noble philosophical poete in Englissh" because of the discussion of Boethian determinism in *Troilus and Criseyde.*[12] Thomas Hoccleve, writing in 1412, portrays Chaucer as a "Mirour of fructuous entendement" (*Regiment of Princes* 1963), emphasizing by "entendement" Chaucer's rational qualities of judgment, intellect, and understanding.[13] William Caxton's epilogue to his edition of the *House of Fame* (ca. 1483) expresses admiration for Chaucer's extraordinary image of true and false tidings checked and melded together at the exits of the Wicker House, "whyche werke as me semeth is craftyly made." Chaucer, he says, "Towchyth in it ryght grete wysedom & subtyll vnderstondynge."[14]

The "subtyll vnderstondynge" that Caxton praises is taken up in Stephen Hawes's description of Chaucer in *The Example of Vertu* (1504?) as "expert / In eloquent terms subtle and couert."[15] Hawes's comment is directed not just at a facility for rhetorical adornment ("eloquent terms") but at the conceptual and expressive resonance of Chaucer's language, which generates complex poetic meaning ("subtle") under a figurative covering ("couert"). The idea reappears in the Proem to Hawes's *Comfort of louers* (1515), which credits poets with expressing truth "under cloudy fygures" and covering it "subtylly."[16] Hawes follows Caxton, too, in seeing the *House of Fame* as a book that "he drewe hymselfe on his owne inue[n]cyon" (*Pastime of Pleasure* 1325).[17] Sir Brian Tuke,

---

9. Robert R. Edwards, "Lydgate and the Trace of Gower," 156–70.

10. Gilroy-Scott, "John Gower's Reputation," 33; see also Pearsall, "Gower Tradition," 179–97.

11. Martin, "Responses to the Frame Narrative of John Gower's *Confessio Amantis*," 561–77.

12. Usk, *Testament of Love,* 266.

13. *MED,* s.v. entendement 1a, glossed as "fertile intellect." Hoccleve, *Regiment of Princes,* ed. Blyth.

14. Chaucer, *Book of fame made by Gefferey Chaucer,* sig. D3r; cited in Spurgeon, *Five Hundred Years of Chaucer Criticism and Allusion,* 1:61.

15. Hawes, *Here begynneth the boke called the example of vertu,* sig. H4r; cited in Spurgeon, *Five Hundred Years of Chaucer Criticism and Allusion,* 1:67.

16. Hawes, *Comforte of louers*; Boswell and Holton, *Chaucer's Fame in England,* 25.

17. Hawes, *Pastime of Pleasure,* 55.

in the preface to William Thynne's 1532 edition of Chaucer's *Works*, praises Chaucer for "fresshnesse of inuencion."[18] In our received understanding of Chaucer's influence and reception, it is not until John Dryden's Preface to *The Fables* (1700) that poetic qualities—chiefly character and what Dryden calls Chaucer's "Thoughts"—are recognized as distinguishing features of his poetry.[19] Yet it is clear that writers much earlier than Dryden responded directly to Chaucer's creative powers and ingenuity, as did Gower's readers. Consequently, the simulation of authorship from the fifteenth century onward must be seen as a conscious choice rather than a misreading or failure of understanding. If it is a determinedly selective reading, as I am suggesting, it is also a strategy that creates and makes available a tradition in which later writers might discover or create places for themselves.

The simulation of authorship occurs, moreover, in a political context resonant with self-inaugural moments. As poets, Gower and Chaucer register a complex and finally ambiguous response to Henry IV's deposition of Richard II and usurpation of kingship. Gower's "laureate poems" on Henry's coronation and his *Chronica Tripertita* advance Lancastrian propaganda, but *In Praise of Peace* offers a more wary view. The envoy of Chaucer's "Complaint to His Purse" (attested in a minority of manuscripts containing the poem) rehearses the traditional claims to Lancastrian succession (also made in Gower's *Chronica*) but perhaps with mock seriousness: "O conquerour of Brutes Albyon, / Which that by lyne and free eleccion / Been verray kyng, this song to yow I sende" (22-24).[20] Whatever their circumstances of composition, Gower's and Chaucer's works subsequently circulate as part of a program to identify the English vernacular and English vernacular writing with Lancastrian dynastic interests.[21] In this respect, efforts in the early fifteenth century to establish an authorial lineage from an imagined literary descent and poetic kinship run parallel to those that seek to legitimate political succession by collateral descent and revisionist Plantagenet historiography—the "lyne" confirming Henry Bolingbroke's claims to the throne and English claims to the French monarchy. In both cases, the explanatory logic of succession and stability override genealogical splicing and substitution. Poets and their royal masters assert lines of descent in order to become recognized heirs.

---

18. Chaucer, *Workes of Geffray Chaucer*, sig. A2v; cited in Spurgeon, *Five Hundred Years of Chaucer Criticism and Allusion*, 1:80.

19. Brewer, *Chaucer*, 1:164; Windeatt, "Chaucer Traditions," 15-17; Trigg, *Congenial Souls*, 144-56.

20. Yeager, "Chaucer's 'To His Purse,'" 373-414.

21. Fisher, "Language Policy for Lancastrian England," 1168-80; Strohm, *England's Empty Throne*; idem, "Hoccleve, Lydgate, and the Lancastrian Court," 640-61; Bowers, *Chaucer and Langland*, 183-215.

Thomas Hoccleve and John Lydgate are the pivotal figures in the genealogical fictions that establish literary authorship in early fifteenth-century England in service to the political order. Lydgate knew Hoccleve's writings, but it is less clear whether Hoccleve knew Lydgate's. Their poetic careers overlap and partially duplicate each other.[22] Hoccleve's translation of Christine de Pisan's *L'Epitre au Dieu d'Amours* as "The Letter to Cupid" (1402) dates from the time when Lydgate is generally presumed to have written courtly poems such as "The Complaint of the Black Knight."[23] In the period when Prince Henry exercises but then loses political governance through the royal council (1411–13), Hoccleve composes the *Regiment of Princes* (1411–12) for Henry, and Lydgate receives Henry's commission to begin *Troy Book* (1412–20). In 1414 Lydgate composes his anti-Lollard "Defence of Holy Church," and in 1415 Hoccleve writes "The Remonstrance against Oldcastle," while Sir John Oldcastle was a Lollard fugitive. In the early 1420s, Hoccleve and Lydgate dedicate works to Humphrey, Duke of Gloucester: Hoccleve composes the miscellany titled *The Series* while Lydgate writes his "Epithalamium for the Duke of Gloucester" (1421) and likely the *Siege of Thebes* (1422) and *Serpent of Division* (1422).

FICTIONS OF PATRONAGE

Patronage is a distinctive feature of authorship and a recurring literary device in Hoccleve and Lydgate. Nicholas Watson observes that in late medieval English writing, the figure of the patron "almost has the force of a trope."[24] Typically, a patron authorizes a work by ordering its composition, translation, or compilation. The commission provides a broad cultural warrant for writers and patrons alike. Writers produce their work at the behest of persons of standing and nominally under their protection; the prestige of the patron accrues to the value of the work and conditions its secondary reception. At the same time, a commissioned work reflects and advances the ambitions of its patrons, and furnishes an object with increasing value in gift exchange and circulation. Carol Meale observes that in late medieval England poetic patronage along these standard lines seems to be a comparatively rare practice in high

---

22. Summaries in Hammond, *English Verse between Chaucer and Surrey*, 54–56; and Seymour, *Selections from Hoccleve*, xxx–xxxii.

23. Symons, *Chaucerian Dream Visions and Complaints*, 82–83, reviews arguments for dating the poem before *Troy Book*; Pearsall, *John Lydgate (1371–1449): A Bio-Bibliography*, 31, suggests the period 1427–29.

24. Watson, "Theories of Translation," 82.

literary culture.[25] Hoccleve and Lydgate, however, are striking examples of an engagement with patronage in ways that reflect their differing approaches to authorship. Hoccleve diverges from the usual model by seeking compensation after he composes his poems.[26] The rhetorical force of patronage within his writing is prospective; it evokes the support of patrons within the fiction of composing a work. For this reason, patronage includes not just authorization, favor, and subsidy by elite men and women but petitions, begging, acknowledgments, and presentation of the works—in short, an imagined and performative environment for authorship. By contrast, Lydgate exploits literary commissions as sources that provide a defined occasion for writing and a point of completion outside the work in social, political, and cultural performance. It is in this arena that he functions as a "Lancastrian propagandist" while remaining a monastic commentator on the secular world.[27] Engaged by secular and later religious patrons, his works also carry the prestige of their commissions to secondary audiences as gifts and objects of value. To civic and guild patrons, Lydgate's authorship itself becomes a commodity with exchange value and literary cachet. Both Hoccleve and Lydgate use patronage as a rhetorical and hermeneutic figure in their works. Patronage serves their writing as a fiction of literary decorum and an occasion for addressing the grand topics of public poetry from subordinate and potentially critical positions.

Hoccleve has a recorded literary benefactor in Guy de Rouclif, a senior clerk at the Privy Seal who bequeathed him a copy of a book on the Trojan War in 1392.[28] Hoccleve's minor poems consistently seek a place in the political and administrative sphere by addressing sponsors who can negotiate the monies promised him for writing texts and documents. Petition and the presentation of a first-person, authorial "I" establish an ethos for poetic ingenuity. The *Male Regle* (1405) appeals to Thomas Nevil, Lord Fournival for payment of Hoccleve's annuity as a clerk of the Privy Seal, as do the balade to Thomas Langley, Chancellor and Bishop of Durham 1406–7 (Furnivall XII), and the balade to Henry Somer, a baron of the Exchequer (1408; Furnivall XIII).[29] The former plays on Langley's role as spiritual father and the latter on Somer's name as an occasion to seek a bountiful harvest for Hoccleve and his fellow clerks. A balade from the same period, later directed to John Carpenter, town clerk of London 1417–38, asks the addressee to be a "mene" between Hoccleve

---

25. Meale, "Patronage of Poetry," 8.
26. Ibid., 13.
27. Pearsall, *John Lydgate*, 1; Green, *Poets and Princepleasers*, 189.
28. Burrow, *Thomas Hoccleve*, 9.
29. Texts quoted from *Hoccleve's Works, I: The Minor Poems*, ed. Furnivall; hereafter cited as Furnivall with relevant poem number.

and his creditors.³⁰ A begging poem to Henry V (Furnivall XV) evokes the feudal ethos to seek payment for Hoccleve and two other clerks, "your seruantz of the olde date" (20), styled as "Louynge lige men to your noblesse" (22).

The balades accompanying the *Regiment of Princes* send Hoccleve's major poem to royal patrons and present it as a surrogate for Hoccleve, the deferential and abject subject. In the balade placed at the end of the *Regiment* and likely directed to Prince Henry (Furnivall XIV), the "litil book" (1) bereft of eloquence and poetic craft speaks the author's good intentions. The poem sent with the *Regiment* to John, Duke of Bedford (Furnivall XI) uses the same conceit: "What myn entente is, þat I speke in thee" (22). The "Balade to my gracious Lord of York" (Furnivall IX) may also have accompanied a presentation copy of the *Regiment*; the opening envoy, "Go, little pamfilet," echoes Hoccleve's reference to the poem (*Regiment* 2060). In Hoccleve's poem, a royal household sets the conditions of reading and reception, hence the qualities expected of his work. Hoccleve's poem answers to the Duke's "rootid gentilese," the Duchess's "wommanly excellence" (24), and the judgment of Master Picard, household arbiter of meter and rhetoric, the kind of official who grants access to great dukes.³¹ Hoccleve suggests, moreover, that the Duke already knows his larger body of occasional poems, having asked once at London "to haue of my balades swich plentee / As ther weren remeynynge vn-to me" (13–14).

Hoccleve's *Regiment*, as we shall see in greater detail in chapter 6, stages patronage as an enabling fiction for the poem and its author. Its circulation in manuscript suggests a network that includes royal and aristocratic patrons, colleagues in government, ecclesiastical and university readers, professionals, and possibly the informal circle of writers grouped around metropolitan and provincial patrons.³² Poems composed after the presentation of the *Regiment* reinforce Hoccleve's claims to be an author with patronage and connections. A poem on the accession of Henry V in 1413 (Furnivall IV) silently equates Hoccleve with the "seigneurs" of the realm who do homage to the new king, and it rehearses the instructional elements of the *Regiment*, Hoccleve's good will, and the theme of royal self-governance. The balade on Richard II's reinterment at Westminster in 1413 (Furnivall VIII) and the remonstrance against Oldcastle in 1415 (Furnivall II) align Hoccleve with Henry's religious orthodoxy and opposition to Lollardy (themes that appear, too, in the *Regiment*

---

30. *Hoccleve's Works, I: Minor Poems*, ed. Furnivall, 1.63n, points out that Carpenter's name is written over an erasure; Burrow, *Thomas Hoccleve*, 16, notes that inserting Carpenter's name adds an additional syllable to the meter of the line.

31. Pearsall, "Hoccleve's *Regement of Princes*," 395.

32. Seymour, "Manuscripts of Hoccleve's *Regiment of Princes*," 255–58, surveys the evidence of reception in the manuscript tradition.

and later in the *Series*); in both poems, heresy is rebellion against belief and the social order, including the chivalry that Henry embodies.[33] The double balade addressing Henry and the Order of the Garter in 1416 (Furnivall V and VI) makes the same point by fashioning Henry in the lineage of Christian emperors and imagining the chivalry in "seint Georges liueree" (54). In the 1421 balade to Henry on his return to England as "heir and Regent of France" (Gollancz IX), Hoccleve numbers himself among "youre humble and buxum liges trewe" (3).[34]

Hoccleve produces a complaint of the Virgin (Furnivall I), translated "a commandement de ma dame de Hereford," for Joan FitzAlan, maternal grandmother of Henry V. A balade to Christ and the Virgin (Furnivall XVIII) is translated at the command of Robert Chichele, a member of the Grocers' Company and twice mayor of London. Thomas Marleburgh, London stationer and warden of the Limners and Textwriters Guild in 1423, commissions a miracle of the Virgin. In Hoccleve's autograph manuscript (Durham University Library, MS Cosin V.III.9), the *Series* written for Duke Humphrey ends with an envoy to Joan Beaufort, Countess of Westmorland. Hoccleve's authorship, as these examples suggest, depends not just on composing works as imaginative or expressive forms but on negotiating the conditions of writing and reception.

Lydgate's record of patronage and reception is no less extensive, and it arguably penetrates further into social, political, and cultural institutions than does Hoccleve's.[35] Walter Schirmer observes, "Most of Lydgate's works owe their origin to a commission."[36] The evidence suggests not just a network of affiliations, as in Hoccleve's Westminster and London associations, but a distinct structure of official favor, commissions, and support across social strata in royal, ecclesiastical, and civic administration. In addition, Lydgate had the substantial benefit of John Shirley's efforts as a scribe, anthologizer, annotator, and promoter of his work.[37] Shirley compiled three manuscript miscellanies

---

33. Nuttall, "Thomas Hoccleve's Poems for Henry V" wants to align Hoccleve's poems on orthodoxy with clerical and ecclesiastical rather than royal interests.

34. Text quoted from *Hoccleve's Works, II: The Minor Poems*, ed. Gollancz, 34.

35. Lydgate's canon and chronology, which underlie any account of the patronage, commissions, and influence he enjoyed, are by no means fully established. Standard accounts begin with MacCracken, "Lydgate Canon," 1:v-lviii, and continue through the following: Brusendorff, "Lydgate and Shirley," 453-71; Hammond, *English Verse between Chaucer and Surrey*, 99-101; Schirmer, *John Lydgate*, 264-86; Pearsall, *John Lydgate*, 73-79; and idem, *John Lydgate (1371-1449): A Bio-bibliography*.

36. Schirmer, *John Lydgate*, 23.

37. Connolly, *John Shirley*. See also Hanna, "John Shirley and British Library, MS Additional 16165," 95-105; Boffey and Thompson, "Anthologies and Miscellanies," 279-315. Shirley served in the retinue of Richard Beauchamp, Earl of Warwick, with whom Lydgate is closely associated from his time in Paris beginning in 1426.

(British Library MS Additional 16165; Cambridge, Trinity College MS R.3.20; and Oxford, Bodleian Library MS Ashmole 59) that link Lydgate with Chaucer as a courtly and religious author writing for a coterie; a fourth manuscript, now lost, served as an exemplar for two other extant witnesses (British Library MS Additional 34360 and Harley 2251).[38] Shirley's introductions and rubrics provide some of the contextual materials typically conveyed in the academic *accessus* for school authors. His manuscripts effectively begin a vernacular textual tradition for Lydgate's shorter works that carries forward to the sixteenth-century London antiquary John Stow, who owned Shirley manuscripts, and to the circulation of Lydgate's poems in print culture.[39]

Lydgate's first recorded instance of royal favor dates from the period 1406–8, when the Prince of Wales writes the abbot of Bury, asking him to extend Lydgate's time of study ("continuer a les Ecoles"), presumably at Gloucester College, the Benedictine house at Oxford.[40] Lydgate's commission from Henry to write *Troy Book* (1412–20) may stem in some ways from Lydgate's time at university, as do other Lydgate poems associated with Henry in the period of *Troy Book*'s composition—"A Defence of Holy Church" (1413) and *The Life of Our Lady* (in the period 1415–22). As Anthony Bale points out, Lydgate establishes for himself an authorial presence that is at once political and religious, "devout monk and princely mentor."[41] Also from this comparatively early period are translations of Psalms 86 and 103 for Edmund Lacy, who was appointed dean of the Royal Chapel by Henry in 1414 and later became Bishop of Exeter (1420–55). The rubric for Fable 7 of *Isopes Fabules* says, on Shirley's authority, that the tale was "translatyd by Iohn Lydgat, made in Oxforde."[42]

Duke Humphrey is the likely recipient of the works composed after *Troy Book*—*The Siege of Thebes* (1421–22) and the *Serpent of Division* (December 1422)—and he is the patron of *Fall of Princes* (1431–38). Taken together, these three works comprise an "epic project" directed to English royalty, surveying the complete "Matter of Rome," which provided an underlying mythology to English national identity.[43] Lydgate's "Letter to Gloucester," a "litil bille" (3) written during the composition of the *Fall*, reprises the begging poems

---

38. See Pearsall, *John Lydgate*, 76, for further manuscript anthologies in which Lydgate's poem are featured.

39. For discussion of Lydgate's poems as items of circulation in manuscript transmission, see Mooney, "John Shirley's Heirs," 182–98; and Boffey, "Short Texts in Manuscript Anthologies," 69–82.

40. Text in Pearsall, *John Lydgate (1371–1449): A Bio-bibliography*, 56–57.

41. Bale, "John Lydgate's Religious Poetry," 76.

42. *Minor Poems of John Lydgate*, ed. MacCracken, 2:598.

43. On Lydgate's "epic project," see Robert R. Edwards, "John Lydgate and the Remaking of Classical Epic," 465–86.

exemplified by Chaucer's "Purse" and Hoccleve's verse petitions for payment; the rubric in two witnesses makes explicit the pose of authorial deference that Lydgate cultivates as his poetic signature: "The auctour makith a lenvoie excusyng hym selff of his writyng."[44] During Henry VI's minority, in which Humphrey served as protector of the realm, Lydgate composed a Christmas disguising for the king's feast at Hertford in 1427 "at þe request of þe Countre Roullour Brys slayne at Loviers" (probably John Brice, the royal household cofferer) as well as Christmas mummings for Henry and Katherine, the king's mother, at Eltham in 1428 and at Windsor in 1430.[45] "On a New Year's Gift of an Eagle," presented at Hertford, may have served, as Julia Boffey surmises, as "high-class gift wrapping" for the signet ring given Henry.[46] Comparable public functions are served by Lydgate's four poems on Henry's coronation in 1429, while "King Henry's Triumphal Entry into London" on his return from France in 1432 is a memorial piece composed from a Latin letter written by John Carpenter, town clerk of London. John Stow's collection of poems by Lydgate and others (British Library, MS Additional 29729) prefaces "That Now is Hay Some-time was Grase," a poem on the mutability of both beauty and world accomplishments, with the note that it was "made at þe commaundement of þe Quene Kateryn."[47] Stow also names Lydgate as the author of verses made for Queen Margaret's entry into London in 1445.[48]

Lydgate's aristocratic and noble patrons turn to him as an author for poems on matters of state and personal attachments, particularly the devotional interests of elite women. From these works as much as the long, dynastic poems on Troy and Thebes, Lydgate emerges as a court poet serving as an unofficial apologist and propagandist of the Lancastrian regime. Derek Pearsall proposes, "The decisive moment in his new career was most probably the commissioning by the earl of Warwick in 1426 of *The Title and Pedigree of Henry VI* . . . , a poem designed to accompany a genealogy demonstrating the claim of Henry VI to the throne of France."[49] Warwick's commission coincides with Lydgate's stay in Paris, beginning in 1426, a period that brought Lydgate directly into the orbit of royal administration. The poem translates and so duplicates in English a French poem on the same topic by Laurence Calot, clerk, notary, and king's secretary, originally compiled from chronicles

---

44. Text in Hammond, *English Verse between Chaucer and Surrey*, 149–50.
45. MacCracken, *Minor Poems of John Lydgate*, 2:275; cf. *John Lydgate: Mummings and Entertainments*, ed. Sponsler, 85–87.
46. Boffey, "Short Texts in Manuscript Anthologies," 70.
47. Text in MacCracken, *Minor Poems of John Lydgate*, 2:809.
48. Brown, "Lydgate's Verses on Queen Margaret's Entry into London," 225–34; Withington, "Queen Margaret's Entry into London," 53–57.
49. Pearsall, *John Lydgate (1371–1449): A Bio-bibliography*, 25.

on commission from the Duke of Bedford, regent of France. The Prologue to *The Title and Pedigree* shows Warwick acting in the political sphere "the right for to magnifie / Of him that is to him moste souerain" (28–29), while Lydgate resolves in a belated literary sphere to "folow my maistre douteles, / Calot, and be not recheles / Liche his writyng my stiel to direct" in his translation (67–69). The ending of the poem repeats the theme of parallel political and literary descent, with an extended astrological dating, as in *Troy Book*, of Lydgate's commission. The effect of Lydgate's enclosing the poem in these authorial gestures, as Scott-Morgan Straker suggests, is to direct the poem to his patron rather than the French audience that Calot originally envisioned.[50] In 1426, Bedford's deputy, Thomas Montagu, earl of Salisbury and second husband of Alice Chaucer, commissioned Lydgate to begin a translation of the second redaction of Guillaume de Deguileville's *Pelerinage de la vie humaine*. A tinted drawing of Lydgate (or perhaps Deguileville) presenting his work to Salisbury serves as the frontispiece to a collection of works by Hoccleve and Lydgate (BL MS Harley 4826), though Lydgate's *Pilgrimage* is not included.

Lydgate's poems for women patrons in this period occupy the same sphere as those commissioned by men in royal administration, and the explanatory materials surrounding them emphasize the work of authorship. John Stow reports that "The Fyfftene Ioyes of Oure Lady" was translated by Lydgate from French "at þinstance of þe worshipfull Pryncesse Isabelle nowe Countasse of Warr' lady Despenser."[51] "The Legend of Seynt Margarete" is written in the period 1429–30 at the "commaundement" (70) of Lady March, who directs Lydgate to compile the poem from French and Latin sources.[52] Shirley notes that "þat solempne religious Lidegate" made "An Invocation to Seynte Anne" "at the commaundement of my Ladie Anne Countasse of Stafford."[53] "The Interpretation and Virtues of the Mass" is written for Alice Chaucer after her marriage to William de la Pole, Duke of Suffolk in 1430 ("ad rogatum domine Countesse de Suthefolchia").[54] Lady Margaret Talbot, Countess of Shrewsbury and first daughter of the Earl of Warwick, commissioned Lydgate to write *Guy of Warwick* as a memorial "of þat moste worþy knyght Guy of Warwike, of whos bloode shee is lyneally descendid"; the poem aligns Lydgate with dynastic history and also functions, as Schirmer remarks, as an affirmation of

---

50. Straker, "Propaganda, Intentionality, and the Lancastrian Lydgate," 118–19.
51. MacCracken, *Minor Poems of John Lydgate*, 1:260.
52. Ibid., 1:176; Pearsall, *John Lydgate (1371–1449): A Bio-bibliography*, 31.
53. MacCracken, *Minor Poems of John Lydgate*, 1:130; Pearsall, *John Lydgate (1371–1449): A Bio-bibliography*, 32.
54. MacCracken, *Minor Poems of John Lydgate*, 1:87.

the institution of monarchy.⁵⁵ The "Epistle to Sibille," written for Lady Sibille Boys of Holm Hale in Norfolk, imitates and amplifies Proverbs 31 in rhyme royal stanzas on the figure of the *mulier fortis*. The poem describes the "vertuous besynesse" (Lydgate's refrain echoing Chaucer's Melibee, Clerk's Tale, and Second Nun's Tale) of governing a stable household of worldly abundance that both supports a husband and directs him away from the need to "robbe or spoyle" (31).⁵⁶ Its ideology and evocation of a domestic environment, as Bale points out, are "informed by the most prestigious habits of gentry reading and commissioning" in a social world that was "cosmopolitan and well connected."⁵⁷

Patronage for Lydgate comes, too, from ecclesiastical institutions closely aligned with royal authority. During his Paris stay, Lydgate reports, "frensshe clerkis" urged him "to translatyn al / Outte of þe frensshe machabres daunce" (22–24) as depicted on the walls of the cemetery of Les Saints Innocents.⁵⁸ He follows the conventions of authorial and political translation "not worde by worde but folwynge þe substaunce / And fro Paris to Engelonde it sente" (666–67). In 1430 John Carpenter requested that the verses be inscribed on the walls of Pardon churchyard at St. Paul's Cathedral.⁵⁹ Lydgate composed *The Lives of St. Edmund and St. Fremund* at the direction of William Curteys, abbot of Bury St. Edmunds, to commemorate Henry VI's extended visit from Christmas 1433 to Easter 1434 and to demonstrate the close links between the abbey and the monarchy. In 1439 John Whetheamstede, abbot of St. Albans, commissioned and paid for *St. Albon and St. Amphibalus*, a poem that matches Bury's claims to tradition and royal favor. In these commissioned poems, Lydgate effectively invents a new hagiographical form, the double saints' life.⁶⁰ Lydgate's conclusion to "On De Profundis" (Pslam 129) says that the poem was composed at the "comaundement" of Abbot Curteys "in myn oold dayes."

In the civic sphere, Lydgate functions as a commissioned author for ceremonial works that parallel the royal entertainments in the later 1420s. Shirley's information about these pieces suggests that Lydgate has made himself into something of a literary brand or trademark. Claire Sponsler's critical reap-

---

55. Schirmer, *John Lydgate*, 93–94; see also Pearsall, *John Lydgate*, 71.
56. MacCracken, *Minor Poems of John Lydgate*, 1:14–18.
57. Bale, "Norfolk Gentlewoman and Lydgatian Patronage," 270, 271. See also Oosterwijk, "'Fro Paris to Inglond'?"; and Pearsall, "Signs of Life," 58–71. Mortimer, *John Lydgate's Fall of Princes*, 48–49, finds the influence of the poem in Lydgate's treatment of Fortune and undeserved misfortune in *Fall of Princes*.
58. Text in Hammond, *English Verse between Chaucer and Surrey*, 124–42.
59. Pearsall, *John Lydgate (1371–1449): A Bio-bibliography*, 26–27.
60. Reimer, rev. of *John Lydgate's* Lives of Sts Edmund & Fremund *and the* Extra Miracles of St Edmund, 78.

praisal of Lydgate's mummings and disguisings situates them at the convergence of ceremony and writing, directed to the overlapping realms of city, court, and monastery.[61] The "Disguising at London" is presented "to fore þe gret estates of þis lande, þane being at London, made by Lidegate Daun Iohan, þe Munk of Bury," possibly in connection with the opening of Parliament in 1427. Its analysis of mutability applies the aristocratic ethos and literary resources of Lydgate's earlier "epic project" to the "comune proufyte" (251), which is glossed in the margin as "republica."[62] The "Mumming for the Mercers of London," presented as a letter in ballad form to William Eastfield, Lord Mayor of London, opens with the dense mythographic allusions, aureate diction, and freighted syntax of *Troy Book* and the *Siege of Thebes*. The companion "Mumming for the Goldsmiths of London," also presented to Eastfield, joins the figure of the biblical ark to the theme of civic government. The "Mumming at Bishopswood" for the sheriffs of London represents springtime renewal as a pattern of harmony for all social estates and offices. Lydgate composed "The Legend of Saint George" for the London armorers and "Bycorne and Chychevache" as a device to be painted on a cloth displayed within a household "at þe request of a werþy citeseyn of London." In all these works, Lydgate's authorial signature is inseparable from the commonplace public themes he develops. His authorship carries the cachet of earlier patrons, links classical to biblical and Christian motifs, and expounds aristocratic values from a position that claims some relative critical distance from them. Lydgate begins his final work for Henry VI, a translation of the pseudo-Aristotelian *Secrees of old Philisoffres*, "ffor tacomplysshe your comaundement" (28; cf. 458).[63] His Prologue connects Henry and Alexander in their respective claims to "tweyne Crownys" (45), Henry to England and France, Alexander to Persia and Macedon. In the logic of his comparison, the performative gesture of Lydgate's teaching Henry is the counterpart to Aristotle's fictional instruction of Alexander.

---

61. Sponsler, *Queen's Dumbshow*, 10. Sponsler proposes that Lydgate's dramatic and paradramatic canon counters the poetic tradition derived from Chaucer and other fourteenth-century writers.

62. Text in MacCracken, *Minor Poems of John Lydgate*, 2:689. For the extension of aristocratic into national rather than specifically civic values, see Maura Nolan, *John Lydgate and the Making of Public Culture*, 130–54; and Benson, "Civic Lydgate," 147–68.

63. Lydgate and Burgh, *Secrees of old Philisoffres*, 2, 16.

CHAPTER 6

Thomas Hoccleve

"Sum of the doctrine"

IN HIS POETRY, Thomas Hoccleve fills all the positions conventionally associated with medieval authorship. He is a scribe who produces autograph manuscripts of his poems and a portion of Gower's *Confessio Amantis*.[1] He acts as a commentator in the *Series* by adding moralizations to the stories of "Jereslaus's Wife" and "Jonathas," and to the devotional extract "Lerne to Die." He compiles and translates from French and Latin sources, especially in the "Letter of Cupid," the *Regiment*, and the *Series*. His extensive self-presentation in the *Male Regle* and the *Regiment* employs a distinctive feature of vernacular authorship developed by poets like Machaut, Deschamps, Froissart, and Christine de Pisan. The holograph manuscripts of shorter poems (Huntington Library, MSS HM 111 and 744) and the *Series* (Durham University Library, MS Cosin V.iii.9) approximate the single-author codices of contemporary French poets and those of the preceding generation.[2] The Huntington manuscripts have been seen as perhaps an effort to create a collected edition of minor poems.[3] The layout of key manuscripts of the *Regiment* (British Library,

---

1. Doyle and Parkes, "Production of Copies of the *Canterbury Tales* and the *Confessio Amantis*," 182–85.

2. Burrow, "Hoccleve and the Middle French Poets," 40–43.

3. Bowers, "Hoccleve's Huntington Holographs," 30–34. Burrow, *Thomas Hoccleve*, 31, traces the suggestion to Doyle and Parkes, "Production of Copies of the *Canterbury Tales* and the *Confessio Amantis*," 182n38.

Arundel 38 and British Library, Harley 4866) replicates that of the Ellesmere *Canterbury Tales*.[4] Hoccleve's range of religious, courtly, and didactic poetry serves the tastes and interests of Lancastrian patrons. His topics have important precursors in Ricardian poetry, but Hoccleve adopts the intensified, ideological forms such writing takes in the early fifteenth century after Henry Bolingbroke's usurpation and campaigns against dissent. Thus religious writing asserts its orthodox views in matters of doctrine, courtly convention is appropriated to masculinized chivalry, and instruction aims to mirror and celebrate rather than form its royal and aristocratic subjects. Paul Strohm suggests that Hoccleve functioned "as a semi-official commentator, a kind of proto-laureate" in Henry V's political ascendancy.[5] Sarah Tolmie has proposed that Hoccleve attempts to create a secular poet, "a professional subject" between aristocratic-courtly and religious-clerical positions.[6] Hoccleve takes on the roles and supplies the expected materials, however, by writing works calculated to be partial and defective. He works inside authorial functions, poetic sources, and intertexts not simply to exploit the unexpressed possibilities of invention and imitation but to produce copies that circulate as visible reproductions and substitutes.

The "Letter of Cupid" (1402) provides an early example of the distinctive approach Hoccleve takes to simulating authorship. His source text is Christine de Pisan's *Epistre au dieu d'Amours*. Christine adapts the conceit of Cupid's writing to his loyal servants in order to publish the complaints of women about the betrayal, abuse, and ill fame they have suffered from men, specifically "les faulx amans" (64).[7] The letter follows the form of letters patent and other documents, such as those Hoccleve executed as a clerk of the Privy Seal, his professional station for virtually all his adult life. The complaints give occasion to rehearse commonplace arguments in the medieval defense of women and to reject the cultural textualization of misogyny in authors like Ovid and Jean de Meun and in those clerks who set the initial conditions of reading "en premiere science / De gramairë" (292–93). As the letter continues, in a voice that subtly shifts from the god's directive to the poet's pro-feminine argument, women emerge as ideal courtly subjects whose nature and behavior do not threaten the social order with violence, deceit, or desire. The threats reside instead in masculine desires and the erotic-political vices of defaming and dissembling, transgressions that merit separation from Cupid's court.

---

4. Horobin, "Forms of Circulation," 22.
5. Strohm, *England's Empty Throne*, 181.
6. Tolmie, "Professional: Thomas Hoccleve," 342–47.
7. *Poems of Cupid*, 36.

Hoccleve's poem is as much a redaction as a translation of Christine. His reworking is apparent not just in reducing the original by roughly half its original length but also in his conscious effort to write within the framework of Christine's poem. Hoccleve begins passages with close renderings of Christine's rhymed couplets but completes his rhyme royal stanzas with materials of his own devising.[8] He adds half a dozen passages of his own, including one that introduces St. Margaret as an unexpected figure of constancy admired by Cupid: "But this leeueth wel yee: / Hir louyng hert and constant to hir lay, / Dryue out of my remembrance we nat may" (432–34).[9] In *L'Epistre*, Christine makes France, once a defender and shield for women, a particularly hostile terrain. Hoccleve shifts the locale to England in its mythological and dynastic formulation: women complain "passyng alle londes on this yle / That clept is Albioun" (15–16). Christine finds a French vernacular tradition of lyric poets supporting women, which Hoccleve matches with Chaucer, Thomas Usk, and John Clanvowe. In one interpolated passage, Chaucer's *Legend of Good Women* becomes for Cupid "our legende of martirs" (316). Hoccleve overwrites Christine's signature dating of Cupid's letter (May Day 1399) with his own: "The yeer of grace ioieful & iocounde, / M.CCCC. and secounde" (475–76). With these changes, he presents himself as the English court poet that Christine declines to be—an author-arranger whose self-inaugurating courtly work addresses and serves royalty by reforming the cultural and linguistic practices of its chivalric agents, men who need regulation.

In the *Male Regle*, another early poem (dated 1405–6), Hoccleve presents a first-person authorial persona that will feature prominently in succeeding works. It is a poetic voice that registers concrete experience through convention and develops its complications as an extended literary preface.[10] Here and elsewhere, as A. C. Spearing observes of the Prologue to the *Regiment of Princes*, the effect of the spoken word uttered by a first-person speaker comes from writing.[11] The *Male Regle* adapts the conventions of penitential lyric to a begging poem that aims ostensibly to restore Hoccleve's moral and financial health but paradoxically returns the poet-petitioner to the starting point of his illness.[12] It also relocates the poetic "I" from the imagined centers of courtly

---

8. Ibid., 161.

9. Text in Gollancz, *Hoccleve's Works, II: The Minor Poems*, ed. Gollancz, 20–34.

10. Burrow, "Autobiographical Poetry in the Middle Ages," 223–46, offers the most incisive discussion of autobiography and convention in Hoccleve's poems.

11. Spearing, *Medieval Autographies*, 144, 164–66.

12. Thornley, "Middle English Penitential Lyric," 295–321. Knapp, *Bureaucratic Muse*, points out that Hoccleve's poem works at cross purposes with penitential writing. Malo, "Penitential Discourse," 277–305, suggests that Hoccleve uses penitential discourse to argue for identity, sanity, and a spiritual equivalent to the good intentions he expresses elsewhere.

environment in French poetry to the adjacent domains of royal administration and urban life in the king's affinity.[13] The immediate petition is to the allegorical figure Health, whose favor Hoccleve metaphorically seeks to regain while sketching his youthful dissipation in drink, muted sensuality, and self-deceit. The pursuit of favor, even restored favor, miscarries, however, in the effort itself. The flattery of tradesmen and laborers, to which Hoccleve succumbs in the narrative of his dissipation, is largely identical in kind to the courtier's disingenuous praise of his lord. The satirical reproof of flattery—"fauele, of lesynges Auctour" (223)—includes, if only implicitly, Hoccleve's own petition. In this way, Hoccleve's confession of "outrage & excesse, and verray waast" (371) struggles to find a rhetorical position beyond the doubleness of courtly speech that it ostensibly deplores. Petition and complaint, Hoccleve suggests, plainly display authorial motives, while their open assertion of what they want makes them persuasive.

In the *Regiment of Princes,* Hoccleve exploits the compound structure of self-presentation and petition to create a poem that supplies its own occasion for writing and develops authorship within the experience of dependence and vulnerability. As in the *Male Regle,* he describes his straitened financial condition and provides a number of biographical details, including his marriage and glimpses of professional life at the Privy Seal. But his earlier "mysreule" gives way here to an account of subjectivity stemming from the contingency of poverty and the anxiety it produces. This first-person portrayal, beginning with Hoccleve's inwardness and elaborated through his dialogue with the figure of the Old Man, forms the first major structural division of the poem (1–2016). The Old Man's counsel, in turn, makes Hoccleve's composition of a mirror for princes for Prince Henry (2017–5463) the fictional and historical remedy for Hoccleve's distress: "Wryte to him a goodly tale or two, / On which he may desporten him by nyght, / And his free grace shal upon thee lyght" (1902–4).[14] Manuscripts of the *Regiment* generally mark these divisions, though Prologue is applied in some to the address to Henry (2017–156) that precedes the mirror proper. Ethan Knapp observes that poetic authority is the common issue in both halves of the poem, as Hoccleve deprecates himself, hovers uncomfortably close to flattery, and feels the dread of addressing the prince.[15]

As he positions himself rhetorically through the commonplaces of humility and subordination, Hoccleve compiles a work from multiple sources and discursive forms that lend significant literary capital as well as materials for

---

13. Burrow, "Hoccleve and the 'Court,'" 71.
14. The *Regiment* is quoted from Blyth, *Regiment of Princes.*
15. Knapp, "Thomas Hoccleve," 197.

writing. His opening account of psychological turmoil focuses on the effects of "Thought," one of the "small-scale personifications" that feature in his poems, and his "musynge" (1, 33) recalls the "sorwful ymaginacioun" and melancholy that begin the *Book of the Duchess* in a passage that Chaucer imitates from Froissart.[16] Hoccleve's reflections on "the welthe unseur of every creature" (16) and Fortune's mutability resituate the mechanism of *de casibus* tragedy from the falls of great men and women down the social hierarchy, to the paradoxical "sikirnesse" (44) that poverty guarantees to mankind as a whole. As he begins his dialogue with the Old Man, he adapts the model of Boethius's *Consolation of Philosophy*, a connection noted in manuscript marginalia.[17] Confession, as in Gower, and complaint, as in Chaucer's minor poems, serve as generic supplements to Boethian dialogue in Hoccleve's framing fiction.[18] When he turns to princely advice in the second half of the poem, Hoccleve draws on the pseudo-Aristotelian *Secretum Secretorum*, the *De regimine principum* of Egidius Romanus, and Jacobus de Cessolis's *De Ludo Scachorum*. Though some manuscripts attribute the poem to Hoccleve, a number identify it as Egidius's work and some as Hoccleve imitating or commenting on Egidius: "hokcleue super Egidium de Regimine Principum."[19] The connection to learned writing is strengthened by the Latin marginal glosses accompanying the text, which are largely authorial.[20]

Hoccleve simulates authorship by producing a work that furnishes a partial version of his sources, a visible reproduction that stands in for the original. The *Regiment* not only brings together different sources but also condenses, concentrates, and concordances them. Hoccleve describes it as a "pamfilet" (2060) and recommends it to Henry as a summation of what he has read and knows intuitively: "In short yee mowen beholde heer and rede / That in hem thre is scatered fer in brede" (2134–35). The histories recounted in the *Regiment* offer profit, and "they been good for to dryve foorth the nyght" (2141). On this view, exemplary, didactic narrative replaces the "romaunce" (48) of

---

16. Spearing, *Medieval to Renaissance*, 119, suggests the influence of *Piers Plowman* in Hoccleve's "small-scale personifications" and of Gower on Hoccleve's plain style. On Chaucer's imitation of Froissart, see Robert R. Edwards, *Dream of Chaucer*, 68–71.

17. Perkins, *Hoccleve's Regiment of Princes*, 180–81.

18. Watt, "Thomas Hoccleve's *Regiment of Princes*," 50.

19. Oxford, Bodleian Library, Selden Supra 53; Oxford, Bodleian Library, Ashmole 40; Cambridge, Fitzwilliam Museum, McClean 182; British Library, Royal 17 C.XIV (rubric in upper margin of fol. 2); British Library, Royal 17 D.XIX (rubric in upper margin of fol. 2); British Library, Additional 18632 (with Aristotle and Jacobus); New Haven, Yale University, Beinecke Library, MS 493; Princeton, Princeton University Library, Garrett MS 137 (Hoccleve on Egidius); Philadelphia, Rosenbach Museum and Library, MS 1083/30 (Hoccleve on Egidius).

20. Blyth, *Regiment of Princes*, 202.

the *Book of the Duchess* used by the Chaucerian narrator "to rede and drive the night away" (49). The paradigmatic scene of reading shifts from a distraught Ricardian poet-narrator to the dutiful Lancastrian reader consolidating the lore and virtues of a princely office. The significance of performing this scene, as scholars note, shifts with historical contexts and circulation. Hoccleve begins the *Regiment* during a period when Prince Henry effectively administered the kingdom through the royal council. He likely presents the work after the Prince has lost power and so benefits from being seen to accept guidance and advice.[21] The work also circulates beyond Henry in royal and aristocratic circles, including a deluxe copy for John Mowbray, Duke of Norfolk (British Library, Arundel 38) and a holograph executed by Hoccleve for John, Duke of Bedford (British Library, Royal 17.D.XVIII) in 1412, with changes in the text that reflect Henry's new political circumstances.[22]

Hoccleve makes a distinctive claim to authorship in the *Regiment* by representing himself as a worker within a network of textual production. Writing, he tells the Old Man, is the integrated labor of "mynde, ye, and hand" (997), differing from the work of other "artificers" (1009) by its isolation and absolute demand of concentration: "We labour in travaillous stilnesse" (1013). The body is the site that registers the labor of writing: "It smertith him ful sore / In every veyne and place of his body" (1025–26). For the Old Man, the linguistic medium of production—Latin, French, or English—is indifferent because Hoccleve's occupation requires him to move across languages: "Of alle thre thow oghtest be wel leerid, / Syn thow so long in hem labouréd haast—/ Thow of the Pryvee Seel art old iyeerid" (1856–58). When Hoccleve resolves to follow the Old Man's advice by writing in order to seek remedy, he reprises the endings of Chaucer's dream visions but removes the aporia that presents those poems as the expected but delayed product of visionary experience. The *Book of the Duchess* ends with the poet-narrator's promise to transform the dream vision to an art work: "I wol, be processe of tyme, / Fonde to putte this sweven in ryme" (1331–32). The *Parliament of Fowls* closes with the narrator's intention "to rede so some day / That I shal mete som thyng for to fare / The bet" (697–99). By contrast, Hoccleve mobilizes himself for the text-making that produces the princely instruction of the *Regiment*: "On the morwe sette I me adoun / And penne and ynke and parchemeyn I hente" (2012–13).

Two authorial passages bracket Hoccleve's instruction. The first (2017–156) conveys the compiler's words and addresses Henry as an authorizing patron who allows Hoccleve to disclose "myn inward wil" (2027) by means of writ-

---

21. Pearsall, "Hoccleve's *Regement of Princes*," 386–410.
22. Harris, "Patron of British Library MS Arundel 38," 462–63; Mooney, "Holograph Copy of Thomas Hoccleve's *Regiment of Princes*," 263–96.

ing. Hoccleve makes clear his subordination and devotion. He also sketches unstable relations based on his sources. Aristotle's letters to Alexander witness "the tendre love and the fervent cheertee / That this worthy clerk ay to this kyng beer" (2045–46), while translating Egidius leaves him "childissh" (2058) and Jacobus has taught him only one move in chess. In the second authorial passage, at the end of the *Regiment*, Hoccleve again as compiler addresses the book as his surrogate. As in the first passage, Henry warrants the presence of the work "unclothid" and naked of eloquence through his patronage. The repeated term for Hoccleve's intention is "hardynesse," the nervy gambit of a supposedly inadequate subordinate to position his lord as a sponsor bestowing his grace. Whatever his professed limitations in "endytynge" (5458), Hoccleve consistently asserts his "good herte" (5461) as the *intentio auctoris* that matters.

Chaucer is the authorial presence woven through the *Regiment* in poetic forms and phrasing. His presence becomes visible at four points. Hoccleve's naming himself to the Old Man is linked immediately with Chaucer: "Sone, I have herd or this men speke of thee; / Thow were aqweyntid with Chaucer, pardee" (1867–68). Spearing observes that in this passage Hoccleve's acquaintance with Chaucer is "represented as being Hoccleve's claim to recognition and almost to identity."[23] In the first of three passages of commendation, Chaucer is the master to Hoccleve's disciple, able to furnish "conseil and reed" (1960) and inspire deep attachment: "O maistir deere and fadir reverent" (1961). Though Hoccleve is preceded by Deschamps and Usk in his praise of Chaucer, he effectively sets the terms of Chaucer's afterlife in the English tradition. Chaucer exhibits three characteristics: eloquence ("flour of eloquence" [1962]), conceptual achievement ("fructuous entendement" and "science" [1963–64]), and moral virtue, especially prudence (1965). The last of these connects Chaucer with Gower (1975) and guarantees his fame beyond death "with bookes of his ornat endytyng / That is to al this land enlumynyng" (1973–74).

The second passage of commendation occurs in the compiler's words to Henry that preface the didactic portion of the *Regiment*. Hoccleve rehearses his affection while fashioning the commonplaces of praise as succession in a national tradition. Chaucer's rhetoric is the equivalent to Cicero's "amonges us" (2086); his learning is "heir in philosophie / To Aristotle in our tonge" (2087–88). Recalling the end of *Troilus and Criseyde*, Hoccleve makes Chaucer in effect an English Statius: "The steppes of Virgile in poesie / Thow folwedist eek" (2089–90). Hoccleve does not name himself Chaucer's successor in any of these qualities, but he positions himself as disciple to "my deere maistir" and son to "fadir, Chaucer" (2077–78). He occupies the place of expectation,

---

23. Spearing, *Medieval Autographies*, 130.

to which succession must inevitably head, just as the Princes of Wales anticipates kingship. Hoccleve's performance of affection and deference to Chaucer demonstrates his good-faith commitment to the patron he solicits.

The final passage to invoke Chaucer cites him as a source "in case semblable and othir mo" (4979) for the equation of royal obedience to God with the power to incline subjects to the royal will. Chaucer is the figure who consolidates Hoccleve's description of his rhetorical and conceptual powers. Hoccleve's phrasing—"the firste fyndere of our fair langage" (4978)—reproduces the rhythm of Theseus's final speech in the Knight's Tale: "The Firste Moevere of the cause above" (I.2987). Hoccleve's summoning of Chaucer extends, moreover, to memory and resemblance. Hoccleve transfers his fresh memory of Chaucer's likeness, its "lyflynesse" (4993), to the text of his poem: "I have here his liknesse / Do make" (4995–96). In British Library, Harley 4866, the miniature executed at Hoccleve's instigation is set alongside the stanza. Shannon Gayk, concentrating on fifteenth-century debates over images, proposes that the miniature "vivifies Chaucer. Further, it affects and acts upon and in Hoccleve, incarnating Chaucer within Hoccleve."[24] The figure of Chaucer points to the lines that specifically convey Hoccleve's intention in commissioning the portrait: "To þis ende in sothfastnesse / þat þei þ[a]t hane of him left þought & mynde / By þis peynture may ageyn him fynde" (4996–98; fol. 88r). As the multiple meanings of "fynde" suggest, the portrait is a means for recovery and invention. Its author is Thomas Hoccleve, who has exercised his position to commission it and assert his custody. Hoccleve, in effect, authorizes the continuing presence of Chaucer's image, while, as Spearing notes, "the painted Chaucer points back at the text" in a self-reflexive gesture that closes a circuit of authorship.[25]

Hoccleve's *Series* is regularly seen as a distant companion piece to the *Regiment of Princes*, separated by the half decade of Hoccleve's recovery from madness, the "wyldhede" (Dialogue 52) that he suffered in 1414. It regularly appears in manuscripts with the *Regiment* and Lydgate's *Danse of Machabre*. Like the *Regiment*, the *Series* employs a compound structure of first-person Complaint and then Dialogue with a Friend (these are the first two poems in the sequence) to construct a fictional framework for the didactic and narrative works that follow.[26] The didactic work is a partial translation of Henry

---

24. Gayk, *Image, Text, and Religious Reform*, 50.
25. Spearing, *Medieval Autographies*, 164.
26. Hanna, "*Speculum Vitae* and the Form of *Piers Plowman*," 130, describes a structure of segmented narrative blocks contained within a shaping device and repeating actions rather than achieving narrative closure. Burrow, *Thomas Hoccleve*, 28, and Spearing, *Medieval Autographies*, 173, associate the *Series* with the French *dits*.

of Suso's *Horologium Sapientiae* entitled "Lerne to Dye," supplemented by a prose account of the joys of heaven; the narratives are two tales from the *Gesta Romanorum* bracketing "Lerne to Dye," the "Tale of Jereslaus's Wife" and the "Tale of Jonathas," both accompanied by prose moralizations. Hoccleve's holograph (Durham University Library, MS Cosin V.iii.9), dated to 1421–26, adds an envoy to Joan, Countess of Westmorland, Chaucer's niece through his wife's sister, Katherine Swynford. As Lee Patterson points out, the topics and themes of "Jereslaus's Wife" and "Jonathas" are ill-suited and impolitic choices for a powerful noblewoman deeply involved in reordering dynastic power and possessions; and so the appearance of Lydgate's poem in manuscript transmission may serve to resituate the *Series* within the conventions of didactic writing, as against inadvertent topical satire.[27]

For Hoccleve, the *Series* is a work of recovery on multiple levels. Hoccleve foregrounds a recovery of self and identity in the Complaint and Dialogue. He seeks to regain a place in the textual community centered in the Privy Seal and London more generally and in a courtly setting shaped by princely decorum and women's sensibility and reading. He stages an imaginative renewal of patronage bonds with Humphrey, Duke of Gloucester, as he works off a literary debt left outstanding by his bout of madness and presumably canceled now with the composition of the didactic and narrative poems in the *Series*. Knapp points out, however, that the narrative of recovery attached to the *Series* includes the prospect that Hoccleve's madness has not been surmounted and that social connections with the world of the Privy Seal have not been severed entirely.[28] Recomposing the facets of recovery involves not just Hoccleve's recuperation of a psychological and social identity but also, I shall argue, a reclaiming of authorship. Indeed, authorship is, effectively, the means for negotiating personal and social identity in the *Series*.

Hoccleve's overt gestures of authorship evoke Gower and Chaucer. In the Dialogue, Hoccleve answers the Friend's concern about the potential risk of relapse from the "labour" of writing by adapting Gower's exordial pose of eschewing "grete thinges" to write about love at the beginning of the *Confessio Amantis*: "I may noght strecche up to the hevene / Min hand" (1.1–2). Hoccleve assures the Friend, "I nat medle of matires grete, / Therto nat strecche may myn intellect" (D 498–99).[29] More pervasive are the selective echoes of Chaucerian set pieces. The Complaint opens the *Series* by inverting the figure

---

27. Patterson, "Beinecke MS 493 and the Survival of Hoccleve's *Series*," 92–103.
28. Knapp, *Bureaucratic Muse*, 163.
29. I quote the Complaint (C) and Dialogue (D) from *Thomas Hoccleve's Complaint and Dialogue*, ed. Burrow, and other poems in the *Series* from Furnivall, *Hoccleve's Works, I: Minor Poems*.

of springtime renewal in the General Prologue to the *Canterbury Tales* to an image of winter blight and desolation, a reversal that finds later expression of the "dooly season" that Robert Henryson remarks at the opening of the *Testament of Cresseid*. The figurative melancholy elaborated at the start of the *Book of the Duchess* is made literal by Hoccleve: "My spiryt / To lyue no lust hadde ne delyt" (C 27–28). Hoccleve finds himself in a House of Rumor in Westminster and London where the words of those uncertain of his recovery "cam to myn ere" (91). In the Dialogue, Hoccleve's Friend reproves him for allegedly defaming women and suggests he undertake a project of literary repentance, much as Cupid rebukes Chaucer and sets him the task of writing about virtuous women and treacherous men in the Prologue to the *Legend of Good Women*. (That the source of Hoccleve's supposed offense—*The Letter of Cupid*—is a translation of Christine de Pisan's *Epistre* is an irony evidently lost on the Friend and not developed overtly in the poem.) One recurring phrase borrowed from Chaucer shows Hoccleve's determined repurposing of language and context. The merchant and his wife in the Shipman's Tale reckon accounts in a world of credit and exchange to determine "how that it stant with me" (VII.120; cf. 114). In the Complaint (398) and Dialogue (29, 59, 318, 468), Hoccleve and the Friend use the phrase repeatedly to address Hoccleve's inner state and emotional control and thereby calculate the benefits of his resuming authorship.

Hoccleve's madness is described in the Complaint through textual images. Hoccleve presents himself as an unformed reader lacking access to the texts that shape the virtues required for moral functioning: "Neuere yit / Was I wel lettrid prudent and discreet" (C250–51). His change of fortune and loss of self-hood are expressed as the erasure of a text: "Out of your tables me planed han yee" (C268). He is removed from the "liueree" (C 271) and "retenance" (C 272) "of my felawes of the priuee seel" (C 296). He finds some measure of consolation in an epitome of the *Synonyma* of Isidore of Seville, a meditative dialogue between man and reason on the topic of salvation, which he inserts into his text in partial translation. Though the owner requires him to return the book, Hoccleve reports, "Yit haue I caght / Sum of the doctrine by Resoun taght" (C 375–76), so that he sets less value in rumors of his illness.

These allusions to authoring and reading texts point toward the question that Hoccleve debates with his Friend throughout the Dialogue—how is Hoccleve's madness to be interpreted? Hoccleve insists that its meaning is exemplary—a demonstration of God's power to afflict and restore mankind—and therefore a "miracle" (D 95) worth publishing. The Friend sees it as a potentially damaging return to a topic that has lost currency. The question quickly comes down to the issue of what to do with the Complaint as an authorial text.

Hoccleve views the Friend as a well intentioned but inaccurate reader: "But greet meruaille haue I of you þat yee / No bet of my conpleynte auysed be" (D 39–40). When the Friend at length asks what might accompany the poem, Hoccleve proposes to translate "Lerne to Dye" as a coda to the Complaint and a means to expiate his guilt. This combination of exemplary and instructional writing will mark, at least provisionally, the end of authorship: "And whan þat endid is I neuere thynke / More in Englissh aftir be occupied" (D 239–40).

The authorial program that Hoccleve actually plans is regulated by a new method of working according to a "fressh lust" (D 505) that moves him internally to write. Its immediate occasion is Duke Humphrey's return from France, which promises to renew literary sponsorship and link patron and author in parallel projects of conquest and composition. Humphrey possesses "a worthy style" (D 579), and Hoccleve finds himself inadequate to recount Humphrey's heroic self-inscription: "Euery act þat his swerd in steel wroot there" (D 583). He rejects translating the military author Vegetius on the grounds that Humphrey's knighthood is beyond improvement. Humphrey's resemblance to Mars in this passage casts him implicitly as a counterpart to Henry V, whom Lydgate's *Troy Book* fashions in similar terms. Humphrey proves an exemplar ("a mirour" [D 608]) in knighthood, the ethical norm of the *Regiment* composed for Henry, just as Hoccleve is an exemplar of divine grace in recovering himself. What is practicable and decorous for Hoccleve to offer, as the Friend urges, is "good auys" (D 633), the "good mateere and vertuous" (D 637) appropriate to a prince. This program is a project of rhetoric and poetic invention. The Friend invokes the architectural metaphor of invention that Geoffrey of Vinsauf gives in the *Poetria nova* and that Pandarus famously redirects to the plan for seducing Criseyde in *Troilus and Criseyde*:

> Thow woost wel / who shal an hous edifie
> Gooth nat therto withoute auisament
> If he be wys / for with his mental ye
> First is it seen / purposid / cast & ment,
> How it shal wroght been / elles al is shent.
> (D 638–42)

Recontextualizing the passage, the Friend presents Galfradian invention as a form of literary and moral prudence for an author. He advises, "Certes for the deffaute of good forsighte / Mistyden thynges þat wel tyde mighte" (D 643–44). It is "in thy makynge / A good mirour" (D 645–46) to delay writing precipitately ("heedlynge") "or thow auysed be wel" (D 647–48). An author, he says, maintains internal discipline and rule so that "no thyng shal out from him breke / Hastily ne of rakil negligence" (D 654–55). The last phrase here clearly echoes Chaucer's phrasing for Geoffrey of Vinsauf's description of artistic deliberation before composition (*manus impetuosa*): "rakel hond" (*Troilus and Criseyde* [1.1067]). By invention, then, the well-governed author regains the virtue that Hoccleve claims to lack in his remarks on madness in the Complaint.

The transition prepared at the end of the Dialogue exploits Chaucer's authorship to establish a frame for the two narratives and didactic work that complete the *Series*. Hoccleve follows the Friend's guidance to expiate his alleged offenses against women by writing in their honor and praise. The Wife of Bath serves as an "auctrice" (D 694) for the view that women resent writers who impute vice to them. Her theme of women's sovereignty structures the relation of the penitent writer to his female audience in a way that belies the authority of gender, textuality, and poetic forebears.[30] Like Chaucer's narrator in the *Legend*, Hoccleve denies intentional guilt: "Considereth thereof was I noon auctour. / I nas in þat case but a reportour / Of folkes tales as they seide, I wroot" (760–62). His language invokes the principle of telling a tale after a man that Chaucer uses in the General Prologue in order to excuse churlish, not misogynistic, speech: "Whoso þat shal reherce a mannes sawe / As þat he seith moot he seyn & nat varie" (D 764–65; cf. *Canterbury Tales* I.731–36). The authorial function that Hoccleve exercises as a "reportour" gives a name to Chaucer's imitation of speech, style, and performance, and it elaborates the medieval juridical sense of authorship, which tracks responsibility for a work to its source of composition. Moreover, says Hoccleve, "I spak conpleynyngly" (D 772)—that is, within a transferred sense. In the fiction of the *Series*, Hoccleve may not be a competent agent to assume authorial responsibility until the work of recovery is completed. He accordingly writes under correction and supervision, as the Friend promises to oversee the work. In the concluding stanzas directed to his female audience, he presents himself as "your freend" (D 810) and asserts to them what he earlier claims to the "felawes" in the trade of textual production who shunned him: "I am al othir to yow than yee weene; / By my wrytynge hath it, & shal, be seene" (D 811–12).

The three works that complete Hoccleve's self-described "book" (D 541) in the *Series* present a counterfeit Chaucerian miscellany. They are, in effect, an analogue to Fragment VII of the *Canterbury Tales*, the so-called "literary fragment" that collects a variety of genres.[31] The Roman imperial setting, betrayals, sexual menace, travels, and hidden identity of the Empress in the "Tale

---

30. Knapp, *Bureaucratic Muse*, 60.

31. Gaylord, "*Sentence* and *Solace*," 226–35, proposes the fragment as the "Literature Group" concerned with the art of storytelling.

of Jereslaus's Wife" recall the blend of hagiography and romance in the Man of Law's Tale, which ends with Constance's restoration to her husband and to royal standing in a Christian Anglo-Roman empire. "Lerne to Dye" is in the same penitential tradition as the Parson's Tale. The "Tale of Jonathas" turns, as does the Squire's Tale, on three magical objects whose effects lie not just in their wondrous powers but in their capacity to change social and moral life by attracting friends and commanding worldly goods.

All three works position Hoccleve in the roles associated with medieval authorship. "Jereslaus's Wife" is framed as a tale to expiate his alleged offense against women, and so it stands as a counterpart (and answer) to the tales of betrayed women in Chaucer's *Legend*. The Friend who comes to inspect Hoccleve's tale when it is completed approves the narrative but observes, "Heere is a greet substance aweye: / Where is the moralizynge" (11–12). Moralization, he says, is an expected "parcel" (20) of the complete text; when he subsequently furnishes it from his own holdings, Hoccleve is able to join ("knyt" [28]) the moralization to the tale in English prose. He thereby proves an author by producing a work accompanied by commentary, even if both elements are translations by his own hand. In "Lerne to Dye," Hoccleve asks for "sotil matires" to "trete" (13–14); and when he stops short, completing only one of four parts of Suso's *Ars moriendi*, he appends the lesson for All Hallows' Day and shows himself as a compiler. In the larger fiction of the *Series*, Hoccleve defers the end of writing when the Friend returns to "translate & make" (7) the "Tale of Jonathas." The immediate aim is to produce a text to help govern the Friend's son, who is "sauage / and wylde" (26–27), as Hoccleve earlier depicts himself in the *Male Regle*. The exemplary aim potentially runs the risk of offending women by its portrayal of Fellicula, Jonathas's faithless mistress. But the Friend gives him a literary decorum—"To goode wommen shal it be no shame, / Al thogh þat thow vnhonest wommen blame" (62–63)—and again furnishes the text, which Hoccleve translates with a moralization appended. Hoccleve's reconstruction as an author thus corresponds throughout the *Series* to his remaking as a subject and social personality.

CHAPTER 7

John Lydgate and the "Stile Counterfet"

IN THE PROLOGUE to his *Troy Book,* John Lydgate marks what seems to be a precise inaugural moment for his literary authorship. According to the dating and astrological allusions in the poem, he received the commission from Henry, Prince of Wales to translate and compile an English version of the Troy story at four in the afternoon of Monday, 31 October 1412.[1] The inaugural moment is, of course, a transition as much as a starting point. The commission Lydgate received requires a considerable body of earlier writing and—equally important—a history of reception among elite readers like Henry. The consensus of literary historians is that the so-called "courtly poems" in the Lydgate corpus likely provide evidence of Lydgate's general fitness for the commission and his access to an audience that would indeed recognize the significant cultural and political work that *Troy Book* undertakes on behalf of its patron and its author.[2] These "courtly poems" include *The Complaint of the Black Knight, The Flower of Courtesy, The Temple of Glass,* and a number of shorter pieces. None of them is dated securely, though many subsequently achieve some prominence in the minor canon of Lydgate's poems that cir-

---

1. *Lydgate's Troy Book,* ed. Bergen, 1:ix, citing W. W. Skeat's calculation.
2. Schirmer, *John Lydgate,* 31–41; Pearsall, *John Lydgate,* 83–121; Ebin, *John Lydgate,* 20–38. Pearsall, *John Lydgate (1371–1449): A Bio-bibliography,* 31, suggests the laureate period 1426-32 as a time when close contact with the court would explain the writing of the love poems.

culated in the fifteenth and sixteenth centuries, often with Chaucer's minor poems but separately from Lydgate's long works, which were frequently transmitted in *de luxe* manuscripts. The courtly poems behind *Troy Book* have typically raised the problem of reconciling their stylized love themes with Lydgate's monastic profession. Yet the critical issue, I believe, is not the alignment of love poetry and religious life but what the courtly poems reveal about the practice of authorship. If the chronology of the Lydgate canon is largely secure for the ambitious, "public poems" but conjectural otherwise, the literary strategy remains consistent across the corpus: Lydgate writes himself into literary culture by simulating the authorship appropriate to genre and other discursive forms.[3] He creates a "stile counterfeit"—a visibly partial reproduction of narratives, themes, and characteristic modes of expression with established cultural authority.[4]

In what follows, I want to look briefly at Lydgate's invention of authorship within courtly poetry, a form he exploits and then helps to supersede. Next, I turn to his "epic project" of writing the narratives of Thebes, Troy, and Rome. Finally, I consider the authorship developed under the pressure of Duke Humphrey's patronage in *Fall of Princes*, which bears some of the structural features of Warwick's commission to write *The Title and Pedigree of Henry VI* in the "laureate period" of the mid-1420s and early 1430s. Lydgate's authorship in his largest and last major poem is set off by the role he creates for himself in two ecclesiastical commissions, the *Lives of Saints Edmund and Fremund* and *Saint Albon and Saint Amphibalus*.

The defining feature of Lydgate's courtly writings is their partial re-creation of Chaucer's court poetry.[5] The *Complaint of the Black Knight* evokes the frame tale of the *Book of the Duchess* to present a complaint that corresponds to the one delivered by Chaucer's man in black and to Chaucer's free-standing formal lyric complaints by mythological and courtly figures. As Pearsall points out, Lydgate's poem is suffused with other echoes of Chaucer's poetry, and the *Roman de la Rose* is the continuing intertext.[6] The *Floure of Curtesy* tropes the setting of the *Parliament of Fowls* to frame another complaint, an extended description in praise of the beloved that leads, as in the *Parliament*, to a concluding balade. The *Temple of Glas* appropriates the prologue and first narrative

---

3. "Public poems" is the term applied to *Troy Book* and the *Siege of Thebes* by Ebin, *John Lydgate*, 39.

4. Simpson, *Reform and Cultural Revolution*, 52, points out that Lydgate's writing is an amalgamation of many discursive fields.

5. Bianco, "Black Monk," 60–68, argues for direct French influence and emphasizes Chaucer and Lydgate as writers whose careers at least partially overlap.

6. Pearsall, *John Lydgate*, 84–97.

section of the *House of Fame* but replaces Chaucer's *ekphrasis* of the *Aeneid* with the central figure of Venus and the lovers who seek her intervention; it focuses thereafter on a woman seemingly fixed in a love that cannot be remedied or realized and then on a lover held back in his affection for her by his inner constraints and her resistance. Venus succeeds in uniting them in a ritual that formalizes both their love and its deferral. What Lydgate achieves with these poems is twofold. His "courtly poems" effectively replicate the corpus of Chaucer's dream poems by offering partial equivalents of them in a form of heuristic imitation.[7] Implicitly, Lydgate has retraced the path that led Chaucer to works of larger scope and ambition, such as *Troilus and Criseyde* and the *Legend of Good Women*. At the same time, he has also tracked a larger shift in late medieval English literary culture mapped by Richard Firth Green. Green describes both the rise of amateur poets, insiders who participate directly and knowingly in the polite entertainments of court culture, and the replacement of these poets by educated literary authors who engage public topics central to the court and political institutions; this second group works most often through compilation and translation yet remains distinct from the historians and chroniclers who furnish many of the materials.[8]

In this context, Lydgate's "courtly poems" serve as counterfeits, forged papers in a fiction and social performance of courtly address, in which Lydgate can participate only as a writer working solely within tradition. The narrator of the *Complaint of the Black Knight* moves through a visionary landscape that removes the underlying dangers of the *Roman de la Rose* and the *dits amoureux*—above all, the chance that desire, appetite, and catastrophe might slip beyond the control of language. The well he finds contains water "so holsom, and so vertuous" (85); it is distinguished explicitly from the "mirrour perilous" (Chaucer, *Romaunt of the Rose* [1601]) of Narcissus, the inspiration associated with Pegasus and the fountain of Hippocrene, and the fierce chastity of Diana's bath. The arbor he enters is the site for a complaint that the narrator can transcribe only as "a skryuener / That can no more what that he shal write, / But as his maister beside dothe endyte" (194–96). At the end of the complaint, he reprises the role with a devoted literalism distinctly unlike the efforts promised by Chaucer's narrator "to put this sweven in ryme" in the *Book of the Duchess* (1332): "A penne I toke and gan me faste spede, / The woful pleynt of this man to write, / Worde be worde, as he dyd endyte" (598–600). Lydgate

---

7. Greene, *Light in Troy*, 38–40.
8. Ibid., 111–34. If Lee Patterson is right in locating the invention of literature in court figures like John Clanvowe, writers like Hoccleve and Lydgate resituate a significant dimension of court literature in the public sphere; see Patterson, "Court Politics," 56–83.

goes, too, past the disclaimers of the modesty topos to separate himself from courtly poets and the writers of *formes fixes* who "knowe felyngly / Cause and rote of al such malady" (188–89) and share courtly "sentement" (197) as do the amateur poets and readers of the *Legend of Good Women*, "Ye lovers that kan make of sentement" (F 69). The advocacy of the lover's "trouthe" that he undertakes with Venus and the Black Knight's beloved at the end of the *Complaint* is on behalf of the convention that he has made a text. His own imagined predicament in "Lenvoye de quare," in which he says he remains beyond hope of finding a remedy "of myn adversite" (681), is the awkward intrusion into the poetic fiction that exposes the rhetorical artifice behind the dream of courtly desire.

The *Floure of Curtesy* follows in the same direction of taming Chaucerian materials. The lark's song that begins the poem on Valentine's Day calls to both paired lovers and those "at your large" (15). The former are to renew and confirm fidelity and the latter to serve Venus and Cupid without "varyaunce" (25)—presumably, without breaking trust. The narrator's isolation from this regulated desire is the occasion for his complaint. He delivers it from a position "vnder a laurer grene" (45)—a place for the poet laureate, Machaut's narrator in the courtly *dits,* and Chaucer's comic writerly persona in the Prologues to the *Legend of Good Women*. The description he offers of a woman supposedly made unavailable to him by Daunger, Male-bouche, and Enuye stands as his poetic service to love. The virtues he describes are those that effectively remove her from eroticized courtly play and from narratives of love's fulfillment or disappointment. She is not an imagined figure but Lydgate's poetic material itself. The examples he links her with are the textual heroines of antiquity, the Bible, and Chaucer's narrative corpus (190–217). His deference to her is matched by his deference to dead Chaucer "that had suche a name / Of fayre makyng" (236–37). It is in the distance from Chaucer that Lydgate defines his writing with nuance and sophistication: "We may assay for to countrefete / His gaye style, but it wyl not be" (239–40). Lydgate's authorship, like his deference and literary succession, operates precisely as a "countrefete" that does not succeed. It remains a simulation detectable in style and conception, and valuable within late medieval literary culture because it is detectable—that is, seen for the literary artifact and authorial vehicle it is.

The *Temple of Glas* develops the salient features of Lydgate's "countrefete" at greater length. Seth Lerer aptly characterizes the poem as "an allegory of reading an anthology" in the manuscript literature containing poems by Chaucer and Lydgate: "It tells a tale of trying to explain the many texts collected and transmitted by Chaucerian authority."[9] Larry Scanlon locates the poem within an effort to simulate Petrarch's laureate poetics through the Clerk's Tale on a smaller scale.[10] Lydgate's disposition of the literary furnishings evokes the *House of Fame* as the poetic locale, but the pictorial images of lovers adorning the interior wall are scenes familiar from the ekphrastic passages of the *Parliament of Fowls* and the Knight's Tale, while the petitioners who mimic the painted scenes within the temple are the counterparts of those who petition the goddess Fame for good reputation in the *House of Fame*. Venus's role differs, however, from Fame's in its benevolent moral discipline: there is nothing to suggest the random caprice of Chaucer's poem, the radical instability that emanates from Fame's assignments of reputation or the melding of truth and error in the Wicker House. The woman who complains of her predicament in the *Temple* receives Venus's assurance of the outcome, just as the male lover who remakes himself according to Venus's instructions receives her promise that she will incline the beloved's heart toward him. These moments of address are at the center of the poem, and they are fully removed from any pressures of narrative context, such as we find in the crushing power of tyrannical, centralizing monarchy and chivalric duplicity that frames complaint in Chaucer's *Anelida and Arcite*. Lydgate constructs a hybrid Chaucerian setting to stage occasions of elaborated complaint and petition. His techniques enact through amplification the delay that Venus requires of the lovers in the poem as patterns of social and moral conduct. The address to the beloved that Venus enjoins on the lover—"Withoute spech thou maist no merci have" (912)—is reproduced in its emotional dimensions by the narrator's quaking pen. Later, in his waking state, the narrator resolves "to maken and to write / A litil tretis and a processe make" (1379–80) that serves as a memorial and placeholder for a full account of the vision, one that will "expoune my forseid visioun, / And tel in plein the significaunce" (1389–90). The suspension of meaning, like the corrections sought in the final lines as the book is sent to its female reader, is the vanishing point of Lydgate's imitation of courtly poems. The "plein significaunce" (whether "plein" means unadorned or complete or both) will never arrive because another meaning already has displaced it—a reproduction of the work of court amateurs who prescribe and examine conduct and decorum as erotic performance.

It would be a mistake to read Lydgate's courtly poems merely as an apprenticeship in the techniques that feature prominently in the "epic" works associated with a decade of Lancastrian sponsorship (1412–22) or with the

---

9. Lerer, *Chaucer and His Readers*, 68.
10. Scanlon, "Lydgate's Poetics," 80–91.

"laureate" compositions that date from the mid-1420s. Rather, Lydgate learns the art of simulating authorship by recrafting the expected modes of address required by genre, topic, and context. The decisive commission to write *Troy Book* accordingly requires an adjustment in all three elements—a triangulation of the *heroicum carmen*, the matter of antiquity, and the rhetorical situation of offering princely advice. The epic machinery of *Troy Book* is visible from its opening address to "Myghty Mars" (Prol 1) and invocation of the epic muse Calliope (Prol 46), here seen as a muse of music and eloquence.[11] The tradition of chronicle history, invoked through Clio (Prol 40), provides the comprehensive narrative of Troy's fall from its remote origins in Jason's quest for the Golden Fleece through Ulysses's death after his return from his prolonged wanderings. Troy's destruction is "þe gynnyng and occasioun" (1.812) for Aeneas's wanderings, the founding of Rome, and the *translatio imperii* that ends in Brutus's founding of Britain. The literature of counsel, for which "Othea, goddesse of prudence" (Prol 38) is the titular deity, teaches the twin lessons of self-governance and statecraft within the imagined foundation of the institution of chivalry and through its instrumental form, *kny3thod*. Henry's commission thus pushes Lydgate into a novel configuration of authorship for court poetry: a vernacular writer composing in an elevated, "classical" form with materials derived from a historical record and directed to the conduct of royal and aristocratic power. The discrete elements of this formula already existed separately in Latin and vernacular heroic poems; in histories written in Latin, French, and English; and in models of advice such as the *Secretum Secretorum*, Book 7 of Gower's *Confessio Amantis*, Chaucer's Melibee, and Hoccleve's *Regiment*.[12] Lydgate brings them together in a work whose reception is underwritten by patronage from the outset and whose effect, as Green describes, is to expand the topics and aim of court poetry beyond the fictions of courtly poetry.

Lydgate's Prologue to *Troy Book* and his self-reflexive commentary throughout the poem set out a literary mode (*forma tractandi*), a tradition of authorship, and a final cause that serves patron and author alike. The poem negotiates between the claims of history to present *res gestae* and the charge that poetry can produce only *fabula* in which truth is hidden by "false transumpcioun" (Prol 264) under a cloud or misty veil. Lydgate thus turns to the chronicle history of Troy emanating from late antique *auctores* and consolidated in Guido delle Colonne's *Historia Destructionis Troiae*; accordingly, he rejects the account of Troy's fall in Homer and much of the material in Vergil

---

11. *Lydgate's Troy Book*, ed. Bergen, 1.1.
12. Ferster, *Fictions of Advice*, provides a critical overview of the mirror for princes.

and Ovid. Henry's commission ostensibly defines Lydgate's modes of authorial composition:

> Whyche me comaunded the drery pitus fate
> Of hem of Troye in englysche to translate,
> The sege also and the destruccioun,
> Lyche as the latyn maketh mencioun,
> For to compyle, and after Guydo make,
> So as I coude.
> (Prol 105–10)

Translate, compile, make—these are the *formae tractandi* for writing *Troy Book*, and each term carries a distinctive resonance. Translation both renders the Troy story in English and situates it within other English versions of the Troy story (*The Seege or Batayle of Troye*, John Clerk's alliterative *Gest Historiale of the Destruction of Troy*, and the *Laud Troy Book*). Compilation draws together multiple sources for recounting the siege and destruction within an inventional frame devised by an author. This inventional frame (*forma tractatus*) shows in the five-book structure Lydgate gives to the story, following the example of Chaucer's *Troilus and Criseyde*, while the additions, amplifications, and digressions he introduces have precedents within epic. Making after Guido involves following the outline of his comprehensive story as a belated writer, much as Statius sends his *Thebaid* to follow Vergil's *Aeneid* at a reverential distance. It also means, as Statius makes clear, to emulate and rival his source by imitation, by creating a functional analogue to the original. Lydgate's overt qualification at the end of this passage—"So as I coude"—signifies the array of gestures that accompanies belated authorship and the poetics of imitation. Modesty, conveyed through the rhetorical topic of inability and deference, is the most prominent of these gestures. It is closely tied to the gesture of inscription (to follow the trace of the source text or direct the author's stylus to follow its tracks) and to the gesture of citation (to write as "myn auctor" says or as the books tell). The authorial figure who carries out these multiple functions is a clerk rather than historian or poet. His office is to shape and preserve memory: "Clerkis wil write, and excepte noon, / The pleyne trouthe whan a man is goon" (Prol 192–93). Clerks as *auctores* preserve the essential truth of things passed, and "thoruȝ writyng þei be refresched newe" (Prol 166). In their works, rhetorical figures "enlumyne" the truth of history and make it comprehensible to later readers.

The historical record that Lydgate sets against poetry proves, however, less a foundation than an imaginative and ideological context for writing and authorship—a fiction of authorship. Lydgate asserts that Dares and Dictys "were present and seyen eueryedel" (Prol 314) of the actions they recount; Guido calls them "fidelissimi relatores."[13] Their works are Latin compositions from Late Antiquity that circulate as counterfeit sources claiming an eye-witness authority lacking in Homer and the poets. A fictitious letter ascribed to the Roman biographer Cornelius Nepos prefaces Dares's sixth-century *De Excidio Troiae Historia* and recounts Nepos's alleged discovery of Dares's autograph copy of the work in Athens. His verbatim translation from Greek to Latin, done without adding or omitting anything, is intended, he says, specifically to cancel any claim that he might be the author of the text ("alioquin mea posset videri").[14] Dictys's fourth-century *Ephemeridos Belli Trojani* has two prefatory sections by its translator, Lucius Septimius; they vary in the details describing the text. The first reports that the work was preserved in the Phoenician alphabet and had to be transliterated by experts; the second adds the detail that an intermediary translation into Greek was made after the transliteration but before the Latin translation. Septimius translates the work, he says, to fill his leisure time ("ut otiosi animi desidiam discuteremus").[15] Both accounts present a textual romance, in which Dictys's journal is buried in his tomb at Knossos, recovered much later by shepherds seeking treasure, and then passed along a chain of civic authority until it reaches the Emperor Nero. Lydgate, following Guido, thinks that Cornelius translated both works but complains that he "left moche be-hynde / Of the story, as men in bokys fynde" (Prol 325–26). For this reason, he turns to Guido as a master "whom I schal folwe as ny3e as euer I may" (Prol 375).

Lydgate's Troy material derives, then, from a literature of forged authority devised as an alternative to the poetic tradition and used to produce the effect of the pseudoantique.[16] It claims, at one level, to offer a more reliable account than Homer; it appeals, at another, to fantasies of recovery and transmission. Nepos writes that he found Dares's original text written in his own hand ("historiam Daretis Phrygii ipsius manu scriptam"). The shepherds who discover the strongbox containing Dictys's text in his ancient, collapsed tomb recover cultural capital rather than the treasure they expected to find. Nero oversees the transliteration and translation of the text, recognizes its value to a true account of the Trojan War, and arranges for its eventual deposit in a Greek library as an authorized narrative. The textual romance allows Lydgate, in turn, to participate in the fiction of authorship that guides the transmis-

---

13. Guido delle Colonne, *Historia Destructionis Troiae*, ed. Griffin, 4.
14. Dares, *Daretis Phrygii de Excidio Troiae Historia*, ed. Meister, 1.
15. Dictys, *Dictys Cretensis Ephemeridos Belli Trojani*, ed. Meister, 1.
16. Robert R. Edwards, "John Lydgate and the Remaking of Classical Epic," 470–73.

sion of the story from Dares and Dictys to Nepos and Guido. (The afterlife of *Troy Book* in the sixteenth and seventeenth centuries proves the continuing vitality of the fiction.) The governing metaphor in this authorial succession is descent: an ongoing *translatio* joins writers over time in a common project of narrative and cultural transmission. In Lydgate's account, literary descent runs parallel to the motives of his patron and operates, in both cases, by asserting continuities that obscure not just gaps but suppression in the transmission of an authorized narrative.

Henry's commission, as Lydgate reports it, recognizes that the Troy story exists in Latin and vernacular versions, but *Troy Book*'s literary genealogy largely erases the French tradition as an imaginative possibility. Guido does not name Benoît de Sainte-Maure's *Roman de Troie* as his source, but when he cites Dares he refers to Benoît, just as the citations of Dictys refer to Joseph of Exeter's *De Bello Trojano*.[17] In the Prologue, Lydgate presents French only as a language transmitting the Troy material, which English must emulate so that the story is "y-writen as wel in oure langage / As in latyn and in frensche it is" (Prol 114–15). The erasure of Benoît cancels a powerful model and potential disruption. It is Benoît who rewrites the counterfeit antiquity of Dares and Dictys within the social, political, and ethical forms that provide its exemplary value and capacity for reflection to medieval readers, among them Henry II and Eleanor of Aquitaine, Benoît's likely patrons.[18] Yet the *Roman de Troie,* like the other *romans antiques,* recontextualizes antiquity in the political framework of the second feudal age, whose focus on baronial prerogatives would hardly be congenial to a Lancastrian monarchy that faced rebellion from great lords after Henry Bolingbroke's usurpation and continuing challenges to its concentration of state power in the figure of the king. Benoît is the intertext that potentially complicates the ideological assignment given Lydgate by the Prince of Wales. As Lydgate explains, "The fyn of his entencioun" (Prol 118), hence the *causa finalis* attached to Lydgate's writing and authorship, is to make the "noble story openly" (Prol 112) known to all social classes ("h3ye and lowe") in a common tongue. The "noble story" communicates a singular national paradigm of aristocratic heroism and conduct uniting all conditions

---

17. Guido delle Colonne, *Historia Destructionis Troiae,* trans. Meek, xx. Meek observes that Guido claims to present what is contained in Dares and Dictys (xviii). Wiggington, "Nature and Significance of the Medieval Troy Story," demonstrates Guido's reliance on Joseph of Exeter.

18. The evidence of patronage appears in the allusion to "riche dame de riche rei" (*Roman de Troie* [13468]). Barbara Nolan, *Chaucer and the Tradition of the* Roman Antique, 14–118, provides an insightful appraisal of the thematic possibilities Benoît discovers in adapting Dares and Dictys; see also Desmond, "Trojan Itineraries," 251–68; and Rollo, "Benoît de Sainte-Maure's *Roman de Troie,*" 191–225.

through a narrative commissioned out of dynastic motives.[19] It is not by chance that the defining elements of Lydgate's authorship—description of his mode of writing and his patron's intent—follow immediately from his identification of Henry as a patron who embodies hopes of dynastic succession. Henry follows his father "of maneris and of name" (Prol 100), and it is Henry "to whom schal longe by successioun / For to gouerne Brutys Albyoun" (Prol 103–4) and who "is iustly born / To regne in Fraunce by lyneal discent" (5.3390–91). As Henry stands to succeed his father (and French father-in-law) as monarch, Lydgate stands to succeed Guido as an author.[20] Both genealogies assert the explanatory logic of descent to argue for continuities and the stable transmission of authority, which overwrite narratives of rebellion and resistance.

Lydgate's participation in the fiction of authorship underwriting the Troy story involves both deference and resistance. Guido is "myn auctour" because he is a source for the "substaunce" (Prol 359, 5.3543) of the narrative and a means to invoke the authority of Dares and Dictys (5.3360–61). He holds a place in Lydgate's story against the competing accounts that figures like Ovid might offer not just as disavowed poets but also as textual authorities on mythography. He provides the warrant (*Historia* Book 10) for a digression on idolatry (2.5409–40) because "he sawe þe mater was nat knowe / I-liche wel, boþe to hiȝe and lowe" (5929–30), the national audience for the Trojan narrative. Yet Lydgate resists Guido's misogyny at several junctures in the story through rhetorical gestures that finally display their own ambivalence.[21] The description of Medea's desire for Jason contains the charge that women are duplicitous and unstable (1.2072–96). Lydgate comments, "Þus liketh Guydo of wommen for tendite" (1.2097), and he goes on to reprove Guido and offer the remedy of penance for his salvation (1.2097–137). Helen's desire for Paris is described as feminine curiosity advanced by the tactics described by Ovid in his love elegies. Lydgate notes Guido's "cursid fals delit" (2.3555) in defaming women and again repudiates "Þe felle wordis in his boke y-founde" (2.3561). In both instances, the commonplaces of misogyny directly follow from narrative action before they are ascribed to Guido and then earnestly repudiated. The same ambivalence, as commentators have remarked, informs Lydgate's treatment of Criseyde.[22] Lydgate expands Guido's reproach to Troilus for

---

19. Nall, *Reading and War,*" 94–96, connects the need for unity portrayed within *Troy Book* to the political discourse of Henry's war with France.

20. As Strohm observes, "The Lancastrian artist recasts the problematic of succession at various expressive levels," asserting both continuity and displacements (*England's Empty Throne,* 188–89).

21. Lydgate shows a similar treatment of Boccaccio's antifeminism (*De casibus virorum illustrium* [1.18 "In mulieres"]) in *Fall of Princes* 1.6511–706.

22. See Mieszkowski, "Reputation of Criseyde," 117–26, for the contradictions in Lydgate's reproof of Guido. Torti, "From 'History' to 'Tragedy,'" 177, proposes that Lydgate "puts still more

trusting Briseida (*Historia* Book 19) to an excursus on women's "doubilness" (3.4369, 4297), amplifying the original *suasoria* by casting women as hidden serpents and as prostitutes peddling themselves when they have no "chapman" (3.4321—Guido's term *solicitator* means tempter or seducer). Lydgate forcefully dissociates himself from these views—"Þus techeþ Guydo, God wot, & not I!" (3.4343)—and offers a standard defense of women's virtue, before returning to argue Guido's major point ("For ʒif wommen be double naturally, / Why shulde men leyn on hem þe blame? [3.4408-9]) and excusing Criseyde's betrayal of Troilus for Diomede as "only kyndes transmutacioun, / Þat is appropred vn-to hir nature, / Selde or neuer stable to endure" (3.4442-44). Lydgate's repeated assertion that he follows the substance of his author applies not just to translating a source but to producing a replica of it even while denying some of the commonplaces it entails.

Chaucer is a more complex presence in *Troy Book* than Guido. He serves Lydgate as a literary source and a model of authorship that potentially carries beyond Guido and the confected genealogy of ancient sources. His poetry provides narrative materials, as in the retelling of *Troilus and Criseyde* that begins with portraits in Book 2 and weaves through the movement toward Hector's death in Book 3; it furnishes language and phrasing used sometimes with allusive significance and sometimes isolated from its original context. Chaucer is "þe noble Rethor þat alle dide excelle" (3.553) and a national poet: "Noble Galfride, poete of Breteyne" (2.4697), "chefe poet / Þat euere was ʒit in oure langage" (3.4256-57), the founding figure whose rhetoric illuminates "oure rude langage" (2.4700). Lydgate specifically connects these rhetorical features in Chaucer: "He owre englishe gilte with his sawes" (3.4237) and took a language "but of litel reputacioun, / Til þat he cam, &, þoruʒ his poetrie, / Gan oure tonge firste to magnifie" (3.4240-42). His status—"þe laurer of oure englishe tonge" (3.4246), comparable to Petrarch's laureation—is worthy of memory. As in Hoccleve's portrait in the *Regiment,* Chaucer is remembered as a beneficent master, whose generosity to his disciples anticipates what Lydgate hopes from his readers, "Suffring goodly of his gentilnes / Ful many þing enbracid with rudnes" (5.3525-26). Chaucer thus constructs models for Lydgate of the authorship required to carry out the royal commission of writing an English Troy book emulating the Latin and French books. Lydgate writes the "Troian gestes" that Chaucer explicitly turns away from in *Troilus and Criseyde* (1.145). He imitates Guido's materials while mobilizing Chaucer's rhetorical achievements not just to reveal the truth of events (the aim of Guido's

---

subtle and ambiguous emphasis on Criseyde's inconstancy" than Guido. See also Watson, "Outdoing Chaucer," 89–108.

rhetorical adornment) but to express exemplary history in a national idiom elevated to a language of classical transmission.

The other components of Lydgate's epic project during this period—the *Siege of Thebes* and *Serpent of Division*—offer a more direct engagement with Chaucer by devising analogues to his works rather than his imagined mode of composition. The *Siege* is a companion piece to *Troy Book* and follows on its completion. Lydgate frames it as a conspicuously apocryphal Canterbury Tale, presented as the first tale recounted on the return trip of the pilgrims from Canterbury to Southwark. Lydgate presents himself as the first-person narrator who relates both the frame tale and his own tale. In the first instance, he has replaced Chaucer as the figure who describes the pilgrims and recounts the beginning of their journey back; he also completes the pilgrimage to Thomas Becket's shrine, which none of Chaucer's pilgrims, including the narrator, accomplishes. In the second, he has overgone Chaucer by telling the background story of the Knight's Tale, which is the disastrous rivalry between Oedipus's sons, Eteocles and Polynices, and the tyranny of Creon. Chaucer, following Boccaccio, had filled the inventional space left open at the end of Statius's *Thebaid* with the romance-epic of Palamon and Arcite's rivalry for Emily, the sister of Theseus's conquered wife, Hippolyta. In *Troy Book*, Lydgate cites Statius as the author of the Theban story (Prol 226–44), which regularly accompanied the Troy story as its precursor and dark underside. In the *Siege*, Lydgate goes beyond Statius and his vernacular successors in the *Roman de Thebes* and in its prose redactions to start the poem with the double founding of Thebes by Amphion and Cadmus as recounted in Boccaccio's mythographic compendium ("myn auctour" [199]), the *Genealogie deorum gentilium*.[23] He thus orchestrates an elegant reversal in which the belated author follows his masters while placing his work before them at a point from which their narratives originate.

Lydgate simulates a Canterbury Tale in the *Siege* by evoking but not reproducing the Chaucerian original. His opening (1–66) amplifies the crafted syntactic balance of Chaucer's initial theme of natural and spiritual renewal (1–18) into a medley of Chaucerian allusion unsustained grammatically by a main verb. He mistakes distinguishing features of the individual pilgrims he mentions from the General Prologue. He praises Chaucer as "Floure of Poetes thorghout al breteyne" (40), but the language of praise repeats the idiom he had already devised in *Troy Book*. Praise of Chaucer is thus inseparable from Lydgate's figuration of Chaucer for his own readers, and it is a Chaucer largely composed from works that precede the *Canterbury Tales*. Moreover, Chau-

---

23. Text in *Lydgate's Siege of Thebes*, ed. Erdmann and Ekwall. See Battles, *Medieval Tradition of Thebes*, 145–57, for discussion of literary sources.

cer is known in the *Siege* only through Lydgate's allusion and autocitation. Lydgate does not give Chaucer's name until the end of the *Siege*, where "my mayster Chaucer" (4501) is identified at the point that the Theban story joins the Knight's Tale (4524, 4531). The story that Lydgate tells in the interim and moralizes at the end is one that opens up the questions about political order seemingly though incompletely resolved in Chaucer's Knight's Tale.[24]

The *Siege* has no designated patron or recipient, though Humphrey or possibly Henry may be the reader Lydgate imagines.[25] It hovers uncertainly between the triumphalist ending of *Troy Book* in 1420 and the trauma of Henry's death in 1422—or perhaps in the aftermath, when the kingdom and the dual monarchy were ruled by conciliar government and the uneasy alignment of Henry VI's uncles.[26] Pearsall remarks that it is Lydgate's most political poem.[27] Whether read for its moral coherence and political precepts or seen as the monitory example of Theban chaos beneath the chivalric virtues attributed to Trojan history, the *Siege* consolidates the position of a clerkly author compiling, translating, and redacting Latin and vernacular sources to address the foundational values of a court audience. This is a position, however it may be appropriated, that necessarily remains at some distance from the princes, aristocrats, and gentry it is designed to instruct. The *Siege*, in reproducing the frame tale of the Canterbury pilgrimage and supplementing the Knight's Tale, squarely raises the question of literary succession. Lydgate, like Hoccleve, creates Chaucer as father and master so that he can be son, heir, and disciple. As Spearing points out, however, Chaucer's literary paternity involves both troubled fatherhood and questionable inheritance—the first in Chaucer's obscuring his poetic precursors and the second in his skepticism about passing down literary virtues.[28] The *Siege* is a response to this ambivalence at its source. Lydgate goes past the figuration of Chaucer as an authorial mode—as rhetorician and founder of a national tradition—to engage him substantively by composing a Chaucerian imitation compiled from Latin and vernacular sources. He does so by addressing political power directly as a clerk rather than obliquely as the court amateur that Chaucer presents in his poetry before the *Canterbury Tales*.

---

24. Discussion in Spearing, "Lydgate's Canterbury Tale," 333–64; Allen, "*Siege of Thebes*: Lydgate's Canterbury Tale," 122–42; Lawton, "Dullness and the Fifteenth Century," 761–99; and Simpson, "'Dysemol daies and fatal houres,'" 15–33.

25. Seymour, *Selections from Hoccleve*, xxxn20, suggests that no fifteenth-century poet would undertake a work like the *Siege* without a patron.

26. Simpson, "'Dysemol daies and fatal houres,'" 15–16, argues for composition after Henry's death.

27. Pearsall, "Lydgate as Innovator," 15.

28. Spearing, *Medieval to Renaissance*, 98.

Lydgate again links clerkly *compilatio* and translation with Chaucerian imitation in the *Serpent of Division*, his only extant prose work. Ostensibly a retelling of the Roman civil war from Lucan's *Bellum Civile*, the *Serpent* reflects the vernacular classicism that recontextualizes antiquity through intermediate redactions and translations of the ancients in the late Middle Ages.[29] For his sources, Lydgate turns to French treatments of Lucan, Sallust, and Suetonius, augmented by portions of Vincent of Beauvais's *Speculum Historiale* and supplemented by other authorities. He names Lucan, Eusebius, Vincent, Valerius, and Chaucer as authors and masters; but, as Maura Nolan points out, these invocations "reveal far less about the background of *Serpent of Division* than about Lydgate's vision of cultural authority."[30] His theme of division—the fracture of unity in the body politic for singular profit—has vernacular precedent in Gower's *Confessio* and in Lydgate's epic project. In *Troy Book*, Lucifer is the originary figure of the serpent who divides the unity of creation (2.5834–924). In the *Siege*, he reappears as the serpent that "hath the Cokkyl sowe" (4668), the figure of Lollardy (glossed marginally as "lollium") and division. Division has a strong resonance in the period immediately after Henry's death in 1422, when the *Serpent* was composed "bi commaundemente of my moste worschipfull maistere & souereyne," usually taken to be Duke Humphrey.[31] It represents the danger of rivalry within the kingdom during Henry VI's minority, the rivalry of magnates in the shared power of conciliar government, and the unresolved conflicts that persisted despite the official acknowledgment of English claims to the French throne. The court culture to which Lydgate's writing addressed its narratives and advice was different from the political context behind *Troy Book* and the *Siege*, shaped by historical forces but also conditioned ideologically to understand itself through Lydgate's remaking of epic into an instrument of learning and reflection.

The *Serpent* is a monitory tale that charts the shift from republican to imperial forms as the vehicle of ambition. Like *Troy Book* and the *Siege*, it reckons the cost of war and chivalric heroism to all belligerents, Caesar and Pompey, above all. But it goes beyond the tragic loss of heroes—the moral and affective center of the earlier poems—to register the damage to the body politic and common profit: "The cite of Rome not onely made bare and bareyne of þer olde richesis and spoiled of here tresowre on þe too side, but destitute and desolate bi deþe of here kniȝthod on þe toþer side; whiche me semyth owȝte Inow suffise to exemplifie what hit is to begynne a werre, & specially to

---

29. See Galloway, "John Lydgate and the Origins of Vernacular Humanism," 445–71.

30. Maura Nolan, *John Lydgate and the Making of Public Culture*, 39. Ibid., 36–43, provides a critical review of Lydgate's sources.

31. Lydgate, *Serpent of Division*, ed. MacCracken, 66.

considre þe irrecuperable harmes of division."[32] Lydgate gestures throughout the *Serpent* to the authorities who recount the changing fortunes of great men driven by pride, envy, and covetousness. He depends on Chaucer to give his narrative a framework. The *Serpent* begins—"Whilome, as olde bookis maken mencion" (50)—with a clear evocation of the Knight's Tale: "Whilom, as olde stories tellen us" (I.859). He ends with his signature representation of Chaucer as "flowre of poetis in owre englisshe tonge" (65) and the first to illuminate the language with rhetoric and eloquence. At this point, however, he cites as Chaucer's a text that conflates the passage on Caesar's death in the Monk's Tale with a passage on Hercules. Lydgate's imitation charts the distance between the triumphal opening of the Knight's Tale and the obsessive repetition of tragic falls that the Knight intervenes to stop in the *Canterbury Tales*. He takes the position of a reader of antiquity in its noblest self-imagination in order to present himself as an author who can abstract the lessons of heroic ambition to instruct his patron and immediate circle of readers as well as "þe wise gouernours of euery londe and region" (65).

Fall of Princes (1431–39) represents Lydgate's most complex negotiation of authorship. As with the *Title and Pedigree of Henry VI* (1426), Lydgate is commissioned to translate a work initially directed to an aristocratic French audience—in this case, the second version of Laurent de Premierfait's *Des Cas des nobles hommes et femmes*, which was completed in 1409 for the royal patron Jean de France, Duc de Berry, uncle of Charles VI. Laurent's work translates and amplifies the B-redaction of Boccaccio's *De casibus virorum illustrium*, completed in 1373. Boccaccio's literary form—*de casibus* tragedy—is immediately recognizable for Lydgate as the one that Chaucer adapted to verse in the Monk's Tale and that Lydgate imitated in his poetic contrafactum at the end of the *Serpent of Division*. Boccaccio's interview with Fortune (his "horridum monstrum illud" becomes Lydgate's "monstruous ymage" [6.18]) in the *De casibus* formalizes the central theme of mutability that Lydgate reiterates throughout the *Fall*, as in his earlier writing; it also illustrates the irony, made apparent when Boccaccio solicits Fortune, that writers warning about Fortune's sudden changes of favor harbor their own ambitions for literary fame.[33] Nicholas Watson observes that Lydgate writes with the threefold mediation of Laurent, Boccaccio, and Chaucer, which moves the *Fall* toward the status of an independent literary composition.[34] Scanlon identifies the points of authority

---

32. Ibid., 65–66.
33. Flannery, *John Lydgate and the Poetics of Fame*, 13–37, argues that Lydgate asserts a distinctive control over fame and Fortune not evident in earlier writers like Chaucer.
34. Watson, "Theories of Translation," 83–85.

as Laurent, Chaucer, and Humphrey.[35] Besides Chaucer, Lydgate evokes a classical and humanist canon that includes Seneca, Cicero, and Petrarch. He cites his own poems, especially *Troy Book* (1.5937–6041) and the *Siege* (1.3724), as authorities for the fall of classical figures. For Arthurian materials, which Boccaccio finds recorded in annals, Lydgate adds the *Brut* tradition and Geoffrey of Monmouth as sources (8.3022, 3099).

Lydgate's commission from Duke Humphrey not only authorizes composition of the *Fall* but bears on its meaning and politics of reception. Once the project is underway, Humphrey intervenes (Prol 2.141–54) to direct Lydgate to insert envoys after each narrative to point the moral and expound the significance. In effect, this prescribed commentary extends Laurent's shift from private morality and conduct in Boccaccio to the body politic, and it carries Lydgate's poem toward the prophetic social voice of Gower's public poetry.[36] Humphrey intervenes more deeply than did Henry in establishing the final cause of *Troy Book*. Alessandra Petrina suggests that he intends "to propose an image of himself as the true, spiritual inheritor of Henry V's legacy."[37] His instructions mark the *Fall* as a compendium of exempla with a stable hermeneutic apparatus to control the meanings to be derived from the narratives and from the complaints that serve as a characteristic mode of expression. His patronage, meanwhile, positions Lydgate, the poem, and Humphrey himself as counterparts and rivals to the massive program of translation for aristocratic audiences undertaken by the Valois monarchy, most prominently through Laurent's translations of Aristotle and Cicero. Whether Humphrey qualifies as an early patron of humanism is perhaps less an issue than his effort to use authorship as an instrument of policy and cultural ambition.[38]

Laurent gives Lydgate a *forma tractandi* that explicitly sets out principles of authorship that Lydgate had earlier found in the supplements that Guido adds to the sources of *Troy Book*. Laurent proposes: "Selon raison et bonnes meurs l'omme soy exerçant en aucune science speculative ou aultre puet honnestement muer son conseil ou propost de bien en mieulx, attendue la mutation des choses et des temps et des lieux. Et aussi puest un potier casser et rumpre aulcun sien vaissel, combien qu'il soit bien fait, pour lui donner aultre

---

35. Scanlon, *Narrative, Authority, and Power*, 327.

36. Hedeman, *Translating the Past*, 17–21; and Armstrong, *English Boccaccio*, 57–60, track Laurent's widening of Boccaccio's original aristocratic audience. Lydgate's envoys are excerpted in manuscripts circulating separately; see *Lydgate's Troy Book*, ed. Bergen, 4:105. They are printed with Chaucer's "Truth" and "Fortune" and two of Lydgate's didactic poems in *Prouerbes of Lydgate*; see Pearsall, *John Lydgate*, 12, 207, and 251.

37. Petrina, *Cultural Politics*, 353.

38. Summit, "'Stable in study,'" 209–31, reads Lydgate's poem and Humphrey's ambitions as mutually reinforcing rather than opposed.

forme qui lui samble meilleur" [According to reason and good habits, a man practicing a speculative science or any other science can honestly change his view or intention from good to better, given the change of things, times, and places. And a potter can also shatter and break any of his vessels, regardless of how well made it is, to give it another form that seems better to him].[39] Lydgate's rendering of the image emphasizes the artisanal over the speculative features of Laurent's precept:

> In his prologe affermyng off resoun,
> Artificeres hauyng exercise
> May chaunge and turne bi good discrecioun
> Shappis, formys, and newli hem deuyse,
> Make and vnmake in many sondry wyse,
> As potteres, which to that craft entende,
> Breke and renewe ther vesselis to a-mende.
> (Prol 8–14)

Laurent's description of his process has as its objective a fuller realization of the potential of a work; it moves forward "de bien en meiulx." Armstrong sees in it both aesthetic and social ends.[40] By contrast, Lydgate emphasizes permutations and recombinations—making and unmaking in different formal structures without an imagined terminus. Lydgate goes on to situate the potter's refinement of aesthetic structure within a tradition of literary production: "Thyng that was maad of auctours hem beforn, / Thei may off newe fynde and fantasie" (Prol 22–23). The warrant for such revision lies in the image of renewal that Chaucer describes as a principle of poetic making in the Prologues to the *Legend* (F 73–77, G 61–65): "Out of old chaff trie out ful cleene corn, / Make it more fressh and lusti to the eie" (Prol 24–25). Laurent insists that the governing moral warrant for revision and renewal is charity rooted in the heart of the author. Scanlon points out nonetheless that Laurent's precept allows "an almost unlimited latitude for innovation."[41]

Lydgate regards Laurent as a model for the kind of literary production he will offer in the *Fall*—revisionary poetic invention within a decorum of rhetorical submission and moral purpose directed to princes and kings. His "auctour," however, is Boccaccio who remains the source for the "mater" (Prol 267) gathered from the biographies of illustrious men and women who experience reversals of Fortune. Although Lydgate refers to Boccaccio as a "noble

---

39. *Laurent de Premierfait's "Des Cas des nobles hommes et femmes,"* ed. Gathercole, 88–89.
40. Armstrong, *English Boccaccio*, 58.
41. Scanlon, *Narrative, Authority, and Power*, 330.

poete" (4.3493), his primary description emphasizes Boccaccio as a recognized source for narrative exempla. Boccaccio also places Lydgate within an authorial succession. At the start of Book 8, Petrarch appears to urge Boccaccio to continue writing, and Boccaccio addresses him as his "cheeff exaumplaire" (8.78) for writing books by compilation, a role confirmed at the start of Book 9. In this way, Lydgate's writing reaches back through Boccaccio to Petrarch, who serves in the *Fall* as the author linking moderns and ancients. Meanwhile, Lydgate's "maistir" (Prol 246) is Chaucer, whose writings Lydgate enumerates in an extended and amplified passage (Prol 274–357) based on Chaucer's own description of his works in the Prologues to the *Legend* and the Retraction at the end of the *Canterbury Tales*. Chaucer, as elsewhere in Lydgate, is the dead and unrecoverable "cheeff poete off Breteyne" (Prol 247, 2.979); and as a poet who "whilom made ful pitous tragedies" (Prol 249), he is linked to Seneca, Cicero, and Petrarch as the author of *De Remediis Utriusque Fortunae*. The ancients, thus broadly construed, furnish the precedent of writers who not only advise princes but guide their study and reading. Caesar's fictitious attendance at the school of Cicero and his hearing Cicero's lectures (Prol 365–71) prepare in turn for a comparison with Duke Humphrey as the patron of Lydgate's translation and compilation. The comparison invites the extended parallel that connects power, learning, and moral instruction: Caesar is to Humphrey, as Cicero is to Lydgate. Moreover, as he turns to recounting Boccaccio's "tragedies" (Prol 466), Lydgate introduces a separate frame that continues to foreground his role as a belated author. The *Fall* is presented as a description of what is contained in Boccaccio's *De casibus*.[42] Its governing fiction is that Lydgate narrates a reading and writing of Boccaccio's book.

As in other poems, Lydgate fashions clerks as writers of histories and custodians of memory. Amplifying Boccaccio's remarks on proud kings (*De casibus* 2.5) to a disquisition on good government, Lydgate traces "the famous cleer shynyng" (2.813) of emperors, "ther laude in reportyng" (2.815), conquests, and triumphs to the work of clerks as "writeris" (2.819). The Prologue to Book 4 extends the memorial function of authors to the remedy of separation and loss: "Thus frut of writyng hath his auauntages, / Of folk ferr off to presente the images" (4.20–21). Writing preserves, says Lydgate, law, religion, and "ordre of good lyuyng" (4.24); it provides a continuing foundation for civil society and religious tradition. To a degree not developed in the earlier works, writing is described not just as preservation against time—as it is with saving Prosper of Aquitaine's epigrams, Seneca's tragedies, Vegetius's mili-

---

42. The title of the 1494 *editio princeps* of the *Fall* (STC 3175) preserves Lydgate's frame: Here begynnethe the boke calledde Iohn bochas descriuinge the falle of princis princessis [and] other nobles.

tary doctrine, or Persius's satires—but active renewal, the replenished "foode of our inward reffut" (4.52), which is also the ground of moral and political knowledge.

Lydgate's citation of Christian and classical writers by genre and topic here suggests the importance of authorial canons as well as an author's individual works. One of the ways authorial fame, which Lydgate identifies as laureation, preserves a writer's name is by enumerating a canon. For Vergil, Lydgate lists "thre famous bookis this auctour list compile" (4.71); unlike Gower, who recognizes a poetic *cursus honorum*, he sees Vergil's poetry as a stylistic and rhetorical achievement. Ovid's *Metamorphoses* is a compendium of "the grete wondres, the transmutaciouns, / The moral menyng, [th]vnkouth conclusions" (1.95–96) of ancient myth; it stands alongside the writings from exile, the *Heroides*, and the erotodidactic poems. Lydgate presents a catalogue of Petrarch's Latin writings. Writing renews Homer and the Troy story, Aesop, and Juvenal. Dante's writing is kept alive and "sunge among Lumbardis in especial, / Whos thre bookis the grete wondres tell / Of heuene aboue, of purgatorie & hell" (4.138–40). Hagiography and medicine are paired as areas of knowledge made available by writing. Cicero's canon is remembered through Vincent of Beauvais's *Speculum Historiale* (6.3158–74). Boccaccio's authorship, says Lydgate, is driven by the twin motives of assuring that learning is "onli ordeyned to our auauntages" (4.153) and securing fame "onli by writyng to geten hym a name" (4.168).

Lydgate's equation of authors with canons is closely connected to the kind of humanism that he produces for Humphrey in the *Fall*. Galloway, Nolan, and Summit have usefully reformulated the question of Lydgate's relation to humanism, directing it away from commonplaces generally applied to the Renaissance (a revival of classical learning, a renewed dignity for mankind, nationalism) and toward the instrumental uses of the past serving patron and poet alike. Humanism, in this sense, reflects not a program or set of principles but a use value, cultural capital that advances the ambitions and prestige of those who control means of transmission as well as production. What Lydgate offers in the *Fall* is a conception of authorship that complements and advances Humphrey's view of himself as a learned prince operating in an elite European framework with practical models in Italian humanism.

The authorship that Lydgate simulates to these ends appears in Book 2 of the *Fall*, with the story of Lucrece, whose republican politics are an object of continual reshaping to the aims of princely power. Lydgate recognizes that Chaucer wrote the "legende soueroyne" (2.979) of Lucrece's life, and he associates it with stories such as that of Dido and Aeneas from the *Legend*. He goes on, however, to supplement Chaucer's unsurpassed narrative with the

Declamatio composed by the Florentine humanist Coluccio Salutati and furnished by Humphrey.[43] Mortimer points out that Lydgate's supplement is an important departure from Laurent's translation and that it is an account that likewise resists Salutati's Augustinian legalism, which focused on Lucrece's guilt as a suicide. The effect of the supplement, in the arguments of the male kinsmen and then Lucrece's reply from the *Declamatio*, is to foreground ethics rather than the historical-political consequences of tyranny, as derived from the story by medieval writers from Jean de Meun onward.[44] In this way, as Summit argues, the potential lesson of republican freedom from tyranny is displaced to a lesson on the need for order and hierarchy whose basis lies in princely governance.[45]

The appeals to persuasion and debate over courses of action in the Lucrece story point to the rhetorical foundation of Lydgate's version of humanism. Rhetoric in this context signifies something beyond style and eloquence, the commonplaces of Lydgate's standard praise for writers as rhetoricians. In the interview with Fortune in Book 6, Lydgate's Boccaccio represents mutability as discord, hence the cause of "dyuersite" (6.352) and division. The remedy to the discord that Fortune instigates is "speche & fair langage." Boccaccio asserts, "Folk be thi fraude fro grace ferr exilid, / Wer be fair speche to vnite reconcilid" (6.376–78). But speech in the social and political sphere serves as more than an instrument of remedy and reconciliation; it is, in the first instance, constitutive. Lydgate treats classical antiquity and the *translatio imperii*—"Peeplis of Grece, of Roome & off Cartage, / Next in Itaille, with many a regeoun" (6.379–80)—as the cultural products of discourse. Civil society is founded in moments of public discussion, as peoples "haue togidre ther conuersacioun, / To beelde castellis & many roial toun" (6.382–83) in order to live under law and in "oon accord" (6.396). Later in Book 6, Lydgate expands Boccaccio's attack on the misuse of rhetoric (*De casibus* 6.13) to an exposition of rhetoric as part of "rational" philosophy, which teaches what should be done or avoided. He rehearses the five canons of rhetoric, but his stress falls on the social effects of discourse. Rhetoricians, he says, are adaptive in their means yet consistent in their objectives: "Be wise exaumplis & prouerbis pertynent / Tenduce the parties to been of oon assent" (6.3457–58). They assume the duties of comforting the desolate and mitigating angry tyrants. The underlying power of their discourse is the harmony of music, so it is not by chance that Lydgate ends his excursus by invoking Amphion who, as in the *Siege*, is presented as a musician and city founder.

---

43. Hammond, "Lydgate and Coluccio Salutati," 49–57.
44. Mortimer, *John Lydgate's Fall of Princes*, 61–78.
45. Summit, "'Stable in study,'" 224.

Lydgate's civic humanism limits itself to the principles and mythography that Cicero lays out in the *De inventione* and that intermediate writers like Brunetto Latini disseminate in the vernacular. Human reason and conversation, Lydgate contends, are the means for negotiating conflict and creating institutions. On this view, authors hold a brief not just for the application of historical exempla to the conduct of rulers but for the order and internal cohesion of institutions, which represent the rational and social qualities that distinguish mankind. As Lydgate's poem approaches its final examples, these issues take shape in commitments to the nation. Lydgate disputes Laurent's praise of French eminence as unwarranted by his source: "Thes woordis be nat take out of myn auctour" (9.1884). He cites the capture of King John at Poitiers as a moment in which "hihe prowesse and prudent pollicie" converge: "Mars and Mercurie aboue ech nacioun / Gouerned that tyme Brutis Albioun" (9.3152–54). He rehearses the English claims to the French throne as an argument decided by the divine "tokne" (9.3219) of Edward's victory, whose significance princes weigh in reaching a consensus that puts the matter beyond further dispute.

At the end of the *Fall*, Lydgate stands as an author who replicates the anxiety that Boccaccio earlier expressed in the face of his daunting task of recounting princely tragedies. His work as a commissioned translator and compiler places him in a literary succession that moves through Chaucer to Boccaccio to Petrarch, whence presumably to the ancients whose writings provide the materials of the exempla and tragedies they gather. His gestures of valediction mark both his model and his difference as an author. The Chaucerian gesture he partially enacts as the translator addressing his work—"Go kis the steppis of them that wer forthring . . . thy makyng" (9.3605-7)—imagines not the school of epic poets named in *Troilus and Criseyde* (5.1791–92) but "laureat poetes, which hadde souereynte / Of elloquence" (9.3606-7). These are the kind of court writers that Lydgate helped bring to prominence in his epic project and public poetry. Their treatment of mutable, worldly goods teaches princes the lessons of virtue through a rhetoric situated in civic humanism with registers of "compleynt & moornyng" (9.3621) whose reproduction marks Lydgate as an author and moral authority.

AFTERWORD

~

The Afterlife of Medieval Authorship

MEDIEVAL ENGLISH writers from the twelfth century onward invented what we might describe as a field of authorship. The field comprises an array of self-inaugurating models that allowed writers to position themselves in relation to classical and vernacular traditions, literary forebears, authoritative texts, intertexts, genres, and other discursive forms as well as institutional structures. Their sources for authorship lie in both the formal structures of exegesis and pedagogy and the practices of invention and imitation. As we have seen, these formal structures become the topics of invention and imitation. Across the multiple forms and expressions of authorship, the defining feature is agency. Writers, I have argued, exercise agency externally, with respect to literary culture, and internally, with respect to poetic creation. These two aspects are not serial but mutually defining, for practices of writing inevitably transform theories of authorship, just as theories hold new possibilities of practice. To describe a field of authorship is, of course, not the same thing as describing authorship for a particular writer. The differences between Walter Map and Marie de France, John Gower and Geoffrey Chaucer, or Thomas Hoccleve and John Lydgate reflect alternatives for authorship within the fields they inhabited individually and shared to a greater or lesser degree. Still, several features remain visible, if not constant, within these differences. In post-Conquest England, authorship is revisionary. Writers modify rather than establish literary culture at an imagined founding moment; in doing so, they work selectively and partially. Their efforts are performative and depend as much on reception as representation. Whatever their *materia,* medieval writers are tacticians of belatedness, adapting succession and subordination to their own ends, much as they adapt the institutions of readership and patronage.

I have contended that medieval inventions of authorship obliquely fashion literary history as a secondary effect of agency. From the middle of the fifteenth century onward, as evidenced by the repeated invocations of Gower, Chaucer, and Lydgate as "primier poetes of this nacion" or the later, encyclopedic antiquarian writings of John Leland, John Bale, and others, authorship, even if it is reduced to the names of writers and their works, proves foundational to any narrative of an English literary tradition.[1] For Scots writers, authorship is the governing fiction of the *Kingis Quair* early in the fifteenth century, and it serves later *makars* near the turn of the sixteenth century by providing a literary precedent for their tradition and a continuing formal influence.[2] In George Puttenham's *The Art of English Poesy* (1598), the English national tradition is a succession of authors, structured by the reigns of monarchs, ending with Queen Elizabeth, who surpasses all. By way of conclusion, I want to examine several moments in the afterlife of medieval English authorship when it encounters and serves to constitute the emerging modernity of Renaissance literary culture.

In our standard accounts of literary history, the line of demarcation between late medieval and Early Modern authorship moves steadily backward through the sixteenth century. E. K.'s *Epistle* in Edmund Spenser's *The Shepheardes Calender* (1579) is frequently cited as a vanishing point for medieval authorship; it might be taken instead as a starting point for the regression. As A. C. Spearing observes, for Spenser, Chaucer is "a poet of the past—admirable and worthy of imitation, but no longer threatening in his superiority." In Spenser's historical moment, he is, Spearing adds, "now an archaic poet."[3] Chaucer "the olde famous Poete" is sufficiently distant to mark a historical break that defines Spenser's modernity. Attended by his "scholler" Lydgate in E. K.'s description and tutored by Gower according to the explanatory materials of early print editions, he represents not just an idealized genealogy but a recognized literary system. Robert Meyer-Lee moves the line a generation or so closer toward a late medieval point of transition, finding in Sir Thomas Wyatt's poetry an underground tradition comprising Lydgate, Hoccleve,

---

1. Simpson, *Reform and Cultural Revolution,* 24, notes that Leland and Bale construct a bio-bibliographical literary history with few literary texts.
2. See Elliott, "Scottish Writing," 587–89, for parallel canons of English and Scottish poets.
3. Spearing, *Medieval to Renaissance,* 329.

and Stephen Hawes. Wyatt, on this reading, displaces the tensions of official patronage and laureate poetics by writing courtly lyrics and evoking Chaucer directly rather than relying on Chaucer's heirs and fifteenth-century intermediaries.[4] Seth Lerer argues that William Caxton and print culture generally serve as a middle term between Early Modern and medieval authorship because Caxton makes Chaucer a figure to invoke and name but not imitate as a poet. Chaucer is part of "a pantheon of English and antique *auctores*," cited but not reproduced with the rise of laureate poetics and courtly amateurs during the Tudor monarchy.[5] A. S. G. Edwards proposes that in some respects the line between past and present may vanish in the claims of Renaissance modernity itself: "For the first time in the sixteenth century, contemporary poets are seen as points of reference comparable with those figures of undisputed past greatness."[6] In a recent overview of sixteenth-century poetry, Patrick Cheney links John Skelton, Wyatt, and Henry Howard, Earl of Surrey forward to Spenser and the Elizabethans and backward to Chaucer and his successors "within a single genealogy" of a national poet.[7]

Hawes's *Pastime of Pleasure* (1506) and John Skelton's *Garlande or Chapelet of Laurell* (1495, printed 1523) anchor much of the critical discussion about the shift between medieval and Early Modern forms of authorship. The two authors are configured in an unlikely contrast: Hawes, presumably looking backward to medieval models, is an author exclusively within print culture; all his works were printed by Wynkyn de Worde, who lavished the attention to presentation in print seen for earlier poets in *de luxe* manuscripts. Skelton, by contrast, strives to create a humanist or protohumanist, politically aligned authorship based on the older technologies of manuscript production and oratory. Within the novel and contrasting formations that each devises, however, medieval authorship is as much a point of recursion as departure. The court and patronage remain the contexts of writing. Hawes exploits the Lancastrian linkage between instruction and state chivalry in his dream visions. Skelton moves between and among the medieval poetic roles of adviser, prophet, *auctor*, and translator; he negotiates the claims of innate and delegated authority into a dynamic process of literary meaning for the poet and his readers.[8] (Thomas Wharton proposes that Skelton's Latin poetry follows the example of Walter Map.[9]) In the material presentation of works by both writers, ana-

---

4. Meyer-Lee, *Poets and Power*, 220–32.
5. Lerer, *Chaucer and His Readers*, 175.
6. A. S. G. Edwards, "Beyond the Fifteenth Century," 225.
7. Cheney, *Reading Sixteenth-Century Poetry*, 117.
8. Griffiths, *John Skelton and Poetic Authority*, 10–17.
9. A. S. G. Edwards, *Skelton: The Critical Heritage*, 82.

logues to medieval paratexts appear in the textual machinery of rubrics, initials, woodcuts, and (for Skelton) glosses.

Hawes's commitment to Lydgate as an authorial model is evident not just in his overt recognition of "the monke of Bury floure of eloquence" (27) and his echoes of Lydgate's lines but in a conspicuously belated reproduction of the poetry that characterizes Lydgate as a Lancastrian propagandist and unofficial laureate.[10] Hawes draws the parallel between Lydgate's writing for Henry V and his own service to Henry VII, who, like his Lancastrian counterpart, descends "by the ryghtfull lyne" (15) to claim legitimate kingship for himself and for an heir who waits to succeed him. He thus retools the genealogical splicing that Lydgate employs to displace the ruptures of descent by patterns of succession. Lydgate delivers "fatall fyccyons" (33), works of historical importance, to Hawes's "fayned fable" (44), imaginative narratives. But he becomes, as Hawes presents him, a writer for whom misty speech and cloudy figures denote allegorical composition rather than elevated style. Allegory, Hawes insists, is the venerable *modus tractandi* of literary discourse, "the guyse in olde antyquyte / Of the poetes olde" (51–52). In this, he follows the commonplace announced in the final books of Boccaccio's *Genealogie deorum gentilium* that poetry is characterized by an allegorical veil.

Hawes, like Lydgate, sees in his royal addressee the princely determination to avoid sloth and embrace an active life consonant with virtue. He asserts, too, the value of common profit that Ricardian and Lancastrian poets extolled as an article of political consensus. Where he differs from Lydgate is in his conception of the idealized reader to be shaped by his work. In *Troy Book*, Lydgate finds in Henry's "manhode" an informing pattern of aristocratic identity that is underwritten by the examples of antiquity and potentially transferrable to all social orders in the nation who read or hear the story in their native tongue. In the *Pastime*, Hawes's protagonist Grande Amoure is a courtier, and his education in the Seven Liberal Arts—a reprise of Book 7 of Gower's *Confessio Amantis*—serves a lover whose erotic quest for La Bell Pucell signifies the desire of the courtly subject as a writer and political subordinate in the secular realm. In the love allegory and encyclopedia, as Daniel Wakelin notes, Hawes combines two familiar early Tudor genres, but their roots lie in medieval forms that give both poetic themes and models of social performance.[11]

Throughout his poem, Hawes appropriates and reapplies the lexicon of authorship from Lydgate. He invokes "my mayster Lydgate" (48, 1163, 1338,

---

10. Text in Hawes, *Pastime of Pleasure*, ed. Mead.
11. Wakelin, "Stephen Hawes and Courtly Education," 56.

1373, 1395, 1402, 5812), echoing the phrase that Lydgate applied to Chaucer. He follows Lydgate's "trace" (47, 1395, 5812), just as Lydgate followed his *auctores* in compiling and translating texts. The extended catalogue of Lydgate's works (1338–65) at the end of the section on rhetoric in the *Pastime* not only outstrips the listing for Chaucer and the bare citation of "morall gower" (1317); it also stands as a counterpart to the catalogues that Chaucer inserts in his own works. But if Lydgate is a model for Hawes to emulate, he is also a figure who sets a boundary for authorship and for Hawes's narrative. Hawes alludes to the image used by Chaucer's Clerk for Petrarch in lamenting that Lydgate "is now wrapte in cheste" (1378). Rather than liberate invention and exegesis, as Petrarch's death does for the Clerk's Tale, Lydgate's demise means the end of serious authorship ("They fayne no fables pleasaunt and couerte" [1389]), as poets direct their talents to "makyng balades of feruent amyte / As gestes and tryfles without fruytfulness" (1391–92). Their work is the literary equivalent of sloth, and it represents the courtly amateur who will return in figures like Wyatt to reclaim the prestige, audience, and political connections from which Lydgate and other clerks had earlier displaced them.

Lydgate returns for the last time in Hawes's poem in a complex narrative movement that begins with Grande Amoure's death. Dame Fame arrives to associate his name with the Nine Worthies for his achievements as a lover and warrior. Time and then Eternity blunt her claims to preserve his name in books against the mutability of worldly achievements. Hawes ends his poem by aligning himself with Lydgate in the authorial "besynes" (5809) of compiling books of moral virtue, a return that Gower had staged for himself at the end of the *Confessio Amantis*. He aims, then, not to succeed medieval authorship but to reproduce and sustain it in a continuous present and to do so, like Lydgate, from a position that transcends the immediate rhetorical contexts of his writing.

Skelton's *Garlande* claims precisely the fame that Hawes abandons to Time and Eternity at the end of the *Pastime*. The Queen of Fame is Skelton's initial advocate for "the laurell grene" (68) traditionally awarded to poets for their service as authors eschewing "slowthfull ydelnes" (120).[12] Dame Pallas replaces Time and Eternity as the constraining force on literary fame. When she accedes to Fame's petition on behalf of Skelton, she reactivates the frantic scenes from Chaucer's *House of Fame* where petitioners seek renown and reputation. Skelton sees "a thousand poetes assembled togeder" (286) to form in the ensemble of ancient and modern authors a full humanist curriculum. The central tableau of the *Garlande* is the encounter of Poeta Skelton (so des-

---

12. Text in *John Skelton: The Complete English Poems*, ed. Scattergood.

ignated in the woodcut and rubrics) with Maysters Gower, Chaucer, and Lydgate, whose "collage above the sterry sky" (403) holds a place for him. In this account, Skelton has earned his "enplement" (402) because he has carried on the project of refining the language, which was traditionally attributed to the "Primier poetes." Gower explicitly makes the point that Skelton is the genealogical link to medieval authorship "that welny was loste when that we were gone" (406). Skelton thus represents a project of restoration as well as the completion of his own trajectory toward full recognition as a laureate. His status is singular in its self-promotion yet cumulative in imagining that he carries forward England's three recognized medieval authors in his own laureation.[13] Thus restored, English poets connect Skelton to the classical and vernacular *auctores* and ratify within the long chain of tradition the poetic eminence ascribed to him by contemporaries beginning with Erasmus.[14]

The ceremonial objects of the *Garlande* symbolize the nature of authorship in Skelton's fantasy. The chaplet sown for him by Elizabeth Howard, Countess of Surrey, and the aristocratic women of her household is the aesthetic and material figure of the courtly context of his writing. Manufactured by its conventional love objects and arbiters of decorum, it displaces the classical garland and thus links the poet's art to women's domestic artistry.[15] The list of works that Occupacyon reads from the book carried under her arm is a canonical arrangement by an author published to the world at large, evidently with a few regrets for works Skelton would now erase from the compendious volume.[16] The recital of the authorial canon provides as well an occasion to refute his detractors and, more important, to register the cries of triumph from poets and orators at the end of the recitation. Skelton goes on to claim an eminence for his Latin compositions that complements his English writings, and he ends with a trilingual translation of the conventional topic "abuses of the age" that insists thematically on his acknowledged role as a satirist. His Latin admonition to all trees to give place to the laurel claims a modern authorship that Skelton asserts he alone can exercise. At the same time, the claim emanates from a dream of fame and reputation; the form reveals itself

---

13. Breen, "Laureation and Identity," 352, argues that the laurel is "a symbol of continuing poetic and historical service" and notes that it is not self-generated but "conferred through a process of evaluation, deliberation, and election" that places Skelton in a social tradition.

14. For Erasmus's "Carmen Extemporale" (1499), equating Skelton with Homer and Vergil as representing a poetic tradition as well as comments by Skelton's contemporaries, see A. S. G. Edwards, *Skelton: The Critical Heritage*, 44–53.

15. Tarnoff, "Sewing Authorship," 415.

16. Griffiths, *John Skelton and Poetic Authority*, 117–28, finds the ambivalence of Skelton's text, particularly its obscured links to patronage, reproduced in the glosses to it, which concentrate around the figure of Occupacyon.

as desire. Skelton can be a modern only by submitting to the mutability situated in Fame's palace and, unlike Chaucer's Geffrey in the *House of Fame*, by giving his name to the contingencies and distortions of language and rumor. The paradox and self-directed energy of the *Garlande* is Skelton's unintended figure for the stubborn presence of medieval authorship within Early Modern poetic ambition.

BIBLIOGRAPHY

PRIMARY SOURCES

Accessus ad auctores; Bernard d'Utrech; Conrad d'Hirsau, Dialogus super auctores. Revised ed. Edited by R. B. C. Huygens. Leiden: Brill, 1970.

Accessus ad auctores: Medieval Introductions to the Authors (Codex latinus monacensis 19475). Edited and translated by Stephen M. Wheeler. Kalamazoo, MI: Medieval Institute Publications, 2015.

Augustine. *Confessionum libri XIII.* Edited by M. Skutella. Revised by Lucas Verheijen. CCSL 27. Turnhout: Brepols, 1981.

———. *De civitate Dei.* Edited by B. Dombart and A. Kalb. Corpus Christianorum, Series Latina, 47-48. Turnhout: Brepols, 2003.

Bede. *Bede's Ecclesiastical History of the English People.* Edited by Bertram Colgrave and R. A. B. Mynors. Oxford: Oxford University Press, 1969.

———. *In Lucae Evangelium Expositio.* In *Bedae Venerabilis Opera,* Pars II, 3: Opera Exegetica. Edited by D. Hurst. Corpus Christianorum, Series Latina 120. Turnhout: Brepols, 1960.

———. *The Old English Version of Bede's Ecclesiastical History of The English People.* Edited by Thomas Miller. EETS OS 95-96. London: Oxford University Press, 1891.

Boccaccio, Giovanni. *Il Filostrato.* Edited by Vittore Branca. In *Tutte le opere di Giovanni Boccaccio.* Vittore Branca, general editor. 12 vols. Milan: Mondadori, 1964-83.

———. *Genealogie deorum gentilium.* Edited by Vincenzo Romano. 2 vols. Bari: Gius. Laterza & Figli, 1951.

Boethius. *In porphyrii Isogogem Porphyrii commenta.* Edited by G. Schepss and S. Brandt. CSEL 48. Vienna: Tempsky, 1906.

Buridan, John. *Quaestiones in decem libros Ethicorum Aristotelis ad Nicomachum.* Oxford: Henry Cripps, Edward Forrest, Henry Curtayne, and John Wilmot, 1637.

Chaucer, Geoffrey. *The book of fame made by Gefferey Chaucer.* Westminster: William Caxton, 1483.

———. *The Riverside Chaucer.* 3rd ed. Edited by Larry D. Benson. Boston: Houghton Mifflin, 1987.

———. *The workes of Geffray Chaucer.* London: Thomas Godfray, 1532.

Dares. *Daretis Phrygii de Excidio Troiae Historia.* Edited by Ferdinand Meister. Leipzig: Teubner, 1873.

Dictys. *Dictys Cretensis Ephemeridos Belli Trojani.* Edited by Ferdinand Meister. Leipzig: Teubner, 1872.

Gower, John. *The Complete Works of John Gower.* Edited by G. C. Macaulay. 4 vols. Oxford: Clarendon Press, 1899–1902.

———. *John Gower: Confessio Amantis.* 2nd ed. Edited by Russell A. Peck. 3 vols. Kalamazoo, MI: Medieval Institute Publications, 2006–13.

———. *John Gower: The French Balades.* Edited and translated by R. F. Yeager. Kalamazoo, MI: Medieval Institute Publications, 2011.

———. *John Gower: The Minor Latin Works.* Edited and translated by R. F. Yeager. With *In Praise of Peace.* Edited by Michael Livingston. Kalamazoo, MI: Medieval Institute Publications, 2005.

———. *John Gower: Poems on Contemporary Events, The 'Visio Anglie' (1381) and 'Cronica tripertita' (1400).* Edited by David R. Carlson. Translated by A. G. Rigg. Toronto: Pontifical Institute of Mediaeval Studies, 2011; Oxford: Bodleian Library, 2011.

———. *The Major Latin Works of John Gower.* Translated by Eric W. Stockton. Seattle: University of Washington Press, 1962.

———. *Mirour de l'Omme (The Mirror of Mankind).* Translated by William Burton Wilson. Revised by Nancy Wilson Van Baak. East Lansing, MI: Colleagues Press, 1992.

Guido delle Colonne. *Historia Destructionis Troiae.* Edited by Nathaniel Edward Griffin. Cambridge, MA: Mediaeval Academy of America, 1936.

———. *Historia Destructionis Troiae.* Translated by Mary Elizabeth Meek. Bloomington: University of Indiana Press, 1974.

Guillaume de Lorris and Jean de Meun. *Le Roman de la Rose.* Edited by Daniel Poirion. Paris: Garnier-Flammarion, 1974.

Hawes, Stephen. *The comforte of louers.* London: Wynkyn de Worde, 1515.

———. *Here begynneth the boke called the example of vertu.* London: Wynkyn de Worde, [1504?].

———. *The Pastime of Pleasure.* Edited by William Edward Mead. EETS OS 173. London: Oxford University Press, 1928 for 1927.

Hoccleve, Thomas. *Hoccleve's Works, I: The Minor Poems.* Edited by F. J. Furnivall. EETS ES 61. London: Kegan Paul, Trench, Trübner & Co., 1892.

———. *Hoccleve's Works, II: The Minor Poems.* Edited by Israel Gollancz. EETS ES 73. London: Oxford University Press, 1925.

———. *Regiment of Princes.* Edited by Charles R. Blyth. Kalamazoo, MI: Medieval Institute Publications, 1999.

———. *Thomas Hoccleve's Complaint and Dialogue.* Edited by J. A. Burrow. EETS OS 313. Oxford: Oxford University Press, 1999.

Laurent de Premierfait. *Laurent de Premierfait's "Des Cas des nobles hommes et femmes."* Edited by Patricia May Gathercole. Chapel Hill: University of North Carolina Press, 1968.

Lydgate, John. *John Lydgate: Mummings and Entertainments.* Edited by Claire Sponsler. Kalamazoo, MI: Medieval Institute Publications, 2010.

——. *Lydgate's Siege of Thebes.* Edited by Axel Erdmann and Eilert Ekwall. 2 vols. EETS ES 108, 125. London: Kegan Paul, Trench, Trübner & Co., 1911, 1930.

——. *Lydgate's Troy Book.* Edited by Henry Bergen. 4 vols. EETS ES 97, 103, 106, and 126. London: Kegan Paul, Trench, Trübner & Co., 1906–8; London: Oxford University Press, 1935.

——. *The Minor Poems of John Lydgate.* Edited by Henry Noble MacCracken. 2 vols. EETS ES 107 and 109. London: Kegan Paul, Trench, Trübner & Co., 1911; London: Oxford University Press, 1934.

——. *The Prouerbes of Lydgate.* London: Wynkyn de Worde, 1510.

——. *Serpent of Division.* Edited by Henry Noble MacCracken. London: Oxford University Press, 1911.

——, and Benedict Burgh. *Secrees of old Philisoffres.* Edited by Robert Steele. EETS ES 60. London: Kegan Paul, Trench, Trübner & Co., 1894.

Map, Walter. *Contes des courtisans: Traduction du De nugis curialium de Gautier Map.* Translated by Marylène Perez. Lille: Centre d'études médiévales et dialectales, Université de Lille III, 1988.

——. *Gualteri Mapes De Nugis Curialium Distinctiones Quinque.* Edited by Thomas Wright. London: Camden Society, 1850.

——. *Master Walter Map's Book, De nugis curialium (Courtiers' Trifles).* Translated by Frederick Tupper and Marbury Bladen Ogle. London: Chatto & Windus, 1924.

——. *De Nugis Curialium.* Edited by Montague Rhodes James. Anecdota Oxoniensia, Mediaeval and Modern Series: Part XIV. Oxford: Clarendon Press, 1914.

——. *De Nugis Curialium; Courtiers' Trifles.* Edited and translated by M. R. James. Revised by C. L. N. Brooke and R. A. B. Mynors. Oxford: Clarendon Press, 1983.

Marie de France. *The Fables of Marie de France.* Translated by Mary Lou Martin. Birmingham, AL: Summa Publications, 1984.

——. *Les Lais de Marie de France.* Edited by Jean Rychner. Paris: Champion, 1971.

——. *The Lais of Marie de France.* 2nd ed. Translated by Glyn S. Burgess and Keith Busby. London: Penguin, 1999.

——. *The Life of Saint Audrey: A Text by Marie de France.* Edited and translated by June Hall McCash and Judith Clark Barban. Jefferson, NC: McFarland, 2006.

——. *Saint Patrick's Purgatory: A Poem by Marie de France.* Translated by Michael J. Curley. Tempe, AZ: Medieval & Renaissance Texts & Studies, 1993.

Petrarch, Francis. *Lettres de la Vieillesse XVI–XVIII / Rerum Senilium XVI–XVIII.* Edited by Elvira Nota. Translated by Jean-Yves Boriaud and Pierre Laurens. Paris: Les Belles Lettres, 2013.

Piramus, Denis. *La vie seint Edmund le rei: Poème anglo-normand du XIIe siécle par Denis Pyramus.* Edited by Hilding Kjellman. Gothenburg: Elanders, 1935; Geneva: Slatkine, 1974.

Poems of Cupid, God of Love: Christine de Pizan's Epistre au dieu d'Amours *and* Dit de la Rose, *Thomas Hoccleve's* The Letter of Cupid, *editions and translations with George Sewell's* The Proclamation of Cupid. Edited by Thelma S. Fenster and Mary Carpenter Erler. Leiden: Brill, 1990.

Servius. *In Vergilii Bucolica et Georgica Commentarii.* Edited by Georg Thilo. Leipzig: Teubner, 1887.

Sidney, Sir Philip. "Defence of Poesie." In *Sir Philip Sidney.* Edited by Katherine Duncan-Jones. Oxford: Oxford University Press, 1989.

Skelton, John. *John Skelton: The Complete English Poems.* Edited by John Scattergood. New Haven: Yale University Press, 1983.

Strengleikar: An Old Norse Translation of Twenty-One Old French Lais. Edited by Robert Cook and Mattias Tveitane. Oslo: Kjeldeskriftfondet, 1979.

Suetonius. "Vita Virgili." In *Suetonius.* Edited by John C. Rolfe. 2 vols. Cambridge, MA: Harvard University Press, 1914.

Usk, Thomas. *The Testament of Love.* Edited by R. Allen Shoaf. Kalamazoo, MI: Medieval Institute Publications, 1998.

Virgil. *Virgil.* Revised ed. Translated by H. Rushton Fairclough. 2 vols. Cambridge, MA: Harvard University Press, 1974.

SECONDARY SOURCES

Aers, David. "Reflections on Gower as 'Sapiens in Ethics and Politics.'" In *Re-Visioning Gower,* edited by R. F. Yeager, 185–201. Asheville, NC: Pegasus Press, 1998.

Allen, Rosamund. "*The Siege of Thebes:* Lydgate's Canterbury Tale." In *Chaucer and Fifteenth-Century Poetry,* edited by Julia Boffey and Janet Cowen, 122–42. London: King's College, Centre for Late Antique and Medieval Studies, 1991.

Anderson, David. *Before the Knight's Tale: Imitation of Classical Epic in Boccaccio's Teseida.* Philadelphia: University of Pennsylvania Press, 1988.

Armstrong, Guyda. *The English Boccaccio: A History in Books.* Toronto: University of Toronto Press, 2013.

Ascoli, Albert. *Dante and the Making of a Modern Author.* Cambridge: Cambridge University Press, 2008.

Ashe, Laura. *Early Fiction in England: From Geoffrey of Monmouth to Chaucer.* London: Penguin, 2015.

———. *Fiction and History in England, 1066–1200.* Cambridge: Cambridge University Press, 2007.

Atkinson, Jenkins T. "Deschamps' Ballade to Chaucer." *MLN* 33 (1918): 268–78.

Bale, Anthony. "From Translator to Laureate: Imagining the Medieval Author." *Literature Compass* 5 (2008): 918–34.

———. "John Lydgate's Religious Poetry." In Boffey and Edwards, *A Companion to Fifteenth-Century English Poetry,* 73–86.

———. "A Norfolk Gentlewoman and Lydgatian Patronage: Lady Sibylle Boys and Her Cultural Environment." *Medium Ævum* 78 (2009): 394–413.

Barbaccia, Holly. "The Woman's Response in John Gower's *Cinkante Balades.*" In Dutton et al., *John Gower, Trilingual Poet,* 230–38.

Barthes, Roland. "La mort de l'auteur." In *Le bruissement de la langue, Essais critiques IV,* 61–67. Paris: Seuil, 1984.

Bates, A. K. "Walter Map and Giraldus Cambrensis." *Latomus* 31 (1972): 860–75.

Battles, Dominique. *The Medieval Tradition of Thebes.* New York: Routledge, 2004.

Bennett, R. E. "Walter Map's Sadius and Galo." *Speculum* 16 (1941): 34–56.

Benson, C. David. "Civic Lydgate: The Poet and London." In Scanlon and Simpson, *John Lydgate: Poetry, Culture, and Lancastrian England,* 147–68.

Bestul, Thomas. "Gower's *Mirour de l'Omme* and the Meditative Tradition." *Mediaevalia* 16 (1993): 307–28.

Bezzola, Reto R. *Les origines et la formation de la littérature courtoise en occident (500–1200)*. 3 vols. Paris: Champion, 1984.

Bianco, Susan. "A Black Monk in the Rose Garden: Lydgate and the *Dit Amoureux* Tradition." *Chaucer Review* 34 (1999): 60–68.

Bloch, R. Howard. *The Anonymous Marie de France*. Chicago: University of Chicago Press, 2003.

———. "The Wolf in the Dog: Animal Fables and State Formation." *differences* 15 (2004): 69–83.

Boffey, Julia. "Short Texts in Manuscript Anthologies: The Minor Poems of John Lydgate in Two Fifteenth-Century Collections." In *The Whole Book: Cultural Perspectives on the Medieval Miscellany*, edited by Stephen G. Nichols and Siegfried Wenzel, 69–82. Ann Arbor: University of Michigan Press, 1996.

Boffey, Julia, and A. S. G. Edwards, eds. *A Companion to Fifteenth-Century English Poetry*. Cambridge: D. S. Brewer, 2013.

Boffey, Julia, and John J. Thompson. "Anthologies and Miscellanies: Production and Choice of Texts." In *Book Production and Publishing in Britain 1375–1475*, edited by Jeremy Griffiths and Derek Pearsall, 279–315. Cambridge: Cambridge University Press, 1989.

Boswell, Jackson Campbell, and Sylvia Wallace Holton. *Chaucer's Fame in England: STC Chauceriana 1475–1640*. New York: Modern Language Association of America, 2004.

Bowers, John M. *Chaucer and Langland: The Antagonistic Tradition*. Notre Dame, IN: University of Notre Dame Press, 2007.

———. "Hoccleve's Huntington Holographs: The First 'Collected Poems' in English." *Fifteenth-Century Studies* 15 (1989): 30–34.

Braet, Herman. "Note sur Marie de France et Ovide (Lai de *Guigemar*, vv. 233–44)." In *Mélanges de philologie et de littératures romanes offerts à Jeanne Wathelet-Willem*, 21–25. Liège: Marche romane, 1978.

Breen, Dan. "Laureation and Identity: Rewriting Literary History in John Skelton's *Garland of Laurel*." *Journal of Medieval and Early Modern Studies* 40 (2010): 347–71.

Brewer, Derek. *Chaucer: The Critical Heritage*. 2 vols. London: Routledge and Kegan Paul, 1978.

Brown, Carleton. "Lydgate's Verses on Queen Margaret's Entry into London." *Modern Language Review* 7 (1912): 225–34.

Brugnoli, Giorgio, and Fabio Stok, eds. *Vitae vergilianae antiquae*, Scriptores graeci et latini. Rome: Istituto Polygraphico, 1997.

Brusendorff, Aage. "Lydgate and Shirley." In *The Chaucer Tradition*, 453–71. London: Oxford University Press, 1925.

Burgess, Glyn S. *The Lais of Marie de France: Text and Context*. Athens: University of Georgia Press, 1987.

Burrow, John A. "Autobiographical Poetry in the Middle Ages: The Case of Thomas Hoccleve." In *Middle English Literature: British Academy Gollancz Lectures*, edited by J. A. Burrow, 223–46. Oxford: Oxford University Press, 1989.

———. "Hoccleve and the 'Court.'" In *Nation, Court and Culture: New Essays on Fifteenth-Century English Poetry*, edited by H. Cooney, 70–80. Dublin: Four Courts Press, 2001.

———. "Hoccleve and the Middle French Poets." In *The Long Fifteenth Century: Essays for Douglas Gray*, edited by Helen Cooper and Sally Mapstone, 35–50. Oxford: Clarendon Press, 1997.

———. *Medieval Writers and Their Works: Middle English Literature and its Background, 1100–1500.* Oxford: Oxford University Press, 1982.

———. "The Portrayal of Amans in 'Confessio Amantis.'" In *Gower's 'Confessio Amantis': Responses and Reassessments,* edited by Alastair J. Minnis, 5–24. Woodbridge, Suffolk: D. S. Brewer, 1983.

———. "Sinning against Love in *Confessio Amantis.*" In Dutton et al., *John Gower, Trilingual Poet,* 217–29.

———. *Thomas Hoccleve,* Authors of the Middle Ages 4. Aldershot, Hampshire: Ashgate, 1994.

Butterfield, Ardis. "Articulating the Author: Gower and the French Vernacular Codex." *Yearbook of English Studies* 33 (2003): 80–96.

———. *The Familiar Enemy: Chaucer, Language, and Nation in the Hundred Years War.* Oxford: Oxford University Press, 2009.

———. "French Culture and the Ricardian Court." In *Essays on Ricardian Literature in Honour of J. A. Burrow.* Edited by Alastair J. Minnis, Charlotte C. Morse, and Thorlac Turville-Petre, 82–120. Oxford: Clarendon Press, 1997.

Caie, Graham D. "'I do not wish to be called auctour, but the pore compilatour': The Plight of the Medieval Vernacular Poet." *miscelánea* 29 (2004): 9–22.

Cairns, Francis. "Varius and Vergil: Two Pupils of Philodemus in Propertius 2.34?" In *Vergil, Philodemus, and the Augustans,* edited by David Armstrong, Jeffrey Fish, Patricia A. Johnston, and Marilyn B. Skinner, 299–321. Austin: University of Texas Press, 2004.

Caiti-Russo, Gilda. "Situation actuelle de Gautier Map, Écrivain fantastique." *Revue des langues romances* 101 (1997): 125–43.

Calin, William. "Deschamps's 'Ballade to Chaucer' Again, or the Dangers of Intertextual Medieval Comparatism." In *Eustache Deschamps, French Courtier-Poet: His Work and His World,* edited by Deborah M. Sinnreich-Levi and Stephen G. Nichols, 73–83. New York: AMS Press, 1998.

Cannon, Christopher. *The Grounds of English Literature.* Oxford: Oxford University Press, 2004.

Cargo, Robert T. "Marie de France's *Le Laustic* and Ovid's *Metamorphoses.*" *Comparative Literature* 18 (1966): 162–66.

Carlson, David R. "Chaucer's Boethius and Thomas Usk's *Testament of Love*: Politics and Love in the Chaucerian Tradition." In *The Centre and Its Compass: Studies in Honor of Professor John Leyerle,* edited by Robert A. Taylor, 29–70. Kalamazoo, MI: Medieval Institute Publications, 1993.

———. *Chaucer's Jobs.* New York: Palgrave Macmillan, 2004.

———. "The Parliamentary Source of Gower's *Cronica Tripertita* and Incommensurable Styles." In Dutton et al., *John Gower, Trilingual Poet,* 98–111.

———. "A Rhyme Distribution Chronology of John Gower's Latin Poetry." *Studies in Philology* 104 (2007): 15–55.

Carruthers, Mary. *The Book of Memory: A Study of Memory in Medieval Culture.* Cambridge: Cambridge University Press, 1990.

Cartlidge, Neil. "Masters in the Art of Lying? The Literary Relationship between Hugh of Rhuddlan and Walter Map." *Modern Language Review* 106 (2001): 1–16.

———. "Narrative and Gossip in Chaucer's *Troilus and Criseyde.*" In *Narrative Developments from Chaucer to Defoe,* edited by Gerd Bayer and Ebbe Klitgård, 221–34. New York: Routledge, 2011.

Cheney, Patrick. "Introduction: 'Jog on, jog on': European Career Paths." In Cheney and de Armas, *European Literary Careers,* 3–23.

———. *Reading Sixteenth-Century Poetry.* Oxford: Blackwell, 2011.

Cheney, Patrick, and Frederick A. de Armas, eds. *European Literary Careers: The Author from Antiquity to the Renaissance.* Toronto: University of Toronto Press, 2002.

Chenu, M. -D. "Auctor, Actor, Autor." *Bulletin du Cange* 3 (1927): 81–86.

Clanchy, Michael. *From Memory to Written Record: England 1066–1307.* 2nd ed. Oxford: Blackwell, 1979.

Clarke, K. P. *Chaucer and Italian Textuality.* Oxford: Oxford University Press, 2011.

Coffman, George R. "John Gower in his Most Significant Role." In *Elizabethan Studies and Other Essays in Honor of George F. Reynolds,* edited by E. J. West, 52–61. Boulder: University of Colorado, 1945.

———. "John Gower, Mentor for Royalty: Richard II." *PMLA* 69 (1954): 953–64.

Coldiron, A. E. B. *Canon, Period, and the Poetry of Charles of Orleans: Found in Translation.* Ann Arbor: University of Michigan Press, 2000.

Connolly, Margaret. *John Shirley: Book Production and the Noble Household in Fifteenth-Century England.* Aldershot, Hampshire: Ashgate, 1998.

Cooper, Helen. *The Canterbury Tales,* Oxford Guides to Chaucer. Oxford: Oxford University Press, 1989.

———. "Chaucer's Poetics." In *New Readings of Chaucer's Poetry,* edited by Robert G. Benson and Susan J. Ridyard, 31–50. Cambridge: D. S. Brewer, 2003.

———. "Choosing Poetic Fathers: The English Problem." In *Medieval and Early Modern Authorship,* edited by Guillemette Bolen and Lukas Erne, 29–50. Tübingen: Narr, 2011.

———. "The Four Last Things in Dante and Chaucer: Ugolino in the House of Rumour," *New Medieval Literatures* 3 (1999): 39–66.

———. "The Frame." In Correale and Hamel, *Sources and Analogues to the Canterbury Tales,* 1: 1–22.

———. "'This worthy olde writer': *Pericles* and the Other Gowers, 1592–1640." In Echard, *A Companion to Gower,* 99–113.

Copeland, Rita. "Insinuating Authors." In *Taking Liberties with the Author: Selected Essays from the English Institute,* edited by Meredith L. McGill. ACLS Humanities E-Book. Cambridge, MA: English Institute, 2013. Accessed 10/22/2015. http://quod.lib.umich.edu.ezaccess.libraries.psu.edu/cgi/t/text/text-idx?c=acls;idno=heb90058.0001.001;rgn=div2;view=text;cc=acls;node=heb90058.0001.001%3A5.1.

———. *Rhetoric, Hermeneutics, and Translation in the Middle Ages: Academic Traditions and Vernacular Texts.* Cambridge: Cambridge University Press, 1991.

Cornish, Alison. *Vernacular Translation in Dante's Italy: Illiterate Literature.* Cambridge: Cambridge University Press, 2011.

Correale, Robert M., and Mary Hamel, eds. *Sources and Analogues of the Canterbury Tales.* 2 vols. Cambridge: D. S. Brewer, 2002–5.

Cottrell, Robert D. "*La Lai du Laustic:* From Physicality to Spirituality." *Philological Quarterly* 47 (1968): 499–505.

Cotts, John D. *The Clerical Dilemma: Peter of Blois and Literature Culture in the Twelfth Century.* Washington, DC: Catholic University of America Press, 2009.

Coxon, Sebastian. *The Presentation of Authorship in Medieval German Narrative Literature 1220–1290.* Oxford: Oxford University Press, 2001.

———. "Wit, Laughter, and Authority in *De nugis curialium*." In Partridge and Kwakkel, *Author, Reader, Book*, 38–55.

Crane, Susan. "Anglo-Norman Cultures in England, 1066–1460." In Wallace, *The Cambridge History of Medieval English Literature*, 35–60.

Cummings, Brian, and James Simpson, eds. *Cultural Reformations: Medieval and Renaissance in Literary History*. Oxford: Oxford University Press, 2010.

Degregorio, Scott, ed. *The Cambridge Companion to Bede*. Cambridge: Cambridge University Press, 2010.

Desmond, Marilynn. "Trojan Itineraries and the Matter of Troy." In *The Oxford History of Classical Reception in English*. Volume 1: The Middle Ages, edited by Rita Copeland, 251–68. Oxford: Oxford University Press, 2015.

Dictionnaire du Moyen Français, version 2010. ATILF CNRF—Nancy Université. www.atilf.fr/dmf.

Downes, Stephanie. "After Deschamps: Chaucer's French Fame." In *Chaucer and Fame: Reputation and Reception*, edited by Isabel David and Catherine Nall, 127–42. Cambridge: D. S. Brewer, 2015.

Downing, Eric. "Anti-Pygmalion: The *Praeceptor* in *Ars Amatoria*, Book 3." In *Constructions of the Classical Body*, edited by James I. Porter, 235–51. Ann Arbor: University of Michigan Press, 1999.

Doyle, A. I., and M. B. Parkes. "The Production of Copies of the *Canterbury Tales* and the *Confessio Amantis* in the Early Fifteenth Century." In *Medieval Scribes, Manuscripts and Libraries: Essays Presented to N. R. Ker*, edited by M. B. Parkes and A. G. Watson, 163–210. London: Scolar Press, 1978.

Dronke, Peter. *The Medieval Poet and His World*. Rome: Edizioni di storia e letteratura, 1984.

Dutton, Elisabeth, with John Hines and R. F. Yeager, eds. *John Gower, Trilingual Poet*. Cambridge: D. S. Brewer, 2010.

Ebin, Lois. *John Lydgate*. Boston: Twayne, 1985.

Echard, Siân. "Gower's 'bokes of Latin': Language, Politics, and Poetry." *Studies in the Age of Chaucer* 25 (2003): 123–56.

———. "Last Words: Latin at the End of the *Confessio Amantis*." In *Interstices: Studies in Middle English and Anglo-Latin Texts in Honour of A. G. Rigg*, edited by Richard Firth Green and Linne R. Mooney, 99–126. Toronto: University of Toronto Press, 2004.

———. "Map's Metafiction: Author, Narrator and Reader in *De Nugis Curialium*." *Exemplaria* 8 (1996): 287–314.

———. "With Carmen's Help: Latin Authorities in the *Confessio Amantis*." *Studies in Philology* 95 (1998): 1–40.

———, ed. *A Companion to Gower*. Cambridge: D. S. Brewer, 2004.

Edwards, A. S. G. "Beyond the Fifteenth Century." In Boffey and Edwards, *A Companion to Fifteenth-Century English Poetry*, 225–36.

———. "The Early Reception of Chaucer and Langland." *Florilegium* 15 (1998): 1–22.

———. *Skelton: The Critical Heritage*. London: Routledge & Kegan Paul, 1981.

———. "The Unity and Authenticity of *Anelida and Arcite*: The Evidence of the Manuscripts." *Studies in Bibliography* 41 (1988): 177–88.

Edwards, Robert R. "Authorship, Imitation, and Refusal in Late-Medieval England." In *Medieval and Early Modern Authorship,* edited by Guillemette Bolen and Lukas Erne, 51–73. Tübingen: Narr, 2011.

———. *Chaucer and Boccaccio: Antiquity and Modernity.* New York: Palgrave Macmillan, 2006.

———. "The Desolate Palace and the Solitary City: Chaucer, Boccaccio, and Dante." *Studies in Philology* 94 (1999): 394–416.

———. *The Dream of Chaucer: Representation and Reflection in the Early Narratives.* Durham, NC: Duke University Press, 1989.

———. "Faithful Translations: Love and the Question of Poetry in Chaucer." In *The Olde Daunce: Love, Friendship, Sex, and Marriage in the Medieval World,* edited by Robert R. Edwards and Stephen Spector, 138–53. Albany: State University of New York Press, 1991.

———. "Gower's Poetics of the Literal." In Dutton et al., *John Gower, Trilingual Poet,* 59–73.

———. "John Lydgate and the Remaking of Classical Epic." In *The Oxford History of Classical Reception in English Literature.* Volume 1: 800–1558, edited by Rita Copeland, 465–86. Oxford: Oxford University Press, 2016.

———. "Lydgate and the Trace of Gower." *South Atlantic Review* 79 (2015): 156–70.

———. "Notes toward the Angevin Uncanny." In *Other Nations: The Hybridization of Medieval Insular Mythology and Identity,* edited by Wendy Marie Hoofnagle and Wolfram R. Keller, 87–101. Heidelberg: Winter, 2011.

Elliott, Elizabeth. "Scottish Writing." In *The Oxford Handbook of Medieval Literature in English,* edited by Greg Walker and Elaine Treharne, 574–93. Oxford: Oxford University Press, 2010.

Ellis, Roger. "Translation." In *A Companion to Chaucer,* edited by Peter Brown, 443–58. Oxford: Blackwell, 2000.

Enenkel, Karl. "Modelling the Humanist: Petrarch's *Letter to Posterity* and Boccaccio's Biography of the Poet Laureate." In *Modelling the Individual: Biography and Portrait in the Renaissance, with a Critical Edition of Petrarch's "Letter to Posterity,"* edited by Karl Enenkel, Betsy de Jong-Crane, and P. Th. M. G. Liebregts, 11–49. Amsterdam: Rodopi, 1998.

Evans, Ruth, Andrew Taylor, Nicholas Watson, and Jocelyn Wogan-Browne. "The Notion of Vernacular Theory." In Wogan-Browne et al., *The Idea of the Vernacular,* 314–30.

Farrell, Joseph. "Greek Lives and Roman Careers in the Classical *Vita* Tradition." In Cheney and de Armas, *European Literary Careers,* 24–46.

Farrell, Thomas J. "The Clerk's Tale." In Correale and Hamel, *Sources and Analogues of the Canterbury Tales,* 1:101–29.

Ferster, Judith. *Fictions of Advice: The Literature and Politics of Counsel in Late Medieval England.* Philadelphia: University of Pennsylvania Press, 1996.

———. "O Political Gower." *Mediaevalia* 16 (1993): 33–53.

Fisher, John H. *John Gower: Moral Philosopher and Friend of Chaucer.* New York: New York University Press, 1964.

———. "A Language Policy for Lancastrian England." *PMLA* 107 (1992): 1168–80.

Fitz, Brewster. "The Prologue to the *Lais* of Marie de France and the *Parable of The Talents*: Gloss and Monetary Metaphor." *MLN* 90 (1975): 558–64.

Flannery, Mary C. *John Lydgate and the Poetics of Fame.* Cambridge: D. S. Brewer, 2012.

Fleming, John V. *Classical Imitation and Interpretation in Chaucer's* Troilus. Lincoln: University of Nebraska Press, 1990.

Frantzen, Allen J. "The Englishness of Bede, from Then to Now." In Degregorio, *The Cambridge Companion to Bede*, 229–42.

Freeman, Michelle A. "Marie de France's Poetics of Silence: Implications for a Feminine *Translatio*." *PMLA* 99 (1984): 860–83.

Foucault, Michel. "Qu'est-ce qu'un auteur?" *Bulletin de la société française de philosophie* 63 (1969): 73–104; rpt. in *Dits et écrits: 1954–1988*, edited by Daniel Defert, François Ewald, and Jacques Lagrange, 4 vols., 1:789–821. Paris: Gallimard, 1994.

Fumo, Jamie C. "The God of Love and Love of God: Palinodic Exchange in the Prologue of the *Legend of Good Women* and the 'Retraction.'" In *The Legend of Good Women: Context and Reception*, edited by Carolyn P. Collette, 157–75. Cambridge: D. S. Brewer, 2006.

Galloway, Andrew. "Gower in His Most Learned Role and the Peasants' Revolt of 1381." *Mediaevalia* 16 (1993): 327–47.

———. "John Lydgate and the Origins of Vernacular Humanism." *Journal of English and Germanic Philology* 107 (2008): 445–71.

———. "Reassessing Gower's Dream-Visions." In Dutton et al., *John Gower, Trilingual Poet*, 288–303.

Gayk, Shannon. *Image, Text, and Religious Reform in Fifteenth-Century England*. Cambridge: Cambridge University Press, 2010.

Gaylord, Alan T. "*Sentence* and *Solace* in Fragment VII of the *Canterbury Tales:* Harry Bailey as Horseback Editor." *PMLA* 82 (1967): 226–35.

Gertz, SunHee Kim. "Echoes and Reflections of Enigmatic Beauty in Ovid and Marie de France." *Speculum* 73 (1998): 372–96.

Gillespie, Vincent. "Authorship." In *A Handbook of Middle English Studies*, edited by Marion Turner, 137–54. London: John Wiley & Sons, 2014.

Gillingham, John. *The English in the Twelfth Century: Imperialism, National Identity, and Political Values*. Woodbridge, Suffolk: Boydell and Brewer, 2000.

Gilroy-Scott, Neil. "John Gower's Reputation: Literary Allusions from the Early Fifteenth-Century to the Time of 'Pericles.'" *Yearbook of English Studies* 1 (1971): 30–47.

Ginsberg, Warren. *Chaucer's Italian Tradition*. Ann Arbor: University of Michigan Press, 2002.

Godefroy, Frédéric. *Dictionnaire de l'ancienne langue française et de tous ses dialectes du IX au XV siècle*. 10 vols. Paris: Ministère de l'éducation nationale, 1937.

Grady, Frank. "The Lancastrian Gower and the Limits of Exemplarity." *Speculum* 70 (1995): 552–75.

Green, Richard Firth. *Poets and Princepleasers: Literature and the English Court in the Late Middle Ages*. Toronto: University of Toronto Press, 1980.

Greene, Thomas. *The Light in Troy: Imitation and Discovery in Renaissance Poetry*. New Haven, CT: Yale University Press, 1986.

Griffiths, Jane. *John Skelton and Poetic Authority: Defining the Liberty to Speak*. Oxford: Clarendon Press, 2006.

Guillory, John. *Cultural Capital: The Problem of Literary Canon Formation*. Chicago: University of Chicago Press, 1993.

Gust, Geoffrey. *Constructing Chaucer: Author and Autofiction in the Critical Tradition*. New York: Palgrave Macmillan, 2009.

Hagedorn, Suzanne. *Abandoned Women: Rewriting the Classics in Dante, Boccaccio, and Chaucer*. Ann Arbor: University of Michigan Press, 2003.

Hammond, Eleanor. *English Verse between Chaucer and Surrey*. Durham, NC: Duke University Press, 1927.

———. "Lydgate and Coluccio Salutati." *Modern Philology* 25 (1927): 49–57.

Hanna III, Ralph. "*Compilatio* and the Wife of Bath: Latin Backgrounds, Ricardian Texts." In *Latin and Vernacular: Studies in Late-Medieval Texts and Manuscripts*, edited by Alastair J. Minnis, 247–57. Cambridge: D. S. Brewer, 1989.

———. "John Shirley and British Library, MS Additional 16165." *Studies in Bibliography* 49 (1996): 95–105.

———. "Rolle and Related Works." In *A Companion to Middle English Prose*, edited by A. S. G. Edwards, 19–31. Cambridge: D. S. Brewer, 2004.

———. "*Speculum Vitae* and the Form of *Piers Plowman*." In *Answerable Style: The Idea of the Literary in Medieval England*, edited by Frank Grady and Andrew Galloway, 121–39. Columbus: The Ohio State University Press, 2013.

Hanna III, Ralph, Tony Hunt, R. G. Keightley, Alastair J. Minnis, and Nigel F. Palmer. "Latin Commentary: Tradition and Vernacular Literature." In *The Cambridge History of Literary Criticism, Volume II: The Middle Ages*, edited by Alastair J. Minnis and Ian Johnson, 363–421. Cambridge: Cambridge University Press, 2005.

Hanna III, Ralph and Traugott Lawler. "The Wife of Bath's Prologue." In Correale and Hamel, *Sources and Analogues of The Canterbury Tales*, 2:351–403.

Hanning, Robert W. "Courtly Contexts for Urban *cultus*: Responses to Ovid in Chrétien's *Cligès* and Marie's *Guigemar*." *Symposium* 35 (1981–82): 34–56.

———. "The Talking Wounded: Desire, Truth Telling, and Pain in the *Lais* of Marie de France." In *Desiring Discourse: The Literature of Love, Ovid through Chaucer*, edited by James J. Paxson and Cynthia A. Gravlee, 140–61. Selinsgrove, PA: Susquehanna University Press, 1998.

Harkins, Jessica. "Chaucer's *Clerk's Tale* and Boccaccio's *Decameron* X.10." *Chaucer Review* 47 (2013): 247–73.

Harris, Kate. "The Patron of British Library MS Arundel 38." *Notes and Queries* 229 (1984): 462–63.

Hedeman, Anne D. *Translating the Past: Laurent de Premierfait and Boccaccio's* De Casibus. Los Angeles: J. Paul Getty Museum, 2008.

Helgerson, Richard. *Self-Crowned Laureates: Spenser, Jonson, Milton and the Literary System*. Berkeley: University of California Press, 1983.

Hinton, James. "Walter Map's *De Nugis Curialium*: Its Plan and Composition." *PMLA* 32 (1917): 81–132.

Hoepffner, Ernest. "Marie de France et l'*Eneas*." *Studi medievali* n.s. 5 (1932): 272–308.

Horobin, Simon. "Forms of Circulation." In Boffey and Edwards, *A Companion to Fifteenth-Century English Poetry*, 21–32.

Hudson, Anne. "Epilogue: The Legacy of *Piers Plowman*." In *A Companion to Piers Plowman*, edited by John A. Alford, 251–66. Berkeley: University of California Press, 1988.

Hume, Cathy. "Why Did Gower Write the *Traitié*?" In Dutton et al., *John Gower, Trilingual Poet*, 263–75.

Hunt, R. W. "The Introduction to the 'Artes' in the Twelfth Century." In *Studia Mediaevalia in honorem admodum Reverendi Patris Raymundi Josephi Martin*, 85–112. Bruges: De Tempel, 1948.

Irvin, Matthew W. *The Poetic Voices of John Gower: Politics and Personae in the* Confessio Amantis. Cambridge: D. S. Brewer, 2014.

Jaeger, C. Stephen. *The Origins of Courtliness: Civilizing Trends and the Formation of Courtly Ideals 939–1210*. Philadelphia: University of Pennsylvania Press, 1985.

Jenkins, T. Atkinson. "Deschamps' Ballade to Chaucer." *MLN* (1918): 268–78.

Johnson, W. R. "The Problem of the Counter-Classical Sensibility and Its Critics." *California Studies in Classical Antiquity* 3 (1970): 123–51.

Kelly, Douglas. *The Conspiracy of Allusion: Description, Rewriting, and Authorship from Macrobius to Medieval Romance*. Leiden: Brill, 1999.

———. "The Scope of the Treatment of Composition in the Twelfth- and Thirteenth-Century Arts of Poetry." *Speculum* 41 (1966): 261–78.

———. "Theory of Composition in Medieval Narrative Poetry and Geoffrey of Vinsauf's *Poetria Nova*." *Mediæval Studies* 31 (1969): 117–48.

———, ed. *The Medieval Opus: Imitation, Rewriting, and Transmission in the French Tradition*. Leiden: Brill, 1996.

Kendall, Calvin B. "Bede and Education." In Degregorio, *The Cambridge Companion to Bede*, 201–15.

Kittredge, G. L. Review of George C. Macaulay's edition of *The Complete Works of John Gower*. *The Nation* 71, 1839 (1900): 254–55.

Knapp, Ethan. *The Bureaucratic Muse: Thomas Hoccleve and the Literature of Late Medieval England*. University Park: Pennsylvania State University Press, 1997.

———. "Thomas Hoccleve." In *The Cambridge Companion to Medieval English Literature 1100–1500*, edited by Larry Scanlon, 191–204. Cambridge: Cambridge University Press, 2009.

Kuczynski, Michael P. "Gower's Virgil." In *On John Gower: Essays at the Millennium*, edited by R. F. Yeager, 161–87. Kalamazoo, MI: Medieval Institute Publications, 2007.

Lapidge, Michael. "The Saintly Life in Anglo-Saxon England." In *The Cambridge Companion to Old English Literature*, edited by Malcolm Godden and Michael Lapidge, 243–63. Cambridge: Cambridge University Press, 1986.

Lawler, Traugott. "Medieval Annotation: The Example of the Commentaries on Walter Map's *Dissuasio Valerii*." In *Annotation and Its Texts*, edited by Stephen A. Barney, 94–107. Oxford: Oxford University Press, 1991.

Lawton, David. "Dullness and the Fifteenth Century." *ELH* 54 (1987): 761–99.

Lees, Clare A., ed. *The Cambridge History of Early Medieval English Literature*. Cambridge: Cambridge University Press, 2012.

Lerer, Seth. *Chaucer and His Readers: Imagining the Author in Late-Medieval England*. Princeton, NJ: Princeton University Press, 1993.

———. "Epilogue: Falling Asleep over the History of the Book." *PMLA* 121 (2006): 229–34.

———. "Literary Histories." In Cummings and Simpson, *Cultural Reformations*, 75–94.

———. "Old English and Its Afterlife." In Wallace, *The Cambridge History of Medieval English Literature*, 7–34.

———. *Tradition: A Feeling for the Literary Past*. Oxford: Oxford University Press, 2016.

Levine, Robert. "How to Read Walter Map." *Mittellateinische Jahrbuch* 23 (1988): 91–105.

Lewis, Charlton T., and Charles Short. *A Latin Dictionary*. Oxford: Clarendon Press, 1879.

Lucken, Christopher. "Eloge de l'Ane." *Reinardus* 11 (1998): 95–116.

MacCracken, Henry Noble. "The Lydgate Canon." In Lydgate, *The Minor Poems of John Lydgate*, 1:v–lviii.

Machan, Tim. "Chaucer as Translator." In *The Medieval Translator,* edited by R. M. Ellis, J. Wogan-Browne, S. Medcalf, and P. Meredith, 55–67. Cambridge: D. S. Brewer, 1989.

Mahoney, Dhira. "Courtly Presentation and Authorial Self-Fashioning." *Mediaevalia* 21 (1996): 97–160.

———. "Gower's Two Prologues to *Confessio Amantis*." In *Re-Visioning Gower,* edited by R. F. Yeager, 17–37. Ashville, NC: Pegasus Press, 1998.

Malo, Robyn. "Penitential Discourse in Hoccleve's *Series*." *Studies in the Age of Chaucer* 34 (2012): 277–305.

Maranini, Anna. "'Proprie quidem compilare est aliena dicta suis intermiscere': Il riutilizzo di fonti antiche e coeve in tradizione medievale." In *Auctor et Auctoritas in Latinis Medii Aevi Litteris. Author and Authorship in Medieval Latin Literature,* edited by Edoardo D'Angelo and Jan Ziolkowski, 675–89. Florence: SISMEL, Edizioni del Galluzzo, 2014.

Martin, Joanna M. "Responses to the Frame Narrative of John Gower's *Confessio Amantis* in Fifteenth- and Sixteenth-Century Scottish Literature." *Review of English Studies* 60 (2009): 561–77.

McCash, June Hall. "*La vie seinte Audree*: A Fourth Text by Marie de France?" *Speculum* 77 (2002): 759–63.

McDonough, Christopher M. Review of Walter Map, *De nugis curialium; Courtiers' Trifles. Mittellateinische Jahrbuch* 20 (1985): 294–302.

McGerr, Rosemarie P. "Retraction and Memory: Retrospective Structure in the *Canterbury Tales*." *Comparative Literature* 37 (1985): 97–113.

McGregor, James J. *The Image of Antiquity in Boccaccio's "Filocolo," "Filostrato," and "Teseida."* New York: Peter Lang, 1991.

Meale, Carol. "The Patronage of Poetry." In Boffey and Edwards, *A Companion to Fifteenth-Century English Poetry*, 7–20.

Meecham-Jones, Simon. "Prologue: The Poet as Subject: Literary Self-Consciousness in Gower's *Confessio Amantis*." In *Betraying Our Selves: Forms of Self-Representation in Early Modern English Texts,* edited by Henk Dragstra, Sheila Ottway, and Helen Wilcox, 14–30. New York: St. Martin's, 2000.

Meyer-Lee, Robert. *Poets and Power from Chaucer to Wyatt.* Cambridge: Cambridge University Press, 2007.

Mickel, Emanuel J., Jr. "A Reconsideration of the *Lais* of Marie de France." *Speculum* 46 (1971): 39–65.

Middleton, Anne. "The Idea of Public Poetry in the Reign of Richard II." *Speculum* 53 (1978): 94–114.

———. "Thomas Usk's 'Perdurable Letters': The *Testament of Love* from Script to Print." *Studies in Bibliography* 51 (1998): 63–116.

———. "William Langland's 'Kynde Name': Authorial Signature and Social Identity in Late Fourteenth-Century England." In *Literary Practice and Social Change in Britain, 1380–1530,* edited by Lee Patterson, 15–82. Berkeley: University of California Press, 1990.

Mieszkowski, Gretchen. "The Reputation of Criseyde, 1155–1500." *Transactions of the Connecticut Academy of Arts and Sciences* 43 (1971): 117–26.

Miller, Mark. *Philosophical Chaucer: Love, Sex, and Agency in The Canterbury Tales.* Cambridge: Cambridge University Press, 2004.

Miller, Thomas. *A Collation of Four MSS of the Old English Version of Bede's Ecclesiastical History of The English People.* EETS OS 110–11; part 2 of *The Old English Version of Bede's Ecclesiastical History of The English People.* London: N. Trübner and Co., 1898.

Minnis, Alastair J. *Chaucer and Pagan Antiquity.* Woodbridge, Suffolk: Boydell & Brewer, 1982.

———. *Fallible Authors: Chaucer's Pardoner and Wife of Bath.* Philadelphia: University of Pennsylvania Press, 2008.

———. "John Gower, Sapiens in Ethics and Politics." *Medium Ævum* 49 (1980): 207–29.

———. "Literary Theory in Discussions of *Formae Tractandi* by Medieval Theologians." *New Literary History* 11 (1979): 133–45.

———. *Medieval Theory of Authorship: Scholastic Literary Attitudes in the Later Middle Ages.* 2nd ed. Philadelphia: University of Pennsylvania Press, 1988.

———. *The Shorter Poems*, Oxford Guides to Chaucer. Oxford: Oxford University Press, 1995.

———. *Translations of Authority in Medieval English Literature: Valuing the Vernacular.* Cambridge: Cambridge University Press, 2009.

———. "The Trouble with Theology: Ethical Poetics and the Ends of Scripture." In Partridge and Kwakkel, *Author, Reader, Book,* 20–37.

Mitchell, J. Allan. *Ethics and Exemplary Narrative in Chaucer and Gower.* Cambridge: D. S. Brewer, 2004.

Mooney, Linne R. "A Holograph Copy of Thomas Hoccleve's *Regiment of Princes.*" *Studies in the Age of Chaucer* 33 (2011): 263–96.

———. "John Shirley's Heirs." *The Yearbook of English Studies* 33 (2003): 182–98.

Mortimer, Nigel. *John Lydgate's* Fall of Princes: *Narrative Tragedy in Its Literary and Political Contexts.* Oxford: Clarendon Press, 2005.

Müller, Jan-Dirk. "Auctor—Actor—Author: Einige Anmerkungen zum Verständnis vom Autor in lateinischen Schriften des frühen und hohen Mittelalters." In *Der Autor im Dialog. Beiträge zu Autorität und Autorschaft,* edited by Felix Philipp Ingold and Werner Wunderlich, 17–31. St. Gallen: Fachverlag für Wissenschaft und Studium [UVK], 1995.

Murphy, James J. *Rhetoric in the Middle Ages: A History of Rhetorical Theory from St. Augustine to the Renaissance.* Berkeley: University of California Press, 1974.

Muscatine, Charles. *Chaucer and the French Tradition.* Berkeley: University of California Press, 1957.

Nall, Catherine. *Reading and War in Fifteenth-Century England: From Lydgate to Malory.* Woodbridge, Suffolk: D. S. Brewer, 2012.

Nelson, Deborah. "Eliduc's Salvation." *French Review* 55 (1981): 37–42.

Nicholson, Peter. "Gower's Revisions in the *Confessio Amantis.*" *Chaucer Review* 19 (1984): 123–43.

———. *Love and Ethics in Gower's* Confessio Amantis. Ann Arbor: University of Michigan Press, 2005.

———. "Poet and Scribe in the Manuscripts of Gower's *Confessio Amantis.*" In *Manuscripts and Texts: Editorial Problems in Later Middle English Literature,* edited by Derek Pearsall, 130–42. Cambridge: D. S. Brewer, 1987.

Nolan, Barbara. *Chaucer and the Tradition of the Roman Antique.* Cambridge: Cambridge University Press, 1992.

Nolan, Maura. *John Lydgate and the Making of Public Culture.* Cambridge: Cambridge University Press, 2005.

Nowlin, Steele. *Chaucer, Gower, and the Affect of Invention.* Columbus: The Ohio State University Press, 2016.

Nuttall, Jenni. "Thomas Hoccleve's Poems for Henry V: Anti-Occasional Verse and Ecclesiastical Reform." In *Oxford Online Handbooks* (2015). doi: 10.1093/oxfordhb/9780199935338.013.61.

Nykrog, Per. "The Rise of Literary Fiction." In *Renaissance and Renewal in the Twelfth Century,* edited by Robert L. Benson and Giles Constable, 593–614. Cambridge, MA: Harvard University Press, 1982.

Obermeier, Anita. "Chaucer's Retraction." In Correale and Hamel, *Sources and Analogues of the Canterbury Tales,* 2: 775–808.

———. *The History and Anatomy of Auctorial Self-Criticism.* Amsterdam: Rodopi, 1999.

Olson, Glending. "Geoffrey Chaucer." In Wallace, *The Cambridge History of Medieval English Literature,* 566–88.

Olsson, Kurt. "The Cardinal Virtues and the Structure of John Gower's *Speculum Meditantis.*" *Journal of Medieval and Renaissance Studies* 7 (1977): 113–48.

———. *John Gower and the Structures of Conversion: A Reading of the* Confessio Amantis. Cambridge: D. S. Brewer, 1992.

Oosterwijk, Sophie. "'Fro Paris to Inglond'? The Danse Macabre in Text and Image in Late-Medieval England." PhD diss., Leiden University, 2009.

Otter, Monika. *Inventiones: Fiction and Referentiality in Twelfth-Century English Historical Writing.* Chapel Hill: University of North Carolina Press, 1996.

Paratore, E. *Virgilio.* 2nd ed. Florence: Sansoni, 1954.

Parkes, Malcolm B. "The Influence of the Concepts of *Ordinatio* and *Compilatio* on the Development of the Book." In *Scribes, Scripts and Readers: Studies in the Communication, Presentation and Dissemination of Medieval Texts,* 35–70. London: Hambledon Press, 1991.

Partridge, Stephen. "'The Makere of this Boke': Chaucer's *Retraction* and the Author as Scribe and Compiler." In Patridge and Kwakkel, *Author, Reader, Book,* 106–53.

Partridge, Stephen, and Erik Kwakkel, eds. *Author, Reader, Book: Medieval Authorship in Theory and Practice.* Toronto: University of Toronto Press, 2012.

Patterson, Lee. "Beinecke MS 493 and the Survival of Hoccleve's *Series.*" In *Old Books, New Learning: Essays on Medieval and Renaissance Books at Yale,* Yale University Library Gazette, Occasional Supplement 4 (January 2001): 92–103.

———. *Chaucer and the Subject of History.* Madison: University of Wisconsin Press, 1991.

———. "Court Politics and the Invention of Literature: The Case of Sir John Clanvowe." In *Culture and History, 1350–1600: Essays on English Communities, Identities and Writing,* edited by David Aers, 7–41. Detroit, MI: Wayne State University Press, 1992.

———. "Genre and Source in *Troilus and Criseyde.*" In *Acts of Recognition: Essays on Medieval Culture,* 198–214. Notre Dame, IN: University of Notre Dame Press, 2010.

Pearsall, Derek. "The Gower Tradition." In *Gower's Confessio Amantis: Responses and Reassessments,* edited by Alastair J. Minnis, 179–97. Cambridge: D. S. Brewer, 1983.

———. "Gower's Latin in the *Confessio Amantis*." In *Latin and Vernacular: Studies in Late-Medieval Texts and Manuscripts*, edited by Alastair J. Minnis, 13–25. Cambridge: D. S. Brewer, 1989.

———. "Hoccleve's *Regement of Princes*: The Poetics of Royal Self-Representation." *Speculum* 69 (1994): 386–410.

———. *John Lydgate*. Charlottesville: University Press of Virginia, 1970.

———. *John Lydgate (1371–1449): A Bio-Bibliography*. Victoria, BC: English Literary Studies, 1997.

———. "Lydgate as Innovator." *Modern Language Quarterly* 53 (1992): 5–22.

———. "Signs of Life in Lydgate's Danse Macabre." In *Zeit, Tod und Ewigkeit in der Renaissance Literatur*, edited by James Hogg, 58–71. Salzburg: Institut für Anglistik und Amerikanistik, 1987.

Peck, Russell A. *Kingship and Common Profit in Gower's* Confessio Amantis. Carbondale: Southern Illinois University Press, 1978.

———. "The Politics and Psychology of Governance in Gower: Ideas of Kingship and Real Kings." In Echard, *A Companion to Gower*, 215–38.

Perkins, Nicholas. *Hoccleve's* Regement of Princes: *Counsel and Constraint*. Cambridge: D. S. Brewer, 2001.

Petrina, Alessandra. *Cultural Politics in Fifteenth-Century England*. Leiden: Brill, 2004.

Pickens, Rupert T. "History and Narration in Froissart's *Dits*: The Case of the *Bleu chevalier*." In *Froissart across the Genres*, edited by Donald Maddox and Sarah Sturm-Maddox, 119–54. Gainesville: University Press of Florida, 1998.

Prior, Sandra Pierson. "'Kar des dames est avenu / L'aventure': Displacing the Chivalric Hero in Marie de France's *Eliduc*." In *Desiring Discourse: The Literature of Love, Ovid through Chaucer*, edited by James J. Paxson and Cynthia A. Gravlee, 123–39. Selinsgrove, PA: Susquehanna University Press, 1998.

Quain, E. A. "The Mediaeval *Accessus ad auctores*." *Traditio* 3 (1945): 228–42.

Reimer, Stephen. Review of *John Lydgate's Lives of Sts Edmund & Fremund and the Extra Miracles of St Edmund*, edited by Anthony Bale and A. S. G. Edwards. *Journal of English and Germanic Philology* 111 (2012): 252–56.

Renevey, Denis. *Language, Self and Love: Hermeneutics in the Writings of Richard Rolle and the Commentaries on the Song of Songs*. Cardiff: University of Wales Press, 2001.

Richards, Earl J. "Les Rapports entre le *Lai de Guigemar* et le *Roman d'Eneas*: Considérations génériques." In *Le Récit bref au moyen âge*, edited by Danielle Buschinger, 45–55. Paris: Champion, 1980.

Rigg, A. G. "Anglo-Latin in the Ricardian Age." In *Essays on Ricardian Literature in Honour of J. A. Burrow*, edited by Alastair J. Minnis, Charlotte C. Morse, and Thorlac Turville-Petre, 121–41. Oxford: Clarendon Press, 1997.

———. *A History of Anglo-Latin Literature 1066–1422*. Cambridge: Cambridge University Press, 1992.

———. Review of *De nugis curialium; Courtiers' Trifles*. *Speculum* 60 (1985): 177–82.

Robertson, Howard S. "Love and the Other World in Marie de France's *Eliduc*." In *Essays in Honor of Louis Francis Solano*, edited by Raymond J. Cormier and Urban Tigner Holmes, 167–76. Chapel Hill: University of North Carolina Press, 1970.

Robertson, Kellie. "Authorial Work." In *Middle English*, Oxford Twenty-First Century Approaches to Literature, edited by Paul Strohm, 441–58. Oxford: Oxford University Press, 2007.

Rollo, David. "Benoît de Sainte-Maure's *Roman de Troie*: Historiography, Forgery, and Fiction." *Comparative Literature Studies* 32 (1995): 191–225.

———. *Glamorous Sorcery: Magic and Literacy in the High Middle Ages.* Minneapolis: University of Minnesota Press, 2000.

Rossi, Carla. *Marie de France et les érudits de Cantorbéry.* Paris: Garnier, 2009.

Scanlon, Larry. "Lydgate's Poetics." In Scanlon and Simpson, *John Lydgate: Poetry, Culture, and Lancastrian England,* 61–97.

———. *Narrative, Authority, and Power: The Medieval Exemplum and the Chaucerian Tradition.* Cambridge: Cambridge University Press, 1994.

Scanlon, Larry, and James Simpson, eds. *John Lydgate: Poetry, Culture, and Lancastrian England.* Notre Dame, IN: University of Notre Dame Press, 2006.

Scase, Wendy. "Latin Composition Lessons, *Piers Plowman,* and the *Piers Plowman* Tradition." In *Answerable Style: The Idea of the Literary in Medieval England,* edited by Frank Grady and Andrew Galloway, 40–47. Columbus: The Ohio State University Press, 2013.

Schirmer, Walter. *John Lydgate: A Study in the Culture of the Fifteenth Century,* translated by Ann E. Keep. Berkeley: University of California Press, 1961.

Schullian, Dorothy M. "Valerius Maximus and Walter Map." *Speculum* 12 (1937): 516–18.

Schwebel, Leah. "Redressing Griselda: Restoration through Translation in the *Clerk's Tale.*" *Chaucer Review* 47 (2013): 274–99.

Segre, Cesare. "Piramo e Tisbe nei *Lai* de Maria di Francia." In *Studi in onore di Vittorio Lugli e Diego Valeri,* 2 vols., 2:845–53. Venice: N. Pozza, 1961.

Seymour, M. C. "The Manuscripts of Hoccleve's *Regiment of Princes.*" *Edinburgh Bibliographical Society Transactions* 4 (1974): 255–58.

———, ed. *Selections from Hoccleve.* Oxford: Clarendon Press, 1981.

Shepherd, G. T. "The Emancipation of Story in the Twelfth Century." In *Medieval Narrative: A Symposium,* edited by Hans Bekker-Nielsen, Peter Foote, Andreas Haarder, and Preben Meulengracht Sørensen, 44–57. Odense, DK: Odense University Press, 1979.

Shippey, Thomas A. "Listening to the Nightingale." *Comparative Literature* 22 (1970): 46–60.

Simpson, James. "'Dysemol daies and fatal houres': Lydgate's *Destruction of Thebes* and Chaucer's *Knight's Tale.*" In *The Long Fifteenth Century: Essays for Douglas Gray,* edited by Helen Cooper and Sally Mapstone, 15–33. Oxford: Clarendon Press, 1997.

———. *Reform and Cultural Revolution.* The Oxford English Literary History, Volume 2: 1350–1547. Oxford: Oxford University Press, 2002.

Sinex, Margaret. "Echoic Irony in Walter Map's Satire against the Cistercians." *Comparative Literature* 54 (2002): 275–90.

Sobecki, Sebastian. "*Ecce patet tensus:* The Trentham Manuscript, *In Praise of Peace,* and Gower's Autograph Hand." *Speculum* 90 (2015): 925–59.

Spearing, A. C. "Lydgate's Canterbury Tale: The *Siege of Thebes* and Fifteenth-Century Chaucerianism." In *Fifteenth-Century Studies: Recent Essays,* edited by Robert F. Yeager, 333–64. Hamden, CT: Archon, 1984; rpt. in *Medieval to Renaissance in English Poetry,* 66–88.

———. *Medieval Autographies: The "I" of the Text.* Notre Dame, IN: University of Notre Dame Press, 2012.

———. *Medieval to Renaissance in English Poetry.* Cambridge: Cambridge University Press, 1985.

Spitzer, Leo. "Note on the Poetic and the Empirical 'I' in Medieval Authors." *Traditio* 4 (1946): 414–22.

Sponsler, Claire. *The Queen's Dumbshow: John Lydgate and the Making of Early Theater*. Philadelphia: University of Pennsylvania Press, 2014.

Spurgeon, Caroline F. E. *Five Hundred Years of Chaucer Criticism and Allusion, 1357–1900*. 3 vols. Cambridge: Cambridge University Press, 1925.

Staley, Lynn. *Languages of Power in the Age of Richard II*. University Park: Pennsylvania State University Press, 2005.

Stapleton, M. L. "*Venus Vituperator*: Ovid, Marie de France, and *Fin'Amors*." *Classical and Modern Literature* 13 (1993): 283–95.

Stok, Fabio. "Virgil between the Middle Ages and the Renaissance." *International Journal of the Classical Tradition* 1:2 (1994): 15–22.

Stow, George B. "Richard II in John Gower's *Confessio Amantis*: Some Historical Perspectives." *Mediaevalia* 16 (1993 for 1990): 3–31.

Straker, Scott-Morgan. "Propaganda, Intentionality, and the Lancastrian Lydgate." In Scanlon and Simpson, *John Lydgate: Poetry, Culture, and Lancastrian England*, 98–128.

Strohm, Paul. *England's Empty Throne: Usurpation and the Language of Legitimation, 1399–1422*. New Haven, CT: Yale University Press, 1998.

———. "Hoccleve, Lydgate, and the Lancastrian Court." In Wallace, *The Cambridge History of Medieval English Literature*, 640–61.

Summit, Jennifer. "'Stable in study': Lydgate's *Fall of Princes* and Duke Humphrey's Library." In Scanlon and Simpson, *John Lydgate: Poetry, Culture, and Lancastrian England*, 209–31.

———. "Women and Authorship." In *The Cambridge Companion to Medieval Women's Writing*, edited by Carolyn Dinshaw and David Wallace, 91–109. Cambridge: Cambridge University Press, 2006.

Swan, Mary. "Old English Textual Activity in the Reign of Henry II." In *Writers of the Reign of Henry II: Twelve Essays*, edited by Ruth Kennedy and Simon Meecham-Jones, 151–68. New York: Palgrave Macmillan, 2006.

Symons, Dana M., ed. *Chaucerian Dream Visions and Complaints*. Kalamazoo, MI: Medieval Institute Publications, 2004.

Tarnoff, Maura. "Sewing Authorship in John Skelton's *Garlande or Chapelet of Laurell*." *ELH* 75 (2008): 415–38.

Thornbury, Emily V. *Becoming a Poet in Anglo-Saxon England*. Cambridge: Cambridge University Press, 2014.

Thornley, E. A. "The Middle English Penitential Lyric and Hoccleve's Autobiographical Poetry." *Neuphilologische Mitteilungen* 68 (1967): 295–321.

Thorpe, Lewis. "Walter Map and Gerald of Wales." *Medium Ævum* 47 (1978): 6–21.

Tolmie, Sarah. "The Professional: Thomas Hoccleve." *Studies in the Age of Chaucer* 29 (2007): 341–73.

Torti, Anna. "From 'History' to 'Tragedy': The Story of Troilus and Criseyde in Lydgate's *Troy Book* and Henryson's *Testament of Cresseid*." In *The European Tragedy of Troilus*, edited by Piero Boitani, 171–97. Oxford: Clarendon Press, 1989.

Treharne, Elaine. "Categorization, Periodization: The Silence of (the) English in the Twelfth Century." *New Medieval Literatures* 8 (2006): 247–73.

Trigg, Stephanie. *Congenial Souls: Reading Chaucer, Medieval to Postmodern*. Minneapolis: University of Minnesota Press, 2002.

Tudor, A. P. "The Religious Symbolism in the 'Reliquary of Love' in *Laustic*." *French Studies Bulletin* 46 (1993): 1–3.

Türk, Egbert. *Nugae curialium: Le règne d'Henri II Plantagenêt (1145–1189) et l'éthique politique*. Geneva: Droz, 1977.

Turville-Petre, Thorlac. *England the Nation: Language, Literature, and National Identity, 1290–1340*. Oxford: Clarendon Press, 1996.

Van Dyke, Carolynn. *Chaucer's Agents: Cause and Representation in Chaucerian Narrative*. Madison, NJ: Fairleigh Dickinson University Press, 2005.

Vàrvaro, Alberto. *Apparizioni fantastiche: Tradizioni folcloriche e letteratura nel medioevo: Walter Map*. Bologna: Il Mulino, 1994.

Vessey, Mark. "From *Cursus* to *Ductus*: Figures of Writing in Western Late Antiquity (Augustine, Jerome, Cassiodorus, Bede)." In Cheney and de Armas, *European Literary Careers*, 47–119.

Wakelin, Daniel. "Stephen Hawes and Courtly Education." In *The Oxford Handbook of Tudor Literature: 1485–1603*, edited by Mike Pincombe and Cathy Shrank, 53–68. Oxford: Oxford University Press, 2011.

Wallace, David. "Chaucer and Deschamps, Translation and the Hundred Years' War." *The Medieval Translator* 8 (2003): 179–88.

———. *Chaucer and the Early Writings of Boccaccio*. Cambridge: D. S. Brewer, 1985.

———. *Chaucerian Polity: Absolutist Lineages and Associational Forms in England and Italy*. Stanford: Stanford University Press, 1997.

———, ed. *The Cambridge History of Medieval English Literature*. Cambridge: Cambridge University Press, 1999.

Wallace-Hadrill, J. M. *Bede's Ecclesiastical History of the English People: A Historical Commentary*. Oxford: Clarendon Press, 1968.

Watson, Nicholas. "Outdoing Chaucer: Lydgate's *Troy Book* and Henryson's *Testament of Cresseid* as Comparative Imitations of *Troilus and Criseyde*." In *Shifts and Transpositions in Medieval Narrative: A Festschrift for Dr. Elspeth Kennedy*, edited by Karen Pratt, 89–108. Woodbridge, Suffolk: D. S. Brewer, 1994.

———. *Richard Rolle and the Invention of Authority*. Cambridge: Cambridge University Press, 1991.

———. "Theories of Translation." In *The Oxford History of Literary Translation in English: Vol. 1 to 1550*, edited by Roger Ellis. Oxford: Oxford University Press, 2008.

Watt, David. "Thomas Hoccleve's *Regiment of Princes*." In Boffey and Edwards, *A Companion to Fifteenth-Century English Poetry*, 47–58.

Webster, K. G. T. "Walter Map's French Things." *Speculum* 15 (1940): 272–79.

Westgard, Joshua A. "Bede and the Continent in the Carolingian Age and Beyond." In Degregorio, *The Cambridge Companion to Bede*, 201–15.

Wetherbee, Winthrop. *Chaucer and the Poets: An Essay on Troilus and Criseyde*. Ithaca, NY: Cornell University Press, 1984.

———. "Classical and Boethian Tradition in the *Confessio Amantis*." In Echard, *A Companion to Gower*, 181–96.

———. "John Gower." In Wallace, *The Cambridge History of Medieval English Literature*, 589–609.

———. "Latin Structure and Vernacular Space: Gower, Chaucer, and the Boethian Tradition." In *Chaucer and Gower: Difference, Mutability, Exchange*, edited by R. F. Yeager, 7–35. Victoria, BC: University of Victoria Press, 1991.

Whalen, Logan E. *Marie de France and The Poetics of Memory*. Washington, DC: Catholic University of America Press, 2008.

———. "The Prologues and Epilogues of Marie de France." In *A Companion to Marie de France*, edited by Logan E. Whalen, 1–30. Leiden: Brill, 2011.

Wheatley, Edward. "The Manciple's Tale." In Correale and Hamel, *Sources and Analogues of the Canterbury Tales*, 2:749–73.

Wiggington, Waller B. "The Nature and Significance of the Medieval Troy Story: A Study of Guido Delle Colonne's 'Historia Destructionis Troiae.'" PhD diss., Rutgers University, 1964.

Wimsatt, James I. *Chaucer and His French Contemporaries: Natural Music in the Fourteenth Century*. Toronto: University of Toronto Press, 1993.

———, ed. and trans. *Chaucer and the Poems of "Ch."* Revised ed. Kalamazoo, MI: Medieval Institute Publications, 2009.

Windeatt, Barry. "Chaucer Traditions." In *Chaucer Traditions: Studies in Honour of Derek Brewer*, edited by Ruth Morse and Barry Windeatt, 1–20. Cambridge: Cambridge University Press, 1990.

———. *Troilus and Criseyde*, Oxford Guides to Chaucer. Oxford: Oxford University Press, 1992.

Withington, Robert. "Queen Margaret's Entry into London, 1445." *Modern Philology* 13 (1915): 53–57.

Wogan-Browne, Jocelyn, Nicholas Watson, Andrew Taylor, and Ruth Evans, eds. *The Idea of the Vernacular: An Anthology of Middle English Literary Theory, 1280–1520*. University Park: Pennsylvania State University Press, 1999.

Wogan-Browne, Jocelyn, Thelma Fenster, and Delbert W. Russell, eds. *Vernacular Literary Theory from the French of Medieval England: Texts and Translations, c. 1120–c.1450*. Cambridge: D. S. Brewer, 2016.

Wormald, Patrick. "Anglo-Saxon Society and Its Literature." In *The Cambridge Companion to Old English Literature*, edited by Malcolm Godden and Michael Lapidge, 1–22. Cambridge: Cambridge University Press, 1986.

Wright, Herbert G. *Boccaccio in England, Chaucer to Tennyson*. London: Athlone, 1957.

Yeager, R. F. "Chaucer's 'To His Purse': Begging, or Begging Off?" *Viator* 36 (2005): 373–414.

———. "English, Latin, and the Text as 'Other': the Page as Sign in the Work of John Gower." *Text* 3 (1987): 251–67.

———. "Gower's French Audience: The *Mirour de l'Omme*." *Chaucer Review* 41 (2006): 111–37.

———. "John Gower's Audience: The Ballades," *Chaucer Review* 40 (2005): 81–105.

———. *John Gower's Poetic: The Search for a New Arion*. Cambridge: D. S. Brewer, 1990.

Zanoni, Mary-Louise. "'Ceo Testimoine Precïens': Priscian and the Prologue to the *Lais* of Marie de France." *Traditio* 36 (1980): 407–15.

Ziolkowski, Jan M. "Cultures of Authority in the Long Twelfth Century." *Journal of English and Germanic Philology* 108 (2009): 421–48.

Zumthor, Paul. *Essai de poétique médiévale*. Paris: Seuil, 1972.

INDEX

Acca of Hexham, 6
Accessus ad auctores, xxii, xxiv, 42; and Chaucer, 106, 112–13, 125; and Gower, 78–79, 81; and Lydgate, 158; and Marie de France, 38
Adamnan, 5n10
Aers, David, 63n2
Aesop, xiiin1, 38–39, 194
Albertus Stadensis, 83n38
Aldhelm, 4n2, 5n10, 7
Alfred (king of England), 39
Ambrose, Saint, 6
Anastasius, Saint, 4, 6
Anne, Countess of Suffolk, 160
Apollonides, King, 23
Apollonius of Tyre, Old English poem, 8; story in Gower, *Confessio Amantis*, 46, 115
Aquinas, Thomas, 68n14
Aristotle, 15n27, 65, 74, 169; and Gower, 65, 74, 88; translations of, 191
Armstrong, Guyda, 150n6, 191n36, 192
Arundel, Richard, Earl of, 83
Arundel, Thomas, Archbishop of Canterbury, 78
Ashe, Laura, xiiin4, xivn10, xxviin53, xxviiin56
Augustine, Saint: and Bede, 4, 5, 5n8, 6; and Chaucer, 115, 135; and Gower, 68n14; and Marie de France, 39; and Walter Map, 15, 16, 17, 18
Aulus Gellius, 109

Authorship: counter-authorship, 16–19, 24, 35; critical approaches, xvi–xxvi; defined, xi–xvi, xxxii–xxxiii, 5, 6, 197–98; and gender, xxn28, 37; juridical, xix, xx, xv–xvi, 15, 30, 36, 118, 137–38, 174, 177, 179, 181; simulation of, xxxi, 124, 150–53, 164–65, 167–68, 179, 194–95; Vergilian model of, 96–98, 194

Baldwin of Worcester, 18n36
Bale, Anthony, xxv, 158, 161
Bale, John, 198, 198n1
Barclay, Andrew, 152
Barthes, Roland, xvi–xviii
Bartholomew of Exeter, 18n36
Bates, A. K., 11n14
Beauchamp, Richard, Earl of Warwick, 157n37, 159–60
Beaufort, Joan, Countess of Westmorland, 157
Becket, Thomas, 13n20, 80, 187
Bede, xiii, xiiin6, xviii, xxvii, 3–8
Bennett, R. E., 11n12, 24n52
Benoît de Sainte-Maure, 35, 184
Benson, C. David, 162n62
Bernard, Saint, 15
Bernard of Utrecht, xiiin7
Bestul, Thomas, 67n11
Bezzola, Reto R., 13n19
Bianco, Susan, 177n5
Bloch, R. Howard, 13, 33n1, 37, 58

Index

Boccaccio, xxxi, 98n16; and Chaucer, 112, 113, 116, 117, 125, 126–27, 128–29, 131, 132, 141–43, 150, 187; and Lydgate, 185n21, 190–96; and Hawes, 200

Boethius, xiin1, xxx, 15n27, 18n35, 91, 116, 117, 118–19, 128, 130, 137, 167; and Usk and Chaucer, 107

Boffey, Julia, 158n39, 159

Bonaventure, xix, xx, xxi, xxin33, 5n11

Bothewald, 11n14

Bowers, John M., 149n2

Boys, Lady Sibille, 161

Braet, Herman, 41

Breen, Dan, 202n13

Brice, John, 159

Brooke, C. N. L., 11, 11n14, 14n25, 15n26

Brusendorff, Aage, 157n35

Burgess, Glyn S., 47

Buridan, John, 65n8

Burrow, John, xii, xiin2, xviii, xx, xxi, 156n30, 163n3, 165n10, 170n26

Butterfield, Ardis, 100n74, 108, 108n12, 150n5

Caedmon, 5, 5n10, 7–8

Caie, Graham, xxiv

Caiti-Russo, Gilda, 20

Callimachus, 130–31

Calot, Laurence, 159–60

Cannon, Christopher, xiiin5, xxvii, xxviii

Carlson, David R., 103n81, 151n8; and Rigg, 79n32, 82n36

Carpenter, John (Town Clerk of London), 155–56, 159, 161

Carruthers, Mary, 88n50

Cartlidge, Neil, 124n35

Cassiodorus, 6

Cato, 74, 118, 133

Caxton, William, 152, 199

Ceolwulf, 6n12

Charles d'Orléans, 150

Chaucer, Alice, 160

Chaucer, Geoffrey, xxiii, xxv, xxvi, xxx, xxxi, xxxii, xxxiii, 9, 11, 105–46, 150, 151–53, 197–99, 201, 203; and Gower, 65, 70, 70n18, 73, 74, 76, 79, 79n30, 80, 87, 92–93, 95n59; and Hoccleve, 163–64, 165, 167–70, 171–72, 173–75; and Lydgate, 159, 177–80, 181, 182, 186–88, 189–91, 192, 193, 194, 196; and Map, 17, 26, 26n55; and poetic triumvirate, xxxii, 64, 197, 201–2

Cheney, Patrick, 199

Chenu, M.-D., xviii

Chichele, Robert, 157

Christine de Pizan, 109, 150, 154; translation of L'Epitre, 164–65

Cicero, 15n29, 18n34, 72, 74; and Chaucer, 117, 118, 124–25; and Hoccleve, 169; and Lydgate, 191, 193–94, 196

Clanvowe, Sir John, 107, 107n9, 151, 165

Clarke, K. P., 143n70

Claudian, 123

Coffman, George R., 65n6

Conrad of Hirsau, xiin1, xiiin7

Cooper, Helen, 120, 143n71, 144n74

Copeland, Rita, xviii, xxi–xxii, xxiii–xxiv, xxv–xxvi, 85n43, 106, 112; on Gower, 64

Cotts, John P., 10n6

Couronnement de Renart, 35n9

Coxon, Sebastian, xviii, 10

Crane, Susan, 13n19

Curteys, William, 161

Cuthbert, Saint, 4–5, 6

Dante, xiiin8, xx, xxiii, xxiv–xxv, xxxiii, 37–38, 125, 126, 133, 140, 150, 194

Dares, 123–24, 130, 131, 183–85

Deguileville, Guillaume de, 160

Deschamps, Eustache, 108–9, 119, 150, 169

Desmond, Marilynn, 184n18

Despenser, Isabel le, Countess of Warwick, 160

Dictys, 123–24, 130, 131, 183–85

Donatus, xii, 97

Downes, Stephanie, 109

Dronke, Peter, 10n7

Dryden, John, 153

Eastfield, William, 162

Ebin, Lois, 177n3

Echard, Siân, 12, 13n20, 14n25, 25, 87n48

Edwards, A. S. G., 127n43, 149n1, 199, 202n14

Edwards, Robert R., 126n41, 158n43, 167n16

Egidius Romanus, 167, 169

Elliot, Elizabeth, 198n2

Ellis, Roger, xxin33

Ethics, xx, 65–66, 126

Eusebius, 189
Évangile aux femmes, 35n9

Felix, Saint, 4
Ferster, Judith, 181n12
Fisher, John H., 81n34, 101n75
FitzAlan, Joan, 157
Flannery, Mary C., 190n33
Fleming, John V., 126, 131, 132
Foliot, Gilbert, 18n36
Foucault, Michel, xvi–xviii, xviiin20
Freeman, Michelle, 57
Froissart, Jean, 85, 116, 119, 120–21, 150, 167
Furnivall, F. J., 156n30

Galloway, Andrew, 77n26, 194
Gayk, Shannon, 170
Geoffrey of Monmouth, xii, 124, 131, 191
Geoffrey of Vinsauf, 173–74
Gerald of Wales, 10, 11n14
Gertz, SunHee Kim, 41, 42
Gesta Romanorum, 171
Gest Historiale of the Destruction of Troy, 182
Giles of Rome, 65n8
Gillespie, Vincent, xxiv–xxv
Gillingham, John, xivn11
Ginsberg, Warren, 143
Godwine, Earl, 23, 24
Gower, John, xxiii, xxv, xxix–xxxi, xxxn59, xxxii, 11, 63–104; and Chaucer, 108, 110, 112, 115, 125, 149–53; and Hoccleve, 163, 167, 169, 171; and Lydgate, 181, 189, 191, 194; and Marie de France, 35; *Confessio Amantis*, 66, 73, 84–94, 94–95, 101, 103; *Cronica Tripertita*, 77–78, 83–84, 103–4; minor poems, 98–104; *Mirour de l'Omme*, 66–76, 82, 85, 91, 93, 94, 103; paratexts, 94–98; *Vox Clamantis*, 76–84
Green, Richard Firth, 178, 181
Gregory of Tours, 5
Gregory the Great, 5n10, 68n14; and Marie de France, 39
Griffiths, Jane, 202n16
Guido delle Colonne, 124, 131, 133, 134–35, 181–87
Guillaume de Lorris, xiv, 75, 113, 117
Guillory, John, xxviiin58
Guy de Rouclif, 155

Hammond, Eleanor, 154n22, 157n35
Hanna III, Ralph, xiin3, 170n26
Hanning, Robert W., 38, 41, 47
Harkins, Jessica, 143n71
Hawes, Stephen, xiv, xxxii, 151, 152, 199–201
Hedeman, Anne D., 191n36
Hélinant de Froidmont, 74
Henry I (king of England), 21–22
Henry II (king of England), xxviii, 9–10, 10n5, 12–13, 13n19, 21, 27–28, 37, 184
Henry IV (king of England), 77–78, 78n29, 84, 88–89, 98–100, 101–2, 150, 153, 164, 184, 200
Henry V (king of England), 156–57; and Hoccleve, 164, 166, 168, 170, 173; and Lydgate, 158, 176, 180, 182, 184–85, 188–89, 200
Henry VI (king of England), 159, 162, 188–89
Henry VII (king of England), 200
Henry of Saltrey, 36
Henry of Suso, 171, 175
Henryson, Robert, 172
Hinton, James, 11, 15n26
History, literary, xxvi–xxviii, xxviiin58, xxxi–xxxii, 12–13, 151, 198–99
Hoccleve, Thomas, xxvi, xxxi–xxxii, 107n9, 152, 163–75, 197–98; and Chaucer, 163–64, 167–70, 171–72, 173–75; and Gower, 169, 171; and Machaut, Deschamps, Froissart, Christine de Pizan, 163; and Map, 17; and patronage, 154–58; poetic triumvirate, 197; *Male Regle*, 165–66; *Regiment of Princes*, 166–70; *Series*, 170–75; translation of *L'Epitre au Dieu d'Amours*, 164–65
Homer, 123–24, 131–32, 181–83, 194, 202n14
Horace, 17, 26, 131–32
Howard, Elizabeth, Countess of Surrey, 202
Howard, Henry, Earl of Surrey, 199
Hudson, Anne, 149n1
Hue de Rotelande, 20, 35
Hume, Cathy, 101n77
Humphrey, Duke of Gloucester, xxxi, 154, 157–59, 171, 173, 177, 188, 189, 191; and *Fall of Princes*, 191n38, 193–95
Hunt, Tony, xxn29

Imitation, xvi, xxii, xxxii–xxxiii, 7, 64, 102, 106, 136, 164, 178, 182
Innocent III, Pope, 111–12

Invention, xi, xv–xvi, xxi–xxii, 7, 20, 33–34, 64, 105, 150–51
Irvin, Matthew W., 69, 90n53
Isidore of Seville, 15n29, 18, 172

Jacobus de Cessolis, 167, 169
Jaeger, C. Stephen, 10n5
James, M. R., 11, 15n26, 21, 28n57
Jean de France, duc de Berry, 190
Jean de la Mote, 119–20
Jean de Meun, xiv, 76, 113, 164, 195
Jerome, Saint, xvii, 4, 5, 6, 139–40
Joan, Countess of Westmorland, 171
John, Duke of Bedford, 156, 160, 168
John of Salisbury, 10, 13, 13n20, 15n27, 16n32
Johnson, W. R., 16n33
Joseph of Exeter, 184
Juvenal, 194

Katherine of Valois, 159
Kelly, Douglas, xviii, 21n46
Kempe, Margery, xxv
Kendall, Calvin B., 6n14
Kingis Quair, 198, 198n1
Kittredge, G. L., 67
Knapp, Ethan, 165n12, 166, 171

Lactantius, 15n29
Lacy, Edward, Bishop of Exeter, 158
Laȝamon, xviii
Langland, William, xii, xxv, xxxi, 149, 149n1, 149n2
Langley, Thomas (Lord Chancellor of England and Bishop of Durham), 155
Lapidge, Michael, 5n7
Latini, Brunetto, 65, 196
Laud Troy Book, 182
Laurent de Premierfait, xxxi, 190–92, 191n36; and Lydgate, 195–96
Lawler, Traugott, 23–24, 24n48
Lees, Clare H., xiiin9
Leland, John, 198, 198n1
Lerer, Seth, xvn13, xxvi, xxviin51, xxviiin58, 179–80, 199
Levine, Robert, 12, 20n40
Livre du Chevalier de la Tour Landry, Le, 143
Livre Griseldis, 143

Livy, 72, 135
Lombard, Peter, xix, 68n14
Louis VII (king of France), 23, 27–28
Lucan, 72, 83n38, 123, 189–90
Lucken, Christopher, 16n32
Lucretius, 18n34
Lydgate, John, xxv, xxvi, xxxi–xxxii, 151, 154–55, 176–96; and Chaucer, 124, 177–82, 177n5, 186–96; and Gower, 99; and Hawes, 200–201; and Hoccleve, 170, 173; and Map, 17; and patronage, 157–62; and poetic triumvirate, xxxii, 64, 151, 198, 202; *Fall of Princes*, 190–96; *Serpent of Division*, 189–90; *Siege of Thebes*, 187–88, 195; *Troy Book*, 181–88

Macaulay, G. C., 68n14, 79n32, 84n39, 87n49
MacCracken, Henry Noble, 157n35
Machaut, Guillaume de, xxv, 85, 150, 179; and Chaucer, 109, 116, 119, 120–21
Macrobius, 117, 122, 124
Mahoney, Dhira, 66n9
Malo, Robyn, 165n12
Mandeville, John, xxv
Map, Walter, xiii–xiv, xxviii–xxix, xxx, 9–32, 88, 139–40, 197, 199; and Marie de France, 33, 35–36
Marie de France, xiii–xiv, xxix, xxx, 33–60, 197; and Map, 33, 35–36
Marleburgh, Thomas (London stationer), 157
McDonough, Christopher M., 10n4
McGregor, James J., 126n41
Meale, Carol, 154–55
Meek, Mary Elizabeth, 184n17
Ménagier de Paris, Le, 143
Meyer-Lee, Robert, xxvi, 198–99
Mickel Jr., Emanuel J., 57–58
Middleton, Anne, 65n6, 108, 149n1
Mieszkowski, Gretchen, 185n22
Miller, Mark, 139n64
Minnis, Alastair, xviii–xxi, xxiii–xxiv, 64n4, 106, 126, 136, 139, 141n66
Mitchell, J. Allan, 65n8
Montagu, Thomas, Earl of Salisbury, 160
Mooney, Linne R., 158n39
Mortimer, Anne, Countess of March, 160
Mortimer, John, 161n57, 195
Mowbray, John, Duke of Norfolk, 168

Index

Murphy, James J., 36n13
Muscatine, Charles, 128n48

Nall, Catherine, 185n19
Nennius, xviiin24
Nevil, Thomas, Lord Fournival, 155
Nicholson, Peter, 65n7, 65n8, 103n81
Nicole de Margival, 119
Nigel of Canterbury, 10
Nolan, Barbara, 184n18
Nolan, Maura, 162n62, 189, 189n30, 194
Nowlin, Steele, xvn16
Nun of Barking Abbey (possibly Clemence of Barking), 33n2
Nuttall, Jenni, 157n33

Obermeier, Anita, 115n22
Olsson, Kurt, 67n11, 88n50
Oresme, Nicholas, 65
Oton de Grandson, 109, 120
Otter, Monika, 8n23, 22n47
Ovid, 8, 26; and Chaucer, xxiv, 106, 108n10, 109, 114, 117, 120–21, 122–23, 125, 128–29, 131, 132–36, 138–39, 142–45; and Gower, xxiii, 79, 86, 92, 95, 96, 98, 108n10; and Hoccleve, 164; and Lydgate, 182, 185, 194; and Marie de France, xxix, 34, 39–59

"Pamphilus de amore" (pseudo-Ovid), 74
Partridge, Stephen, xxiv, 115n21
Patterson, Lee, 107n8, 127, 128, 128n48, 130, 171, 178n8
Paul, Saint, 4, 5, 26n55, 72, 106; and Chaucer, 115
Paulinus, 4
Pearsall, Derek, 94n58, 154n23, 157n35, 158n38, 159, 176n2, 177, 188
Peck, Russell, 65n6, 87n49
Perez, Marylène, 21n43, 22n47
Persius, 194
Peter of Blois, 10, 10n6
Petrarch, Francis, xxv, 97, 150, 180, 201; and Chaucer, 117, 126, 132, 141–44; and Lydgate, 186, 191, 193–94, 196
Petrina, Alessandra, 191
Philippe de Mézières, 143
Piramus, Denis, 35, 37
Plantagenet, Geoffrey, 15

Plato, 118, 137
Plautus, 29
Pliny, 68n15
Prior, Sandra Pierson, 54
Priscian, 26, 37
Propertius, 97
Prosper of Aquitaine, 193
pseudo-Aristotle. See *Secretum Secretorum*
Publilius Syrus, 118
Puttenham, George, 198

Quain, xxn29
Quixley, Robert de, 101n76

Renevey, Denis, xiin3
Richard II (king of England), 77, 77n28, 78n29, 84, 88, 156
Ridewall, John, 9
Rigg, A. G., 10n4, 11–12, 11n12, 26, 26n55, 79n31
Robertson, Kellie, xxv
Rolle, Richard, xii, xiin3
Rollo, David, 8n23, 184n18
Roman de la Rose, xiv; and Chaucer, 108–9, 111–13, 116, 117, 121, 125, 139, 164; and Gower, 74–76, 74n24, 79, 85, 102; and Lydgate, 177–78
Roman d'Eneas, 38
Roman de Thèbes, 38, 130, 187
Rychner, Jean, 41

Saint-Pierre, Jean de, 102
Sallust, 189
Salutati, Coluccio, 195
Scanlon, Larry, 73n22, 180, 190–91, 192
Schirmer, Walter, 157, 160
Schullian, Dorothy M., 19n37
Scogan, Henry, 151
Secretum Secretorum, 91, 162, 167, 169, 181
Seege or Batayle of Troy, The, 182
Seneca, 74, 109, 191, 193
Servius, 97
Seymour, M. C., 154n22, 156n32, 188n25
Shakespeare, William, 64–65
Shepherd, G. T., 12
Shippey, Thomas A., 57
Shirley, John, 157–58, 160, 161

Sidney, Sir Philip, 105
Silvius Italicus (*Punica*), 83n38
Simpson, James, xxvi, 177n4, 188n26, 198n1
Sinex, Margaret, 16n30
Skelton, John, xiv, xxxii, 199–203
Sobecki, Sebastian, 100n71
Socrates, 109
Solomon, 118, 145
Somer, Henry, Baron of the Exchequer, 155
Spearing, A. C., xxvi, 126, 149n1, 165, 167n16, 169, 170, 170n26, 188, 198
Spenser, Edmund, xxxii, 198–99
Spitzer, Leo, xv, xvii
Sponsler, Claire, 161–62, 162n61
Stapleton, M. L., 42–43
Statius, xxxiii, 38; and Chaucer, 127–28, 130, 169, 182, 187
Stockton, Eric W., 84n39
Stow, George B., 77n28
Stow, John, 158, 159, 160
Straker, Scott-Morgan, 160
Strengleikar, 34, 34n4
Strohm, Paul, 164, 185n20
Sudbury, Simon, 80
Suetonius, 97, 189
Summit, Jennifer, xxn28, 191n38, 194, 195
Swan, Mary, xxviin51
Symons, Dana M., 154n23

Talbot, Lady Margaret, Countess of Shrewsbury, 160–61
Tertullian, 18
Theophrastus, 139, 140
Thomas, Duke of Gloucester, 83
Thomas, Earl of Warwick, 83–84
Thornbury, Emily V., 3–4
Thorpe, Lewis, 11, 11n14, 20n40, 24
Tolmie, Sarah, 164
Torti, Anna, 185n22
Translation, xxi–xxiii, 5, 7, 64
Treharne, Elaine, xxviin51
Trevet, Nicholas, 9, 129, 130
Trigg, Stephanie, xxv, 106, 107n6

Tuke, Sir Brian, 152–53
Tupper, Frederick, 21, 22n47
Türk, Egbert, 9n1, 13
Turville-Petre, Thorlac, xivn11

Usk, Thomas, 107, 107n9, 108, 151, 152, 165, 169

Valerius Flaccus, 134
Valerius Maximus, 19n37, 21–22, 117, 189
Van Dyke, Carolynn, xvn14
Vàrvaro, Alberto, 20, 29n58
Vegetius, 193–94
Vergil, 5, 8, 38, 83n38, 95–97, 98, 112, 117, 122–23, 130, 133–34, 181, 194, 202n14
Vessey, Mark, xviin19
Vincent of Beauvais, 133, 189, 194

Wace, xviii, 35, 38
Wakelin, Daniel, 200
Wallace, David, 108–9, 142
Walton, John, 152
Watson, Nicholas, 154, 185n22, 190
Webster, K. G. T., 14n25
Westgard, Joshua A., 4n3
Wetherbee, Winthrop, 132
Whalen, Logan E., 36n14
Wharton, Thomas, 199
Wheatley, Edward, 144n74
Whetheamstede, John, 161
Wiggington, Waller B., 184n17
Wimsatt, James I., 109n16
Wogan-Browne, Jocelyn, xiin2, xv, xxiv, xxxn59
Worde, Wynkyn de, 199
Wright, Thomas, 11
Wyatt, Sir Thomas, 198–99, 201

Yeager, R. F., 66n10, 73n22, 74n24, 79n32, 95n59, 101n75

Zanoni, Marie-Louise, 37n16
Ziolkowski, Jan, xix
Zumthor, Paul, 57

INTERVENTIONS: NEW STUDIES IN MEDIEVAL CULTURE
Ethan Knapp, Series Editor

Interventions: New Studies in Medieval Culture publishes theoretically informed work in medieval literary and cultural studies. We are interested both in studies of medieval culture and in work on the continuing importance of medieval tropes and topics in contemporary intellectual life.

Invention and Authorship in Medieval England
    ROBERT R. EDWARDS

Challenging Communion: The Eucharist and Middle English Literature
    JENNIFER GARRISON

Chaucer on Screen: Absence, Presence, and Adapting the Canterbury Tales
    EDITED BY KATHLEEN COYNE KELLY AND TISON PUGH

Chaucer, Gower, and the Affect of Invention
    STEELE NOWLIN

Fragments for a History of a Vanishing Humanism
    EDITED BY MYRA SEAMAN AND EILEEN A. JOY

The Medieval Risk-Reward Society: Courts, Adventure, and Love in the European Middle Ages
    WILL HASTY

The Politics of Ecology: Land, Life, and Law in Medieval Britain
    EDITED BY RANDY P. SCHIFF AND JOSEPH TAYLOR

The Art of Vision: Ekphrasis in Medieval Literature and Culture
    EDITED BY ANDREW JAMES JOHNSTON, ETHAN KNAPP, AND MARGITTA ROUSE

Desire in the Canterbury Tales
    ELIZABETH SCALA

Imagining the Parish in Late Medieval England
    ELLEN K. RENTZ

Truth and Tales: Cultural Mobility and Medieval Media
    EDITED BY FIONA SOMERSET AND NICHOLAS WATSON

Eschatological Subjects: Divine and Literary Judgment in Fourteenth-Century French Poetry
    J. M. MOREAU

Chaucer's (Anti-)Eroticisms and the Queer Middle Ages
    TISON PUGH

Trading Tongues: Merchants, Multilingualism, and Medieval Literature
    JONATHAN HSY

Translating Troy: Provincial Politics in Alliterative Romance
  ALEX MUELLER

Fictions of Evidence: Witnessing, Literature, and Community in the Late Middle Ages
  JAMIE K. TAYLOR

Answerable Style: The Idea of the Literary in Medieval England
  EDITED BY FRANK GRADY AND ANDREW GALLOWAY

Scribal Authorship and the Writing of History in Medieval England
  MATTHEW FISHER

Fashioning Change: The Trope of Clothing in High- and Late-Medieval England
  ANDREA DENNY-BROWN

Form and Reform: Reading across the Fifteenth Century
  EDITED BY SHANNON GAYK AND KATHLEEN TONRY

How to Make a Human: Animals and Violence in the Middle Ages
  KARL STEEL

Revivalist Fantasy: Alliterative Verse and Nationalist Literary History
  RANDY P. SCHIFF

Inventing Womanhood: Gender and Language in Later Middle English Writing
  TARA WILLIAMS

Body Against Soul: Gender and Sowlehele *in Middle English Allegory*
  MASHA RASKOLNIKOV

www.ingramcontent.com/pod-product-compliance
Lightning Source LLC
Chambersburg PA
CBHW030109010526
44116CB00005B/167